Taking SIDES

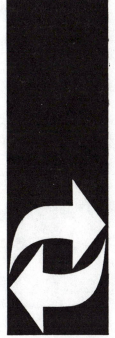

Clashing Views on Controversial Issues in World Politics

Sixth Edition

Taking SIDES

Clashing Views on Controversial Issues in World Politics

Sixth Edition

Edited, Selected, and with Introductions by

John T. Rourke
University of Connecticut

The Dushkin Publishing Group, Inc.

For my son and friend—John Michael

Photo Acknowledgments

Part 1   UN PHOTO 159207/S. Whitehouse
Part 2   The Dushkin Publishing Group, Inc.
Part 3   United Nations/Photo by Sygma
Part 4   Colorado Tourism Board

Cover Art Acknowledgment

Charles Vitelli

Library of Congress Cataloging-in-Publication Data

Main entry under title:
    Taking sides: clashing views on controversial issues in world politics/edited, selected, and
    with introductions by John T. Rourke.—6th ed.
    Includes bibliographical references and index.
    1. World politics—1989–. I. Rourke, John T., *comp.*
        D860.T357   909.82—dc20
        1-56134-324-2   94-33209

 Printed on Recycled Paper

The Dushkin Publishing Group, Inc.

PREFACE

In the first edition of *Taking Sides,* I wrote of my belief in informed argument:

> [A] book that debates vital issues is valuable and necessary.... [It is important] to recognize that world politics is usually not a subject of absolute rights and absolute wrongs and of easy policy choices. We all have a responsibility to study the issues thoughtfully, and we should be careful to understand all sides of the debates.

It was gratifying to discover in the success of *Taking Sides* that so many of my colleagues share this belief in the value of a debate-format text.

The format of this edition is the same as the last. There are 20 issues on a wide range of topics in international relations. Each issue has two readings: one pro and one con. Each is also accompanied by an issue *introduction,* which sets the stage for the debate, provides some background information on each author, and generally puts the issue into its political context. Each issue concludes with a *postscript* that summarizes the debate, gives the reader paths for further investigation, and suggests additional readings that might be helpful.

I have continued to emphasize issues that are currently being debated in the policy sphere, and the authors of the selections are a mix of practitioners, scholars, and noted political commentators. In order to give the reader a truly international perspective on the issues of world politics, the authors of the selections represent many nations, including Bosnia, China, Egypt, France, Great Britain, Poland, and Singapore, as well as the United States.

Changes to this edition   The dynamic, constantly changing nature of the world political system and the many helpful comments from reviewers have brought about significant changes to this edition. Fifteen of the 20 issues are completely new: *Has the World Become a More Dangerous Place Since the End of the Cold War?* (Issue 1); *Should the West Give Massive Foreign Aid to Russia?* (Issue 2); *Should the Arms Embargo on Bosnia Be Lifted?* (Issue 4); *Is Africa Heading Toward Disaster?* (Issue 7); *Is the United States Unfairly Pressing Japan to Adopt Managed Trade?* (Issue 8); *Is Free Trade a Desirable International Goal?* (Issue 10); *Does Immigration Strain Society's Resources?* (Issue 11); *Should a Permanent UN Military Force Be Established?* (Issue 12); *Should the United States Forcefully Oppose North Korea's Nuclear Weapons Program?* (Issue 13); *Is It Time to Terminate the CIA?* (Issue 14); *Does the World Have to Have Nuclear Weapons at All?* (Issue 15); *Is There a Global Environmental Crisis?* (Issue 17); *Is the United Nations Advocating Objectionable Policies to Control World Population Growth?* (Issue 18); *Is Self-Determination a Right of All Nationalities?* (Issue 19); and *Are U.S. Efforts to Promote Human Rights Culturally Biased and Self-*

Serving? (Issue 20). Three other issues have been recast to reflect changing emphasis: *Should the United States Abandon Its Superpower Role?* (Issue 3); *Is Islamic Fundamentalism a Threat to Political Stability?* (Issue 5); and *Should the Developed North Increase Aid to the Less Developed South?* (Issue 9). Thirty-four of the 40 readings are new, and of the 40 readings, the majority are from publications dated 1992 or later.

For this edition I have redoubled my efforts to select lively articles and pair them in such a way as to show clearly the controversies of a given issue. (See, for example, Issue 12 on the military role of the United Nations.)

A word to the instructor An *Instructor's Manual With Test Questions* (multiple-choice and essay) is available through the publisher for instructors using *Taking Sides* in the classroom. A general guidebook, *Using Taking Sides in the Classroom,* which discusses methods and techniques for integrating the pro-con approach into any classroom setting, is also available through The Dushkin Publishing Group.

A note especially for the student reader You will find that the debates in this book are not one-sided. Each author strongly believes in his or her position. And if you read the debates without prejudging them, you will see that each author makes cogent points. An author may not be "right," but the arguments made in an essay should not be dismissed out of hand, and you should work at remaining tolerant of those who hold beliefs that are different from your own.

There is an additional consideration to keep in mind as you pursue this debate approach to world politics: To consider objectively divergent views does not mean that you have to remain forever neutral. In fact, once you are informed, you ought to form convictions. More importantly, you should try to influence international policy to conform better with your beliefs. Write letters to policymakers; donate to causes you support; work for candidates who agree with your views; join an activist organization. *Do* something, whichever side of an issue you are on!

Acknowledgments I received many helpful comments and suggestions from colleagues and readers across the United States and Canada. Their suggestions have markedly enhanced the quality of this edition of *Taking Sides.* If as you read this book you are reminded of a selection or issue that could be included in a future edition, please write to me in care of The Dushkin Publishing Group with your recommendations.

My thanks go to those who responded with suggestions for the sixth edition:

Caren Addis
Rutgers University

Paul Angelini
Sheridan College

Roger Crownover
Madonna University

Douglas M. Dent
Madonna University

Cheng Tian Kuo
University of
  Wisconsin–Milwaukee

Wei-chin Lee
Wake Forest University

Timothy J. Lomperis
Duke University

Theodore Reller
Canada College

John W. Schmaltz
Northern Iowa Area
  Community College

Kristine Thompson
Concordia College

I would also like to thank the publisher for the Taking Sides series, Mimi Egan, for her help in refining this edition.

John T. Rourke
University of Connecticut

CONTENTS IN BRIEF

CONTENTS

Patrick Glynn, a former official in the U.S. Arms Control and Disarmament Agency, contends that post–cold war political and social fragmentation is making the world a more dangerous place. Francis Fukuyama, a consultant at the RAND Corporation, argues that the current period of post–cold war instability does not necessarily mean that we face a more dangerous future.

Rex A. Wade, a professor in the history department at George Mason University, contends that because the policies and actions of the West will help determine the nature of the political regime in Russia, the United States and other industrialized countries should extend massive aid to Russia and to the other former Soviet republics. Karen LaFollette, a research associate at the Institute for Political Economy in Washington, D.C., argues that the West should resist the urge to pour aid into Russia.

Doug Bandow, a former special assistant to U.S. president Ronald Reagan, argues that the United States should bring home its military forces and curtail expensive foreign aid programs. Anthony Lake, special assistant for national security affairs in the Clinton administration, maintains that U.S. national interests make full international engagement imperative.

Ejup Ganic, the vice president of the Republic of Bosnia and Herzegovina, contends that in order to allow the Bosnian army to more evenly match the weaponry of the rebel Bosnian Serb forces, and thereby permitting the "legitimate and recognized government to defend itself," U.S. leaders should lift the arms embargo on Bosnia. Jean Claude Mallet, testifying on behalf of the French Ministry of Defense, argues that lifting the arms embargo on Bosnia would only escalate the fighting and further endanger the United Nations forces in the country.

Political researcher and writer Judith Miller argues that the radical Islamic movement in the greater Middle Eastern region threatens domestic and international political stability. John Esposito, director of the Center for Muslim-Christian Understanding at the School of Foreign Service, Georgetown University, holds that it is wrong to view Islam as an organized whole whose adherents are mostly dangerous fanatics.

Zhao Xiaowei, a prominent member of the Democratic Liberal Party, predicts that as China modernizes and becomes more stable domestically, it is likely to engage in an arms race designed to build itself up to a regional, even global, superpower. Political science professor Samuel S. Kim maintains that China is a weak state that will be hard pressed to survive the multiple threats from within.

Robert D. Kaplan, a contributing editor of *The Atlantic Monthly,* argues that scarcity, crime, overpopulation, tribalism, and disease are rapidly destroying the social fabric of many African countries. Michael Chege, a visiting scholar at the Center for International Affairs at Harvard University, contends that a more balanced, less hysterical examination of Africa shows that there has been considerable social, economic, and political progress.

Jagdish Bhagwati, who is the Arthur Lehman Professor of Economics at Columbia University, argues that Washington's attempts to institute managed trade with Japan are neither economically nor politically wise. Roger C. Altman, deputy secretary of the U.S. Department of the Treasury, maintains that the United States is not pressing Japan for managed trade, but he holds that the two countries must come to an agreement about how to reduce Japan's merchandise trade surplus with the United States.

United Nations executive James Grant contends that one way to jumpstart solutions to many of the world's problems is to extend more assistance to impoverished countries. The editors of *The Economist,* a well-known British publication, suggest that the usual ways in which international aid is distributed and spent make it a waste of resources.

Peter F. Drucker, a professor of social science and management at the Claremont Graduate School, contends that global economic integration is the only basis for an effective international trade policy. Historian Jeremy Brecher argues that unrestricted, unregulated trade is threatening the economic well-being of working people.

Daniel James, an analyst and author who writes on social issues, contends that a tidal wave of immigration is hitting U.S. shores and is threatening the U.S. economy and sense of cultural cohesiveness. Stephen Moore, an economist with the Cato Institute in Washington, D.C., maintains that the net gains that the country reaps from the contributions of immigrants far outweigh any social costs.

United Nations Secretary-General Boutros Boutros-Ghali contends that the extent of the UN's military capabilities should be expanded significantly in the interest of world peace. John F. Hillen III, a lieutenant in the U.S. Army, criticizes the idea of a permanent UN army and argues that such a force is unworkable.

U.S. Senator John McCain (R-Arizona) advocates taking strong action to force North Korea to open itself to international inspection and to give up its nuclear weapons program. Doug Bandow, a senior fellow at the Cato Institute in Washington, D.C., argues that there is little clear information available about the nuclear capability or intentions of North Korea, and so it would be wise for the United States to avoid taking drastic measures.

Marcus Raskin, cofounder of the Institute for Policy Studies, argues that the CIA and other intelligence agencies of the United States should be dismantled or transformed. R. James Woolsey, U.S. Director of Central Intelligence, contends that the United States continues to need an effective intelligence capability.

Sir Michael Quinlan, former permanent under-secretary of state at the British Ministry of Defense, contends that a good case can be made to support the maintenance of nuclear weapons capability by the United States and others. Lincoln Wolfenstein, a member of the U.S. National Academy of Sciences, argues that the collapse of the former Soviet Union and other destabilizing changes in world politics makes now the right time to pursue complete nuclear disarmament.

Former U.S. secretary of state Cyruse R. Vance contends that a commitment to human rights must be a central principle of foreign policy. Former U.S. secretary of state George Shultz asserts that foreign policy must avoid idealism if it conflicts with the national interest.

Hilary F. French, a senior researcher at the Worldwatch Institute in Washington, D.C., warns that countries cannot continue doing business as usual without dire environmental consequences. Julian L. Simon, a professor of economic and business administration, asserts that the current gloom and doom about the "crisis" of our environment is not supported by scientific facts.

John Paul II, pontiff of the Roman Catholic Church, charges that the draft document for the United Nations International Conference on Population and Development (ICPD) contains concepts and wording that, if pursued and promoted, could cause a moral decline. Jessica J. Kulynych, a doctoral student in political science at the University of Connecticut, replies that the proposals before ICPD empower women and represent an important, necessary, and humane change for population programs.

Michael Lind, executive editor of *The National Interest*, writes that for practical, strategic reasons, and for reasons of principle, the United States should support legitimate efforts at self-determination. Amitai Etzioni, a professor of sociology at George Washington University, contends that self-determination movements are destructive.

Bilahari Kausikan, director of the East Asian and Pacific bureau of the Ministry of Foreign Affairs of Singapore, contends that international human rights advocates seek to impose rules that reflect the "individualistic ethos of the West" on the more "consensus-seeking" societies of East and Southeast Asia. Aryeh Neier, president of the Open Society Fund, an organization that promotes the development of civil society in formerly repressive countries, argues that there are fundamental human rights that transcend the cultural values of any one society.

INTRODUCTION

World Politics and the Voice of Justice

John T. Rourke

Some years ago, the Rolling Stones recorded "Sympathy With the Devil." If you have never heard it, go find a copy. It is worth listening to. That theme is echoed in a wonderful essay by Marshall Berman, "Have Sympathy for the Devil" (*New American Review*, 1973). The Stones and Berman's theme was based on Johann Goethe's *Faust*. In that classic drama, the protagonist, Dr. Faust, trades his soul to gain great power. He attempts to do good, but in the end he commits evil by, in contemporary paraphrase, "doing the wrong things for the right reasons." Does that make Faust evil, the personification of the devil Mephistopheles among us? Or is the good doctor merely misguided in his effort to make the world better as he saw it and imagined it might be? The point that the Stones and Berman make is that it is important to avoid falling prey to the trap of many zealots who are so convinced of the truth of their own views that they feel righteously at liberty to condemn those who disagree with them as stupid or even diabolical.

It is to the principle of rational discourse, of tolerant debate, that this reader is dedicated. There are many issues in this volume that appropriately excite passion—for example, the issue on whether or not Islamic fundamentalism represents a threat to political stability or the issue on the population policies of the United Nations. Few would find fault with a commitment to ease population growth. How to get to that end is another matter, however, and we should take care not to confuse disagreement on means with disagreement on ends. In other cases, the debates you will read do diverge on goals. Two authors, for example, argue over whether or not complete nuclear disarmament is desirable. Another issue deals in part with whether or not the former opponents of the former Soviet Union should provide extensive foreign aid to the remaining republics. Two key issues here are whether or not funds would even help and whether or not democracy will survive in the former Soviet republics.

As you will see, each of the authors in all the debates strongly believes in his or her position. If you read these debates with an objective attitude, you will find that each side makes cogent points. They may or may not be right, but they should not be dismissed out of hand. It is also important to repeat that the debate format does not imply that you should remain forever neutral. In fact, once you are informed, you *ought* to form convictions, and you should try to act on those convictions and try to influence international policy to conform better with your beliefs. Write letters to policymakers, donate money to causes you support, work for candidates with whom you agree, or join an activist organization.

On the subject of lethargy and evil, Ethiopia's emperor Haile Selassie (1892–1975) told the United Nations in 1963:

> Throughout history it has been the inaction of those who could have acted, the indifference of those who should have known better, the silence of the voice of justice when it mattered most that made it possible for evil to triumph.

The point is: Become Informed. Then *do* something!

APPROACHES TO STUDYING INTERNATIONAL POLITICS

As will become evident as you read this volume, there are many approaches to the study of international politics. Some political scientists and most practitioners specialize in *substantive topics,* and this reader is organized along topical lines. Part 1 (Issues 1 through 7) begins with a question about the future of the international system, currently an emphasis of many scholars. Beginning with Issue 2, the focus of Part 1 shifts to regional issues and actors. Debates here deal with Russia, the United States, Europe, the Middle East, Asia, and Africa. Part 2 (Issues 8 through 11) focuses on international economic issues, including Japan's international economic strength, North-South development, the desirability of free trade, and the economic impact of immigration. Part 3 (Issues 12 through 15) examines issues surrounding the use of force in international relations, including whether or not countries can give up their nuclear weapons and remain secure, the utility of the CIA in the post–cold war world, and the future of the United Nations' military activities. Part 4 (Issues 16 through 20) examines values and the future operation of the global system. Issues here concern whether or not morality should be a centerpiece of foreign policy formation, whether or not there is an environmental crisis, the UN's population policies, the wisdom of promoting unfettered self-determination, and whether or not Asia's human rights standards are acceptable.

Political scientists also approach their subject from differing *methodological perspectives.* We will see, for example, that world politics can be studied from different *levels of analysis.* The question is: What is the basic source of the forces that shape the conduct of politics? Possible answers are world forces, the individual political processes of the specific countries, or the personal attributes of a country's leaders and decision makers. Various readings will illustrate all three levels.

Another way for students and practitioners of world politics to approach their subject is to focus on what is called the realist versus the idealist debate. Realists tend to assume that the world is permanently flawed and therefore advocate following policies in their country's narrow self-interests. Idealists take the approach that the world condition can be improved substantially by following policies that, at least in the short term, call for some risk or self-sacrifice. This divergence is an element of many of these debates.

DYNAMICS OF WORLD POLITICS

The action on the global stage today is also vastly different from what it was a few decades ago or even a few years ago. Directly related to this condition is the first issue, which asks whether the new world order is a cause for pessimism or optimism. *Technology* is one of the causes of world changes. Technology has changed communications, manufacturing, health care, and many other aspects of the human condition. Technology has also led to the creation of nuclear weapons and other highly sophisticated and expensive conventional weapons. One debate is over whether or not, having created and armed ourselves with these weapons, we can and should reverse the process and disarm. Another dynamic aspect of world politics involves the *changing axes* of the world system. For about 40 years after World War II ended in 1945, a bipolar system existed, the primary axis of which was the *East-West* conflict, which pitted the United States and its allies against the Soviet Union and its allies. Now that the Warsaw Pact has collapsed as an axis of world politics, many new questions have surfaced, particularly with regard to the primary successor state to the Soviet Union, Russia. One issue is whether or not billions of dollars in foreign aid should be extended to Russia; would it benefit the country? Even if the answer is yes, will that mean a friendly, democratic Russia or a reinvigorated opponent? Insofar as containing communism and the Soviet Union were the mainstay of U.S. post–World War II policy, the end of the Soviet threat also brings the United States to a pivotal choice about future foreign involvement. As the issue on the superpower role of the United States explains, there is a growing tide of isolationist sentiment in the United States, but there are also those who argue that abandoning internationalism would be foolhardy.

Technological changes and the shifting axes of international politics also highlight the *increased role of economics* in world politics. Economics have always played a role, but traditionally the main focus has been on strategic-political questions—especially military power. This concern still strongly exists, but it now shares the international spotlight with economic issues.

Another change in the world system has to do with the main *international actors*. At one time, states (countries) were practically the only international actors on the world stage. Now, and increasingly so, there are other actors. Some, such as the United Nations, are global actors, and in one issue, the secretary-general of the UN and a U.S. army lieutenant debate one aspect of the UN's current and future role. Other actors are regional. There is a debate on whether or not China will become a regional superpower. Then two analysts address sub-Saharan Africa and debate whether or not the region is heading toward disaster.

PERCEPTIONS VERSUS REALITY

In addition to addressing the general changes in the world system outlined above, the debates in this reader explore the controversies that exist over many of the fundamental issues that face the world.

One key to these debates is the differing *perceptions* that protagonists bring to them. There may be a reality in world politics, but very often that reality is obscured. Many observers, for example, are alarmed by the seeming rise of radical actions by Islamic fundamentalists. As the issue on Islamic fundamentalism illustrates, the image of Islamic radicalism is not a fact but a perception; perhaps correct, perhaps not. In cases such as this, though, it is often the perception, not the reality, that is most important because policy is formulated on what decision makers *think*, not necessarily on what *is*. Thus, perception becomes the operating guide, or *operational reality*, whether it is true or not.

Perceptions result from many factors. One factor is the information that decision makers receive. For a variety of reasons, the facts and analyses that are given to leaders are often inaccurate or at least represent only part of the picture. Perceptions are also formed by the value system of a decision maker, which is based on his or her experiences and ideology. The way in which such an individual thinks and speaks about another leader, country, or the world in general is called his or her *operational code*. There is an issue, for example, that explores the United States' role in the world. How U.S. presidents and other Americans define their country's role creates an operational code governing relations. Thus far, President Bill Clinton has shown himself to have more of an internationalist operational code than the public does. Clinton, for example, wanted to launch a military intervention into Bosnia and Herzegovina to assist the Muslims who were under attack by Serbian forces there. The American public was opposed to intervention in this civil war, showing much less willingness than the president to cast their country in the role of defender of democracy, of human rights, or of what President George Bush called the "new world order."

Another aspect of perception is the tendency to see oneself as peacefully motivated and one's opponent as aggressive. This can lead to perceptual distortions such as an inability to understand that your actions, perceived by you as defensive, may be perceived as a threat by your opponent and, indeed, may cause your opponent to take defensive actions that, in turn, seem aggressive to you. One issue, for example, focuses on relations with Japan and how Japan's recent economic rise is perceived by some as a prelude to world domination. Such perceptions could lead to economic conflict.

Perceptions, then, are crucial to understanding international politics. It is important to understand objective reality, but it is also necessary to comprehend subjective reality in order to be able to predict and analyze another country's actions.

LEVELS OF ANALYSIS

Political scientists approach the study of international politics from differing levels of analysis. The most macroscopic view is *system-level analysis*. This is a top-down approach that maintains that world factors virtually compel countries to follow certain foreign policies. Governing factors include the number of powerful actors, geographic relationships, economic needs, and technology. System analysts hold that a country's internal political system and its leaders do not have a major impact on policy. As such, political scientists who work from this perspective are interested in exploring the governing factors, how they cause policy, and how and why systems change.

After World War II's end, the world was structured as a *bipolar* system, dominated by the United States and the Soviet Union. Furthermore, each superpower was supported by a tightly organized and dependent group of allies. For a variety of reasons, including changing economics and the nuclear standoff, the bipolar system faded. Some political scientists argue that it is now being replaced by a *multipolar* system. In such a configuration, those who favor *balance-of-power* politics maintain that it is unwise to ignore power considerations. The debate about the future of China as a regional, perhaps global, power affects considerations of how to deal with China over trade disputes, the suppression of democracy by China's government (symbolized by the 1989 massacre at Tiananmen Square), and many other issues.

State-level analysis is the middle, and the most common, level of analysis. Social scientists who study world politics from this perspective focus on how countries, singly or comparatively, make foreign policy. In other words, this perspective is concerned with internal political dynamics such as the roles of and interactions between the executive and legislative branches of government, the impact of bureaucracy (as in the issue on the CIA), the role of interest groups, and the effect of public opinion. There are a number of issues in this reader that are subject to strong domestic pressure on political leaders, such as the issue on immigration.

A third level of analysis, which is the most microscopic, is *human-level analysis*. This approach focuses, in part, on the role of individual decision makers. Political scientists who take this approach contend that individuals make decisions and that the nature of those decisions is determined by the decision makers' perceptions, predilections, and strengths and weaknesses. Human-level analysis also focuses on the nature of humans.

REALISM VERSUS IDEALISM

Realism and idealism represent another division among political scientists and practitioners in their approaches to the study and conduct of international relations. *Realists* are usually skeptical about the nature of politics and, perhaps, the nature of humankind. They believe that countries have opposing interests and that these differences can lead to conflict. They further contend that states (countries) are by definition obligated to do what is beneficial for their own citizens (national interest). The amount of power that a state has will determine how successful it is in attaining these goals. Therefore, politics is, and ought to be, a process of gaining, maintaining, and using power. Realists believe that the best way to avoid conflict is to remain powerful and to avoid pursuing goals that are beyond one's power to achieve. "Peace through strength" is a phrase that most realists would agree with.

Idealists disagree about both the nature and conduct of international relations. They tend to be more optimistic that the global community is capable of finding ways to live in harmony and that it has a sense of collective, rather than national, interest. Idealists also claim that the pursuit of a narrow national interest is shortsighted. They argue that, in the long run, countries must learn to cooperate or face the prospect of a variety of evils, including possible nuclear warfare, environmental disaster, or continuing economic hardship. Idealists argue, for example, that armaments cause world tensions, whereas realists maintain that conflict requires states to have weapons. Idealists are especially concerned with conducting current world politics on a more moral or ethical plane and with searching for alternatives to the present pursuit of nationalist interests through power politics.

Several of the issues address the realist-idealist split. For example, in one issue, Cyrus Vance contends that human rights represent a fundamental principle and should strongly influence policy, while George Shultz contends that morality must be balanced with other factors to determine policy. There is also an idealist-realist element to the issue regarding the degree of aid that the economically developed countries should give to the less developed countries. The debate over intervention in Bosnia, and by extension other troubled countries and places in which modern conflicts may arise, also involves realist-idealist considerations.

THE POLITICAL AND ECOLOGICAL FUTURE

Future *world alternatives* are discussed in many of the issues. The first issue, for example, debates whether or not the current world situation portends anarchy. The debate on the North providing aid to the South is not just about humanitarian impulses; it is about whether or not the world can survive and be stable economically and politically if it is divided into a minority of wealthy nations and a majority of poor countries. Another, more far-reaching, alternative, is if an international organization were to take over some (or all) of the sovereign responsibilities of national governments. To explore this alternative, another issue focuses on the authority of the UN Security Council to assume much more power in the area of peacekeeping. Another possibility for governance falls between current countries (each governed independently) and the possibility of a single global government, represented by the United Nations.

The global future also involves the availability of natural resources, the condition of the environment, and the level of world population, which are addressed in the issues on UN population policy and the environment.

THE AXES OF WORLD DIVISION

It is a truism that the world is politically dynamic and that the nature of the political system is undergoing profound change. As noted, the once primary axis of world politics, the East-West confrontation, has broken down. Yet, the issue on Russia is related to the question of whether or not, in a nonideological context, this axis might be reconstituted by an ultranationalist, hostile Russia.

In contrast to the moribund East-West axis, the *North-South axis* has increased in importance and tension. The wealthy, industrialized countries (North) are on one end, and the poor, less developed countries (LDCs, South) are at the other extreme. Economic differences and disputes are the primary dimension of this axis, in contrast to the military nature of the East-West axis. This is evident in the issue that explores these differences and debates whether or not the North should significantly increase economic aid to the South.

Then there is the question of what, if anything, will develop to divide the countries of the North and replace the East-West axis. The possibility for tension is represented in several issues. Some believe that the remnants of the USSR, especially Russia, will one day again pose a threat to Western Europe. There are also those who argue that the European Community, an Asia organized and dominated by Japan or China, and a North American region that is based on the United States–Canada–Mexico free trade agreement could form the basis of a new split.

INCREASED ROLE OF ECONOMICS

As the growing importance of the North-South axis indicates, economics is playing an increased role in world politics. The economic reasons behind the decline of the East-West axis is further evidence. Economics has always played a part in international relations, but the traditional focus has been on strategic-political affairs, especially questions of military power.

However, political scientists are now focusing increasingly on the international political economy, or the economic dimensions of world politics. International trade, for instance, has increased dramatically, expanding from an annual world total of $20 billion in 1933 to $3.8 trillion in 1992. The impact has been profound. The domestic economic health of most countries is heavily affected by trade and other aspects of international economics. Since World War II, there has been an emphasis on expanding free trade by decreasing tariffs and other barriers to international commerce. In recent years, however, a downturn in the economies of many of the industrialized countries has increased calls for more protectionism. This is related to the debate on Japan's international trading practices.

Another economic issue is whether or not the environment can withstand current and increased economic activity. For people in industrialized countries, the issue is whether or not they can sustain current standards of living without continuing to consume unsustainable levels of energy and other resources and while lowering levels of pollution and other forms of environmental degradation. For people in less developed countries, the issue is whether or not they can develop their economies and reach the standard of living enjoyed by people in wealthy countries without creating vast new drains on resources and vast new amounts of pollution. This concern is a major aspect of the debate on the global environmental crisis.

CONCLUSION

Having discussed many of the various dimensions and approaches to the study of world politics, it is incumbent on this editor to advise against your becoming too structured by them. Issues of focus and methodology are important both to studying international relations and to understanding how others are analyzing global conduct. However, they are also partially pedagogical. In the final analysis, world politics is a highly interrelated, perhaps seamless, subject. No one level of analysis, for instance, can fully explain the events on the world stage. Instead, using each of the levels to analyze events and trends will bring the greatest understanding.

Similarly, the realist-idealist division is less precise in practice than it may appear. As some of the debates indicate, each side often stresses its own standards of morality. Which is more moral: defeating dictatorship or sparing the sword and saving lives that will almost inevitably be lost in the dictator's overthrow? Further, realists usually do not reject moral considerations. Rather, they contend that morality is but one of the factors that a country's decision makers must consider. Realists are also apt to argue that standards of morality differ when dealing with a country as opposed to an individual. By the same token, most idealists do not completely ignore the often dangerous nature of the world. Nor do they argue that a country must totally sacrifice its short-term interests to promote the betterment of the current and future world. Thus, realism and idealism can be seen most accurately as the ends of a continuum—with most political scientists and practitioners falling somewhere between, rather than at, the extremes. The best advice, then, is to think broadly about international politics. The subject is very complex, and the more creative and expansive you are in selecting your foci and methodologies, the more insight you will gain. To end where we began, with Dr. Faust, I offer his last words in Goethe's drama, *"Mehr licht,"* ... More light! That is the goal of this book.

PART 1

Regional Issues and Actors

The issues in this section deal with countries that are major regional powers. In this era of interdependence among nations, it is important to understand the concerns that these issues address and the actors involved because they will shape the world and will affect the lives of all people.

- Has the World Become a More Dangerous Place Since the End of the Cold War?

- Should the West Give Massive Foreign Aid to Russia?

- Should the United States Abandon Its Superpower Role?

- Should the Arms Embargo on Bosnia Be Lifted?

- Is Islamic Fundamentalism a Threat to Political Stability?

- Will China Become an Asian Superpower?

- Is Africa Heading Toward Disaster?

ISSUE 1

Has the World Become a More Dangerous Place Since the End of the Cold War?

YES: Patrick Glynn, from "The Age of Balkanization," *Commentary* (July 1993)

NO: Francis Fukuyama, from "Against the New Pessimism," *Commentary* (February 1994)

ISSUE SUMMARY

YES: Patrick Glynn, a scholar at the American Enterprise Institute in Washington, D.C., and a former official in the U.S. Arms Control and Disarmament Agency, contends that post–cold war political and social fragmentation is destabilizing countries and making the world a more dangerous place.

NO: Francis Fukuyama, a consultant at the RAND Corporation and a former State Department official, argues that the current period of post–cold war instability will not last and does not necessarily mean that we face a more dangerous future.

Nineteen ninety-one was a truly remarkable year. The world watched in awe and anticipation as the Soviet Union began to collapse and then finally ceased to exist altogether. For most of this century, the communist Soviet empire had seemed to most in the West to loom threateningly. For 45 years, from the end of World War II to 1991, the Soviet Union and the United States, each militarily mighty and ideologically hostile to the other, had been locked in a deadly rivalry. Although the two countries never engaged one another in direct combat, a hot war, their struggle was nevertheless intense and potentially apocalyptic, given the two superpowers' nuclear arsenals. Their rivalry and spheres of influence engulfed the entire world system, and *cold war* became the accepted term to describe the tensions that gripped international relations.

And then the foreboding was gone! In December 1991 the Soviet flag atop the Kremlin in Moscow was replaced with the Russian flag. No longer did a monolithic Soviet Union exist; in its place were 11 states linked in a loose confederation and 4 completely independent countries. Russian president Boris Yeltsin pledged democracy and peace with the United States. The cold war is over, U.S. president George Bush told a national audience at the time, and the Americans have won. The world seemed safer. There were pledges of newfound friendship from the capitals of former enemies, several new arms control initiatives and treaties were signed, and there were moves in the United States and elsewhere to slash defense spending.

There was also great optimism about changing the world system for the better. As President Bush put it at the time, "a new world order [is] struggling to be born. . . . [A world] where the rule of law supplants the rule of the jungle. A world in which nations recognize the shared responsibility for freedom and justice. A world where the strong respect the rights of the weak."

Not everyone was so hopeful. Scholar John Mearsheimer warned that we would one day look back nostalgically at the stability of the cold war period. (See "Why We Will Soon Miss the Cold War," *The Atlantic Monthly,* August 1990.) His view, which is shared by many political scientists, is that when there is a change in the number of major powers (called poles) in the international system, or a significant shift in the strength of one or more of the poles, then, according to theory, several destabilizing trends may occur. One is that rising powers and declining powers may clash over territory, control, or resources. Another is that areas of the world once dominated by a fading power may fall into chaos as the declining power's influence dissipates, permitting formerly suppressed rivalries to emerge.

Now that the cold war has ended, the dire image of the future projected by Mearsheimer and others seems to be coming to pass. Nationalism has become the predominate cause of conflict around the world. Several of the republics that established their independence by seceding from the Soviet Union have faced their own secessionist movements. Elsewhere, the efforts of the Kurds to break away from Iraq (and other surrounding countries), the fighting in the Sudan between Muslims in the north and non-Muslims in the south, the clashes among Bosnians, Croats, and Serbs in the former Yugoslavia, the clan warfare in Somalia, and the horrific tribal violence between Hutus and Tutsis in Rwanda have shocked the world. Such national and ethnic-based rivalries are, in the view of some analysts, part of a greater pattern of fragmentation that threatens to destroy the domestic social fabric of many countries. Numerous commentators argue that the national political systems that have so long been at the center of domestic order, and a primary aspect of the international system, are in danger of disintegrating.

There can be little doubt that there is instability in the international system as it seeks a new equilibrium. What is not certain, and what is the subject of this debate, is whether the current state of affairs will continue in the long term, and thus should make us relatively pessimistic about future global stability, or whether the current instability is short-term. Are there also countervailing trends that should make us relatively optimistic about the future? Patrick Glynn and Francis Fukuyama take up that debate. Glynn argues that the world is becoming fragmented; Fukuyama contends that if we look beyond immediate, distressing events, we need not be pessimistic about the future.

YES

Patrick Glynn

THE AGE OF BALKANIZATION

Today a fundamental change is under way in the character of global political life. A new era is in the making. Gone or fading are the great bipolar conflicts —between democracy and fascism, between democracy and Communism, and even perhaps between Left and Right—that shaped war and peace in the 20th century. In their place a new political struggle is emerging—more complex, more diffuse, but nonetheless global in character.

On every continent, in almost every major nation, and in almost every walk of life the overriding political reality today is that of increasing social separatism and fragmentation—a sometimes violent splintering of humanity by ethnic group, race, religion, and even (to a less dramatic extent) such characteristics as gender or sexual orientation. While the causes of this phenomenon are as yet imperfectly understood, its implications could hardly be more far-reaching.

The most dramatic manifestation of the change is found, of course, in the countries that used to be known as Yugoslavia and Czechoslovakia, and it is also showing itself in other parts of the defunct Soviet empire, not to mention the old Soviet Union itself. But the phenomenon is not merely one of Communism giving way to nationalism, nor is it confined to the old Communist world.

Indeed, everywhere one sees well-established nation-states threatened with disunion, and even in countries without explicit separatist movements, the unifying themes of political life are increasingly under attack. Canada copes with Quebec's secessionism, the United Kingdom with Scottish separatists, Italy with increasing tensions between its north and its south. In Germany, as well as in France and Britain, ethnically motivated violence has become a major factor in politics, and rebellious youths are inflamed by a puzzling new ideology of ethnic hatred.

Even in America—the proverbial melting pot—racial, ethnic, and other varieties of separatism are distinctly on the rise. Blacks assert their identity as "African-Americans"; homosexuals discover in their sexual orientation a basis for political action; Christian fundamentalists exert more and more influence as an organized political force.

Nor is this phenomenon merely political. It also finds its reflection in the highest reaches of contemporary culture and intellectual life. The controversial doctrine of "multiculturalist education" and the "postmodernist" philosophy now so current in American universities are both essentially codifications of the new experience of fragmentation.

Side by side with this splintering, paradoxically, has gone a fresh drive for unity. As the cold war was ending, George Bush, then still in the White House, hailed the advent of a Europe "whole and free," and in the lead-up to the Gulf war he spoke hopefully of a "new world order." Since then, European Community leaders have worked to forge a unitary Europe, while Germany's leadership has sought to make one nation out of two. In Russia, Boris Yeltsin fights a parallel battle, desperately trying to hold Russia together while moving toward democracy in the face of radical nationalism and mounting pressures for regional secession.

But these efforts at unification—including the effort to posit a new world order based on common democratic values—have thus far proved unable to stem the powerful counter-currents rooted in separatist identities. For this new cultural struggle is taking place not only within nations, but among them. Attempts to expand the postwar liberal trading order have been frustrated by intensified cultural conflict between America and Japan and, to a lesser extent, between America and Western Europe. Islamic fundamentalism poses a threat to moderate Arab regimes and increases the likelihood of eventual armed conflict between the West and radical Arab states.

Slowly this clash between, on the one hand, ethnic (and other types of) particularism and, on the other hand, what might be called democratic universalism seems to be replacing the old Left-Right and class polarities that have governed political life for nearly a century. It has every appearance of becoming the new bipolarity of global politics, the new dialectic of a new age.

* * *

What are the reasons for this great shift? The most obvious cause would seem to lie in the collapse of Soviet Communism. Communism repressed national differences; indeed, Marxist-Leninist ideology, rooted as it was in Enlightenment economic thinking, defined national and ethnic differences as epiphenomenal, stressing instead the primacy of class. Under Communism, nationalism was either disguised or stifled.

What we have seen since the breakdown of Communism—whether in the former Soviet Union, the former Yugoslavia, or the rest of Eastern Europe—is, to borrow a phrase from Sigmund Freud, a "return of the repressed," a resurgence of powerful national and ethnic feelings which had been simmering angrily beneath the surface.

But if Communist regimes ruthlessly imposed unity on their own peoples, they also evoked a more or less united response from the outside world they threatened. The unitary nature of the Communist threat inspired an unprecedented degree of cooperation—under American leadership—among heretofore uncooperative states. European adversaries laid aside age-old grudges to join NATO. New security relationships were forged among the United States and major Asian nations, including Japan.

To be sure, Woodrow Wilson and Franklin Roosevelt had earlier sought on their own initiative to structure a more or less unified world order, to export America's stated principles of ethnic tolerance, and to bring the many nations of the world together on the basis of common interests and goals. But it is far from clear that, absent the Soviet threat, so many disparate nations would have been so successful in achieving collaboration, not just on trade but on a host of diplomatic and security matters, as they were during the cold war. Long ago the sociologist Georg Simmel posited that human societies were cemented together by the need to cope with outside threats. This was clearly true of what we used to call the "free world."

Even within American politics, the anti-Communist imperative had a powerful unifying effect. It produced, albeit intermittently, bipartisanship in foreign policy. It also, at various times, unified each of the two major parties. In the early years of the cold war, the Democrats, and in the later years, the Republicans, found a basis for party solidarity in the anti-Communist cause. So much was this the case that when the Democrats and then the Republicans experienced ruinous internal division, it was owing in part to a perceived or real diminution of the Soviet threat—for the Democrats during the late 1960's and early 1970's, when many believed the cold war to have become obsolete, and for the Republicans in recent years, when it became plain that the cold war was in fact over.

The Republican case is especially interesting, for what else but fear of the Soviet threat could finally have held together the diverse elements of Ronald Reagan's winning electoral coalition: Christian fundamentalists, Jewish neoconservative intellectuals, free-market libertarians, blue-collar Democrats, and traditional Republican voters? Should it surprise us that with the subsidence of the Soviet threat, old party alignments would weaken? Is it illogical that with external dangers reduced we would turn inward as a society and discover social and political differences among one another that we had previously been willing to overlook?

Yet while the collapse of Soviet Communism remains the signal event of our age, many of the trends we are discussing were apparent before the Berlin Wall came down. Ethnic, national, and racial awareness was already growing, on both sides of the iron curtain. Here in America, for example, the multiculturalist movement—now so famous and controversial for its advocacy of heightened ethnic and racial consciousness in schools—was already making inroads into secondary and higher education. On both sides of the iron curtain, faith in central authority was declining and had been declining for some time. Even before the advent of Mikhail Gorbachev, Western Sovietologists debated whether Communist leaders still actually believed their ideology. Ironically, a weakening in the influence of received values—society's traditional unifying ideas—was apparent in our own culture as well, observed by intellectuals and documented by opinion polls.

* * *

In other words, it is hard to say whether the demise of Soviet Communism is the ultimate cause of the change we are witnessing, or whether Soviet Communism itself fell victim to some vaster trend, some grand Hegelian shift in human consciousness.

Certainly the contemporary experience of social and political fragmentation was foreshadowed by new directions in intellectual life, long before the social consequences were apparent. One of the major proponents of "postmodernist" thinking, Fredric Jameson of Duke University, has written of the postmodern idiom in contemporary literature:

> Perhaps the immense fragmentation and privatization of modern literature —its explosion into a host of distinct private styles and mannerisms— foreshadow deeper and more general trends in social life as a whole. Supposing that modern art and modernism—far from being a kind of specialized aesthetic curiosity—actually anticipated social developments along these lines; supposing that in the decades since the emergence of the great modern styles of society has itself begun to fragment in this way, each group coming to speak a curious private language of its own, each profession developing its own private code or idiolect, and finally each individual coming to be a kind of linguistic island, separated from everyone else?

Behind this new experience of cultural and intellectual fragmentation lies a loss of faith in general truths, and even, at its most radical, a loss of faith in the very possibility of general truths. Notably, the most sophisticated humanities instructors in our major universities today will no longer venture to assert that a proposition is "true," merely that it is "productive" or "intriguing," i.e., a basis for reflection or intellectual play. This premise lends a notable arbitrariness to "postmodern" modes of expression, robbing contemporary literature, criticism, and even philosophy of a certain weight, authority, or seriousness.

The same mixture of posturing and pastiche has become evident in our political discourse (think back to Bush's Gulf war speeches). However glorious the phrases—"freedom," "tyranny," "new world order"—they are uttered today with a certain self-conscious nostalgia.

We have lived through an era when people attached themselves to grand ideas—whether for good or for evil—and fought and sometimes died for them. But for some reason these ideas collectively seem to be losing their force. Such is the defining tendency of our age.

The resulting fragmentation is far from being a propitious development. At stake, one could argue, is the future of civilization itself. The struggle for civilization has always been a struggle for unity, universality, ecumenism. The great ages of civilization have been periods of concord and commonality, when large tracts of the globe were more or less united by common values, and sometimes even by a common language and common laws—the Roman empire, the era of Charlemagne, the Renaissance, the 19th-century Concert of Europe. These periods have been succeeded in turn by periods of fragmentation, factional strife, and relative barbarism: the Dark Ages, the feudal era, the Reformation with its religious wars, and of course the long "civil war" that wrenched Europe between 1914 and 1945. Looking back, one can see that Western history has been marked by a cyclical pattern in which unifying ideas triumph, only gradually to lose their hold on the imagination and to be replaced by factional struggle and particularism.

It is possible that we are on the threshold of a new such cyclical turn.

* * *

At the root of the problem lies the very large and very deep question of human identity. In a sense, the master-idea of Western civilization is the view that the identifying feature of the human being qua [as] human being is the faculty of reason. When the Greek philosophers hit upon this notion of man as the rational animal, they made possible the creation of large political orders on a basis other than that of pure despotism.

Furthermore, as Socrates and his students saw, this conception transcended differences of nationality and race: rational man could not be defined as Athenian or Spartan or even Greek or barbarian. And with this insight, the philosophers ceased to be good citizens of their cities, their *poleis,* at least in the terms of those cities: they became citizens of the rational universe—to use a somewhat later term, cosmopolitans—and they challenged the laws and gods of their fellow citizens....

Periods when [the classical idea of rational man] is in the ascendancy have been the great periods of civilization as we in the West know it. It is during such periods that peace reigns, learning spreads and advances, and the arts flourish. Yet experience shows that this idea does not hold indefinitely.

Perhaps the reason simply has to do with the inherent restlessness of human beings. When it first appears on the scene, the idea of rational man has a demythologizing force; it is an exploder of myth. Socrates' notion of rational man was subversive of the laws, customs, and gods of Athens—which is why he was condemned to death by his fellow citizens. Roman law, too, was subversive of local traditions and local religions; it was the "modern" idea of its era. The Renaissance was anti-traditional in the same sense—introducing ideas from the classics that raised questions about Christian beliefs.

Perhaps human beings have an overriding need for myth, or perhaps the act of demythologization always contains within it the seeds of its own destruction. At any rate, periods of demythologization tend to be followed by periods of remythologization....

Remythologization and reversion to ethnic particularism have tended to go hand in hand. People cease to find satisfactory selfhood in large unities, become alienated from the larger whole, and begin to seek identity in smaller units. Such periods are characterized by diminished will on the part of those who stand for reason to defend reason, by a diminished appeal of reason to the human imagination. Civilization is destroyed by those whose attachment to religious or ethnic identity gives them the zeal which the defenders of reason come to lack. Civilization falls victim to barbarians from without and zealots from within. In such periods, as Yeats famously wrote, "The best lack all conviction, while the worst/ Are full of passionate intensity."

* * *

There are hints of all this in the emerging mood of our own time. The ferocious war in the Balkans is but one manifestation of a reemergent barbarism apparent in many corners of the earth. In the Balkans, the voices of the rational and the tolerant—for example, officials of the secular-minded Bosnian government—have been drowned out by the guns of ethnic fanatics. Efforts to secure democracy on the basis of rational Western principles have been crushed by the bloodthirsty exponents of "ethnic cleansing."

The new barbarians differ fundamentally from the old enemies of liberal democracy in feeling no need to justify themselves before the court of reason. The Communists, too, practiced barbarism, but they harbored a powerful imperative to vindicate themselves on the basis of some general truth: hence their elaborate ideology. Paradoxically, it was to prove they had the truth that they fashioned huge tissues of lies. Much the same was true of the Nazis, who invented the technique of the Big Lie.

The new tyrants—such characters as Slobodan Milosevic, Radovan Karadzic [both are Serbs], or for that matter Saddam Hussein—feel no such pressures. They offer as justification for their actions the thinnest pretexts. Their explanations are less an appeal to reason than a pure gesture of defiance.

Precisely because these tyrants lack intellectual seriousness, we are likely to discount them. But we forget that the great ideological struggle that characterized most of our century was the exception rather than the rule in history. Usually the enemies of civilization have not been so intellectually well-armed as the Communists (and even, in their way, the Nazis) were; but despite this they have often succeeded in prevailing. The once-mighty Romans, after all, were finally defeated by forces culturally, intellectually, and technologically inferior to them....

Nor is this problem merely one of foreign policy or regional conflict. The very idea of rational man—the cardinal concept of our civilization—is, as we have already seen, under explicit attack in our own universities. Our students are today being taught that such categories as "African-American," "female," or "person of color" are in effect more fundamental than the category of American, let alone of rational man, the human being qua [as] human being.

While the motives and consequences may be vastly different in the two cases, the multiculturalist doctrine that is fragmenting our universities as well as our intellectual life, and the "ethnic cleansing" of the Serbs, belong to the same troubling cultural and historical moment.

It is especially disturbing that this should be happening here, for America has always been the most rationally constituted of nations. It is the heir and perfecter of the great Roman idea of the *civis*, a country where nationality has nothing to do with ethnicity, a nation which has fought, through civil war and great domestic turmoil, to realize, however imperfectly, the principle of universality and tolerance.

We are now in an age that will move either toward ever greater fragmentation and violence or toward the ever wider spread of the tolerance and rationality by which we in the West have learned to live and prosper. As was true for most of this century, it is American leadership that will determine the path that history finally takes.

NO

Francis Fukuyama

AGAINST THE NEW PESSIMISM

The end of the cold war has brought about a remarkable consensus between former hawks and doves—at least those professionally involved in some fashion with international affairs, whether they be journalists, academics, or politicians—to the effect that the world has become a much worse place since the demise of the Soviet Union. The pessimistic analysis runs roughly as follows:

In 1989, with the fall of the Berlin Wall, everyone was filled with euphoria over the collapse of Communism and believed that the entire world was turning to democracy. But this expectation proved extraordinarily naive: the collapse of Communism led not to democracy but to the unleashing of virulent nationalism and/or religious passion. Now, about four years later, we see that the world is not progressing toward the "global village" but retreating into atavistic tribalism, whose ugliest expression is the "ethnic cleansing" witnessed in Bosnia.

Nor, according to the pessimistic account, is the former Yugoslavia an isolated case. Rather, Yugoslavia demonstrates that modernity is a very thin veneer indeed; what has happened there portends the resurgence of ethnic passions throughout Eastern Europe and the former USSR. And not just in that region. Even among the apparently stable democracies of Western Europe, attacks on foreign residents and immigrants are just the tip of a larger racist iceberg.

Our international institutions, by this same account, are woefully inadequate to the job of maintaining global order. The United Nations, which many people hoped would become far more effective after the cold war than it was in the days of the Soviet veto, has gotten overextended and is now presiding over policy failures in Bosnia, Somalia, and Haiti. The fecklessness of the European Community (EC) and NATO in failing to stop the slaughter in Bosnia shows how laughable was George Bush's concept of a "new world order." Instead of order we have a world far more dangerous and insecure than that of the cold war. Just as in 1914—so the pessimists conclude—the Balkans in our own day may serve as the tinderbox for a larger European conflict.

This litany, promoted by media and academic pundits around the world, makes the present situation sound very, very bad indeed. But I would argue that it misses the deeper reality of the contemporary situation, and vastly exaggerates the problems we face.

One reason it does so is that the pessimistic outlook is held primarily by Europeans or by Americans focused on European affairs, and represents a highly Eurocentric view. For a "return to tribalism" is not a helpful formula for understanding much of the rest of the world.

* * *

Let us begin at home. After having come through a bruising recession, the United States now leads the industrialized world in economic growth, hitting a rate of close to 4 percent in the fourth quarter of 1993. This latest recession performed the positive function of all recessions: it forced corporations to trim fat and focus on productivity, leaving American companies leaner and more competitive than they have ever been (albeit at a cost in certain jobs). Many of the productivity-enhancing innovations introduced in the 1980's, mostly related to information and communications technology, are now finally showing up on corporate bottom lines, particularly in the service sector. Who today would trade the American semiconductor, computer, aerospace, banking, or biotech industries for their Japanese counterparts? Or, for that matter, the American automobile industry for the German one?

As Henry S. Rowen of Stanford has pointed out, the new reality of the 21st century is that many poor people around the world are going to get rich. This is nowhere more true than in Asia, a region that is hardly descending into tribal violence. Its problems are, rather, ones of adjustment to newfound prosperity. China, the world's largest country, grew an astonishing 13 percent in 1993, and every other country in the region (with the exception of Japan) forged ahead at comparable rates despite the recessions in other parts of the world.

Just as the proponents of modernization theory predicted in the 1950's, democracy has been following in the wake of economic development: the election of Kim Young Sam in South Korea last year represents a final break with that country's authoritarian past, while Taiwan will hold its first completely free elections in the near future. The most remarkable development is occurring in Japan. Despite Karel Van Wolferen's protestations that nothing ever changes in Japan, the Japanese political system is slowly moving away from the corrupt machine politics of the past couple of generations toward a more genuinely pluralistic democracy.

There are, it is true, serious security problems in Asia, the most important being North Korea's nuclear program. Further, the whole region will have to adjust to a very large and dynamic China, which in a decade may have an impact on regional politics comparable to the emergence of a unified Germany after 1871. But the likelihood seems low that in ten years China will still be a unitary, purposeful, authoritarian superpower with external ambitions, given the massive and rapid socioeconomic transformation it is now undergoing. A fragmenting or unstable China would also cause serious problems for the region, but not a balance-of-power threat.

In general, the character of internal relations in East Asia is remarkably different from that of Europe: security concerns have for some time now taken a back seat to economic issues as the chief preoccupation of the region's best minds. This perhaps explains why the countries most directly threatened by North Korean nuclear weapons—South Korea and Japan, as well as China—are decidedly more relaxed about the problem than is the distant United States. They believe that North Korea is one of the world's weakest states, economically and politically, and they maintain that its erratic behavior is the product of weakness rather than strength. Since time is working against the Kim Il Sung regime, it is in their view better dealt with through patience.

Finally, Latin America's prospects look brighter than at any time since the first decades of the century. Despite recent setbacks in Haiti and Venezuela, three of the region's large economies—those of Chile, Mexico, and Argentina—have liberalized substantially over the past decade, and have experienced low inflation and high growth. The code to economic development—a liberal one—has been cracked (or, more properly, relearned after decades of Marxist and Keynesian confusion), and those countries that have mustered the political will to follow its dictates are being rewarded.

Indeed, one of the great slanders of last fall's debate on the North American Free Trade Agreement (NAFTA) was Ross Perot's assertion that Mexicans were desperately poor people who could not afford to buy anything. In the next generation, Americans will have to get used to thinking about Mexico not as a political and economic basket case, but as an avid consumer and increasingly aggressive competitor. Even Peru, by most measures one of the world's most troubled countries, has seen a flood of new investment and positive economic growth since the Fujimori government's arrest of Abimael Guzman, the leader of the Shining Path guerrilla movement. With the passage of NAFTA and the successful conclusion of the Uruguay round of the General Agreement on Tariffs and Trade (GATT), the foundations have been laid for another generation of economic growth in Latin America.

* * *

Now let us turn to Europe. There, it is clear, nationalism and ethnic violence *have* been worse than anyone expected four years ago. Civil or interstate wars have been raging in Georgia, Azerbaijan, and Tajikistan, with many other potential conflicts just beneath the surface. But the chief indictment of the new world order centers, of course, on Bosnia, a horror the like of which has not been seen in Europe since the Holocaust.

The Bosnian conflict has four possible implications for the broader security of Europe. The first is that the war there could spread and involve other Balkan countries, and then the great powers of Europe. The second is that Yugoslavia will set an encouraging precedent for new conflicts among other intertwined ethnic groups in the former Communist world —Hungarians and Romanians, Poles and Lithuanians, Russians and Ukrainians. The third is that ethnic cleansing will legitimate racial and ethnic intolerance even in the apparently stable democracies of Western Europe, undermining their political fabric at a particularly delicate moment. And lastly, the ineffectiveness of international organizations like the EC, NATO, and the UN in dealing with the Yugoslav crisis will damage their credibility and encourage further aggression.

These fears are real, and should not be dismissed lightly. On the other hand, each one can and has been greatly overstated.

Take the question of escalation. The scenarios by which the Yugoslav civil war could lead to a larger conflagration tend to be rather nebulous. Other Balkan countries could indeed get involved if conflict spreads to the Serbian province of Kosovo, or to Macedonia. But of the interested outside powers, Albania—Europe's poorest and most backward country—wields virtually no power, while Greece would likely side with Serbia in crushing Macedonian independence.

Far more important than local Balkan considerations, however, is the absence of a larger great-power rivalry in Europe. In 1914, Europe was divided between two hostile alliances, and if war had not broken out over the Balkans, it could just as well have been sparked by Tangier or the Baghdad Railway. Today, the great powers of Europe are, if anything, struggling to avoid messy foreign entanglements as they try to deal with pressing domestic economic problems. Regional conflicts were of concern during the cold war because the superpower competition left open the constant possibility of superpower intervention and ultimately escalation. But the absence today of larger great-power rivalries means that sectional strife will remain regionalized in its impact, however horrendous the consequences may be for local populations. The ironic result is that even as the world is being united through communications technology, it is being regionalized and *dis*connected politically by the absence of a global great-power rivalry.

The second fear, that the Yugoslav example will be replicated among other ethnic groups, has already been realized in many places. But most of these conflicts, such as those in Transcaucasia and Central Asia, can and have been safely ignored by the outside world. (The only one that will pose direct security concerns for Europe is between Russia and Ukraine, an issue that will be dealt with below.)

The truth is that the mutual hatred of Yugoslavia's constituent groups is in many respects an extreme and atypical situation, and other parts of Eastern Europe look much less bleak. Economically, recent news is encouraging. Virtually all East European countries that have engaged in shock therapy or some variant of radical market reform have seen their inflation rates come down and their production bottom out and then rebound. Poland's GNP stopped falling in the second half of 1992 and is now rapidly on the way up. While recent elections in Poland brought back to power a left-wing coalition including the former Communists, this does not represent a rejection of reform so much as a desire to modulate its pace. Hungary, the Czech Republic, Slovakia, Slovenia, Lithuania, and Latvia are similarly poised for economic turnarounds, much like Western Europe in the early 1950's.

* * *

The third fear—that Bosnia will undermine tolerance and democracy in Western Europe—is supported by the wave of anti-immigrant violence in Germany, Italy, France, and most recently Austria. Nevertheless, the embourgeoisement of West Europeans has gone very far, and their situation is quite different from that of the rural Serbs and Croats driving the current struggle in Yugoslavia. If one scratches the typical Italian, German, or Frenchman of today, one is unlikely to find a vicious nationalist itching to come out. Such individuals certainly exist in Western Europe, but they have thus far been segregated at the margins of their societies. With any degree of sensible leadership, and in the absence of new discontinuities like war or depression, there is no reason to think they will not remain there.

The fourth and final fear concerns the weakness of international institutions in dealing with the war in Yugoslavia. The international community's single most important failure was actually an error of commission rather than omission—that is, the placing of a UN arms embargo on all the combatants in the civil war, and the subsequent failure to lift it so as to give the Bosnian Muslims a chance to defend themselves. An early ending of the embargo was the only policy option that had a chance of stopping Serb aggression at a reasonable cost to the outside world, and the fact that it was so bitterly opposed by the Europeans and so weakly advocated by the United States is both a moral failure and a political mystery.

On the other hand, the failure of various international organizations to intervene actively to promote order in the ways suggested by some does not reflect impotence so much as prudence. It is not self-evident that multinational, or even single-country organizations can intervene effectively and at reasonable cost in many conflicts that are primarily ethnic and/or civil in nature. Those, like Anthony Lewis of the *New York Times*, who argue that appeasement of Serbia encouraged the nationalists in Russia to vote for Vladimir Zhirinovsky in last December's parliamentary election should consider what lessons would have been drawn from a *failed* Western intervention.

The UN cannot function as a serious security organization except when it acts as a cover for unilateral American intervention, as in Korea or the Gulf. It has gotten into trouble in Somalia and Haiti because it did indeed outrun its mandate. As for NATO, it is an effective security organization, but primarily in those canonical big-war scenarios for which it was originally designed. Those who want to extend NATO's functions to include ethnic peacekeeping and the like seriously risk involving it in contingencies for which it is not particularly well suited, thereby unintentionally subverting its ability to execute tasks it is better able to perform. It is true that the world community does not have an effective instrument to promote order and security in regions like Eastern Europe today; but if the chance of escalation is low, this lack will not be critical.

* * *

The gloomy Europeanist assessment of the implications of ethnic conflict would be more cogent if there were an ongoing great-power rivalry. And in fact, many do postulate that one exists, latently if not overtly. Thus, a view is currently coalescing that Russia is well under way toward restoring the old union, using the cause of ethnic Russians stranded in the "near abroad" by the breakup of the Soviet Union to bully and threaten the other Soviet successor states. Some, like Zbigniew Brzezinski, believe it is almost inevitable that President Boris Yeltsin will fall and that Moscow will go back to its authoritarian, expansionist ways. Others, like Henry Kissinger, believe that Yeltsin himself harbors great-power yearnings, while analysts like William Odom argue that Yeltsin has already sold his soul to the Russian military in return for its support in his showdown with parliament....

Ultimately, those who take a jaundiced view of Russian intentions have already written off Yeltsin's democratic experiment. They argue—with much plausibility—that the political situation in Russia is unlikely to stabilize, or the economy to turn around, or democratic institutions to start putting down roots any time soon. Yet the policy question the United States faces is whether *we* want to be the ones to turn out the lights, especially when the new constitution adopted last December at least clears the way for a hyper-presidential regime that has some chance of promoting economic reform and a moderate foreign policy.

* * *

At any given historical moment there are always ominous clouds on the horizon. The current nightmares of specialists in international relations—nationalism or fundamentalism run amok; immigration; a growing gap between rich and poor countries; uncontrolled nuclear proliferation; and the like—many not be as dangerous as they are portrayed. Others less discussed may be more urgent....

* * *

It would be very surprising if the collapse of the largest empire in the world had not caused enormous instability and confusion. We are obviously in the midst of a prolonged transition period as political, economic, and interstate systems transform themselves into something else. But it is vital not to take transitional turbulence for a permanent state of affairs, or to ignore the elements of order that exist while focusing on extreme cases of disorder in relatively unimportant parts of the world.

To be sure, it is primarily specialists in international affairs who are pessimistic; others, like investment bankers, who have to put money on the line behind their views of world order, tend to be much more sanguine. But among people professionally involved with international affairs, the liberals tend to be unhappy with the idea that the West won the ideological struggle of the cold war outright, and are eager to assert that the vindication of capitalism and liberal democracy is only apparent. Many conservatives, for their part, remain wedded to a dour view both of human nature and human institutions.

And then there is a simple matter of prudence: who, liberal or conservative, would not find it safer to be remembered as a Cassandra than as a Pollyanna? A Cassandra proved wrong (and there are many of them populating our TV talk shows and newspaper columns) is never held accountable; indeed, such people retain an aura of moral seriousness for their tragic sense of human history. Naive Pollyannas, by contrast, are routinely held up to ridicule. In the stock market, those who are unduly bearish are punished over the long run. The "market" for views on international affairs is, unfortunately, not quite so self-correcting.

POSTSCRIPT

Has the World Become a More Dangerous Place Since the End of the Cold War?

The end of the Soviet Union, along with the relative decline of the United States compared to its allies Germany and Japan, certainly means that the international system is undergoing momentous change. The system's power structure during the 45 years after the end of World War II can be characterized as bipolar, a system in which there are two dominant poles of power. By the early 1990s the bipolar era was over. It is now in the process of being replaced by a multipolar system, one in which there are four or more significant poles of power. China, Germany, Japan, Russia, and the United States are certainly among those poles, with some other pretenders to big-power status, such as India, appearing on the horizon. The debate among political scientists on the impact such shifts have on stability is extensive and can be reviewed in part by consulting Manus I. Midlarsky, "Polarity and International Stability: Comment," and Ted Hopf, "Polarity and International Stability: Reply," both in the *American Political Science Review* (March 1993).

Is the world more dangerous in the post–cold war era? That depends on your assessment of various threats. Surely there is more local instability in many regions, as the events in Bosnia, Rwanda, and elsewhere attest. But just as surely there is, at least for now, a reduced threat of a potentially civilization-ending nuclear exchange between the United States and its allies and the former Soviet Union and its allies.

A related and even more important question is whether the future will be dark or bright. That also depends. It depends in part on individuals and in part on whole populations of people. Many of the issues that need to be addressed to promote a hopeful future involve two main questions: how active internationally each country should be, and what role it should take (unilaterally or collectively in association with the United Nations) to maintain or restore stability. Issues to be dealt with include how much monetary aid industrialized countries should give to less developed countries to help promote stability, the future desirability of nuclear weapons, and others. There is a great deal of uncertainty in the world. This much is certain, however: the future of the world is not set, and whether the world will be more or less dangerous than it was during the cold war depends in significant part on what governments and individuals alike do to promote or allow instability, on the one hand, or to secure peace, on the other.

To explore the idea of the world system and the momentous forces that are now buffeting it, you might wish to explore such works as James N. Rosenau, *Turbulence in World Politics: A Theory of Change and Continuity* (Princeton University Press, 1992). For a view that the world will continue to be the scene of traditional struggle, see Kenneth N. Waltz, "The Emerging Structure of International Politics," *International Security* (Spring 1993). For an opinion by a political scientist who believes that a new world order is necessary and possible, see Richard Falk, "In Search of a New World Model," *Current History* (April 1993).

ISSUE 2

Should the West Give Massive Foreign Aid to Russia?

YES: Rex A. Wade, from "The United States, Russia and the Republics," *The Soviet and Post-Soviet Review* (vol. 20, nos. 2–3, 1993)

NO: Karen LaFollette, from "Massive Aid to Russia Won't Help," *USA Today Magazine,* a publication of the Society for the Advancement of Education (March 1994)

ISSUE SUMMARY

YES: Rex A. Wade, a professor in the history department at George Mason University, contends that the United States and other industrialized countries should extend massive aid to Russia and to the other former Soviet republics. Because the policies and actions of the West will help determine the nature of the political regime in Russia, such aid should be forthcoming.

NO: Karen LaFollette, a research associate at the Institute for Political Economy in Washington, D.C., argues that the West should resist the urge to pour aid into Russia, especially in light of the rebirth of militant nationalism there.

Russia has experienced two momentous revolutions during the twentieth century. The overthrow of the czar in 1917 began the first. After a brief attempt at democratic rule, Lenin's Bolshevik Communists seized power in 1918 and established a totalitarian government, naming the remade Russian empire the Union of Soviet Socialist Republics.

The seeds of the second revolution were sown with the elevation in 1985 of reform-minded Mikhail Gorbachev to the leadership of the Soviet Communist party. His reforms, including *perestroika* (restructuring) and *glasnost* (openness, including limited democracy) unleashed strong forces within the Soviet Union.

The revolution that Gorbachev's reforms promoted—or at least contributed to—reached a crisis stage in 1991. The old-guard Communist party leaders, whose positions of power were being threatened by both *perestroika* and the demands of many of the Soviet Union's constituent republics for greater autonomy, staged a coup against Gorbachev, by then the Soviet president, on August 18.

The coup collapsed within several days, however, in part because hundreds of thousands of Soviet citizens took to the streets to rally against it. Boris

Yeltsin, the president of Russia (then a Soviet republic), was the most visible symbol of democratic defiance of the old guard.

In the aftermath of the crisis, the already weak Soviet state lapsed into a terminal coma. Central authority dissipated. Real power shifted rapidly to Yeltsin's office in the Russian White House and to the other 14 republics, which moved rapidly toward independence. On December 25, 1991, the Soviet flag was lowered for the last time from atop the Kremlin and the Russian flag was raised in its stead.

Of the former Soviet republics (FSRs), Russia is by far the largest, the most populous, and the most powerful. Russia has retained all of the Soviet Union's tactical nuclear weapons and the vast majority of its strategic-range nuclear weapons. These factors make the future course of Russia a matter of great concern for the world, and Russia's future is the focus of this debate.

The fundamental question is what, if anything, the West should do to assist the former Soviet republics, especially Russia. Most commentators agree that the industrialized countries should encourage Russia to undertake political reforms to secure a democratic system of government and economic reforms to privatize the economy (and shift ownership from the state to private entrepreneurs). Those who advocate the adoption of a market-based economy by Russia believe that economic reform is important for two, interrelated reasons.

The first is that capitalism will lead to economic recovery and an improved standard of living for the Russian people. Second, those who advocate economic reform in Russia assume that better living conditions for citizens will improve the odds of democracy surviving in Russia, thereby decreasing the chances of political instability and the associated possibility of foreign adventurism by Russia. Political scientists generally agree that democracy is most secure in political systems where basic human needs, such as food and housing, are being met. There is also considerable research that demonstrates that democracies seldom if ever go to war with one another.

Thus far, a combination of a lack of a democratic tradition in Russia (which has never before had a sustained democratic government) and poor economic conditions have cast considerable uncertainty on the future of Russian political reform. Throughout the process of struggle and change in Russia and the former Soviet republics over the past couple of years, the West has extended significant aid to Russia and, to a lesser extent, the other FSRs, through grants, loans, trade concessions, and renegotiation of Russian debts to the West. At the July 1993 economic summit of the seven most powerful Western countries (Canada, France, Germany, Great Britain, Italy, Japan, and the United States —the so-called Group of Seven, or G-7, countries), Russian president Boris Yeltsin was granted approximately $3 billion in additional aid.

In the following articles, Rex A. Wade and Karen LaFollette differ over whether or not such massive aid and its continuance are wise. They agree that economic and political reform should be encouraged, but they disagree over whether or not economic aid is the correct approach.

19

YES   Rex A. Wade

THE UNITED STATES, RUSSIA
AND THE REPUBLICS

The Soviet Union has collapsed, it is gone. With it has gone a historical era, both in its own history and the history of international relations. It represented a unique player on the international scene, first in its role since 1917 as advocate of a universal creed and with the avowed goal of fundamentally reshaping the world and the power relationships therein, and second in its role after 1945 as a superpower and in the Cold War. Observers are widely hailing the end of the Cold War. We will hope that they are correct. What was incorrect, certainly, was the belief, widely held about 1989–91, that the end of the Cold War and Soviet universalist claims automatically meant a more peaceful, more democratic, world.

It might yet be such a world, but it might not be. That will depend to a very large degree on events inside Russia and the newly independent republics of the former Soviet Union, but it also will depend at least in part on the policies and actions of the Western countries, and especially the United States, toward Russia and the newly independent republics. Yet, we are uncertain as to what our role should be, for with the passing of the Soviet Union and the Cold War the focus of American, and West European, foreign policy for the past half century passed also. Developing a new one, in general and toward Russia and the New Republics in particular, is urgent.

Simply put, if Russia and the major successor states (Ukraine in particular) can develop stable democracies and populace-oriented, market economies, then the prospects for peace will be vastly improved. That will not remove conflict in the world, for there are too many other sources of strife around the globe. But if America and Russia, the West and the new republics in Eastern Europe, are able to act cooperatively internationally, then those conflicts appear in a very different context, both in terms of the possibility of settlement and in terms of the danger of their escalation into great power conflict. Moreover, the danger of direct superpower conflict is vastly reduced if the main successor to the Soviet Union, Russia, no longer sees itself as fundamentally hostile to the world of liberal democracy, but instead views itself as part of that world. It has become something of a commonplace to say that

From Rex A. Wade, "The United States, Russia and the Republics," *The Soviet and Post-Soviet Review*, vol. 20, nos. 2–3 (1993), pp. 115–128. Copyright © 1993 by *The Soviet and Post-Soviet Review*. Reprinted by permission.

democracies do not go to war against each other. I am not entirely convinced of the absoluteness of that statement, but it certainly seems to contain a strong element of truth.

The problem, the question, is will Russia and the newly independent republics develop stable, democratic, prosperous societies? Or, will they revert to more authoritarian, aggressive governments, ones quite willing and able to direct the resources of the society not to satisfying the material needs of their population but to supporting the military and political ambitions of authoritarian leaders? The answer, while largely dependent upon internal developments, can be influenced by America and the West. How? Let us try to answer that in a two-step manner, by first looking briefly at the problems of political and economic reconstruction in the successor states of the former Soviet Union (understanding those are essential if we are to make intelligent choices about what policies are needed) and then at the lines of action open to America and the West to help resolve those problems. In doing so we must remember that a triple revolution is in process in the former Soviet Union: from authoritarian to democratic government, from command to market economy, and from empire to nation-states. We can look at the problems, and Western action, within the framework of these three revolutions.

At its heart the Soviet system had become dysfunctional by the mid-1980s. First, and perhaps foremost, there was a fundamental economic problem: the command economy no longer worked. . . . By the 1980s, however, the elaborate and rigid system created to provide political and economic control and basic industrialization . . . could not adjust to the realities of late twentieth-century economy. It could *neither* support the great power military pretensions of the Soviet state (its main goal) nor provide a decent quality of life for its citizens (its secondary goal). Indeed, things were getting worse. Change was essential. It quickly became obvious that the economic system had to be transformed into one which addressed itself to the needs and desires of the population rather than the political and military ambitions of the rulers.

This requires a basically free-enterprise market-oriented economy, which alone can produce the desired material well-being. . . .

Second, the political system was equally bankrupt. By the 1980s the Communist Party was a moribund organization . . . [and] it was becoming apparent that the authoritarian political system was incompatible with the growing desire of a better educated population for civil rights and individual freedoms as well as economic progress. This political problem, plus the dramatic economic crisis, led to the collapse of the highly centralized political system. In its place must evolve a more open, pluralistic and democratic system, with emphasis upon the rights of the individual and the rule of law instead of the traditional stress on the rights of the state, the obligations of the individual and autocratic authority.

The transition to a new political culture will not be easy. Democracy is a fragile system, dependent upon a broad range of supporting cultural values and institutions, not easily implanted in an alien soil. Yet, developing it is important. In doing so the people of the former Soviet Union can build on an evolution toward parliamentary democracy in late Imperial Russia and on the growing educated "civil society" and the many interest groups that developed in late Soviet history.

Third, nationalism proved to be a stronger force than anyone... believed. As the central authorities faltered, it reasserted itself vigorously, bringing an end to the ancient Russian/Soviet empire. The empire had been built by conquest, sustained by force and then rebuilt by reconquest after 1918 and sustained by even greater repressive force....

National sentiments continued to exist, however, and indeed were reinforced in a peculiar way: the republics gave a sense of identity and statehood to the larger nationalities. They now were republics, with boundaries and bureaucracies....

The state system of Eastern Europe has to be restructured. This endeavor involves first of all the acceptance of the end of empire.... Ukraine, the Baltic nations and other areas have [repeatedly] shown their unwillingness to be a part of some Muscovite state. Russia must accept that fact....

In addition, acceptance of the independence of the new republics is critically important for Russia's international relations. A Russia launching attacks on its new neighbors will not bode well for international relations. The former East European satellites will regard Russian attempts to reconquer those areas a threat to their own independence. The foreign assistance of various kinds which Russia needs, especially economic, will not be forthcoming to an expansionist Russian dictatorship. Moreover, Russia desperately needs peace for its own internal reasons. It needs to direct its own resources to economic development for consumer goods, not for arms. And especially it needs it if the new attempt at democracy is to succeed.

If, as we suggested earlier, it is in our, as well as their, interest to promote these kinds of economic and political developments in the former USSR, how do we go about it? What should American foreign policy be?

First of all, we must recognize that the US, and especially President Clinton personally, has to take the lead in formulating Western policy toward Russia and the new republics. There was some brave talk in 1990–91 that a new Western Europe collectively might take the lead in dealing with Eastern Europe. But what with its own distractions and enormous difficulty in developing consistent policies, it could not do so.... Still, it seems obvious that both quick help and a coherent long-term strategy will come only if Clinton involves himself in formulating a basic policy and then aggressively presses the G-7 [Canada, France, Germany, Great Britain, Italy, Japan, and the United States] (and others) into accepting and implementing it. Otherwise we will see more of the same process of endless discussions without resolution that has characterized policy toward Eastern Europe for the past three years (with the Bosnian disaster a particularly clear example). Moreover, Russian pride demands that the United States, the other "super power," take the primary role in developing a new Russia-West relationship.

... The US, backed by Europe, needs to make a commitment to *long-term* assistance and consistent policies designed to stabilize the political and economic situation of Russia and Eastern Europe; this will not be a quick fix. Change will be incremental and uneven; we must learn to live with that while keeping our attention fixed on long-term objectives. Unfortunately, we live in an era that conditions us to short attention spans and quick solutions to complex problems.

Overcoming these difficulties is an essential part of political leadership, however, and to that Clinton, with perhaps two terms ahead of him, needs to commit himself. True, he is primarily oriented toward domestic issues, but in an age of global economy the line between domestic economic prosperity (his first priority), and international relations, especially stability, is rapidly disappearing. Clinton must realize that and address the problem directly. Also, he must become aware of the negative side of failing to act: he does not want to be known as the President who "lost" democratic Russia and the end of the Cold War, during whose watch the promise of greater international peace gave way to a new superpower rivalry. In other words, there are some basic political realities which push Clinton toward an activist role in this area.

Unfortunately, other factors can drive him in the opposite direction. One such element, of course, is the very complexity of the problem, the difficulty of identifying the best thing to do and how to do it. Second, the terrible budget constraints make it difficult for the United States (and Europe) to contribute the massive amounts of money necessary to shore up the Russian, not to mention other, economies. Third, the initial efforts to garner West European support for a more vigorous policy in Eastern Europe, in Bosnia especially but generally as well, have been notably unsuccessful, and Clinton has shown a tendency to give way rather than assert American leadership.

Fourth is the basic problem of developing a new foreign policy for the post Cold War world. This will require vision and innovative thinking. . . .

A fifth, final, problem that inhibits an active policy toward Russia is the perverse fact that becoming too deeply involved may work against what we hope to achieve. A growing element in Russia is suspicious of American actions and contends that the United States is responsible, through sabotage and subversion, for the demise of the Soviet Union, and that it is today working for the further destruction of Russia. There are frequent allegations that Gorbachev, Yel'tsin and other reformers were (or are) American CIA agents! This reaction can be attributed in part to the inevitable conspiracy theories. But it also reflects a deeper resentment of the economic reforms, which are seen as Western required or at least Western inspired, and hence a general suspiciousness of the West and its motives. We are in a position where aid, unless done right (and maybe in any event) will be used against the reformers.

Despite these negatives, Clinton probably will be forced into a more active policy toward Russia and the new republics, either *ad hoc* or as part of a larger foreign policy initiative. If so, what specifically might Clinton and the United States (and Western Europe) do to encourage a desirable outcome to the enormous changes underway in the former Soviet Union? We can assess that question through the same three categories of economics, domestic politics and nationalism/new republics.

First, the economic problems, which must be dealt with vigorously. Several things must be done to encourage development of a healthy market economy (we speak here of policy, of types of actions, rather than specific dollar figures).

1. There must be a coherent strategy for economic reconstruction which links together all parts of economic assistance, coordinating bilateral government policies, international agencies, private investment, other initiatives and the necessary Russian policies. This approach must be worked out among American, European and Russian/Republic leaders, but the United States must take leadership and may have to lean hard on some allies. Russia and the republics will require a complex combination of various types of assistance, from broad monetary to very specific technical aid for certain industries, from helping develop economic literacy to investment....

2. It must include significant private capital investment from outside. This sort of investment from the private sector is especially important because it can be self-sustaining and continuous. These economic investments must be sound, justified from a business standpoint. They might involve some governmental guarantees, via agencies such as the Overseas Private Investment Corporation and the European Bank for Reconstruction and Development, but the main force must be private business investment for business reasons. For this purpose, however, Russia and the other republics must create stable legal, monetary and tax systems. Only when businesses can calculate risk, profit, prices, and so on and be assured of their property rights, will they invest in a volume and manner likely to have significant impact.

3. The fundamental ignorance of economics, business practice and related matters in the post-Soviet world must be addressed. Some of this inexperience can be dealt with through government actions, but one of the best ways is to encourage private and volunteer efforts. Non-profit organizations, universities, retired business executives and businesses investing in the former USSR, among others, can work with the new post-Soviet private sector to foster basic marketing and production techniques and values....

4. We must encourage consumer oriented production. This the country desperately needs, and the domestic market can be the motor for driving economic development. Moreover, it will reinforce the political reforms.

5. At the same time, we must facilitate access to international trade markets and systems, through most favored nation status, involvement in the various tariff negotiations and other means. Bringing the Russians, Ukrainians and others into the world trade system is important economically and politically.

6. We must be attuned to local development. Power already has devolved to local regions within Russia as well as to the Republics. Some local leaders are more willing and able to reform, innovate and use assistance, and we should focus on them. Successful specific, local, developments will be very important. We should not look only at the "big picture."

7. There must be priorities for individual countries. It is important to pay attention and be involved in the developments in all the new states, but some are more important than others. Russia must be the main priority simply because of the impact its development, or lack thereof, will have on the others and on the broader world.

It may sound callous, but what happens there is more important than what happens in Estonia or Uzbekistan. What happens in Ukraine is probably next most important. Assistance should be focused on especially important countries, although not to the exclusion of the others.

8. Humanitarian aid is essential to relieve the suffering caused by the economic collapse and the dislocation created by the economic transition. We must assist in providing a "social fund," a safety-net for all the population. This aid could include housing for military forces, especially officers, returning from Eastern Europe. It will not be that expensive, and it is necessary not only for humanitarian reasons but also because it is important to the survival of the economic reforms and democracy.

9. While it is necessary that the US take a leading role, that role must be shared. And not just with the G-7 countries. For example, there is no reason that the Nordic countries should not take a major role in assisting the Baltic states as part of a broader Baltic initiative.

The collapse of the Soviet Union destroyed the "unified economic space," while the end of the command system destroyed the way economic decision making was done without providing a new one. The result is a complex of republics and regions pursuing uncoordinated and often inconsistent policies, and within which there is a vigorous struggle among old economic elites, new entrepreneurs, new and old political leaders, to control and direct the economy. This problem will not be easily resolved even within states, and we can assume quite different systems will emerge among them. However, wise and coordinated economic aid and development programs for all the republics can make a major difference. It must be the focus of American and Western policy.

What about the *political* transformation of Russia and the Republics? What can we do to help the promotion of democracy in Russia and the republics? Here is an even more difficult issue than economic aid. It is perhaps indicative of the problem that discussions about helping Russia and the other republics often include specific recommended economic measures, but say little about how to facilitate political reform.... Yet, the West can play a role. How?

First, the United States and European governments must constantly insist upon the importance of these matters, in theory and practice. Western insistence upon them played a role in opening up the Soviet political system (and thus in its ultimate destruction). We must continue to press the new governments about their actions in this area, despite any objections by local leaders that we are interfering in their affairs (this is especially true of Ukraine and other republics, which often slip below the horizon of news reporting....

Second, we must support those trying to create a more open and democratic society and must encourage the development of cultural values of civil rights, pluralism, representative democracy and tolerance of those with different opinions. These efforts probably will be best made through a multiplicity of initiatives, mostly private, which familiarize Russians and others with these values and their importance....

Third, we must remember that democracy is messy. The political turmoil in Russia between Yel'tsin and Parliament has not been all bad, and we should keep some perspective on it. Political democracy does involve political conflict, why should we expect it to be absent in Russia?...

Fourth, we should not expect immediate, universal, uniform success. The various countries will develop different political systems, differing degrees and types of democracy (and authoritarianism). It really makes little difference to us whether a presidential or parliamentary system emerges, or how many parties appear (as long as there are more than one). I suspect that we will see more of the French model (highly centralized and bureaucratized, weak local government) than of the Anglo-American type (more decentralized, greater emphasis on local government, on individual rights and on restrictions on the power of government). And the process will take time and may, within a given country, be a multistaged evolution. The important thing is progress *toward* political democracy.

Finally, what will the rise of nationalism, the end of empire and the emergence of numerous small republics imply for international relations and security issues, both within the area of the former USSR and East bloc as well as more broadly? Here, America and the West have a vital interest and can play a more active and direct role, almost exclusively via government action.

First, our governments must accept (and they were slow to do so) the end of the Russian empire and must firmly insist that the Russians do so as well. This admission is essential to everything else. Although the political configuration of the territory of the former Soviet Union probably will undergo further changes, its breakup into a number of independent states is a reality for the foreseeable future. It must be made clear to Russia that aggressive, imperialistic actions will carry a very heavy penalty, primarily economic.

Second, at the same time the other successor states should know that they must act responsibly towards Russia. Almost inevitably, the new leaders are tempted to strengthen home support by anti-Russian gestures and actions.... We must make clear to them that we will support their independence, but not irresponsible action. Most of all, they should be fully aware that American or West European troops will not be used to defend their independence.

Third, general encouragement should be given to the survival and development of the Commonwealth of Independent States or something similar because of its importance to the working out of economic problems, its potential value in heading off or settling conflicts between republics and the role it can play in coordinating policies to deal with various common legacies of the Soviet era (such as its environmental problems)....

Fourth, American and every other foreign policy must be aware of certain power realities, the most important being that Russia will remain the great power of the region and will play a special role....

Fifth, it will be important for the United States to continue to treat Russia as a great power, perhaps even a superpower, and an equal. Continued close consultation, even summits, will be important in encouraging Russia to continue to develop a foreign policy based on cooperation, mutual action and the search for mutual interests rather than confrontation. The Russians are very sensitive about the loss of their former power status, and we are well advised to consider that sensitivity.

Sixth, special consideration must be given to security issues and potential sources of conflict in the post-Soviet area. Border issues, treatment of minorities, trade conflicts and the Crimea are among the more dangerous issues that could lead to conflict. In addressing these matters we probably should strongly encourage the use of international organizations —the United Nations and others....

Where does this leave us? America is still trying to develop a general foreign policy framework for the post Cold War era, both in general and specifically toward Russia and the newly independent republics. That effort will take time. The two major issues to be settled, perhaps, are 1) how interventionist American foreign policy will be, and 2) whether it primarily will be reactive to events elsewhere or will act within a broad and well-defined vision of American policy and interests.... In our interdependent world the United States has a strong national interest in encouraging democratic, open societies. Issues of human rights should be seen as part of that broader interest and be supportive of it. We cannot intervene everywhere, however, especially in civil conflicts.... We need some overriding policy to guide our varied responses to these disorders.

We must develop a more comprehensive vision of the post Cold War era and America's role therein, and we must set priorities for our action based upon achieving that vision. We cannot do everything there is to do. Russia remains the second most powerful country, at least militarily, with tremendous ability to destablilize the world. Therefore it, and the major republics such as Ukraine, must be a primary focus of our concerns and policy. The United States must take a leadership role in providing assistance for the economic and political reconstruction of the area, attempting to influence the emergence there of democratic societies, especially in Russia, which would then join the US and Western Europe as a partner in promoting stability and prosperity in the region and the world, and in finding peaceful solutions to world problems.

Nor should we forget that among the problems thereby "solved" are America's own, for our own future well-being demands that we reduce our defense burden and turn more of our resources to solving domestic problems and economic competitiveness. Assisting Russia and the Republics is in our own interest. We should remember that point ourselves, and tell the Russians frankly that it is so. We should assure them that our actions spring not only from traditional American humanitarian impulses and from traditional American interest in the spread of democracy, but also from the fundamental awareness that our own interests as a country, as well as theirs, are served by helping stable, peaceful, prosperous and democratic societies develop where formerly stood the USSR.

NO

Karen LaFollette

MASSIVE AID TO RUSSIA WON'T HELP

The arguments against aid to Russia that would strengthen the old order hold today just as they did when Western policymakers were anxious to save [Soviet president] Mikhail Gorbachev and when they wished to support democratically elected Boris Yeltsin. In 1991, Yeltsin and Moscow Mayor Gavriil Popov opposed financial aid to the U.S.S.R. because they believed that it would be used by the Kremlin to prop up decrepit Soviet institutions. With real money at its disposal, the Soviet government would have been able to repurchase loyalties and subvert or slow the transition to democracy. Once the Soviet institutions began to decay, hard currency would frustrate real economic reform for the simple reason that there would be nowhere for the financial aid to flow except into reviving the very institutions that had caused the U.S.S.R.'s economic problems in the first place.

The West, in its desire to help, should resist the urge to pour in aid indiscriminately, especially in light of the [strength of the ultranationalists in the 1993] Russian elections and the rebirth of militancy. Government-to-government transfers of more than one trillion dollars to the Third World since World War II have not helped those nations to develop. On the contrary, cutting-edge scholars in recipient countries have concluded that the aid has institutionalized corruption, entrenched atavistic institutions, and sidelined the private sector to the black market. In Russia, the danger is that reformers could be distracted by the opportunities for graft presented by large-scale financial transfers, and then there would be no one to undertake the transition.

No aid at all is better than using Western taxpayers' resources to undermine reformers by strengthening institutions that they have to overcome. Policy changes that would stimulate the private sector—deregulation, privatization, lowering the tax burden, and eliminating barriers to trade—can be accomplished without aid. The Russians themselves have to construct a viable market economy.

If the West is determined to help, there appear to be several constructive ways it might assist the transition. The Western nations could encourage the Russians to introduce reforms to stimulate entrepreneurship, enter into free-trade agreements with Russian and other struggling ex-Soviet republics, promote private investment by eliminating disincentives to it in their own countries, help finance mass privatization of the Russian economy, forgive or restructure the foreign debt incurred by the former Soviet Union, and finance the dismantling of nuclear weapons. With most of the Group of Seven [Canada, France, Germany, Great Britain, Italy, Japan, and the United States] countries strapped by budget deficits, those suggestions have the advantage that none of them involve new large-scale financial transfers to the Russian government.

The West should advocate policies that will stimulate the productive area of the Russian economy—the emergent private sector. The focus should be on rapid privatization, deregulation, and the establishment of a favorable business climate based on a sound currency. The government should be advised to establish a regime of low taxation and minimal regulation, uphold and expand private property rights under a rule of law, and establish investment laws and trade policies that would attract foreign capital and stimulate rapid growth of the private sector.

Another way the industrialized nations could help Russia and the other countries of the former Soviet Union is by removing trade barriers. Nations that have received the most Western aid since World War II report that lowering barriers to trade is far more helpful to their development than are large amounts of government-to-government aid....

The industrialized countries further could help the former Soviet republics by eliminating subsidies to export industries to foster a "level playing field" in international trade. Particularly prevalent in agriculture, subsidies result in higher prices for domestic consumers and give an unfair advantage to privileged companies.

For their part, the former Soviet republics unilaterally should lower protectionist trade barriers and endeavor to set up a free-trade area, which eventually could be joined with that created by the North American Free Trade Agreement. Also, Russia should eliminate subsidies to industries and implement its Law on Bankruptcy to allow inefficient industries to expire so that capital can be freed to be reallocated for more productive uses —such as the production of exports for hard currency.

While Russian reformers need to create a good domestic business climate that attracts foreign companies, the West could help the process by dismantling disincentives for businesses to invest overseas. One disincentive is the Foreign Corrupt Practices Act, which prohibits American companies from participating in deals using bribes to speed transactions. Not only is the law naive about the way business is routinely conducted in many areas of the world, it does not take into account the special circumstances in Russia and the U.S. interest in promoting free enterprise in former communist countries....

Western governments should help eliminate barriers to private investment in the former Soviet Union. In the end, however, there is little that government can do. When former senior Russian official Gennadii Burbulis was asked to whom he thought property would belong in one year and then in three years, he replied: "To the quick and the smart." In Russia, private property rights are being defined, through fair means and foul, and American companies' share in the benefits of secure private property in Russia will depend on the extent to which they hustle to operate in today's uncertain environment. Throughout history, private property rights and the infrastructure of a market economy have evolved for the most part independent, and in advance, of government action. Governments tend to codify existing arrangements and *de facto* property rights.

The U.S. government already is spending $13,000,000 to finance—through the voucher system the Russian government initiated on Oct. 1, 1992—an ambitious plan to privatize hundreds of state-owned companies. Reformers aim to rapidly privatize 5,000 large state enterprises. Previously, Russia had virtually no big factories.

The U.S. government is paying the International Finance Corporation of the World Bank and the accounting firm of Price Waterhouse to organize auctions of state-owned businesses in 10 regions of Russia. According to the plan agreed to by each firm, the government will give workers a 51% ownership stake or a 30% ownership stake and auction off a portion of the remaining shares for privatization vouchers.

The voucher plan enables Russians to buy shares in state factories. Each of the 148,000,000 Russians is entitled to one voucher nominally valued at 10,000 rubles ($17.50)....

Another way the West could ease Russia's transaction would be to forgive or restructure the foreign debt incurred by the former Soviet Union. As of Feb. 1, 1993, the U.S. Treasury reported that debt totaled $81,000,000,000, of which $39,000,000,000 is owed to official creditors and $22,000,000,000 to commercial banks. Suppliers' credits of $14,200,000,000 made up the bulk of the remainder.

Lending to the Soviet Union was not commercially wise, and Western banks and governments should have to bear the consequences. Russia's foreign debt is mainly a European headache; 11% of the official debt, or approximately $4,000,000,000, is owed to the U.S. government, compared with 39% owed to Germany alone. Unofficial U.S. Treasury estimates place the non-government-guaranteed debt owed American commercial banks at a maximum of $250–300,000,000. At a meeting of the Group of Seven in Tokyo on April 14 and 15, 1993, the major creditor governments agreed to ease the terms of repayment of Russia's debt. At present, it seems that a combination of debt forgiveness and rescheduling would enable reformers to focus on the immediate task of establishing incentive for production. The transition might occur faster if reformers did not have to worry, at least for now, about sending a large portion of their country's scarce resources to repay a foreign debt that was assumed without the consent of the population.

Finally, there are some 30,000 nuclear weapons in potentially unstable regions. The first Strategic Arms Reduction Treaty (START I), negotiated between the U.S. and the Soviet Union, was signed in July, 1991. Since the breakup of the Soviet Union, the pact has been recast by a series of negotiated appendices to bind the four former Soviet republics that control parts of the nuclear force. START II, confirmed by Pres. George Bush on Dec. 30, 1992, would cut the combined number of warheads in the former Soviet Union and the U.S. to a total of 6,500. The former Soviet Union would be allowed to retain a total of 3,000.

Instability and disputes within the Commonwealth of Independent States have placed compliance with the provisions of START II in doubt. The

$800,000,000 U.S. program to help fund the dismantling of nuclear weapons in Russia has bogged down, according to Joseph Kelly of the General Accounting Office, because of chaos within Russia, Moscow's lingering obsession with secrecy, and its determination to make as much money as it can on the deal.

The U.S. should push for further cuts in the nuclear arsenals, in part to persuade the former Soviet countries to comply with START II. Washington could offer to purchase perhaps 29,500 missiles, send experts to oversee their dismantling, and encourage the Russian government to use the money to help create a ruble-stabilization fund. A relatively low offer of perhaps $200,000,000 could be tied to policy changes in Western countries, such as the elimination of subsidies to export industries, to sweeten the deal. It is understandable that the Russian government and possible that of Ukraine might wish to retain a nuclear capacity, but 500 nuclear missiles still would be a formidable arsenal.

SUPPORTING YELTSIN AND THE REFORMERS

It seems worthwhile at this time for the West to help Yeltsin and his team, who have made seemingly serious commitments to reform and the creation of a market economy in Russia, especially considering the more radical alternatives. At the same time, the West should not pin all its hopes for Russian democracy on one man, a strategy that could backfire if that leader ends up a casualty of International Monetary Fund-sponsored austerity. The reduction or elimination of industrialized countries' trade barriers, debt forgiveness, and the other measures outlined above are perhaps the most effective mans by which the West can support Russian reform.

If the West is determined to provide aid to Russia, the amounts should not be large. Furthermore, any government assistance should be designed to minimize its negative effects on reform. Yeltsin's policies will not be strengthened by providing large-scale economic assistance.

A massive aid program will strengthen state institutions and postpone badly needed reforms, but not help Yeltsin or the Russian people. Western officials should recognize that reformers and hard-liners are engaged in a fierce struggle over property. It is not over privatization *per se*, but about who benefits from privatization.

Reformers are battling the old power structure over how privatization will proceed and who will end up in charge. The stakes are enormous. The assets up for grabs include 46,000 large enterprises and Russia's vast natural resources, including potentially profitable oil fields....

Nomenklatura privatization, whereby functionaries take over state enterprises and convert them to private businesses, is far advanced. In January, 1993, Russian Deputy Prime Minister in charge of privatization Anatoly Chubais asserted that the fiercest struggle would be unleashed by attempts of the "communist opposition" to grant preferential rights and benefits to the employees of the privatized enterprises....

Private property is the basis of a market economy, and granting the population property rights is the key to jump-starting a market economy. Western advice and limited aid should be targeted to help Russian reformers to stimulate the growth of a successful private sector and rapidly privatize the entire economy. Stripped of their control over state enterprises, hard-liners would find themselves forced to respond to the incentives of a thriving market economy and would cease to be a threat.

Agricultural reform is critical to creating a viable economy. In Russia, collective farms still dominate the sector, and official production is falling. According to newspaper reports, collective farmers face problems such as insufficient government credit at preferential interest rates; a disproportionate rise in prices for agricultural inputs, compared with prices for agricultural products; and bad weather, the perennial scapegoat of the old Soviet regime.

The real issue is the paucity of private property in agriculture. The failures of collective farming are well-known, but privatization is proceeding slowly because of resistance from the Russian parliament and local agricultural bureaucrats. A legal framework to protect private property rights in agriculture largely is absent. In December 1992, Yeltsin signed a law that permits citizens to buy and sell private plots, albeit with a feudalistic restriction that prohibits the plots being used for other than originally specified purposes. That is a step in the right direction, but in today's chaotic Russia, laws exist mainly on paper....

HARMFUL WESTERN ADVICE

At present, Russian reformers are receiving conflicting advice from the West, and much of it is counterproductive. The West, with its emphasis on social welfare and redistribution, discourages Russians from establishing the incentives they need. Western governments have given the IMF and the World Bank a leading role in providing advice and aid to governments trying to make the transition to a market economy.

Both the IMF and the World Bank view privatization as merely one of a list of reforms that have to be undertaken. To those institutions, privatization is less important than macroeconomic stabilization, price reforms, and introduction of a convertible currency. Many of the fiscal reforms those institutions advocate —such as tight control over the money supply to combat inflation and the introduction of a convertible currency—will be necessary in due course. The trouble is that both the World Bank and the IMF place the cart before the horse. Rather than press for privatization of the entire economy as quickly as possible, which would eliminate the need for subsidies to bankrupt enterprises and thus help cut inflation, the World Bank recommends that the government subsidize loss-making enterprises during the transition period....

During 1992 and early 1993, the Russian government was trying to meet IMF targets in order to satisfy IMF condition for a formal stabilization plan that large-scale financial transfers depend upon. Although agreements between member governments and the IMF never are made public, they typically entail fiscal restraint (while keeping in place deficit-ridden state enterprises), currency devaluations, and tax increases to cut domestic demand. In December, 1993, the World Bank began exploring options to step up aid for privatization and support for the poor, even if Russia fails to meet IMF inflation targets.

At the behest of Western advisers, in 1992, the Russian government freed many prices in advance of far-reaching reform and levied a series of taxes, including a 28% value-added tax, that, in combination with pre-existing regulations and prohibitions, hobble the nascent private sector or at least keep it in the unofficial economy. In February, 1993, the government heeded the repeated calls of its Western advisers to free prices in the petroleum sector; as a result, natural gas prices nearly trebled for domestic users of heating and nearly doubled for industrial users....

A Russian market economy is being created from the bottom up. While politicians bicker over market reforms, ordinary people are forced to participate in the market economy or perish. Muscovites trade, barter, or sell whatever they can get their hands on to supplement meager salaries that often do not cover even a week's food. The result is thriving commerce on Moscow's streets.

The days of waiting in block-long queues are over for those who can afford high prices. Everything, including imported luxuries that most people never saw during the years of communist rule, is available to those with high incomes—about 20% of the population. The problem is that Yeltsin in following the advice of Russia's official Western advisers, is making the transition more painful than it needs to be. Russians believe most people are becoming worse off than better off at this juncture.

This is a critical moment in Russia's transition, one that could prove dangerous unless it rapidly establishes a market economy to begin to deal with its vast social and political problems. The long-suffering peoples of the former Soviet republics deserve a quick and less painful transition to a market economy. That can be achieved if they set entrepreneurs free to use capital and new ideas to create wealth. With the establishment of economic and political liberty in Russia and the other former Soviet republics, the region can ring in the 21st century with prosperity and hope.

Once and for all, the West should end its outdated reliance on large-scale government-to-government aid. The world can ill afford the consequences of turning Russia into an international welfare dependency. Massive aid to Russia only would entrench unproductive institutions and prolong the crisis. A better solution is to base development on the proven success of free markets and free enterprise.

POSTSCRIPT

Should the West Give Massive Foreign Aid to Russia?

Western aid to Russia continues to be a major international question. Russian president Boris Yeltsin traveled to Italy in July 1994 to ask the leaders of the major industrial powers to increase aid beyond the billions pledged at the 1993 G-7 meeting in Tokyo, Japan. The future of Russia remains an important international concern, in part because the country still controls a strong nuclear arsenal, although several recent arms-control treaties are reducing the number of weapons possessed by the United States, Russia, and the former Soviet republics that have nuclear weapons (Belarus, Kazakhstan, and Ukraine). Idealistic Americans, Canadians, and others who live in democratic countries and believe in democratic principles think the West should help promote democracy in Russia, and elsewhere, as a matter of principle. This is argued, for example, by Larry Diamond in "Promoting Democracy," *Foreign Policy* (Summer 1992).

More pragmatically, there is a strong assumption in the West that a democratic (and capitalist) Russia is more likely to be a friendly Russia. The view that democracies are more peaceable, at least with one another, is supported by academic research. For a recent article discussing this research, see Alex Mintz and Nehemia Geva, "Why Don't Democracies Fight Each Other?" *Journal of Conflict Resolution* (September 1993).

There is an old adage about the proof being in the pudding, and one way to judge whether or not Western aid can help achieve economic and political reform in Russia is to measure its success. Unfortunately, the answer is not yet clear! One reason for this is that a great deal of the aid pledge has not been delivered. For example, of $2.1 billion in U.S. aid approved in 1993, only 25 percent had been made available to Russia by mid-1994. Another reason that it is hard to come to a definitive conclusion about the efficacy of aid is that the results have been mixed. On the positive side, the inflation rate for the ruble dropped tenfold, to 10 percent a month, by 1994, down from the crisis-level of 100 percent a month in 1992–1993. Shortages of nearly everything are still widespread, but mass starvation and a complete economic breakdown have not occurred. Russia survives, albeit poorly.

Since Rex Wade and Karen LaFollette wrote the articles presented here, the Yeltsin government has backed away from a strong economic reform program, the plight of the Russian people remains distressing, crime and corruption mount, Yeltsin's popularity has plummeted, and the rise of ultranationalist forces continues. A recent discussion of the ultranationalists and their controversial leader, Vladimir Zhirinovsky, can be found in Jacob W. Kipp,

"The Zhirinovsky Threat," *Foreign Affairs* (May/June 1994). Some analysts doubt the future of Russian democracy. For one such viewpoint, see Dimitri Simes, "The Return of Russian History," *Foreign Affairs* (January/February 1994). Moreover, the strength of the ultranationalists has pushed Russia (or, some might say, given it an excuse) to begin to meddle in and even assert some control over the other FSRs. The FSRs have come to be termed the "near abroad" in the Russian press, and Russia has come close to claiming a special authority in these regions as part of a Russian sphere of influence. Thus, the future course of Russia's domestic political regime and of its foreign policy remains highly uncertain.

ISSUE 3

Should the United States Abandon Its Superpower Role?

YES: Doug Bandow, from "Keeping the Troops and the Money at Home," *Current History* (January 1994)

NO: Anthony Lake, from "A Quartet of Foreign Policy Speeches," *Foreign Policy Bulletin* (November/December 1993)

ISSUE SUMMARY

YES: Doug Bandow, a senior fellow at the Cato Institute and a former special assistant to U.S. president Ronald Reagan, argues that the United States, while remaining engaged in global affairs, should nevertheless bring home its military forces and curtail expensive foreign aid programs.

NO: Anthony Lake, special assistant for national security affairs in the Clinton administration, maintains that calls from the ideological left and right for the United States to stay at home and disengage from abroad are ill-considered. U.S. national interests make full international engagement imperative.

Isolationism was one of the earliest and most persistent characteristics of U.S. foreign policy. In his 1796 Farewell Address, President George Washington counseled: "Our detached and distant situation invites and enables us ... to steer clear of permanent alliance with any portion of the world, ... taking care always to keep ourselves ... in a respectable defensive posture."

Washington's view played a strong role in U.S. foreign policy making until World War II. It is not true that the country was isolationist until that point and then became internationalist. History is considerably more complex than that, and it is more accurate to say that there has always been among Americans a tension or an ambiguity about isolationism and internationalism. Even during the 1700s and 1800s the world could not be ignored, as U.S. foreign trade, sporadic clashes with other countries, and other factors occasioned U.S. international involvement. In the late 1800s and increasingly in this century, U.S. global interaction increased as trade grew in volume and importance, as U.S. military and economic power gave the country world-class strength, and as the speed of communications, transportation, and military movement shrank the world operationally.

Still, isolationism remained both a strong and respectable policy through the 1930s. World War II brought an end to that. The emergence of the United States from that conflict as the world's richest and most militarily powerful country, and the perceived global threat from communism backed by Soviet military strength, combined to thrust the United States into virtually unchallenged internationalism. The very term *isolationism* became discredited.

Isolationism did not disappear, however. Although it was a distinctly minority view, isolationism did receive public support among Americans, as surveys throughout the cold war period showed. Gallup surveys from 1945 through 1986 indicate that the percentage of Americans surveyed who said the United States should "stay out" of world affairs averaged 27 percent. Over the years, an average 7 percent had no opinion, and 66 percent favored the United States playing an "active part" in world affairs.

In the 1990s the isolationist-internationalist debate has resurfaced. Three factors have been the main (though not only) causes for this renewed debate. One is the end of the cold war and the end of the perceived threat from the Soviet Union. The containment doctrine that countered the communist and Soviet military threat was one of the main thrusts behind U.S. internationalism. That doctrine waned after the Vietnam War, and it has fallen into seeming irrelevance with the collapse of the USSR. Second, U.S. economic power has declined relative to the rest of the world, and the country is experiencing troubling economic conditions. This has focused the attention of many Americans on the home front. Several recent surveys have indicated that the foreign policy goal most often selected by Americans as the most important is the one of ensuring that world trade does not endanger the jobs of U.S. workers. Third, the upsurge in instability around the world, in Bosnia, Somalia, and elsewhere, seems to many Americans to threaten to draw human and financial resources into a never-ending series of potentially expensive, frustrating engagements not directly related to the safety and prosperity of the United States. One could debate the source and gravity of these difficulties, but no matter what the objective truth is, many Americans are convinced that huge defense budgets, gaping trade imbalances, increasing foreign ownership of U.S. economic assets, and other symptoms demonstrate that internationalism has become too expensive a policy to pursue. In particular, they are unwilling to allow the United States to continue to bear the cost of being a hegemon, a dominant superpower.

Doug Bandow is among those who would have the United States step back from superpower status. He argues that the United States should calculate military interventions and foreign aid on a strict cost/benefit basis. If Americans do so, they will see that it is wiser, in most instances, to keep the troops and money at home. Anthony Lake, in opposition, asserts that the prosperity and safety of the United States is inextricably bound up with the economic health and stability of the world. He does not advocate unthinking aid or interventions, but Lake does believe that the United States should remain fully engaged in all areas of international affairs.

YES   Doug Bandow

KEEPING THE TROOPS
AND THE MONEY AT HOME

We are living in exciting times. Who would have believed when George Bush was elected president that a year later the Berlin Wall would fall? That non-Communist governments would take power throughout Eastern Europe, Germany would reunite, and the Soviet Union would disintegrate? That the menace of aggressive Soviet communism would disappear? That the chairman of the Joint Chiefs of Staff Colin Powell would admit, "I'm running out of villains. I'm down to Castro and Kim Il Sung."?

In this dramatically changed world the interventionist stance that has dominated United States foreign policy for nearly five decades must be reexamined. The United States will be a global power, but what kind of power? Should it continue to seek global hegemony, or should it go back to being, in former ambassador to the UN Jeane Kirkpatrick's words, a "normal country"?

THE INTERVENTIONIST'S OUTLOOK

Today the American military is spread around the globe. President Bill Clinton says that 100,000 United States troops in Europe is the minimum required, despite the disappearance of any credible threat to the West and the ability of the prosperous European Community—which includes two nuclear powers, Britain and France—to deter a resurgent Russia in the future. Indeed, George Bush went so far as to state that he did not foresee that "utopian day" when all America's soldiers might come home arriving for perhaps another hundred years.

The Clinton administration, following the lead of its predecessor, also seems committed to retaining at least 100,000 troops in East Asia. Japan is the world's second-ranking economic power and faces no serious military threats; nevertheless, Tokyo apparently is slated to continue as an American defense dependent indefinitely. South Korea has 12 times the GNP [gross national product] and twice the population of Communist North Korea, yet Clinton suggests that United States forces will remain so long as Seoul wants them, which could be forever.

From Doug Bandow, "Keeping the Troops and the Money at Home," *Current History* (January 1994). Copyright © 1994 by Current History, Inc. Reprinted by permission of *Current History*.

And many would like to further expand America's role as global policeman. Three years after the mercifully short war against Iraq in the Persian Gulf, the United States remains entangled in Kuwait, Saudi Arabia, and the affairs of Iraq's Kurdish minority, risking a long-term presence in one of the world's most volatile regions. Bulgaria, the Czech Republic, Hungary, and Poland all want United States defense guarantees, preferably through formal membership in NATO [North Atlantic Treaty Organization]. America is enmeshed in Somalia and has threatened to intervene in the Balkans. Some press for involvement in Liberia's three-sided civil war, to bring peace, or against Haiti's military regime, to bring back democracy. Others write of America's obligation to guarantee Taiwan's security, prevent North Korea, Iran, and others from building weapons of mass destruction, and wage low-intensity conflicts around the world —in Latin America, Asia, the Middle East, and Africa. And columnist Ben Wattenberg wants the United States to go on making weapons simply to stay "Number One."

Given the expansiveness of the United States role abroad, it is time to ask: Is there anything the American people are not forced to pay for? Is there anything young Americans are not expected to die for?

THE IMPORTANCE OF JUSTIFYING POLICY

To answer these questions, one must first decide on the purpose of the national government. But rarely, alas, is this issue even addressed. The current administration speaks of a foreign policy of "enlargement"; hyper-internationalists cite the alleged need to spread democracy and enforce peace; and unreformed cold warriors warn of new enemies and threats requiring a military as large as that which successfully contained the Soviet Union. None consider whether their grand designs are consistent with America's organization of government, however.

Among the primary duties of the United States government, the first is to safeguard the country's security in order to protect citizens' lives and property. (The federal government also has some obligation to attempt to protect American citizens traveling abroad, but ultimately those who do business outside the United States must voluntarily incur the risks of doing so. Thus the formal justification for the entry of the United States into World War I—to uphold the right of Americans to travel on armed belligerent merchantmen carrying munitions through declared submarine zones—was patently absurd.) The government's second primary duty is to preserve the constitutional system and liberties that make America unique and worth living in. Every foreign policy action should be consistent with these two functions, and the president, legislators, and other officials can have no higher goals.

This is not, of course, to say that there are no other important ideals in life. For instance, the apostle John wrote in his first epistle, "This is how we know what love is: Jesus Christ laid down his life for us. And we ought to lay down our lives for our brothers." But the moral duties that individuals acknowledge are very different from duties established by the civil institutions that govern all. John did not suggest that we should force our neighbors—indeed, everyone in our entire country—to lay down their lives for others.

Yet many people no longer perceive any moral dimension to taxing and drafting citizens to implement government policies. Joshua Muravchik of the American Enterprise Institute, for example, sees no problem in promoting "common purposes" so long as such actions "don't involve curtailing the rights of our own citizens, but involve only taxing them." Yet taxation, and conscription, the policy used for years to obtain the needed personnel for Washington's extensive overseas commitments, certainly "involve curtailing the rights of our own citizens." An activist foreign and military policy should, therefore, require a justification that warrants circumscribing—often severely—people's freedom.

A FOREIGN POLICY OF HIGHER PRINCIPLES?

Advocates of an interventionist foreign policy have, of course, advanced many lofty justifications: To promote democracy. To ensure stability. To protect human rights. To stop aggression. To enforce international law and order. To create a new world order. And on and on. Such appeals to higher principles and values are very seductive; suggesting that foreign policy should be based on the promotion of the national interest sounds decidedly cold and selfish in comparison.

The moral goals articulated by many interventionists are important, but citizens should have no illusions about the ability of the United States government to promote, let alone impose, them. Furthermore, recourse to such principles is often simply a rationalization for pursuing strategic or political ends. A cursory survey of activist foreign policy decisions ostensibly taken in the name of higher moral principles reveals ample evidence of both naïveté and sophistry.

For instance, in 1990 policymakers in Washington proclaimed their love of democracy and the free market, but years later there is still little sign of reform in Kuwait City, which was "liberated" during the Gulf War; American troops fought to make the Middle East safe for a monarchy that has largely evaded fulfilling its promises of greater domestic freedom. Despite its professed ideals, the United States used its armed forces to prop up authoritarian regimes in Korea and Vietnam. In two world wars it cultivated grand alliances with, respectively, an authoritarian Russia (although by the time the United States officially declared war, the czar had been overthrown) and a totalitarian Soviet Union. It viewed its bases in and defense treaty with the Philippines as equally important during the presidencies of autocrat Ferdinand Marcos and democrat Corazon Aquino.

Not only has American intervention often been motivated by factors other than disinterested selflessness, but Washington has equally often bungled the job. Financial assistance to a host of third world autocracies has strengthened the enemies of freedom and democracy. Aid and support tied the United States to failing dictatorships in Iran and Nicaragua; the two regimes' collapses resulted in neither democracy nor allies. America's entry into World War I to promote a utopian world order had perhaps the most disastrous consequences of any international meddling by any state ever; by allowing the allies to dictate an unequal and unstable peace, it sowed the seeds of the planet's worst conflagration, which bloomed just two decades later.

Even more important than the question of Washington's sincerity and realism in promoting higher principles in its foreign policy is the question of cost. How much money—and how many lives—should be sacrificed to bring American principles to other countries? Restoring Kuwait's sovereignty proved surprisingly cheap, but there were no guarantees United States and coalition casualties would be so light. How many American lives did policymakers think Kuwait's liberation would be worth? Five thousand? Fifty thousand? And even if Iraq was the aggressor, the deaths of estimated tens and possibly even hundreds of thousands of Iraqis, many of them either civilians or military conscripts, must also be recognized as a very real cost of United States intervention.

How many body bags per foreign life saved would make intervention elsewhere worthwhile? Why did Iraq's earlier brutal assaults on its Kurdish minority not warrant war? What about Syria's depredations in Lebanon? China's swallowing of Tibet? The war between India and Pakistan? Or Pol Pot's mass murder in Cambodia?

If young American males—and now females—are born to give their lives overseas to forestall aggression, protect human rights, and uphold a new world order, should not the United States have gone to war to unseat the two dictators who (unlike, say, Ho Chi Minh, Iraq's Saddam Hussein, or Serbia's Slobodan Milosevic) truly *were* the moral equivalent of Hitler—Stalin and Mao? Why was protecting human rights in these instances not worth war? If the answer is that the cost would have been too great, then those who attempt a moral explanation for sacrificing 58,000 Americans for Vietnam but refusing to offer up some unspecified larger number to free more than 1 billion Chinese need to elucidate their methodology—unless, of course, they believe the United States should have ignited World War III in the name of some more just world order.

In fact, the United States did not intervene to liberate the two largest Communist states because doing so was not perceived to be in America's interest, owing to the catastrophic costs that such actions surely would have entailed. For all the idealism embodied in the moral explanations for United States behavior, American intervention is generally animated by a spirit of realpolitik [politics based on practical factors]....

As unsatisfactory as an emphasis on the national interest may be to some, it is the only proper basis for American policy. Such an approach reflects the purpose of the United States government—to protect the security, liberty, and property of the American people—in a way the international pursuit of utopian ideals does not. Reasons of national interest and security are the only legitimate justification for United States intervention abroad.

WEIGHING COSTS

It is not enough, however, to decide that the United States has one or more interests at stake in some foreign matter, because interests are not of unlimited value. The benefits of gaining desired objectives have to be balanced against the cost of intervention.

Perhaps the most obvious expense is financial. NATO accounts for roughly half the entire United States military budget; the defense of the Pacific runs to about $40 billion. Operation Desert Shield cost

$60 billion or more (though that bill was largely covered by coalition states). Foreign aid adds another $12 billion annually to the deficit. All told, roughly 70 percent of America's military outlays goes to prepare for conventional wars abroad. As General Wallace Nutting, former commander in chief of the United States Readiness Command, has observed, "We today do not have a single soldier, airman, or sailor solely dedicated to the security mission within the United States."

American domestic freedoms also suffer as a result. World Wars I and II resulted in massive assaults on civil liberties, including the suppression of dissent and free speech, and culminated in the incarceration of more than 100,000 Japanese Americans. Much more modest, but still unsettling, was the anti-Arab Sentiment unleashed during the short war against Iraq. Moreover, a panoply of security restrictions that grew out of the cold war continues to limit Americans' freedom.

Both wars also vastly expanded the government's economic powers. Federal spending in 1916 was just $713 million; it shot up to $18.5 billion in 1919, eventually settling back to the $3-billion level throughout the 1920s, more than quadruple its prewar level. Similarly, federal outlays in 1940 were $9.5 billion. Spending increase nearly tenfold, to $92.7 billion, fell to $29.8 billion in 1948—triple prewar figures—and then began its inexorable climb. Burton Yale Pines of the National Center for Public Policy Research argues that "today's mammoth federal government is the product not so much of the New Deal but of the massive power assembled in Washington to wage Wold War II and the Cold War." Some of the government's regulations have never been reversed: New York City, for instance, still suffers from the destructive effects of rent control, a supposedly temporary wartime measure.

Similarly, America's interventionist foreign policy has malformed the domestic constitutional system. We have seen both a centralization of power in the federal government and the aggrandizement of the presidency. How far we have come is reflected by the fact that serious thinkers who purport to believe in jurisprudential interpretation based on the original intent of the framers argue that the president can launch a war against another sovereign state without congressional approval. And although United States participation in formal UN forces is rather limited, it represents an even greater abrogation of congressional authority, since the act allowing participation dispenses with the need for a declaration of war when such troops are involved.

Further, intervention has a great human cost. Woodrow Wilson's fantasies of a new world order drove him to take the country into the mindless European slugfest of World War I, which left 116,000 Americans dead and led to the outbreak within one generation of an even worse war, which killed another 407,000 (mostly young) Americans. Since the end of the second world war, more than 112,000 American citizens have died in undeclared conflicts. It is one thing to ask Americans to die for the United States Republic. It is quite another to expect them to sacrifice their lives in the interest of power-projection politics more characteristic of an empire.

Finally, intervention could one day threaten the very national survival of the United States. Biological, chemical, and nuclear weapons are spreading and ballistic missiles [are] increasingly available. Terrorism has become a fixture of international life. With the growing ability of even small political movements and countries to kill United States citizens and to threaten mass destruction, the risks of foreign entanglements increase. No longer are the high costs limited to soldiers in the field. In coming years the United States could conceivably lose one or more large cities to demented or irrational retaliation for American intervention. A modest Strategic Defense Initiative program would reduce these risks, but it would never be able to provide full protection.

DIFFERENT WAYS AND MEANS

How, then, should the United States formulate a foreign policy? Every action taken abroad should reflect the purpose behind the creation of the government: namely, to serve the interests of American society and the people who live in it. Washington's role is not to conduct glorious utopian crusades around the globe. It is not to provide a pot of cash for the secretary of state to pass out to friendly regimes to increase United States influence abroad. It is not to sacrifice the lives of Americans to minimize other peoples' sufferings. In short, the money and lives of the American people are not there for policymakers, or even the president, to expend for purposes other than defending the American community.

Of course, some analysts argue that promoting moral values, particularly democracy and human rights, advances American national interests by making conflict—or at least war—less likely. The link is tenuous, however. Indeed, in the Middle East, North Africa, and some other states, true democracy is as likely to unleash destabilizing as stabilizing forces, particularly Islamic fundamental-

ism. The end of the totalitarian rule that kept simmering ethnic tensions in eastern Europe under control has already resulted in violent conflict in the Balkans: it was "democratic" decisions to secede from Yugoslavia after free elections in Slovenia and Croatia that sparked war. The best we can say is that democracies generally do not attack their neighbors.

Further, America's ability to advance democratic values is inconsistent at best. There is little the United States can do to make Haiti a free country, for example; sustaining in power a demagogue like Jean-Bertrand Aristide, even an elected one, certainly will not. And Washington's policies often throw United States commitment to democracy into question. Foreign aid, in particular, has assisted authoritarian rulers more often than liberal forces all over the third world. In the absence of any direct link between important United States objectives and the imperative to advance democracy in a particular country, American resources should not be used in this way.

Furthermore, to decide that a specific intervention is consistent with the purpose of the United States government is not enough to justify it. Decisionmakers also need to assess whether there are alternative means of achieving the goal. A free Europe is certainly important to the United States, but keeping 100,000 troops there is not necessary. The Soviet threat has disappeared, while Europe's ability to defend itself has expanded. A sharply reduced potential Russian threat may remain in coming years as Moscow struggles with daunting economic, ethnic, and political problems, but civil war is far more likely than aggression against the West. Indeed, according to the International Institute for Strategic Studies, Russia now spends less than Germany alone on the military. Thus there is no reason the Europeans, with three times the economic strength of a decaying Russia (and a larger gross national product than America) and a new buffer in the former Warsaw Pact states, cannot create their own security system to deter any potential threat.

Indeed, those who should be most concerned about a Russian revival—the Germans—aren't. Last year Chancellor Helmut Kohl announced his nation was going to cut troop levels 40 percent through 1995. If Bonn sees no need to maintain a large military for its protection, there is certainly no cause for America to maintain troops in Germany. Washington is increasingly begging the Europeans for the right to defend them.

Similarly, South Korea is vastly stronger than North Korea by every measure except current military strength. Seoul's growing edge has become increasingly obvious as South Korea has stripped away all of the north's allies, particularly Russia and China. The south is fully capable of eliminating the military imbalance on the peninsula. South Korean officials do not deny their country's ability to sharply increase its defense efforts; instead, they tend to complain about having to bear the added expense. This is hardly a justification for an American presence. Seoul could gradually increase its military spending—which would be unnecessary if the north enters into meaningful arms control negotiations—as United States forces were phased out. The potential North Korean acquisition of a nuclear weapon is serious, but the continued presence of American ground forces will do nothing to stop nuclear proliferation; rather, the troops would simply serve as nuclear hostages....

It might be difficult to fashion alternative solutions that do not involve direct United States intervention, and Washington might not always be fully satisfied with the outcome. But it is unrealistic to expect the United States to assume the responsibility for maintaining global order. Instead, Washington should seek to promote cost-effective policies that yield results most consistent with the government's duty to protect Americans' security and constitutional freedoms.

Even if there appear to be no alternatives to a United States commitment, the United States must weigh benefits against costs before it intervenes, and avoid or extricate itself from tragic but ultimately irrelevant conflicts. For example, more people died in 1993 in Angola than in Bosnia. Starvation stalks Liberia and Sudan, both victims of vicious civil wars. Yet there has been no groundswell for intervention in Angola, and no UN relief mission for the latter two. The Trans-Caucasus is suffering from seven separate conflicts. All are human catastrophes, but none affects a single vital American interest or warrants the death of even one United States soldier. The point is not that American lives are worth more than others', but that the primary duty of the United States government is to safeguard the lives of its own citizens—servicemen included—not sacrifice them for even seemingly worthy causes.

What if United States policymakers concluded that South Korea would not defend itself if Washington pulled out its troops? In fact, Seoul would probably be the last American ally to give up, but what if it decided to do so? A northern takeover of the south would be a tragedy for the latter, but it would have little impact on the United States, whose security would remain largely unchanged and whose economy would suffer only marginally from the loss of a midsize trading partner. The threat to go to war should be reserved for cases involving vital American interests. Korea is a peripheral, rather than a substantial, interest of the United States, and does not justify spending billions of dollars and risking tens of thousands of lives every year, especially if the peninsula goes nuclear.

A similar analysis could have been conducted for the Gulf. Even if the other regional powers had not taken steps to contain Iraq, the likelihood of Saddam Hussein striking Saudi Arabia was overplayed, since this would have left him dangerously overextended. (In fact, United States intelligence knew at the time he was withdrawing his best units to Iraq after seizing Kuwait.)

The consequences even of a highly unlikely conquest of the entire Gulf were overstated. In this fantastic worst-case scenario, Saddam would have controlled about one-fifth of international petroleum production; enough to nudge prices up, to be sure, but not enough to control them or wreck the international economy. Nor did Saddam's invasion of Kuwait threaten America's ally Israel. On the contrary, Iraq only attacked Israel in a desperate attempt to split the coalition; absent the United States presence, Baghdad would surely not have attacked Israel since it was fully capable and willing to retaliate.

THE LUXURY OF UNINVOLVEMENT

The United States enjoys many advantages that provide it with the luxury of remaining aloof from geopolitical conflicts that engulf other countries. American benefits from relative geographic isolation, for example. (This does not insulate it from nuclear attack, of course, which is why it should try to develop some form of missile defense.) The United States is also the world's largest single economic market, which reduces the impact of the loss of one or more trading partners. (Germany and Japan, for example, would suffer far more if the American market was denied them.) Moreover, the United States has a constitutional system and political philosophy that have endured for more than 200 years and have proved to be popular around the world.

This unique status allows America to balance the costs and benefits of intervention differently from most other states. Alliances make a lot more sense among European states threatened by a Soviet Union, for instance, or between Saudi Arabia and its neighbors when they are threatened by Iraq. Observes political commentator and former presidential candidate Patrick Buchanan, "Blessed by Providence with pacific neighbors, north and south, and vast oceans, east and west, to protect us, why seek permanent entanglements in other people's quarrels?"

For this reason, the United States is rarely open to charges of appeasement, such as are sometimes rightly leveled at other countries, for intervention is seldom required to protect its vital interests. For example, had France and Britain accurately perceived the potential threat posed by Nazi Germany, they should have blocked the remilitarization of the Rhineland and they certainly should not have helped dismember Czechoslovakia (through active intervention, it should be noted). Washington's failure to leave its expeditionary force in Europe in 1919 or to raise a new one in 1933, however, did not constitute appeasement. Similarly, it would not be appeasement for the United States to decline to defend a populous and prosperous South Korea; for Seoul to choose not to augment its forces once United States troops were gone, however, would be.

In fact, there is nothing wrong in principle with appeasement, if this means only diplomatic accommodation and avoidance of war. In the late nineteenth and early twentieth centuries, Austria-Hungary, Britain, France, Germany, and Russia all resolved potentially violent disagreements without conflict by making concessions to one another that could be termed "appeasement." The case of Nazi Germany was different, because Hitler wanted far more than could be given to him, and because the allies materially weakened themselves—for example, by eviscerating Czechoslovakia—in attempting to satisfy him.

The end of the cold war has resulted in a new world order, whether or not the United States defines or polices it. The Russian military remains a potent force, of course, but it is far less capable than that possessed by the Soviet Union, and Moscow's will to use it in an aggressive fashion appears to have dissipated. Moreover, the ability of American allies —a Japan that is the second-ranking economic power in the world, a reunited Germany that dominates Europe, and so on—to contain Russia has grown. These two changes alone give the United States an opportunity to refashion its foreign policy.

A new, noninterventionist policy should rest on the following bedrock principles:

- The security of the United States and its constitutional system should remain the United States government's highest goal. Individuals may decide to selflessly risk their lives to help others abroad; policymakers, however, have no authority to risk their citizens' lives, freedom, and wealth in similar pursuits.
- Foreign intervention is usually expensive and risky, and often counterproductive. Many smaller nations may still need to forge preemptive alliances to respond to potentially aggressive regional powers. Because of America's relative geographic isolation and other advantages, however, intervention is rarely necessary to protect our security and free institutions. This is especially true today, with the disappearance of a threatening hegemonic power.
- America's most powerful assets for influencing the rest of the world are its philosophy and free institutions, the ideas of limited government and free enterprise that are now sweeping the globe, and its economic prowess as the world's most productive nation. These factors ensure the nation's influence irrespective of the size of its military and where its soldiers are stationed. The United States can best affect others through private means—commerce, culture, literature, travel, and the like.
- The world will continue to suffer from injustice, terror, murder, and aggression. But it is simply not Washington's role to try to right every wrong —a hopeless task in any event. The American people are entitled to enjoy their freedom and prosperity rather than having their future held hostage to unpredictable events abroad. Their lives and treasure should not be sacrificed in quixotic crusades unrelated to their basic interests.

The world is changing faster today than it has at any time since the end of World War II. As a result, the United States has no choice but to refashion its foreign policy. While Washington should remain engaged throughout the world culturally, economically, and politically, it should bring its military home and curtail expensive foreign aid programs. After bearing the primary burden of fighting the cold war, Americans deserve to enjoy the benefits of peace through a policy of benign detachment. War may still be forced upon them, of course. But as John Quincy Adams observed shortly after the nation's founding, America should not go abroad "in search of monsters to destroy."

NO   Anthony Lake

LAKE'S SPEECH AT THE JOHNS HOPKINS UNIVERSITY, SEPTEMBER 21, 1993

I have come to speak with you today because I believe our nation's policies toward the world stand at an historic crossroads. For nearly half a century America's engagement in the world revolved around containment of a hostile Soviet Union. Our efforts helped block Soviet expansionism, topple Communist repression and secure a great victory for human freedom. Clearly, the Soviet Union's collapse enhances our security. But it also requires us to think anew because the world is new.

In particular, with the end of the Cold War, there is no longer a consensus among the American people around why, and even whether, our nation should remain actively engaged in the world. Geography and history always have made Americans wary of foreign entanglements. Now economic anxiety fans that wariness. Calls from the left and right to stay at home rather than engage abroad are reinforced by the rhetoric of Neo-Know-Nothings.

Those of us who believe in the imperative of our international engagement must push back. For that reason, as President Clinton sought the Presidency, he not only pledged a domestic renaissance, but also vowed to engage actively in the world in order to increase our prosperity, update our security arrangements and promote democracy abroad.

PURSUING AMERICAN INTERESTS ABROAD

... Since he took office, President Clinton has pursued those goals vigorously. We have completed a sweeping review of our military strategy and forces. We have led a global effort to support the historic reforms in Russia and the other new states. We have helped defend democracy in Haiti and Guatemala and secured important side agreements that pave the way for enactment of the North American Free Trade Agreement. We have facilitated major advances in the Mideast peace process, working with our Arab partners while strengthening our bonds with Israel. We have pursued steps with our G-7 partners to stimulate world economic growth. We have placed our relations with Japan on a new foundation and set a vision of a New Pacific Community.

From Anthony Lake, "A Quartet of Foreign Policy Speeches," *Foreign Policy Bulletin* (November/December 1993).

We are putting in place practical policies to preserve the environment and to limit the spread of weapons of mass destruction. We have proceeded with sweeping reductions in nuclear arms and declared a moratorium on testing as we move toward a comprehensive test ban. We have struggled with the complex tragedy in Bosnia. And we have worked to complete our mission of ensuring lasting relief from starvation in Somalia.

But engagement itself is not enough. We also need to communicate anew why that engagement is essential. If we do not, our government's reactions to foreign events can seem disconnected; individual setbacks may appear to define the whole; public support for our engagement likely would wane; and America could be harmed by a rise in protectionism, unwise cuts to our military force structure or readiness, a loss of the resources necessary for our diplomacy—and thus the erosion of U.S. influence abroad.

Stating our purpose is neither academic nor rhetorical. What we do outside our borders has immediate and lasting consequences for all Americans. As the President often notes, the line between foreign and domestic policy has evaporated. Our choices about America's foreign policy will help determine:

- Whether Americans' real incomes double every 26 years, as they did in the 1960s, or every 36 years, as they did during the late 1970s and 1980s.
- Whether the 25 nations with weapons of mass destruction grow in number or decline.
- Whether the next quarter century will see terrorism, which injured or killed more than 2,000 Americans during the last quarter century, expand or recede as a threat.

- Whether the nations of the world will be more able or less able to address regional disputes, humanitarian needs and the threat of environmental degradation.

I do not presume today to define the Administration's entire foreign policy vision. But... I want to suggest some broad principles, as a contribution to an essential national dialogue about our purpose in the world.

AMERICA'S CORE CONCEPTS: DEMOCRACY AND FREE MARKETS

Let us begin by taking stock of our new era. Four facts are salient.

First, America's core concepts—democracy and market economics—are more broadly accepted than ever. Over the past ten years, the number of democracies has nearly doubled. Since 1970, the number of significant command economies dropped from 10 to 3.

This victory of freedom is practical, not ideological: Billions of people on every continent are simply concluding, based on decades of their own hard experience, that democracy and markets are the most productive and liberating ways to organize their lives.

Their conclusion resonates with America's core values. We see individuals as equally created with a God-given right to life, liberty and the pursuit of happiness. So we trust in the equal wisdom of free individuals to protect those rights: through democracy, as the process for best meeting shared needs in the face of competing desires; and through markets as the process for best meeting private needs in a way that expands opportunity.

Both processes strengthen each other: democracy alone can produce justice, but not the material goods necessary for individuals to thrive; markets alone can expand wealth, but not that sense of justice without which civilized societies perish.

Democracy and market economics are ascendant in this new era, but they are not everywhere triumphant. There remain vast areas in Asia, Africa, the Middle East and elsewhere where democracy and market economics are at best new arrivals—most likely unfamiliar, sometimes vilified, often fragile.

But it is wrong to assume these ideas will be embraced only by the West and rejected by the rest. Culture does shape politics and economics. But the idea of freedom has universal appeal. Thus, we have arrived at neither the end of history nor a clash of civilizations, but a moment of immense democratic and entrepreneurial opportunity. We must not waste it.

The **second** feature of this era is that we are its dominant power. Those who say otherwise sell America short. The fact is, we have the world's strongest military, its largest economy and its most dynamic, multiethnic society. We are setting a global example in our efforts to reinvent our democratic and market institutions. Our leadership is sought and respected in every corner of the world.... Around the world, America's power, authority and example provide unparalleled opportunities to lead.

Moreover, absent a reversal in Russia, there is now no credible near-term threat to America's existence. Serious threats remain: terrorism, proliferating weapons of mass destruction, ethnic conflicts and the degradation of our global environment. Above all, we are threatened by sluggish economic growth, which undermines the security of our people as well as that of allies and friends abroad. Yet none of these threats holds the same immediate dangers for us as did Nazi conquest or Soviet expansionism. America's challenge today is to lead on the basis of opportunity more than fear.

The **third** notable aspect of this era is an explosion of ethnic conflicts.... The end of the Cold War and the collapse of various repressive regimes has removed the lid from numerous caldrons of ethnic, religious or factional hatreds. In many states of the former Soviet Union and elsewhere, there is a tension between the desire for ethnic separatism and the creation of liberal democracy, which alone can safely accommodate and even celebrate differences among citizens. A major challenge to our thinking, our policies and our international institutions in this era is the fact that most conflicts are taking place within rather than among nations.

These conflicts are typically highly complex; at the same time, their brutality will tug at our consciences. We need a healthy wariness about our ability to shape solutions for such disputes, yet at times our interests or humanitarian concerns will impel our unilateral or multilateral engagement.

The **fourth** feature of this new era is that the pulse of the planet has accelerated dramatically and with it the pace of change in human events. Computers, faxes, fiber optic cables and satellites all speed the flow of information. The measurement of wealth, and increasingly wealth itself, consists in bytes of data that move at the speed of light.

The accelerated pace of events is neither bad nor good. Its sharp consequences can cut either way. It means both doctors and terrorists can more quickly share their technical secrets. Both pro-democracy activists and skinhead anarchists can more broadly spread their views. Ultimately, the world's acceleration creates new and diverse ways for us to exert our influence, if we choose to do so—but increases the likelihood that, if we do not, rapid events, instantly reported, may overwhelm us. As the President has suggested, we must decide whether to make change our ally or allow ourselves to become its victims.

FROM CONTAINMENT TO ENLARGEMENT

In such a world, our interests and ideals compel us not only to be engaged, but to lead. And in a real-time world of change and information, it is all the more important that our leadership be steadied around our central purpose.

That purpose can be found in the underlying rationale for our engagement throughout this century. As we fought aggressors and contained communism, our engagement abroad was animated both by calculations of power and by this belief: to the extent democracy and market economics hold sway in other nations, our own nation will be more secure, prosperous and influential, while the broader world will be more humane and peaceful.

The expansion of market-based economics abroad helps expand our exports and create American jobs, while it also improves living conditions and fuels demands for political liberalization abroad. The addition of new democracies makes us more secure because democracies tend not to wage war on each other or sponsor terrorism. They are more trustworthy in diplomacy and do a better job of respecting the human rights of their people.

These dynamics lay at the heart of Woodrow Wilson's most profound insights; although his moralism sometimes weakened his argument, he understood that our own security is shaped by the character of foreign regimes. Indeed, most Presidents who followed, Republicans and Democrats alike, understood we must promote democracy and market economics in the world—because it protects our interests and security and because it reflects values that are both American and universal.

Throughout the Cold War, we contained a global threat to market democracies; now we should seek to enlarge their reach, particularly in places of special significance to us. The successor to a doctrine of containment must be a strategy of enlargement—enlargement of the world's free community of market democracies.

During the Cold War, even children understood America's security mission; as they looked at those maps on their schoolroom walls, they knew we were trying to contain the creeping expansion of that big, red blob. Today, at great risk of oversimplification, we might visualize our security mission as promoting the enlargement of the "blue areas" of market democracies. The difference, of course, is that we do not seek to expand the reach of our institutions by force, subversion or repression.

We must not allow this overarching goal to drive us into overreaching actions. To be successful, a strategy of enlargement must provide distinctions and set priorities. It must combine our broad goals of fostering democracy and markets with our more traditional geostrategic interests. And it must suggest how best to expend our large but nonetheless limited national security resources: financial, diplomatic and military.

In recent years, discussions about when to use force have turned on a set of vital questions, such as whether our forces match our objectives, whether we can fight and win in a time that is acceptable, whether we have a reasonable exit if we can not, and whether there is public and congressional support. But we have overlooked a prior, strategic question—the question of "where"—which sets the context for such military judgments.

I see four components to a strategy of enlargement.

First, we should strengthen the community of major market democracies—including our own—which constitutes the core from which enlargement is proceeding.

Second, we should help foster and consolidate new democracies and market economies, where possible, especially in states of special significance and opportunity.

Third, we must counter the aggression—and support the liberalization—of states hostile to democracy and markets.

Fourth, we need to pursue our humanitarian agenda not only by providing aid, but also by working to help democracy and market economics take root in regions of greatest humanitarian concern.

A host of caveats must accompany a strategy of enlargement. For one, we must be patient. As scholars observe, waves of democratic advance are often followed by reverse waves of democratic setback. We must be ready for uneven progress, even outright reversals.

Our strategy must be pragmatic. Our interests in democracy and markets do not stand alone. Other American interests at times will require us to befriend and even defend non-democratic states for mutually beneficial reasons. Our strategy must view democracy broadly—it must envision a system that includes not only elections but also such features as an independent judiciary and protections of human rights. Our strategy must also respect diversity. Democracy and markets can come in many legitimate variants. Freedom has many faces.

[In the next section, not included here, Lake outlines the value of fostering democracy in other regions also.—Ed.]

ENGAGEMENT VS. ISOLATIONISM

I believe there is a more fundamental foreign policy challenge brewing for the United States. It is a challenge over whether we will be significantly engaged abroad at all. As I suggested at the outset, in many ways we are returning to the divisions and debates about our role in the world that are as old as our Republic. On one side is protectionism and limited foreign engagement; on the other is active American engagement abroad on behalf of democracy and expanded trade.

The last time our nation saw that classic division was just after World War II. It pitted those Democrats and Republicans whose creativity produced the architectures of postwar prosperity and security against those in both parties who would have had us retreat within the isolated shell we occupied in the 1920s and 1930s. The internationalists won those debates, in part because they could point to a unitary threat to America's interests and because the nation was entering a period of economic security.

Today's supporters of engagement abroad have neither of those advantages. The threats and opportunities are diffuse, and our people are deeply anxious about their economic fate. Rallying Americans to bear the costs and burdens of international engagement is no less important. But it is much more difficult.

For this reason, those who recognize the value of our leadership in the world should devote far more energy to making the case for sustained engagement abroad and less energy to debates over tactics. To be sure, there will be disagreements over tactics: we expect to be held accountable for our policy decisions, and our critics can expect us to respond where we disagree. But all of us who support engagement should be careful to debate tactics in a way that does not prevent us from coming together in common cause around the fundamental importance of that goal.

All of us have come out of the Cold War years having learned distinct lessons about what not to do—don't go to war without a way to win; don't underestimate the role of ideas; don't minimize the power of nationalism. Yet we have come into the new era with relatively few ways to convince a skeptical public that engagement abroad is a worthwhile investment. That is why a national dialogue over our fundamental purposes is so important.

In a world of extraordinary complexity, it would be too easy for us in the internationalist camp to become "neo-Marxists" —not after Karl, but after Groucho, who once sang, "Whatever it is, I'm against it." It is time for those who see the value of American engagement to steady our ranks; to define our purpose; and to rally the American people. In particular, at a time of high deficits and pressing domestic needs, we need to make a convincing case for our engagement or else see drastic reductions in our military, intelligence, peacekeeping and other foreign policy accounts.

In his farewell address in January 1953, Harry Truman predicted the collapse of Communism. "I have a deep and abiding faith in the destiny of free men," he said. "With patience and courage, we shall some day move on into a new era."

Now that era is upon us. It is a moment of unparalleled opportunity. We have the blessing of living in the world's most powerful and respected nation at a time when the world is embracing our ideals as never before. We can let this moment slip away. Or we can mobilize our nation in order to enlarge democracy, enlarge markets, and enlarge our future. I am confident that we will choose the road best travelled.

POSTSCRIPT

Should the United States Abandon Its Superpower Role?

The past five years have radically altered the previous four decades of world politics and the accompanying assumptions about U.S. foreign policy. Not only have the bipolar era and the cold war come to an end, but so has the Soviet Union. The anticommunist foreign policy consensus has been replaced with discord. What role should the United States play in the world? What are the country's vital interests, and how much internationalism can Americans afford? For further debate on these issues, valuable insights are provided by two articles in *International Security* (Spring 1993): Robert Jervis, "International Primacy: Is the Game Worth the Candle?" and Samuel P. Huntington, "Why International Primacy Matters."

There are several dimensions to opinions about what the U.S. world role should be. A recent source that explains the various ideological divisions within the U.S. population, and many other aspects of foreign policy opinion, is Ole R. Holsti, "Public Opinion and Foreign Policy: Challengers to the Almond-Lippman Consensus," *International Studies Quarterly* (December 1992). There can be little doubt, however, that one impact of the recent world changes has been a rise in isolationist opinion—or at least advocacy of a considerable reduction of the U.S. political and military presence in the world. Surveys show that a strong majority of Americans still favor an active, global role for the United States, but there are limits to just how active a role Americans will support. A 1991 survey showed that only 21 percent of Americans polled wanted their country to play the role of "world policeman," or "globocop" as it has become popularly known. A survey taken in 1993 that asked respondents whether the United States should "take a leading role" in world affairs or "reduce its involvement" revealed that 70 percent favored the less involved option. John Rielly explores public sentiments of both American leaders and the public in "Public Opinion: The Pulse of the '90s," *Foreign Policy* (Spring 1991).

Yet, it is incontestable that "fortress America" is not a viable option. The United States has global political and economic interests, and in a world that has not forsaken force, those interests may sometimes require military defense. Furthermore, there are vast and pressing environmental and human needs that can only be addressed through global cooperation. Can the United States abandon its role as an international leader?

In his Inaugural Address, President John F. Kennedy said that Americans should be prepared to "pay any price, bear any burden" to preserve the free world. No one argues for that sort of unrestrained, internationalistic, *Pax*

Americana approach anymore. *Interventionist* is an uncomfortable label. Similarly, there is no responsible sentiment for abandoning *all* U.S. international involvement. *Isolationism* is also an uncomfortable label. To determine your own position and to evaluate the positions of others, identify specifically what U.S. interests are or should be and then what you and others are or should be willing to do to maintain them.

ISSUE 4

Should the Arms Embargo on Bosnia Be Lifted?

YES: Ejup Ganic, from "Statement to the Senate Armed Services Committee," *Congressional Record* (July 1, 1994)

NO: Jean Claude Mallet, from "Statement to the Senate Armed Services Committee," *Congressional Record* (July 1, 1994)

ISSUE SUMMARY

YES: Ejup Ganic, the vice president of the Republic of Bosnia and Herzegovina, in a passionate appeal to members of Congress, asks the United States to end the prohibition on sending arms to Bosnia. In order to allow the Bosnian army to more evenly match the weaponry of the rebel Bosnian Serb forces, and thereby permitting the "legitimate and recognized government to defend itself," Ganic calls on U.S. leaders to lift the arms embargo.

NO: Jean Claude Mallet, testifying on behalf of the French Ministry of Defense, argues that lifting the arms embargo on Bosnia would only escalate the fighting and further endanger the United Nations forces in the country. In addition, a unilateral end to the arms embargo by the United States would violate a UN mandate and set a dangerous precedent.

The Balkans refers to the countries that occupy the Balkan Peninsula, which is located in southeastern Europe: Albania, Bulgaria, Greece, Macedonia, Romania, the part of Turkey that lies in Europe, and Yugoslavia. Beginning in the spring of 1991, many of the states and territories that made up Yugoslavia declared independence; Yugoslavia dissolved, and there now exists the separate states of Croatia, Slovenia, and Bosnia and Herzegovina (often referred to simply as Bosnia). Present-day Yugoslavia consists of the former republics of Serbia and Montenegro. The region is slightly larger than the state of Texas and is home to about 70 million people. The Balkans are a place of significant diversity: there are, for example, eight major languages, three major religions, and many ethnic groups.

Balkan history is a tale of frequent turbulence that has often spread to include outside powers. From the 1460s until the 1870s, all or part of the Balkans were ruled by the Ottoman Empire, centered in Turkey. Greece gained its independence in the 1920s. Other provinces gained degrees of autonomy in the ensuing years.

Into the twentieth century, the Balkans continued to convulse. In 1908 after Austria annexed Bosnia and Herzegovina, general warfare was barely averted. Peace in the region was fleeting, however, and was ended by the First Balkan War (1912: Bulgaria, Greece, and Serbia versus Turkey), then by the Second Balkan War (1913: Bulgaria, Romania, and Turkey versus Serbia and Greece). World War I, the "war to end all wars," was ignited in Sarajevo, the capital of Bosnia.

In 1918, after World War I, the victorious powers created Yugoslavia (the name means Land of the South Slavs), which included Serbia, Montenegro, Bosnia and Herzegovina, Croatia, Slovenia, and several other areas populated by ethnic groups with ties to peoples in countries bordering the newly formed Yugoslavia.

The bipolar confrontation between the United States and the Soviet Union during the long years of the cold war brought relative, if tense, stability to the region. Now the cold war is over and once again the Balkans are aflame. In May of 1991, caught up in ethnic and nationalistic sentiments, Bosnia and Herzegovina declared independence from Yugoslavia. However, the largely Serbian-led Yugoslav military attacked the breakaway republic, and the area has been at war ever since.

The people of Bosnia and Herzegovina are an ethnically and religiously mixed group. Of the major groups, about 44 percent are Bosnian Muslims, 31 percent Eastern Orthodox Serbs, and 17 percent largely Roman Catholic Croatians. Croatia, it should be noted, has pockets of Serbs, who make up 10 percent of the Croatian population. This ethnic and religious mix has proved volatile with the dissolution of Yugoslavia. Bosnian and Croatian Serbs, backed by the Serbs who control the reduced Yugoslavia, launched military attempts to secede from Bosnia and Herzegovina and from Croatia. Croats in Bosnia and Herzegovina have also moved to secede. The warfare has been hellacious. The Serbs have generally prevailed, although they have not gained complete victory.

The international community has tried several approaches to restore peace. The United Nations has dispatched peacekeeping forces, and NATO has threatened, and occasionally used, limited force to protect some Bosnian Muslim areas from the Bosnian Serbs. The UN and NATO have backed various mediation attempts, and the United Nations has imposed economic sanctions on Yugoslavia and an arms embargo on the entirety of what had been Yugoslavia.

Bosnia's vice president, Ejup Ganic, argues that it is time to lift the arms embargo because it unfairly favors the Bosnian Serbs, who, Ganic claims, get heavy weapons from the Yugoslav army. French general Jean Claude Mallet strongly opposes such moves on the grounds that it would undercut U.S. global standing and leadership and only serve to intensify the fighting—which would be to the detriment of all the Bosnians as well as the French and other UN peacekeepers serving there.

YES Ejup Ganic

STATEMENT TO THE SENATE ARMED SERVICES COMMITTEE

On behalf of the Republic of Bosnia and Herzegovina thank you for this opportunity to testify on the issue that is so vital to our future: the arms embargo on our country. I arrived this morning from Sarajevo to be here for the Senate's consideration of legislation of the arms embargo.

Just two days before, Mozart's Requiem was performed by the Sarajevo Philharmonic Orchestra conducted by Mr. Zubin Mehta, in the burnt-out building of the National Library that was almost totally destroyed by the heavy artillery of the Yugoslav army.

It has been three years since the Yugoslav army led by Serbian generals, and under political control of the Belgrade regime, launched aggression on those republics of the former Yugoslavia in which people voted to join the western democracies. Most of the aggression and destruction has been perpetrated against the Bosnian country and people. As a result of the arms embargo imposed on former Yugoslavia, we have over two hundred thousand of our civilians killed in Bosnia and Herzegovina, close to 2 million displaced and about 66% of our territory occupied. Crimes against humanity have been committed by the Yugoslav army and their allies and surrogates. The arms embargo against the legitimate and recognized Government of the Republic of Bosnia and Herzegovina was the policy—in effect the "therapy" that the international community imposed on Bosnia for the last two years to respond to aggression. This therapy created a catastrophe for my country. It has failed simply because the patient is dying. This therapy has to be changed.

The illegal and invalid arms embargo has deprived us of our right of self-defense. This right to self-defense was taken from us, and with it the ability to protect our citizens, and defend the sovereignty and integrity of our country. Belgrade and its well-armed surrogates ignored their pledges, signatures, and promises they made in all negotiations—at the London conference, in Geneva, New York, Brussels, Athens—because they wanted to and knew they could dictate events in the negotiating process by telling us, straight to our face—we have arms, you don't—that is the reality. If

From Ejup Ganic, "Statement to the Senate Armed Services Committee," *Congressional Record* (July 1, 1994).

you want your homes back, your land back, you have to push us back out.

Bosnia and Herzegovina is a small European country of multiethnic character, which existed as a state in various forms, for close to one thousand years. Before the aggression on Bosnia, we asked the United Nations, most specifically, Mr. Cyrus Vance, Special Representative of the UN Secretary General at that time, to deploy UN troops on the borders of Bosnia and Herzegovina and therefore to prevent aggression from being initiated against this multiethnic country. The request was turned down. I recall that one of Vance's advisers told me: You have to have war first. There will be casualties and then some kind of cease fire, at least temporarily, and then we would come. He was unfortunately right.

About two weeks ago, the world celebrated the D-day. We saw many, now older American veterans, who took part in that heroic battle against fascism. We also saw many European leaders shaking hands and taking pictures with them. These same European leaders we saw during the D-day celebration once again seem unable or unwilling to assume the task of confronting fascism. Fifty years after the defeat of fascism, what is happening in Bosnia today is fascism again, this time of the Belgrade regime. The Belgrade regime planned and executed massive ethnic cleansing with genocide, with brutalities not seen in Europe since the end of World War II. Massive rapes of women and girls, and other forms of terror had been instilled to drive the population out, taking over their private property, destroying historical buildings, industrial infrastructure, cultural and religious monuments, so that the population might never return. This repression and genocide against the non-Serbian population is the program of creating a "Greater Serbia" through the idea of ethnic purity. Unfortunately, fifty years later in Europe, we have fascism again on the rise. I ask if the world is prepared to act and stop the Serbian fascism as was done fifty years ago. At least say no to fascism by letting us defend ourselves.

We are asking you to lift the arms embargo so that we may defend ourselves and secure a durable peace. We have not lost the war. The Serbs tried by all means to destroy our country and finish with us, but they have not succeeded, yet. Our people are talented and educated, and with our bare hands we resist and still hold under our control the major cities and vital industrial areas. We organized our army to defend in every cell of our society. Unfortunately, not more than thirty percent of the soldiers have light weapons.

We are asking you to lift the arms embargo in order to create conditions for peace and for negotiations through balance in weaponry. We had in fact asked you to lift the arms embargo from the first day of aggression. You said that the peace was coming. Now, more than two years later, the Serbian troops, loyal to Belgrade regime, occupy 66% of the territory, they killed more than two hundred thousand people, and we are asking again, we are begging you to lift the arms embargo because the peace is not possible under the present environment of weapons imbalance. It is NOT too late. Lift the arms embargo with a program to achieve peace. We need arms to survive, not for victory, because of the losses that we had and genocide we went through, we can never talk about victory.

We repeat over and over again: We are not asking for your troops to fight for us on the ground. That is our job and our task. But please, do not combine any more big words with small deeds. God will not forgive you if you do nothing. Doing nothing creates tragedy in Bosnia every day.

For almost twenty-six months, your Administration is in something like Hamlet-like dilemma: to be or not to be. But this Hamlet-like dilemma, and the spirit of hesitation have unfortunately allowed for dead bodies all over, as in Shakespeare's tragedies. Stop this Hamlet's dilemma because there is no more space for dead bodies in Bosnia. The peace that we have been waiting for the last twenty-six months is not coming without your action.

The United Nations are responsible for ineffective results. Its resolutions are being ignored. The UN declared "safe areas" have become the most unsafe places in Bosnia and Herzegovina. Remember Gorazde, over one hundred NATO jets were on the disposal of the Secretary General and his Special Representative, Mr. Akashi, to protect this safe area and give a lesson to the Serbs that the buck stops somewhere. Mr. Akashi, supported by many of the same political leaders who sat before you today, first allowed the Serbian tanks to penetrate the safe area lines established by the UN itself by declaring that there was no real danger to the civilian population because the tanks were too far from the potential victims. Then, when the Serbian tanks came within a few yards of the Gorazde hospital and other residential areas, the same man claimed that it was technically not possible to confront the tanks because they were too close to the residential areas and the civilian victims. The Serbian generals instructed by the Belgrade regime did

not allow General Michael Rose to go to Gorazde and declared him the voluntary prisoner of their army until they destroyed most of Gorazde. Some UN generals who spoke openly, like General Razek and General Morillon, that the peace will not come in Bosnia as long as the situation is handled by those who oppose lifting the arms embargo were immediately sent home.

America is a country of hard-working people. If you cannot help us, then do not prevent the lifting of the arms embargo. We know that Americans are against ethnic cleansing, against genocide, against massive rapes and torture of our people. We know that Americans are and have always been against fascism. Oppose fascism of the Belgrade regime on Bosnia. No consensus is required to oppose fascism.

We count on American democracy, we count on the moralism of American people and their commitment to legality. We are looking to the United States Congress for America's leadership. We hope for the proper action from America. The ethnic cleansing as imposed by Belgrade regime destabilized the world. Only in the stable world will the United States of America continue to prosper.

Mr. Chairman, distinguished audience.

Every day in Bosnia we pray for peace. We are hard working people, we are a part of the European civilization. We do not need anyone to work for us, we do not need money from anybody. We need a chance to survive.

At one time I was a lucky Bosnian. As an MIT student, many years ago, I learned from my American roommates that the ethnic purity concept was always fascism for American people. Much of Europe, including its most economically advanced Member States, still do not practice or even understand the concept of a multiethnic state. While your nation strives to perfect this idea, too many European leaders still avoid it as an undesirable contamination of their culture or history. The leadership of American people, demonstrated today in this room, is a hope for all generations in Bosnia for a better future.

Thank you and I am at your disposal for any questions you might have. I just came from Sarajevo after 26 hours of flight, to be here with you today, and I am the one who feels privileged.

NO

Jean Claude Mallet

STATEMENT TO THE SENATE ARMED SERVICES COMMITTEE

I am here on behalf and with the personal trust of the French Minister of Defense Francois Leotard.... I am certain you realize, through this unprecedented gesture, the importance France attaches to your present debate and its potential consequences.

I will give you an in-depth view of the French Government's studies to the issue of lifting of the embargo. It must not be seen or understood that we have just rejected this as a slogan that would not be accepted in France. It has triggered in-depth studies, particularly in the Ministry of Defense....

I have the honor to represent ... a country which has devoted a considerable amount of effort—political, financial, and human—in the Bosnian crisis, sometimes at the expense of the lives of its soldiers since we have had to see about 20 deaths—20 deaths exactly—and about 300 casualties since we first sent military observers in July 1991 at the request of the European Union and CSCE [Conference on Security and Cooperation in Europe], observers, monitors, ground troops, up to 6,000 now, a naval battle group, AWACS [radar planes], reconnaissance, and combat aircraft, even the French Gendarmerie on the Danube are present in and around former Yugoslavia.

This important involvement stems from at least three categories of motives: First, we feel the future of European security is in many respects at stake again with this crisis in the Balkans; second, humanitarian tragedies have triggered, in particular in the summers of 1992 and 1993, an increased effort; and third, we have thought that we needed to design a containment policy in order to avoid the spill-over of the conflict in neighboring countries. 67 percent of the UNPROFOR [United Nations Protection Force] forces are European.

... Why have we been resisting the Bosnian Government appeals for the lifting of the arms embargo; what prospects do we see today for the peace process? Up to a point, those two questions are very clearly closely connected.

I am convinced that the lifting of the embargo would mean the end of any peace process and prospect for a very long period of time. The lifting of the embargo is nothing but a war-helping and nearly war-making measure. It

From Jean Claude Mallet, "Statement to the Senate Armed Services Committee," *Congressional Record* (July 1, 1994).

would ruin, without doubt, any present efforts to build a new momentum towards a peace plan supported... by the United States, Russia, and the European Union powers. I will come back to that later.

The lifting of the embargo—that is my second point—would mean inevitably the withdrawal of UNPROFOR and trigger the resumption of a fierce violence and war throughout Bosnia. In that sense, it would be a tremendous drawback from what has been achieved on the ground in particular since August 1993.

Third, the lifting of the embargo means doubtless increased deeper inevitable involvement of the allies, and among them foremost of the United States of America in a war-like situation. Before dealing with these points, I would like to say a word on the issue of unilateral lifting, which I understand has been a matter of debate here.

... I do not think unilateral lifting, from an international point of view, means leadership. But it is a sure recipe for international disorder in the post–Cold War world. Let me just remind you briefly, the text of the Security Council resolution of September 1991, which is today the legal basis of the arms embargo. It reads in its paragraph 6 that the Council has decided on the basis of Chapter VII of the Charter that the member states will immediately enforce a general and complete embargo, and I quote, until the Security Council decides otherwise, end of quotation.

We have, then, together subscribed to a tax which imposes on us to come back to the Security Council of which U.S. and France and Great Britain in particular are prominent members, if we wanted to change this piece of international law. Could the United States, as such, and

as a permanent member of the Security Council and as a member state of the United Nations, decide solely to place itself above the law it has contributed to create? Could it consider such a clear resolution as a worthless sheet of paper?

This could probably mean the end of the game in the Security Council in the new context, a year before the celebration of the 50th anniversary of the United Nations Charter signature on the 26th of June 1949. It could mean after such a precedent that other members of the Council, permanent or not, could see themselves free not to abide by the resolutions they vote in the highest international body, the body which authorizes or not the use of force and is responsible for peacekeeping. So in that case, in that hypothesis, who is next after U.S.? It would mean, of course, or probably, a tremendous crisis with your European allies and your Russian partner.

Now, if we turn to the lifting of the embargo itself per se, what do we see? We see first, as has been pointed out, a quick, almost immediate decision to withdraw the United Nations forces in this theater, at least in the French Government opinion which I think is shared both by the United Nations and/or allies and partners. Some could say now, does the international community, do the Muslims really care about that? Let me dwell a little bit on UNPROFOR.

Our forces are presently accomplishing a series of missions thanks to which the situation has slowly been stabilized since August 1993. I will just give you a few highlights of these missions:

Humanitarian aid has arrived, and since January 1994, for the first time in the history of this conflict, humanitarian needs are matched by humanitarian flows, and these needs have been met since January 1994....

In the meantime, interposition between the warring factions have multiplied. In Central Bosnia, in Sarajevo, in Gorazde, there the blue helmets stand between two camps and avoid the resumption of fighting.

Third, they are guarding heavy weapons storages, and this is another mission to which a lot of personnel have to be devoted. There are, of course, a few violations of this rule, and things can be improved. But there it is. In several places, particularly Sarajevo, heavy weapons have been withdrawn or stored. Do we want them back in the battlefield?

Fourth, monitoring of the ceasefire or cessation of hostilities is, of course, another mission which requires an important number of units.

So, the lifting of the embargo would make all of these missions impossible for UNPROFOR because it means the contrary.

Humanitarian aid delivery means freedom of movement on roads; free access to airports. Roads and airports would be the place through which heavy weapons would have to be delivered. They would then immediately be the targets of war operations in order for one party to secure the deliveries and for the other party to interdict those deliveries. Communication axes, airfields, would be quickly the target of attacks.

Interposition missions would have to be abandoned for two reasons: first, the resumption of large-scale battles in these sensitive places in which they have to be met; second, the loss of the impartial image of UNPROFOR in the eyes of the Serbs. If we accept weapons deliveries for their enemies we take sides. Withdrawal of UNPROFOR from theses places would

trigger now battles in all places, Sarajevo, Central, Eastern, Northern Bosnia....

Some object that the Muslims are the best place to judge. But you must be aware of their wishes. Prime Minister Siladzic repeated them to the French Government a few weeks ago. The Bosnian Government wants both, both the lifting of the embargo and the maintenance of UNPROFOR presence. Why? First, of course, because the Bosnian Government would like to see UNPROFOR and the allies side by side with them—and that is natural, we can understand that—but also because they know in spite of all that our presence, our corresponding policy, has been a help since at least a year. Let me give you a few illustrations of what happened in the past 10 months.

Humanitarian aid has been progressively and is now surely a success. I have said that. The creation of the safe areas in June 1993 has in effect stopped the Serb progression and offensives, in particular in the Eastern enclaves. The situation in Sarajevo is tremendously improved... since the ultimatum of last February, and the Serbs are no more in a position to seize the Bosnian capital as they were during last winter.

During autumn and winter, the Muslim army extended its hold in Central Bosnia, and you could see on maps the progress they made between July 1993 and February 1994 to control a wider space in Central Bosnia. So, on the whole, it must be admitted that the presence of UNPROFOR has corresponded to a period during which the situation of the Muslims has improved on several aspects. But the lifting of the embargo, which would trigger new combats and very likely an offensive by the Serbs to anticipate Bosnian moves before the Bosnian army gets stronger, would inevitably be the signal for our withdrawal.

This is not the only consequence. The logic in which we, and foremostly, you the United States, would be thrown in is therefore a new buildup of war. I do not see how the United States, having decided or supported the lifting of the embargo, could stay out of the crisis. On the contrary, your country would have to commit itself even more.

Either in effect such a decision is simply a buzz word, a leitmotif, a slogan, you have no intention to be part of the game which is complex and far from here, and this can be understood—but then why interfere with the present efforts on the ground—or it means that you want to help the Muslims and then the United States cannot stop there. You would have to offer air protection, at least for a while, at the scale of the whole battlefield, not only the safe areas as today.

These strikes would accelerate UN-PROFOR's dramatic withdrawal. You would have to help directly or indirectly the Bosnians so that they are trained to use heavy weapons, tanks, et cetera, on a large scale; you would have to commit yourself to avoid any extension of the conflict, in particular if the Serbian army, led by Belgrade, felt itself in a position to support the Bosnian Serbs. Large-scale air campaign, military assistance, containment, these obligations lead certainly to an ever-increased involvement of the United States of America and some of its allies, not the other way around.

I hope these explanations are a help for you to understand why we have been so reluctant to consider the option of lifting of the arms embargo. In our view, this measure pertains to the worst-case scenario and should not be envisaged without having explored at length all the other options. I understand the American administration has come to similar conclusions recently. In our view, it is now time to give all its chances to the peace process which has been relaunched for several weeks.

The French Government policy has always been to build up a consensus between the United States, the Europeans, and the Russians, in order to arrive at a balanced and shared view of a peace settlement. Considerable time and political involvement have been devoted in recent weeks to this objective since the ultimatum of Sarajevo and Gorazde. In that perspective, President Clinton's visit in Europe on the 50th birthday of the D-Day and talks in Paris are considered by my Minister and my Government as a success for both countries. We are close to an agreement on a map, a series of measures, incentives, and disincentives accompanying the plan, and a schedule.

This convergence of the United States, European Union, and Russia, is vital if we want a settlement, if we want peace. If it is put at risk, if the parties think that we are divided, they will exploit this weakness and this at our and your and their expense. On territorial percentages, on the map, on the definition of incentives, we are now closer than ever. If we are united, there is a chance to bring this conflict if not at once to a complete stop at least to a beginning of a settlement. Reiterating the leitmotif of the arms embargo is raising false expectations and is a source of serious misunderstandings and divisions with the Europeans and the Russians.

In 1994, as we are celebrating the liberation of my country by American troops with the help of the French resistance and of the free French, I would like to see the United States of America and its European partners side by side in this resolution of what we consider to be a major crisis. If we achieve unity of vision, if we commit ourselves together both politically and, when the time comes, in the field, we can help to bring peace back in the Balkans.

Believe me, lifting the arms embargo is the worst way to get involved and stuck in the present drama.

Thank you.

POSTSCRIPT

Should the Arms Embargo on Bosnia Be Lifted?

There are many reasons for the world community to be concerned with what happens in Bosnia and Herzegovina. The fighting there has been intense and horrific: there have been reports of so-called ethnic cleansing, to drive people from their homes, and of widespread rape, used as a military tactic to terrorize the population. Most of the allegations have been made against the Bosnian Serbs, but atrocities have been committed by all sides. So for humanitarian reasons, we should be concerned. Ethnic conflict is not limited to Bosnia, and a good account of the subject can be found in Ted Robert Gurr and Barbara Haff's *Ethnic Conflict in World Politics* (Westview Press, 1994). A second reason for worldwide concern over the fighting in Bosnia is that it could spread, as conflicts in the Balkans have in the past. The possibility of a third Balkan war is real. The Serbs are angered by Macedonian independence, and the Greeks fear that the independent Macedonians may soon lay claim to the Greek province of Macedonia, which has heightened tension. Turkey and other Muslim countries are distressed by the slaughter of Bosnian Muslims. The Bosnian Muslims and Croats have settled their differences and are beginning to coordinate military efforts against the Serbs. Hungarians are protective of ethnic Hungarians in the Yugoslav province of Vojvodina. The Russians have also become increasingly concerned, following their tradition of support for their Serbian ethnic cousins. The list of antagonistic permutations in this part of the world could go on, but the point to make is that many observers fear that increasing alliance formation could lead to another world war. A third reason for concern has to do with issues related to the status of the United Nations and the effectiveness of NATO (North Atlantic Treaty Organization): Can these organizations be relied upon in the future for dispute resolutions in the international system?

What to do? The U.S. Congress has twice considered and narrowly rejected overturning the arms embargo. The Senate debates can be found in the *Congressional Record* for May 12 and July 1, 1994. There have also been proposals for and arguments against massive intervention by outside powers to bring peace. In a provocatively entitled article, "If Bosnians Were Dolphins...," *Commentary* (October 1993), Edward N. Luttwak contends that if Bosnians were dolphins, we would be rushing to their rescue rather than standing on the shore. Colin Gray warns against plunging hurriedly into the uncharted waters of interventionism in "Force, Order, and Justice: The Ethics of Realism," *Global Affairs* (Summer 1994).

ISSUE 5

Is Islamic Fundamentalism a Threat to Political Stability?

YES: Judith Miller, from "The Challenge of Radical Islam," *Foreign Affairs* (Spring 1993)

NO: John L. Esposito, from "Political Islam: Beyond the Green Menace," *Current History* (January 1994)

ISSUE SUMMARY

YES: Political researcher and writer Judith Miller argues that the radical Islamic movement in the greater Middle Eastern region has created a combustible mixture that threatens domestic and international political stability.

NO: John Esposito, director of the Center for Muslim-Christian Understanding at the School of Foreign Service, Georgetown University, holds that it is wrong to view Islam as an organized whole that acts as a single unified powerful force, whose adherents are mostly dangerous fanatics.

Islam was founded by the prophet Muhammad late in the sixth century. The word *Islam* means submission to God (Allah), and Muslims (ones who submit) believe that Muhammad received Allah's teachings, which make up the Koran. There are several Islamic political concepts that are important to this issue. Some tend to bring Muslims together; others work to divide them.

One of the forces that serve to promote Muslim unity is the idea of *ummah*, the spiritual, cultural, and political community of Muslims. In part, this means that Muslims are less likely than people from the Western cultural tradition to draw distinct lines between the state, religion, and the individual. Instead, some Muslims believe that the conduct of government and of individuals should be governed by *shari'ah*, that is, Koranic law. *Ummah* implies that faithful believers of Islam should join spiritually and politically into one, great Muslim community. A related unifying element of Islam is that Muslims distinguish between Muslim-held lands ("the house of Islam") and non-Muslim lands ("the house of unbelief"). One of the fundamental tenets of Islam is the jihad, meaning struggle in the name of Allah. A jihad can be peaceful or violent; a jihad can defend Islam against nonbelievers or against individual Muslims or sects deemed to be heretical or disloyal to the true faith. Those who struggle to defend or promote Islam are sometimes called *mujahedin*.

A sense of common history is another factor that works to bring Muslims together. After a triumphant and powerful beginning, which included the spread of Islamic religion and culture into Europe and beyond from its Middle Eastern origins, the political fortunes of Muslims declined slowly after about the year 1500. Part of this decline was due to military losses during the Crusades (1095–1291). The Crusades were military expeditions undertaken by Christian, European powers in the eleventh, twelfth, and thirteenth centuries to win the Holy Land from the Muslims. By the start of the modern era, almost all Muslim lands were under the direct or indirect control of colonial —mostly European, mostly Christian—powers. Muslim history, therefore, includes conflict with Christian powers (especially those of Europe) and the domination of Muslims by others.

There are also strong forces that tend to divide Muslims. One of these is the frequent rivalry between the majority Sunni sect and the minority Shi'ite sect. The origins of this division are not important to our political discussion here, except to point out that the minority Shi'ites tend to be more militant, and they tend to reject the legitimacy of Sunni control of such important Islamic places as Mecca, in Saudi Arabia.

Muslims are also divided over the degree to which they believe in strict adherence to *shari'ah* to govern both religious and civil conduct. Muslim traditionalists (or fundamentalists, according to common usage) want to establish legal systems based on *shari'ah* and reinstitute practices such as banning alcohol and having women cover their faces, which declined under the influence of Western culture.

Other Muslims, who are often called secularists (or less accurately, modernists) believe that religious and civil law should be kept relatively separate. For them, Koranic law is flexible enough to allow changes in tradition. The secularists reject the argument that they are not good Muslims.

Nationalism (primary political loyalty to a national state) is a third factor that divides Muslims. Individual Muslim countries are fiercely nationalistic. Achieving full Muslim political unity would necessarily entail giving up patriotism and other manifestations of nationalism.

Why are the forces of unity and division among Muslims a global concern? Since its low point after World War I, the Muslim world's role on the world stage has been enlarged. There are now many more independent Muslim countries. Moreover, Muslim countries are becoming stronger—a strength based in part on the wealth that petroleum has brought them. And Muslims everywhere have begun to reclaim their heritage in what might be called a Muslim pride movement.

The issue debated here is whether resurgent Islam, especially its traditional, fundamental aspects, represent a threat to political stability. Judith Miller argues that the answer is yes, that the traditionalists are fundamentally antithetical to stability. John L. Esposito disagrees, arguing that the traditionalists are not inherently dangerous and should be viewed within their cultural context.

YES   Judith Miller

THE CHALLENGE OF
RADICAL ISLAM

In April 1991 an unusual meeting was held in the Sudanese capital of Khartoum. For four days, leading Islamic politicians and intellectuals from 55 countries and three continents met to draft a common strategy to establish Muslim states in their respective lands. It was an Islamic star-studded event....

The group ultimately approved a six-point manifesto intended to demonstrate that "whatever the strength of America and the West" in the aftermath of the Gulf War, "God is greater." The manifesto paid lip service to liberalism and democracy, asserting that they were "not incompatible" with *shura* [ruling Muslim council], or Islamic government through consultation. Political pluralism was fine, provided it was not "unlimited" and was subordinate to the need for "unity and the *shura*." Cooperation with the West and existing non-Islamic governments was permissible, if such exchanges were based on new and more equitable principles. "Good regimes," the document states, "will benefit from popular will; bad regimes will be fought." Read in its entirety, the manifesto's underlying message was clear: in Islam's war against the West and the struggle to build Islamic states at home, the ends justified the means.

The gathering received almost no attention in the Western press. But many regard the Islamic Arab Popular Conference, as it was called, as an important event. It marked the first serious effort by an avowedly Islamic state to define with other leading figures of the movement their own vision of a new world order and a strategy for achieving it. The conference also made progress toward Turabi's long-stated goal of overcoming the historic rift between Sunni Muslim states, like Sudan, and a Shiite state, like Iran—that is, toward ending the bitter historic enmity that has separated these two wings of Islam since the seventh century. In addition, the gathering helped fuse formerly secular Arab nationalist movements, which have dominated Arab politics in the anticolonial struggles for independence and statehood for nearly 50 years, with the increasingly more seductive and influential groups espousing the new Islamic rhetoric.

WHAT IS TO BE DONE?

How should the United States and its new administration view the rise of militant Islam in the Middle East? How should Americans react? What, if anything, can be done about the trend?

The Khartoum conference is merely one example of the growing power of militant Islam. Since Islamic revolutionaries led by the Ayatollah Ruhollah Khomeini toppled the shah of Iran in 1979 and swept Islamic militants to power, an avowedly Islamic government has emerged only in impoverished, isolated Sudan. But everywhere, Arab governments are struggling to contain Islamic pressures and respond to a widespread desire among their citizens for more "Islamic" government and society....

Few serious analysts of militant Islam, or Islamic fundamentalism (an inappropriate but widely used term borrowed from American Protestantism to describe the phenomenon), argue that Islamic militant groups constitute a monolith. Fewer still see Islam... as the "Green Menace."... Most sophisticated analysts know that militant Islam is as diverse as the Arabs themselves and the countries in which it is taking hold. They recognize that Islam is not inherently at odds with modernity; the two co-exist comfortably in Muslim societies from Indonesia to Bosnia. Nor do most foes of fundamentalism maintain that the Khartoum conference and other efforts by Islamists to enhance cooperation should be regarded as a new "Khomeintern"—a vast conspiracy led by Iran and Sudan.

However, radical political Islam placed atop the societies of the Middle East has created a combustible mixture. And those who believe in universal human rights (and women's rights in particular), democratic government, political tolerance and pluralism and in peace between the Arabs and Israelis cannot be complacent about the growing strength of militant Islamic movements in most Middle Eastern countries, or about the numerous and increasing ties among such movements and between Iran and Sudan. Western governments should be concerned about these movements and, more important, should oppose them. For despite their rhetorical commitment to democracy and pluralism, virtually all militant Islamists oppose both. They are, and are likely to remain, anti-Western, anti-American and anti-Israeli.

The Bush administration seemed to understand this point, but this recognition was never fully apparent in its policy. The administration tried to draw a distinction between good and bad Islamists, and it wound up fudging a response to the challenge posed by radical Islam....

[The] distinction was politically useful for the administration. It enabled Washington, on the one hand, to oppose any Islamic group that espoused violence and challenged regimes that the United States either liked or needed to do business with, such as Egypt and Saudi Arabia, and on the other, to resist the anti-American Islamic governments in power in Sudan and Iran, which met his criteria of being violent, intolerant and coercive. The doctrine, by extension, also justified American support for "good" Islamic groups—those seeking to overturn communist or tyrannical states (such as the Mujahedeen rebels in Afghanistan and the Mujahedeen-e Khalq, a militant Islamic group that is fighting Iran not only from inside Iraq but also from Washington).

A few analysts challenged the wisdom of America's support for these good Islamic groups. They warned ineffectively, but with keen foresight, that those Islamic factions supported by the West in their fight against Kabul would ultimately make Afghans nostalgic for the good old days of President Najibullah. And others labeled the American-tolerated, if not openly supported, Mujahedeen the "Khmer Rouge of Islamists."

Despite such reservations, the Bush administration's policy seemed fairly straightforward. Of course, the United States would oppose groups such as the violent wing of the Islamic Resistance Movement (Hamas), the Iranian-supported Hezbollah in Lebanon and the four—and still splitting—factions of the Islamic Jihad [holy war], all of which champion violence, terrorism and "holy war" to rid Muslims of the "un-Islamic" governments that oppress Arabs in Israel, Jordan, Lebanon and Egypt. But how would Washington view Islamic groups that pledged to create democratic rule, to respect human rights and pluralism? . . .

What the United States wanted, he explained, was for Middle Eastern nations to broaden political participation in their societies. At the same time . . . Washington would oppose those seeking to use the democratic process to come to power, only to destroy that very process in order to retain power and political dominance. . . .

But how would Washington know which Islamic groups were genuinely committed to democratic principles and peaceful coexistence with its own minorities, women and the West? Here, the statement was diplomatically silent. "We'll know 'em when we see 'em," quipped one American diplomat. But Washington's reluctance to spell out its criteria was a deliberate evasion. . . .

CLERICS IN CIVILIAN CLOTHES?

Why should one suspect the sincerity of the Islamists' commitment to truth, justice and the democratic way? In short, because of Arab and Islamic history and the nature and evolution of these groups. Consider, for one, the FIS [Islamic Salvation Front, an Islamic fundamentalist movement]. In Algeria the FIS won a plurality of the electoral votes in national elections in December 1991, but the group was denied victory by a military coup and the installation of an emergency government that has banned the FIS and ruthlessly hunted down its members ever since.

During parliamentary elections, FIS leaders led a double linguistic life. They offered Algeria's poor and disenfranchised vague slogans of spiritual and, more important, economic salvation through Islam, and to Western journalists and its more Frenchified but politically frustrated middle class, they gave reassurances of their belief in democracy and human rights. Before the first round of voting, in sum, FIS leaders were careful to stress their democratic intentions.

But their tone and message changed abruptly after the FIS scored so well in the first round and seemed destined to secure an overwhelming parliamentary majority in the second voting round. Only then did the supposedly moderate FIS leaders begin emphasizing the party's earlier slogan: "No law. No constitution. Only the laws of God and the Koran." While this linguistic double-talk may not justify the cancellation of elections and surely not the subsequent repression, it raises questions about what the FIS would have done had it been permitted to assume power.

A similar pattern of events occurred in the Sudan. Islam was brought to power there not by the ballot box, but by a military coup. Sudan's leaders now parrot the Islamic values and principles enunciated by the Svengali of the Islamic movement—Hassan Turabi, a Western-trained jurist who is spellbinding in at least three languages. On paper, it was hard to find fault with Turabi. He favored "Islamic" emancipation of women and respect for individual dignity and property. Islam, he said, did not believe in coercion. But the reality of life in his new Islamic state belies these sentiments and reassurances. Since coming to power, the military government has canceled freedom of assembly and the press, banned all non-Islamic parties, forced women to wear Islamic dress or lose their jobs and, according to Amnesty International and other human rights groups, tortured suspected heretics and other political dissidents in what the Sudanese call "ghost houses," which are sprinkled throughout the capital.

Minorities have fared even worse. Catholic bishops have accused the Sudanese government of waging a holy war against the state's Christians (almost ten percent of the population) and those who follow African religions. *Sharia*, or Islamic law, has been reimposed with new vigor: lashings of women for inappropriate dress are now common; so are other corporal punishments, such as amputations for repeated theft, stoning for adultery; the law even allows crucifixion.

Iran is often cited as another example of Islamic "pragmatism" and growing "moderation." While Tehran allows greater freedom of debate and political participation than was permitted under the shah,... no individual or group that questions the basic tenets of the Islamic revolution and theocratic rule is permitted to participate. Iran... remains nonetheless rhetorically and to some extent genuinely hostile to the West, the United States in particular. Finally, its refusal to retract the disgraceful religious ruling—or the bounty on his head—against Salman Rushdie for writing an allegedly blasphemous book, *The Satanic Verses*, reflects more vividly than any other single action Iran's total disregard for basic human rights and international law....

A new, more moderate political Islam may evolve and take root in the region. But many believe that this is unlikely. "Islam is today the language of opposition," says A. Abu Zayd, a Sudanese educator. "To attract the young, Islam must be fierce and militant, opposed to the existing order. So to speak of a moderate political Islam is a contradiction in terms."

Other analysts, such as Martin Kramer, associate director of the Moshe Dayan Center at Tel Aviv University, argue that militant Islamic groups, by nature, cannot be democratic, pluralistic, egalitarian or pro-Western. In a recent *Commentary* article, Kramer notes that Islamic law is not legislated but divinely revealed. It is, therefore, perfect law, which as such is beyond reform, abrogation or alteration. "While it is not above some reinterpretation," Kramer observes, "neither is it infinitely elastic." That law, he continues, stands in stark opposition to the Universal Declaration of Human Rights, which guarantees the freedom to choose, among other things, one's religion and spouse, both of which are restricted in Islamic law. While Islam over the centuries has proven far more tolerant toward minorities and diversity than Christianity (sectarian strife and religious persecution having been atypical and hardly ever as intense as the great persecutions that occurred under Christianity), minorities under Islamic law are given protected, not equal, status.

Bernard Lewis, a noted historian of the Middle East, argues in a recent article in *The Atlantic Monthly* that the nature and history of Islam and the relationship between Islam and temporal power do not make liberal democracy and Islam natural bedfellows. Islam, he explains, has been characterized throughout history by the absence of any legal recognition of corporate persons or the legal person, which is at the heart of the representative institutions embodied in Roman law. The Islamic state was in principle a theocracy, Lewis argues, "not in the Western sense of a state ruled by church and the clergy, since neither existed in the Islamic world, but in the more literal sense of a polity ruled by God." Therefore, devout Muslims believe that legitimate authority comes from God alone. And since the ruler derives his power from God and the holy law, and not from the people, defying authority has been tantamount to defying God. "Disobedience was a sin as well as a crime," Lewis concludes. Against such a backdrop, autocracy has been the norm, and the notions of plurality, self-criticism and disagreement—all essential features of liberal democracy—face an uphill, though not impossible, battle in winning widespread cultural acceptance.

PROMOTE HUMAN RIGHTS, NOT ELECTIONS

... American officials formulating new policies toward Islam and the Arabs should be skeptical of those who seek to liberate Arabs through Islam. First, they should understand that no matter how often and fervently Islamic groups assert their commitment to democracy and pluralism, their basic ideological covenants and tracts, published declarations and interviews (especially in Arabic) appear to make these pledges incompatible with their stated goals of establishing societies under Islamic laws and according to Islamic values. Far too many Middle Easterners, and Islamists in particular, have learned how to mollify the West (and deceive their own potential adherents, many of whom genuinely crave democracy, greater political expression and an end to political repression) by manipulating the words of democracy.

Moreover, to most Islamists, and to many Arabs today, democracy translates as majority rule. There is an almost total disregard for minority rights, an essential component of liberal democracy. If the majority want an Islamic state, Islamists maintain, then the minority or minorities —be they religious, ethnic or female— who do not will have to put up or shut up, or accept a far worse fate.

As it begins to chart its course in foreign policy, the new Clinton administration is likely to feel obliged to promote democracy in the Middle East. It must recognize, however, that the promotion of free elections immediately is likely to lead to the triumph of Islamic groups that have no commitment to democracy in any recognizable, meaningful form. In other words, there seems to be a paradox in America's relentless rhetorical (if not actual) promotion of democracy and pluralism in the Middle East. Because Islamic groups... are currently the best organized opposition and, in some countries, the only organized opposition, given Arab reluctance to openly oppose associations that call themselves Islamic, free elections seem more likely than any other route to produce militant Islamic regimes that are, in fact, inherently anti-democratic....

What the Clinton administration should say is that the establishment of avowedly "Islamic states" risks jeopardizing the principles espoused in the Universal Declaration of Human Rights and codified in the International Covenant on Civil and Political Rights. The ICCPR declaration is not a new form of cultural imperialism, as Islamists argue, but rather a code of values that constitutes the basis of decent and humane government and has been approved by 117 countries. The fact that leading Islamic militants felt obliged to meet in Paris in 1981 to draft an Islamic Declaration of Human Rights, which omitted all freedoms that contradicted *sharia,* should give any policymaker pause about what can be expected from the Islamic radicals, should they come to power.

Consider women. While Islamists speak of the need to honor women and prevent their degradation, the governments most Islamists are promoting would, in accordance with their interpretation of *sharia,* deny women work in many sectors of the economy and deny them equal rights and equal legal standing. In Iran, the government in the name of Islam restored polygamy and child marriage, which the shah had earlier outlawed. This is not simply a different, and hence morally acceptable, way of organizing society. Rather, the systematic denial of women's rights is like binding female children's feet in China—a barbaric practice impeding economic and social development that should be denounced by any self-confident American government. No one is recommending that the United States invade Sudan or Saudi Arabia to liberate women. But neither should the alternative be official American si-

lence about such practices. While there will always be a difficult balance between realpolitik and idealistic values in foreign policy, American administrators should strive toward the latter.

The Bush administration should have said that America would promote elections tomorrow and civil society today —increased participation in public life by a growing number of individuals, groups and associations who genuinely crave liberal democracy—so that the concepts and traditions upon which democracy depends have time to take root, and so that countries that have known little else but one-party authoritarian rule will stand a better chance of developing truly democratic governments. It should have articulated openly the conundrum that is whispered about in the corridors of Foggy Bottom: that America's mindless, relentless promotion of elections immediately is likely for now to bring to power through the ballot box those who would extinguish democracy in the name of Allah. It should have stressed instead more modest goals: increased political participation in government and the need for a freer press and freer public debate in all countries in the region.

Any American policy is likely to be only marginal in affecting developments in the Middle East, given the enormity of economic and political problems facing most Arab governments (though this argument is rarely made when the Arab-Israeli conflict is discussed). But influencing events at the margin is better than not attempting to influence them at all. It is surely better than despairing and saying that nothing can or should be done about the trend toward fundamentalism. Ultimately, the triumph of militant Islam in the Middle East may say as much about the West as about the Arabs and the failure of their existing systems. Islamists, by and large, have come to power when no one is willing to oppose them at home and abroad. In any new world order, Americans should not be ashamed to say that they favor pluralism, tolerance and diversity, and that they reject the notion that God is on anyone's side.

FIGHTING RADICAL ISLAM WITH WORDS

The Clinton administration has an opportunity to speak in direct terms about the prospects for democracy and Islamic government. It can say what is suggested by so many specialists but rarely articulated—that the United States supports as a matter of principle the separation of temporal from spiritual power in government. It should seize the moment not to draw a line in the sand, as Bush did, but to make a firm commitment to democratic, pluralistic values.

Washington, under President Bush, did not take this position. It never said that the West believes that Islam is a great religion, which produced an inspired culture from which the West learned much, but that in the 21st century in the Middle East, in nation states that are ethnically, tribally and religiously heterogeneous, an Islamic state as espoused by most of its proponents is simply incompatible with values and truths that Americans and most Westerners today hold to be self-evident. Perhaps an American government that defines its interest along narrow strategic lines—that is, along access to oil at a steady and acceptable price—cannot afford to say such things. Such statements would surely antagonize American allies such as Saudi Arabia, an avowedly Islamic state that denies basic human rights to half its population and all religious minorities but is dependably pro-Western, considerably less harsh and repressive than many of the states that surround it, and also America's major source of foreign oil.

While the American government cannot and perhaps, from a strict definition of national interest, should not say such things, there are individual Americans who can speak out. In the past decade, human rights activists have addressed many of these concerns. In the Arab world itself, human rights groups and activists are beginning to find their own voices, despite great risks and staunch government opposition.

Islamic militancy presents the West with a paradox. While liberals speak of the need for diversity with equality, Islamists see this as a sign of weakness. Liberalism tends not to teach its proponents to fight effectively. What is needed, rather, is almost a contradiction in terms: a liberal militancy, or a militant liberalism that is unapologetic and unabashed.

The administration can signal its commitment to these principles in many symbolic and practical ways. It can, for example, welcome at the State Department not the Turabis of the region, as the Bush administration did, but rather those who share a commitment to the dignity of individuals and their inherent right to speak out and disagree, such as the Sudanese scholar-in-exile in Washington, Mohammed Khalil, who practically wept when he learned that Turabi was being welcomed on Capitol Hill and at the State Department.

It should reject the assumption that seemed to underlie President Bush's policy toward Islamic forces—namely that such groups are destined to come to power in the region anyway, so the United States should have a dialogue with them now to avoid a repetition of what occurred in Iran in the future.

Washington can also say that the governments of Egypt, Jordan and Saudi Arabia are, for all their many, well-publicized failings, still more tolerant and less repressive than those that the Islamists would most probably establish in their stead. If Washington said this openly, those same governments might well be more receptive to American criticism of practices that Washington finds unacceptable—such as torture in Egypt and the repression of minorities and women in Saudi Arabia.

The Clinton administration should not seek to wage an American or Western secular war against the Islamists. But it should not be embarrassed to call attention to America's accomplishments, or afraid to discuss candidly the failings of an Islamic theocracy. Too often, American administrations, fearful of being accused of cultural imperialism, have remained silent about denials of basic human freedom in the Middle East.

It has been argued that America will not be strategically affected by the triumph of militant Islamic governments in the region. Given America's military might, Islamic governments would probably be reluctant to attack this country openly and directly. And Middle Eastern oil producers, no matter what their political orientation, will always need to sell oil.

But the proliferation of state-sponsored or assisted terrorist groups and of weapons of mass destruction in the region threatens the United States, as well as Israel, Egypt, and other allies. The United States would be hard pressed, given American domestic politics and its long-standing commitment to Israel, to remain aloof from a conflict that endangered the Jewish state. Moreover, a nuclearized Iran might prove to be more than simply a strategic nuisance to the United States. Even without nuclear weapons, Tehran managed to affect an election in this country through its ruthless manipulation of U.S. hostages. Moreover, in the aftermath of the bombing of the World Trade Center in New York City, the United States must acknowledge now that Islamic fervor nurtured overseas is bound to come home.

Finally, even what might be little more than a nuisance for Americans would be a catastrophe for democrats and Western-minded Arabs in the region. How sad it would be for a world emerging from the shackles of communism and a debilitating Cold War to accept a new era of darkness and autocratic rule for the Arabs, who have enjoyed far too little freedom and security.

NO

John L. Esposito

POLITICAL ISLAM: BEYOND THE GREEN MENACE

From Ayatollah Khomeini to Sheik Omar Abdel Rahman, from Iran to the World Trade Center, government leaders and opinion makers in the West and in the Middle East have warned of the dangers of militant Islam. If the 1980s were dominated by images of embassies under siege, American hostages, and hijackings, the 1990s bring prophecies of insurgent movements wielding nuclear weapons and employing urban terrorism. Headlines announce the possibility of a worldwide Islamic uprising and a clash of civilizations in which Islam may overwhelm the West. Television viewers see the bodies of Coptic Christians and tourists killed by Egyptian extremists and take in reports of Algerian militants' pitched battles with police. All fuel alarmist concerns reflected in publications and conferences with titles like "Roots of Muslim Rage," "Islam: Deadly Duel with Zealots," and "Awaiting God's Wrath: Islamic Fundamentalism and the West."

For more than four decades governments formulated policy in the midst of a superpower rivalry that defined the globe and the future in terms of the visible ideological and military threat posed by the Soviet Union. In the aftermath of the cold war, the fall of the Soviet Union and the discrediting of communism have created a "threat vacuum" that has given rise to a search for new enemies. For some Americans the enemy is the economic challenge the Japanese or the European Community represent. For others it is an Islamic world whose 1 billion Muslims form a majority in more the 48 countries and a rapidly growing minority in Europe and America. Some view Islam as the only ideological alternative to the West that can cut across national boundaries, and perceiving it as politically and culturally at odds with Western society, fear it; others consider it a more basic demographic threat.

The 1990s, however, reveal the diversity and complexity of political Islam and point to a twenty-first century that will shake the assumptions of many. While some Islamic organizations engage in terrorism, seeking to topple governments, others spread their message through preaching and social services and demand the right to gain legitimate power with ballots rather than bullets. But what of militant Islam? Is there an international Islamic threat? Will

From John L. Esposito, "Political Islam: Beyond the Green Menace," *Current History* (January 1994). Copyright © 1994 by Current History, Inc. Reprinted by permission of *Current History*. Notes omitted.

humanity witness the rise of a "new Comintern" led by "religious Stalinists" poised to challenge the free world and impose Iranian-style Islamic republics through violence, or through an electoral process that enables Islamic movements to "hijack democracy"?

FAITH, FUNDAMENTALISM, AND FACT

Muslims vary as much in their interpretations of Islam as followers of other faiths with theirs. For the vast majority of believers, Islam, like other world religions, is a faith of peace and social justice, moving its adherents to worship God, obey His laws, and be socially responsible.

Indiscriminate use of the term "Islamic fundamentalism" and its identification with governments and movements have contributed to the sense of a monolithic menace when in actuality political Islam is far more diverse. Saudi Arabia, Libya, Pakistan, and Iran have been called fundamentalist states, but this tells us nothing about their nature: Saudi Arabia is a conservative monarchy, Libya a populist socialist state headed by a military dictator. Moreover, the label says nothing about the state's Islamic character or orientation. Pakistan under General Muhammad Zia ul-Haq embodied a conservative Islam, and Saudi Arabia still does; Islam in Libya is radical and revisionist; clerics dominate in Iran. Finally, although fundamentalism is popularly equated with anti-Americanism and extremism, and Libya and Iran have indeed often denounced America, Saudi Arabia and Pakistan have been close allies of the United States and the mujahideen that resisted the Soviet occupation of Afghanistan received support from Washington for years.

The Iranian revolution of 1978–1979 called attention to a reassertion of Islam in Muslim personal and public life that subsequently came to be referred to by many names: Islamic resurgence, Islamic revivalism, political Islam, and more commonly, Islamic fundamentalism. The totally unexpected ousting of the shah of Iran by an Islamic revolution led by the charismatic Ayatollah Ruhollah Khomeini and the creation of an Islamic republic under the mullahs stunned the world. Fear that Iran would export Islamic revolution to other countries of the Middle East became the lens through which events in the Muslim world were viewed. When Khomeini spoke, the world listened—supporters with admiration, detractors with disdain and disgust or, often, anxiety.

The 1979 takeover of the United States embassy in Teheran and Khomeini's expansionist designs, Libyan leader Muammar Qaddafi's posturing and promotion of a third world revolution, and Egyptian President Anwar Sadat's 1981 assassination by Muslim extremists supported the projection of a militant Islamic fundamentalism. Hostage-taking, hijackings, and attacks on foreign and government installations by groups such as the Islamic Liberation Organization, Jihad, and Takfir wal Hijra (Excommunication and Flight) in Egypt and by the Iranian-funded Hezbollah and Islamic Jihad in Lebanon received enormous publicity. In the late 1970s and throughout the 1980s the prevailing picture of the Islamic world in the West was of militants bent on undermining countries' stability, overthrowing governments, and imposing their version of an Islamic state. The result was the facile equation: Islam = fundamentalism = terrorism and extremism.

THE ROOTS OF RESURGENCE

The reality is that Islamic revivalism was not the product of the Iranian revolution but of a global reassertion of Islam that had already been under way and that extended from Libya to Malaysia.

The causes of the resurgence are many and differ from country to country, but common catalysts and concerns are identifiable. Secular nationalism (whether in the form of liberal nationalism, Arab nationalism, or socialism) has not provided a sense of national identity or produced strong and prosperous societies. The governments in Muslim countries —mostly nonelected, authoritarian, and dependent on security forces—have been unable to establish their political legitimacy. They have been blamed for the failure to achieve economic self-sufficiency, to stem the widening gap between rich and poor, to halt widespread corruption, to liberate Palestine, to resist Western political and cultural hegemony. Both the political and the religious establishments have come under criticism, the former as a westernized, secular elite overly concerned with power and privilege, and the latter (in Sunni Muslim nations) as leaders of the faithful who have been co-opted by governments that often control mosques and religious universities and other institutions....

Islamic revivalism is in many ways the successor to failed nationalist programs. The founders of many Islamic movements were formerly participants in nationalist movements: Hasan al-Banna of the Muslim Brotherhood in Egypt, Rashid Ghannoushi of Tunisia's Renaissance party, and Abbasi Madani of the Islamic Salvation Front in Algeria. Islamic movements have offered an Islamic alternative or solution, a third way distinct from capitalism and communism. Islamists argue that secularism, a modern bias toward the West, and dependence on Western models of development have proved politically inadequate and socially corrosive, undermining the identity and moral fabric of Muslim societies. Asserting that Islam is not just a collection of beliefs and ritual actions but a comprehensive ideology embracing public as well as personal life, they call for the implementation of Sharia, or Islamic law, as a social blueprint. While the majority within the Muslim world seek to work within the system, a small but significant minority believes that the rulers in their countries are anti-Islamic and that they have a divine mandate to unseat them and impose their vision.

In general, the movements are urban-based, drawing heavily from the lower middle and middle classes. They have gained particular support among recent university graduates and young professionals, male and female. The movements recruit from the mosques and on campuses where, contrary to popular assumptions, their strength is not so much in the religious faculties and the humanities as in science, engineering, education, law, and medicine....

In many Muslim countries an alternative elite exists, its members with modern educations but self-consciously oriented toward Islam and committed to social and political activism as a means of bringing about a more Islamic society or system of government. This phenomenon is reflected in the presence—and often dominance—of Islamists in professional associations of lawyers, engineers, professors, and physicians. Where permitted to participate in society, Islamists are found in all sectors, including government and even the military.

FROM PERIPHERY TO CENTER

Demonization of Islam proceeded throughout the 1980s, but by late in the decade a more nuanced, broad-based, diverse Islamic world was increasingly evident. Beneath the radical façade, apart from the small, marginalized extremist groups, a quiet revolution had taken place. While a rejectionist minority had sought to impose change from above through holy wars, many others reaffirmed their faith and pursued a bottom-up approach, seeking a gradual Islamization of society through words, preaching, and social and political activity. In many Muslim countries Islamic organizations had become energetic in social reform, establishing much-needed schools, hospitals, clinics, legal societies, family assistance programs, Islamic banks and insurance companies, and publishing houses. These Islamically oriented groups offered social welfare services cheaply and constituted an implicit critique of the failure of the regimes in the countries to provide adequate services.

Along with social activism went increased political participation. In the late 1980s economic failures led to mass demonstrations and food riots in Egypt, Tunisia, Algeria, and Jordan. Moreover, the demand for democratization that accompanied the fall of the Soviet Union and the liberation of Eastern Europe touched the Middle East as well. Throughout the decade many governments in the Muslim world charged that the Islamic activists were merely violent revolutionaries whose lack of popular support would be evident if elections were held, but few governments showed themselves willing to put this claim to the test. When political systems were opened up and Islamic organiza- tions were able to participate in elections, the results stunned many in the Muslim world and in the West. Although Islamists were not allowed to organize separate official political parties, in Egypt and Tunisia they emerged as the leading opposition. In the November 1989 elections in Jordan they captured 32 of 80 seats in the lower house of parliament and held five cabinet-level positions and the office of speaker of the lower house. Algeria, however, was the turning point.

Algeria had been dominated for decades by a one-party dictatorship under the National Liberation Front (FLN). Because FLN was socialist and had a strong secular elite and feminist movement, few took the Islamic movement seriously; moreover, the movement had been among the least well known of the country's groups outside its borders, even among Islamists. The stunning victory of the Islamic Salvation Front (FIS), an umbrella group, in 1990 municipal elections sent a shock wave around the globe.

Despite the arrest of front leaders Abbasi Madani and Ali Belhadj; the cut-off of state funds to municipalities, often crippling FIS officials' ability to provide services; and gerrymandering to create districts more favorable to itself, the ruling party failed to prevent an even more stunning sweep by the FIS in parliamentary elections held in December 1991. As Islamists at home and across the Muslim world celebrated, the military intervened, forcing the resignation of Algeria's president, arresting FIS leaders, imprisoning more than 10,000 people in desert camps, and outlawing the front, and seizing its assets.

In the face of the repression much of the world stood silent. The conventional wisdom had been blind-sided. While most feared and were on their guard against "other Irans," the Islamic Salvation Front's victory in Algeria raised the specter of an Islamic movement coming to power through democratic elections and ballots worried many world leaders even more than bullets. The justification for accepting the Algerian military's seizure of power was the charge that the FIS really only believed in "One man, one vote, one time." The perceived threat from revolutionary Islam was intensified by the fear that it would capture power from within the political system by democratic means.

THE TRIPLE THREAT

In contrast to other parts of the world, calls for greater political participation and democratization in the Middle East have been met by empty rhetoric and repression at home and by ambivalence or silence in the West. Middle Eastern governments have used the danger posed by Islamic fundamentalism as the excuse for increasing authoritarianism and violations of human rights and the indiscriminate suppression of Islamic opposition, as well as for the West's silence about these actions.

Fear of fundamentalism, like fear of communism, has made strange bedfellows. Tunisia, Algeria, and Egypt join Israel in warning of a regional and international Islamic threat in their bids to win Western aid and justify their repression of Islamists.... Israeli Prime Minister Yitzhak Rabin justified the expulsion of 415 Palestinians in December 1992 by saying that "Our struggle against murderous Islamic terror is also meant to awaken the world, which is lying in slumber... We call on all nations, all peoples to devote their attention to the greater danger inherent in Islamic fundamentalism[, which] threatens world peace in future years ... [W]e stand on the line of fire against the danger of fundamentalist Islam."

Israel and its Arab neighbors have warned that a resurgent Iran is exporting revolution throughout much of the Muslim world, including Sudan, the West Bank and Gaza Strip, Algeria, and Central Asia, as well as to Europe and America; indeed, Egyptian President Hosni Mubarak has urged the formation of a "global alliance" against this menace.

Islam is often portrayed as a triple threat: political, civilizational, and demographic. The fear in the 1980s that Iran would export its revolution has been superseded by the larger fear of an international pan-Islamic movement with Iran and Sudan at its heart. In this decade, despite Iran's relative failure in fomenting revolution abroad, visions of global Islamic threat have proliferated, combining fear of violent revolution and of Algerian-style electoral victories. French writer Raymond Aron's warning of an Islamic revolutionary wave generated by the fanaticism of the Prophet and Secretary of State Cyrus Vance's concern over the possibility of an Islamic-Western war have been succeeded by columnist Charles Krauthammer's assertion of a global Islamic threat of "fundamentalist Koran-waving Khomeiniism" led by Iran.

The Ayatollah Khomeini's condemning of novelist Salman Rushdie to death for blasphemy for his *Satanic Verses*, combined with Iraqi President Saddam Hussein's call for a holy war against the West during the 1991 Persian Gulf War, reinforce fears of a political and cultural confrontation. This is magnified by some who, like Krauthammer, reduce contemporary realities to the playing out of ancient rivalries: "It should now be clear that we are facing a mood and a movement far transcending the level of issues and policies and the governments that pursue them. This is no less than a clash of civilizations—a perhaps irrational but surely historic reaction of an ancient rival against our Judaeo-Christian heritage, our secular present, and the worldwide expansion of both."

Muslim-Western relations are placed in the context of a confrontation in which Islam is again pitted against the West— "our Judaeo-Christian and secular West" —rather than specific political and socioeconomic grievances. Thus the assault on the West is seen as "irrational," mounted by peoples peculiarly driven by their passions and hatred; how can Western countries really respond to this?

The politics of the Middle East refutes theories of a monolithic threat. Despite a common "Islamic" orientation, the governments of the region reveal little unity of purpose in interstate or international relations because of conflicting national interests and priorities. Qaddafi was a bitter enemy of Anwar Sadat and Sudanese leader Gaafar Nimeiry at the very time that all were projecting their "Islamic images." Khomeini's Islamic republic consistently called for the overthrow of Saudi Arabia's Islamic state on Islamic grounds. Islamically identified governments also differ in their stance toward the West. Libya's and Iran's relationships with the West, and the United States in particular, were often confrontational; at the same time, the United States has had strong allies in Saudi Arabia, Egypt, Kuwait, Pakistan, and Bahrain. National interest and regional politics rather than ideology or religion remain the major determinants in the formulation of foreign policy.

The World Trade Center bombing last year gave impetus to a third current, the portrayal of Islam as a demographic threat. The growth of Muslim populations in Europe and the United States has made Islam the second-largest religion in Germany and France and the third-largest in Britain and America. Disputes over Muslim minority rights, demonstrations and clashes during the Salman Rushdie affair, and the Trade Center bombing have been exploited by strident voices of the right—politicians such as France's Jean-Marie LePen, neo-Nazi youth in Germany, and right-wing political commentators in the United States.

NO DEMOCRACY WITHOUT RISKS

For Western leaders, democracy in the Middle East raises the prospect of old and reliable friends or client states transformed into more independent and less predictable nations, which generates worries that Western access to oil could become less secure. Thus stability in the Middle East has often been defined in terms of preserving the status quo.

Lack of enthusiasm for political liberalization in the region has been rationalized by the assertion that Arab culture and Islam are antidemocratic (an issue never raised to a comparable degree with regard to the former Soviet Union, Eastern Europe, or Africa). The proof offered is the lack of a democratic tradition, and more specifically, the glaring absence of democracies in the Muslim world.

The history of that world has not been conducive to the development of democratic traditions and institutions. European colonial rule and postindependence governments headed by military officers, ex-military men, and monarchs have contributed to a legacy in which political participation and the building of strong democratic institutions are of little concern. National unity and stability as well as the political legitimacy of governments have been undermined by the artificial nature of modern states whose national boundaries were often determined by colonial powers and whose rulers were either put in place by Europe or simply seized power. Weak economies, illiteracy, and high unemployment, especially among the younger generation, aggravate the situation, undermining confidence in governments and increasing the appeal of "Islamic fundamentalism."

Experts and policymakers who question whether Islamic movements will use electoral politics to "hijack democracy" often do not appear equally disturbed that few rulers in the region have been democratically elected and that many who speak of democracy believe only in the risk-free variety: political liberalization so long as there is no danger of a strong opposition (secular or religious) and loss of power. Failure to appreciate that the issue of hijacking democracy is a two-way street was reflected in the West's responses to the Algerian military's intervention and cancellation of the election results.

Perception of a global Islamic threat can contribute to support for repressive governments in the Muslim world, and thus to the creation of a self-fulfilling prophecy. Thwarting participatory politics by canceling elections or repressing populist Islamic movements fosters radicalization. Many of the Islamists harassed, imprisoned, or tortured by the regime, will conclude that seeking democracy is a dead end and become convinced that force is their only recourse. Official silence or economic and political backing for regimes by the United States and other Western powers is read as complicity and a sign that there is a double standard for the implementation of democracy. This can create the conditions that lead to political violence that seemingly validates contentions that Islamic movements are inherently violent, antidemocratic, and a threat to national and regional stability.

More constructive and democratic strategies are possible. The strength of Islamic organizations and parties is also due to the fact that they constitute the only viable voice and vehicle for opposition in relatively closed political systems. The strength at the polls of Tunisia's Renaissance party, the Islamic Salvation Front, and Jordan's Muslim Brotherhood derived not only from a hard core of dedicated followers who backed the groups' Islamic agendas but from the many who wished simply to cast their vote against the government. Opening up the political system could foster competing opposition groups and thus weaken the monopoly Islamic parties have on opposition voters. (It must be remembered that the membership of Islamic organizations does not generally constitute a majority of the population.) Finally, the realities of a more open political marketplace—having to compete for votes, and once gaining power having to govern amid diverse interests—could force Islamic groups to adapt or broaden their ideology and programs.

The United States should not in principle object to the involvement of Islamic activists in government if they have been duly elected. Islamically oriented politicians and groups should be evaluated by the same criteria as any other potential leaders or opposition parties. While some are rejectionists, most will be critical and selective in their relations with the United States, generally operating on the basis of national interests and showing a flexibility that reflects understanding of the globally interdependent world. The United States should demonstrate by word and action its belief that the right to self-determination and representative government extends to an Islamically oriented state and society, if these reflect the popular will and do not directly threaten United States interests. American policy should accept the ideological differences between the West and Islam to the greatest extent possible, or at least tolerate them.

All should bear in mind that democratization in the Muslim world proceeds by experimentation, and necessarily involves both success and failure. The transformation of Western feudal monarchies to democratic nation states took time, and trial and error, and was accompanied by political as well as intellectual revolutions that rocked state and church. It was a long, drawn-out *process* among contending factions with competing interests and visions.

Today we are witnessing a historic transformation in the Muslim world. Risks exist, for there can be no risk-free democracy. Those who fear the unknown, wondering how specific Islamic movements will act once in power, have legitimate reasons to do so. However, if one worries that these movements might suppress opposition, lack tolerance, deny pluralism, and violate human rights, the same concern must apply equally to the plight of those Islamists who have shown a willingness to participate in the political process in Tunisia, Egypt, and Algeria.

Governments in the Muslim world that espouse political liberalization and democracy are challenged to promote the development of civil society—the institutions, values, and culture that are the foundation of true participatory government. Islamic movements, for their part, are challenged to move beyond slogans to programs. They must become more self-critical, and speak out not only against local government abuses but against those of Islamic regimes in Iran and Sudan, for example, as well as acts of terrorism by extremists. They are urged to present an Islamic rationale and policy that extend to their opposition and to minorities the principles of pluralism and political participation they demand for themselves. The extent to which the growth of Islamic revivalism has been accompanied in some countries by attempts to restrict women's rights and public roles; the record of discrimination against the Bahai in Iran, the Ahmadi in Pakistan, and Christians in Sudan; and sectarian conflict between Muslims and Christians in Egypt, Sudan, and Nigeria pose serious questions about religious pluralism, respect for human rights, and tolerance in general.

Islamic revivalism has run counter to many of the presuppositions of Western liberal secularism and development theory, among them the belief that modernization means the inexorable or progressive secularization and Westernization of society. Too often analysis and policymaking have been shaped by a liberal secularism that fails to recognize it too represents a world view, not the paradigm for modern society, and can easily degenerate into a "secularist fundamentalism" that treats alternative views as irrational, extremist, and deviant.

A focus on "Islamic fundamentalism" as a global threat has reinforced the tendency to equate violence with Islam, to fail to distinguish between illegitimate use of religion by individuals and the faith and practice of the majority of the world's Muslims who, like adherents of other religious traditions, wish to live in peace. To equate Islam and Islamic fundamentalism uncritically with extremism is to judge Islam only by those who wreak havoc—a standard not applied to Judaism and Christianity. The danger is that heinous actions may be attributed to Islam rather than to a twisted or distorted interpretation of Islam. Thus despite the track record of Christianity and Western countries when it comes to making war, developing weapons of mass destruction, and imposing their imperialist designs, Islam and Muslim culture are portrayed as somehow peculiarly and inherently expansionist and prone to violence and warfare.

There are lessons to be learned from a past in which fear of a monolithic Soviet threat often blinded the United States to the Soviet bloc's diversity, led to uncritical support for (anti-Communist) dictatorships, and enabled the "free world" to tolerate the suppression of legitimate dissent and massive human rights violations by governments that labeled the opposition "Communist" or "socialist." The risk today is that exaggerated fears will lead to a double standard in the promotion of democracy and human rights in the Muslim world as can be witnessed by the Western concern about and action to support democracy in the former Soviet Union and Eastern Europe but the muted or ineffective response to the promotion of democracy in the Middle East and the defense of Muslims in Bosnia and Herzegovina. Support for democracy and human rights is more effective if it is consistent around the world. Treating Islamic experiences as exceptional is an invitation to long-term conflict.

POSTSCRIPT

Is Islamic Fundamentalism a Threat to Political Stability?

The history and beliefs of Muslims are complex and rich, and finding out more about them is not only rewarding, it also counteracts the tendency to stereotype things about which one knows little. To learn more about Islamic history and its relations with Europe, read *Islam and the West* (Oxford University Press, 1993) by Bernard Lewis. Another recent analysis can be found in the symposium issue of *The Annals of the American Academy of Political and Social Science* (November 1993), edited by Charles E. Butterworth and I. William Zartman. It contains 15 articles about Islam and, especially, how it interacts with political ideas and practices.

There can be little doubt that the interplay between Islam and politics remains an important issue in world affairs. Fundamentalism remains strong. A civil war in Yemen in mid-1994 between traditionalists from the north and secularists, with somewhat leftist leanings, in the south was won by the fundamentalists. Fundamentalist Muslims with ties to an Egyptian cleric residing in the United States exploded a bomb in the World Trade Center in New York City, bringing home to Americans the anger and terrorist tactics of some traditionalists. That does not necessarily mean that such events will recur, as suggested by Leon Hadar in "Islamic Fundamentalism Is Not a Threat to U.S. Security," *USA Today* (November 1993).

Amid the turmoil, there are many signs that Muslim countries are adjusting to what is arguably a spreading homogenization (Western or not) of global culture. As elsewhere, democracy has taken hold in some Muslim countries, and it struggles to survive or to begin in others. This poses some interesting dilemmas. Should North American powers support, as in Algeria, traditionalists when they win democratic majorities or secularists who hold or seize power by dint of force? Some aspects of Muslim culture, such as the status of women, which bothers many Westerners, are beginning to change. One symbol of that change is Benazir Bhutto, who is currently the prime minister of Pakistan and is the first woman to head the government of a predominantly Muslim country. And Tansu Ciller, a Muslim woman who holds a Ph.D. in economics from the University of Connecticut, became Turkey's first woman prime minister in 1993. The growing moderation of Muslim policy toward Israel is another new development. Limited Palestinian autonomy has been established in Gaza and in Jericho, and in July 1994 the king of Jordan and the prime minister of Israel met in Washington, D.C., and agreed to end the "state of belligerency" that had existed between their two countries for more than 40 years.

ISSUE 6

Will China Become an Asian Superpower?

YES: Zhao Xiaowei, from "The Threat of a New Arms Race Dominates Asian Geopolitics," *Global Affairs* (Summer 1992)

NO: Samuel S. Kim, from "China as a Regional Power," *Current History* (September 1992)

ISSUE SUMMARY

YES: Zhao Xiaowei, a prominent member of the Democratic Liberal Party, a mainland China political party in exile, predicts that as China modernizes and becomes more stable domestically, it is likely to engage in an arms race designed to build itself up to a regional, even global, superpower.

NO: Political science professor Samuel S. Kim maintains that China is a weak state that will be hard pressed to survive the multiple threats from within. Thus distracted, China is not likely in the foreseeable future to become a regional, much less global, superpower.

China has a history as one of the oldest, most sophisticated, and most powerful countries in the world. Protohuman tool makers (Peking man, *Sinanthropus pekinensis*) inhabited north China a half million years ago. Four thousand years ago, under the semilegendary Emperor Yu of the Hsia dynasty, the Chinese built irrigation channels, domesticated animals, engaged in cultivation, and established a written language. Through 14 Chinese dynasties China built a civilization marked by great cultural and engineering feats. The Great Wall of China, the only human creation visible from space, was begun in about 210 B.C. The great philosophy of Confucianism was soon thereafter established. China also exercised wide political influence, holding sway over a considerable regional area.

As is the way with empires, China's political fortunes waxed and waned and eventually declined. By the 1800s, increasingly ascendant outside powers came to dominate an ever more decaying China. The British provoked the Opium War (1839–1842) over their insistence on the right to sell drugs to the Chinese. China was easily defeated. Hong Kong was seized by the British and leased to them until 1997. British traders grew rich on the desperation of the patrons of Chinese opium dens. Over approximately the next eight decades, China underwent what was to the Chinese a period of humiliation. Huge tracts of their territory were seized by the Russians, the island of Formosa (Taiwan, or Nationalist China) was taken by Japan in 1945, and various European countries and Japan came close to making China a colony by dividing it up into zones of interest that they dominated. During the so-called Boxer Rebellion (1900), Chinese nationalists tried to expel the foreigners, but the Chinese forces were defeated by an international coalition that included American troops. The moribund Manchu dynasty fell in 1911 and was replaced by a republic headed by Sun Yat-sen.

Sun died in 1916, and a struggle for power among various factions led to the establishment in 1926 of a central government under Nationalist Chinese leader Chiang Kai-shek. Although Chiang's government proved corrupt and ineffective in many ways, it did largely consolidate power and moved to edge foreign influences out of China. That trend became even stronger in 1949 when Chiang's government fell to the communists of Mao Zedong. Chiang's government fled to the island of Formosa, now Taiwan, and established a rump Nationalist Chinese government.

For two decades, many in the West perceived China to be part of the communist monolith headed by the Soviet Union. That was never true, and by the late 1960s, China had gained enough strength and showed enough independence that it was obvious that China was a rising power in its own right. An important symbol of that shift was President Richard Nixon's visit to China in 1972. Relations between the United States and China improved even more after Chairman Mao Zedong died in 1976 and Deng Xiaoping came to power.

By many standards, China is already a major power. It has the world's largest population (over 1 billion) and a gross domestic product (GDP) of more than $600 billion. It has the world's eighth largest GDP, and it is growing at the astounding rate of 13 percent annually (1992–1994). Its territory is enormous. Officially, China's defense spending for 1993 was only about $7.3 billion, but many analysts believe the real figure could be two or three times higher. China's 3 million personnel in uniform give it the largest standing military force in the world by that measure. China's conventional forces have not achieved the same level of technological sophistication as Western countries, but the country does possess strategic-range nuclear weapons. China is also a permanent member of the UN Security Council, thus possessing a veto in that organization.

The issue here is what the future of China will be. Some, including Zhao Xiaowei in the first selection, contend that China will become a regional superpower. Others, including former president Richard Nixon, have predicted that China will be a global superpower, perhaps the leading superpower, in the twenty-first century. Others focus on China's many problems, and they forecast that internal travails will prevent China from becoming a superpower and could even lead it into decline. Samuel Kim, in the second selection, is among those who take this latter view.

YES

Zhao Xiaowei

THE THREAT OF A NEW ARMS RACE DOMINATES ASIAN GEOPOLITICS

Asia has been largely eclipsed by the drama played out in Europe where the former Soviet Union, at least in its current incarnations, can no longer support the costs of the vast military machine built by its prior rulers. As a consequence, there has been talk of "the forgotten Far East."

This euphoria is understandable: Since the collapse of Marxism-Leninism in Europe, humankind seemingly has freed itself from the nightmare of a general nuclear conflict that would render the planet uninhabitable. Most of the industrial democracies are now caught up in a scramble to find ways to spend anticipated "peace dividends." The United States defense budget has been significantly reduced—and barring unanticipated changes in the international security environment, further reductions will be forthcoming. "Peace activists" have argued that the absence of adversaries has made the U.S. military obsolete. Many of those charged with the responsibilities of forming public opinion apparently share these convictions about the advent of universal peace—or at least enough peace to allow the United States to pursue some sort of disarmed detachment from the world.

ASIA BY YEAR 2000

Most of this, of course, has been a by-product of changes in Europe. But those who focus on Asia remind Americans that by the year 2000, the nations on the Pacific rim will be peopled by 70 percent of the world's population, will produce more than 50 percent of the world's commodities, will consume 40 percent of the world's production and are expected to account for 70 percent of the world's trade. Neglecting Asia could be fatal to the West's security and prosperity as well as for the masses of Asia.

Where Asia has not suffered from the benign neglect of most Western geopoliticians, the concerns expressed have largely been the result of selective trade tensions. There has been a body of reportage colored by the notion that

From Zhao Xiaowei, "The Threat of a New Arms Race Dominates Asian Geopolitics," *Global Affairs* (Summer 1992). Copyright © 1992 by The International Security Council. Reprinted by permission of *Global Affairs*. Notes omitted.

Japan might emerge as a security threat —as "the only runner in the arms race." From this perspective Japan not only threatened the economy of the United States, it was seen as an "invisible military giant"—a "strong samurai" prepared to overwhelm the world with its arms as it already had with its exports.

While there is little doubt that Japan's defense allocations make it one of the world's major military spenders, few military strategists consider it a current or future security threat. For the foreseeable future Japan's military will serve only as an element of the forward defense policies of the United States.

Furthermore, recently, the declining Japanese defense budget has largely allayed concerns. By the beginning of 1990, there were clear signs of a decreasing commitment to defense expenditures. That Tokyo has reduced its defense outlays appears to confirm what some observers have argued are the determinants of Japan's defense budgets.

Japan's budgets are a result of a process shaped by influences having very little to do with military purposes. Japan's military budget reflects the influence of macroeconomic policy objectives and the management of relations with the United States. For the determinate future, Japan's ties with the United States preclude its emergence as an independent actor in any Asian arms race.

More persuasive in the role of spoilers of the peace of East Asia are the antagonists on the Korean peninsula. The Democratic People's Republic of Korea—North Korea—continues to allocate almost 25 percent of its gross domestic product to maintaining an aggressive force structure that threatens not only the Republic of Korea—South Korea—but the peace of the entire region. South Korea, in turn, apparently will marginally reduce its current and future defense budgets to produce slower growth rather than significant reductions. The reduction in regional threats have reduced domestic arms orders.

The disintegration of the Soviet Union has diminished the overall threat in Northeast Asia—and has complicated the risk assessments of the leadership in Pyongyang. In and of itself, the regime in North Korea could hardly provoke a major change in the threat environment. Best evidence indicates that the economy of the North has been in negative growth for several years; there have been reports of North Koreans fleeing to Communist China to escape the all-pervasive poverty that dominates the countryside. Therefore, it would appear that North Korea could hardly underwrite an increased threat.

There is one aspect of North Korea military developments that is potentially destabilizing and merits attention: its nuclear program. It is an issue that "could have serious implications for the U.S. military/security role in Korea and Northeast Asia, and could threaten peace and stability there."

North Korea has a substantial nuclear program involving a major plant site at Yongbyon about 60 miles north of Pyongyang. One component is a small reactor (about 30-megawatt capability) able to produce about seven kilograms of plutonium annually. This reactor is supplemented by a larger reactor with a capacity to produce enough weapons grade plutonium to arm as many as five nuclear weapons a year. There is some evidence that North Korea may have hidden nuclear weapons sites, similar to those recently exposed in Iraq.

BEIJING'S ROLE AS PROVOCATEUR

It is uncertain how the communist leadership of an impoverished North Korea managed the cost, and developed the technological expertise, to put together the capacity now expected to manufacture its first atomic device in 1992. It is generally accepted that the Soviet Union provided North Korea a small research reactor in the 1960s and may have supplied technological assistance and training into the late 1980s. While there is no direct evidence, many analysts are convinced that Communist China has supplied North Korea major assistance. In the 1950s and 1960s, many North Koreans received training in nuclear technology in China, and the House Republican Research Committee's "Task Force on Terrorism and Unconventional Warfare" has recently reported that an agreement between the PRC and North Korea in October and November 1991 afforded Pyongyang the technological assistance necessary to expedite its program of nuclear arms development.

Should that prove to be the case, it is not North Korea, in and of itself, that threatens the peace and stability of Northeast Asia. It is the regime on China's mainland, the People's Republic of China (PRC), that has not only supplied critical components to North Korea's nuclear arms program, but has provided Pyongyang substantial political and moral support.

This suggests that whatever Beijing's role in the development of North Korea's nuclear arms program might prove to be, attention should be concentrated on Communist China's practices, security doctrine, and international concerns. Even if Beijing has provided no material assistance to Pyongyang, the arms sales practices of the PRC has reinforced North Korea's destabilizing undertakings.

Whether or not Beijing has assisted North Korea with its nuclear program in the past, or continues to do so in the present, it has been confirmed that the PRC has aided, or intends to aid, Iran and Iraq in their pursuit of nuclear arms capabilities. Presently, an agreement between the PRC and Algeria will supply the latter a nuclear reactor large enough to make weapons grade plutonium. Beijing is also prepared to provide Syria a small research reactor. The PRC has not only supplied a design for a reliable nuclear weapon to Pakistan, but has transferred enough enriched uranium for production of at least two atomic devices as well.

More recently, Beijing has assisted Pakistan in its effort to enrich uranium domestically, and sold the tritium gas commonly employed to enhance the yield of fission bombs. There have also been credible reports of an intended sale and transfer of a turnkey 300 megawatt nuclear power facility to Islamabad. Thus, whether or not Beijing is directly involved in the North Korean nuclear arms program, it is certainly a party to the proliferation of nuclear weapons capabilities that make up a substantial part of an emerging arms race in South and Southwest Asia.

CONCERN BY BEIJING'S NEIGHBORS

One result of China's readiness to assist in the development of nuclear weapons capabilities in Northeast, South and Southwest Asia has been to precipitate renewed concern among its neighbors. Early in 1992, [Pakistani] Foreign Secretary Shahryar Khan announced that, thanks to the assistance of the PRC, Pakistan can now assemble its own nuclear device. Involved in a long and volatile boundary dispute with India, Pakistan's announcement has increased tensions throughout South Asia.

All of this has obvious implications for the world power balance and for U.S. policymakers. What is not as obvious is why Beijing would wish to involve itself in such activities. In general, commentators allude to mainland China's preoccupation with domestic concerns—preoccupations that would seem to exclude controversial arms sales that might compromise its internal programs of economic growth and modernization.

Actually, for all its talk of "opening to the industrial democracies" in order to access their import markets and attract capital investments as well as technology transfers, Beijing still conceives the fundamental relationship between a socialist China and market-based democracy as adversarial. At the end of 1991, the Hong Kong publication Cheng Ming reported that the Chinese Communist Party, in a confidential document entitled "Fundamental Policies Toward the United States," identified Washington as China's "principal enemy." As a consequence, Beijing has regularly flouted Western attempts to halt the proliferation of nuclear weapons capabilities.

Together with its sale of nuclear arms components, the PRC has also sold systems suitable for nuclear and chemical weapons delivery. By the end of the 1980s, there were reports that Beijing was negotiating the sale and transfer to both Syria and Pakistan of short-range missiles designed to carry nuclear and chemical warheads. Protests from the United States did nothing to deter the negotiations.

WHAT MOTIVATES BEIJING'S POLICIES

Since that time, the Director of the [U.S.] Central Intelligence Agency has reported that China has been supplying Iran with "battlefield missiles, cruise missiles, ballistic-missile technologies and components, and nuclear technology."

Beijing has supplied destabilizing technologies to real and potential enemies of the industrialized democracies. Even when Beijing's sales have been with allies of those democracies, the sales have nonetheless been destabilizing. They have involved either nuclear weapons technology or ballistic systems that increase security risks wherever they appear.

Whatever assurances Beijing offers the democracies, Gary Milhollin, director of the Wisconsin Project, a Washington-based organization tracing nuclear proliferation, stated that the "past conduct [of the Beijing leadership] indicates that they are very likely to go ahead and break their word." "China," he went on, "is definitely a renegade supplier."

While Chinese arms sales, both conventional and nonconventional, have heightened tensions throughout Asia and the Middle East, there are analysts who have argued that such sales are not strategically motivated. They represent, according to this line of reasoning, a simple search for profit on the part of a capital-poor actor on the world stage. It is certainly true that arms sales are profitable and the Chinese are desperate for foreign exchange. Others have suggested that the pervasive nepotism and corruption that characterize the export sector of the mainland Chinese economy make it impossible for the authorities to halt the flow of arms. The proof that is offered is that arms sales are pursued "aggressively" by "well-connected people, including Deng's son-in-law, He Ping." Chinese arms vending, however offensive and dangerous, it is argued, is simply the result of Chinese greed and corruption.

None of this is convincing when the evidence is examined. It is probable that there will be some "leakage" in any nation's arms sales, but it is equally clear that potentially controversial arms sales would have to be cleared by the highest authorities in Beijing before they could be undertaken. There are few who have studied the details of these transactions who believe that Chinese arms traffic is entirely explained by an inordinate desire for material gain. Chinese sales, in large measure, are an expression of Chinese foreign policy imperatives.

Since the mid-1980s, the People's Republic of China has been guided by a strategy policy that conceives the world divided into progressive and "reactionary" states. Those intrinsically hostile states can "coexist," even "cooperate" with "socialist China"—so long as the "imperatives of history" are recognized and defended. Within such a theoretical perspective, the leadership in Beijing dismisses any real possibility of a general nuclear conflict. In Beijing's judgment, the "imperialist" powers have learned that nuclear conflict is no longer a real policy alternate. Given that reality, China's "international class enemies" are left with only a few tactics to defeat "Chinese socialism." Among those tactics, "peaceful evolution"—the subtle introduction of "bourgeois spiritual values" and "capitalist" modalities into China's "progressive" economy—is currently the most prominent. But, the leadership in

Beijing warns, the "hegemonists" might make an appeal to a certain acceptable level of violence to resist the "inevitable march of socialism."

In this context, Chinese arms sales, particularly those involving nuclear and missile technology, are calculated to undermine the remaining "hostile policies" left to "world imperialism." Thus Chinese arms sales must be seen as inspired by a defense of Chinese ultimate and long-term interests. Beijing sees nuclear proliferation as complicating the "new world order" the democracies hope to see emerge from the collapse of European Marxism-Leninism.

PART OF A BROAD STRATEGY

The sale of missiles and nuclear technology is part of a broad program that would not only make the People's Republic of China a major global power in the twenty-first century, but assure its ultimate victory. Thus the Chinese military budget is among the few in East Asia that has significantly increased in the immediate past. More than that, Western intelligence agencies estimate that the actual budget is 100–150 percent greater than that supplied by official Chinese figures.

In 1991, Beijing negotiated for the purchase of expensive high performance Soviet combat aircraft. The PRC sought to obtain the Sukhoi Su-27 and the Mikoyan MiG-29 air superiority aircraft together with the Sukhoi Su-24 ground attack fighter-bomber. At the same time, Beijing increased the power projection capabilities of its navy. Long considered a coastal defense force, the PRC navy is now capable of undertaking blue water missions far from China's ports. With firepower and firecontrol capabilities enhanced by purchases from Western inventories, Beijing has extended its influence throughout Asia.

Beijing's nuclear and missile technology sales and its extensive force structure modernization destabilize all of Asia and raise legitimate security concerns. In November and December 1991, both the Director of the Central Intelligence Agency and Secretary of Defense Dick Cheney identified the PRC as a long-term potential threat to the security of Asia as well as that of the United States.

None of this has been lost on the nations of Southeast Asia. Until recently, the defense strategies of the Association of South East Asian Nations (ASEAN) were largely devoted to the control of domestic insurgencies. By the end of the 1980s, however, the armed forces of the Southeast Asian nations began to focus on external threats, developing long-range maritime strike and air defense potential, together with some degree of airborne early warning, command and control capability as well. Defense analysts in the region have pointed to long-standing disputes in the South China Sea that threaten regional conflict and to the fact that with the threat of a new arms race, the Chinese Communist military has developed the capabilities that would permit it to pursue a military option should circumstances permit. Beijing has succeeded in arming itself with capabilities superior to those it would face in any regional conflict on its periphery.

The acquisition of new equipment has provided the People's Liberation Army [PLA] with significant increases in power projection and firepower. "Long range bombers, in-flight refuelling, long-distance naval replenishment, amphibious tanks and armored vehicles and a marine corps have all been developed in recent years—all of which suggests that Beijing is not just interested in defending China. The range of PLA operations is steadily being extended outward from China, and to that end the PLA has been mapping all its territory, including those islands and neighbors with which China is in dispute."

The nations of the ASEAN community have responded with a recognition of the objective threat to their national interests. The "recent build-up of Chinese ... forces in the South China Sea [is] seen as Peking's signal that it intends, at a future date, to assert its claims in the area."

The emerging arms race in East Asia is being driven by a strategic policy informed by traditional Marxist-Leninist principles of "international class warfare." Beijing's current military doctrine is predicated on the probability of "small wars" breaking out along its periphery —conflicts of short duration for limited objectives. Convinced that the "internal contradictions of capitalism" will ultimately resolve the historic rivalry between Marxism-Leninism and "imperialism," China's current arms sales policies and military doctrine have increased the magnitude of threat with which the nations of the region, as well as the international community, must contend.

"THE OTHER RING OF FIRE"

These circumstances have led the editors of the *Economist* to speak of Asia, extending from the Northeast to the Southwest, as "the other ring of fire" that threatens the peace and stability of the "new world order." Others have simply recognized that "An arms race in Asia is not just a threat, it is already under way."

That Asia may be compelled to endure yet another arms race is a consequence of the anachronistic views still entertained by the superannuated leadership in Beijing. They have not only aided and abetted the nuclear program that now threatens Northeast Asia, but they have apparently enlisted the collaboration of Pyongyang in their enterprise to unsettle the Middle East and Southwest Asia with a flood of tactical range missiles and nuclear weapons technology.

Beijing persists in its maritime claims in the East China and South China Seas. Not only does that fuel the arms buildup among the nations of Southeast Asia, but on Taiwan [Nationalist China, Formosa] as well. Ultimately, Beijing's territorial pretensions may directly engage the Japanese. Not only does the leadership in Communist China advance claims against Japanese holdings in the East China Sea, it threatens the integrity of Southeast Asia—a region that has been identified as "the key to Japan's prosperity."

Tokyo has reported the fact that "China has strengthened its military presence in the Spratly Islands and Paracel Islands [claimed by several countries] while improving the bases for operation in these islands. As these developments indicate," the Japanese White Paper on Defense continues, "China's moves are seen as expanding its operational area on the ocean." Together with the naval and air threat to the sealines of communication, the long-term strategy of mainland China poses an evolving threat to the security and economic viability of Japan.

Not long ago, Gerald Segal warned the industrial democracies that "while in the short term it may appear that a modernized China is a more stable China, there are disturbing signs that in the medium term China is likely to pose a challenge to international stability—especially in the ever more important Pacific." As the United States is compelled to draw down its forces in East and Southeast Asia as a consequence of domestic priorities and budgetary constraints, the People's Republic of China will probably emerge as a major threat to Asia, and ultimately, to the international community. Barring major changes in the regime that the [former] U.S. Secretary of State James Baker characterizes as "anachronistic," the new arms race that has already commenced will probably accelerate.

NO

Samuel S. Kim

CHINA AS A REGIONAL POWER

What can we say about China's status as a regional power in the post–cold war era? The question seems elementary yet defies an easy answer since, in international relations, the perception of power matters as much as the reality of it. In the Chinese case there persists the belief that China, by dint of its demographic weight or the greatness of its civilization, has a natural and inalienable right to great power status. The country's erratic shifts in foreign policy behavior over the years have been based on the conviction that China's strategic value can never be taken for granted by any external power, for it is both willing and able to play a decisive role in reshaping the structure of global high politics.

Yet while the cold war helped China project power well beyond the Asia-Pacific region, its end stripped away the veil of the China mystique and the semblance of Chinese influence in international life. The ending of the cold war has also shattered the illusion of a consensus on what constitutes a "superpower," made evident by the rise of Japan as a global power of a different kind (a one-dimensional global power), the sudden "third worldization" of the former Soviet Union, and America's heroic but ineffective claim of global leadership without bearing the costs and responsibilities.

Just as Japan is seen as a wallet in search of a global role, China has become an empty seat on the United Nations Security Council searching for a new national identity. Suddenly, Beijing is unsure of its place in a world no longer dominated by superpower rivalry and the country is in the grip of an unprecedented legitimacy—identity crisis. Not since the founding of the People's Republic in 1949 have the questions of internal and external legitimacy—catalyzed by the Tiananmen carnage and the collapse of global communism—been as conflated as in the past three years.

CHINA'S ASIAN IDENTITY

The China threat—the image of a dragon rampant—looms large in the security calculus of every Asian state. Yet China's identity as a regional power is deeply problematic. Although most of the country's external relations pivot

From Samuel S. Kim, "China as a Regional Power," *Current History* (September 1992). Copyright © 1992 by Current History, Inc. Reprinted by permission of *Current History*. Notes omitted.

around the Asia-Pacific region, Beijing has yet to come up with any coherent definition of its place in Asian international relations.

The starting point for understanding China's awkward regional identity—and its inability to maintain any deep and enduring friendship with any Asian state, including North Korea—is to recognize that since the collapse of the traditional Sinocentric world order in the late nineteenth century, this proud and frustrated Asian giant has had enormous difficulty finding a comfortable place as an equal member state in the family of nation-states. During the cold war years the People's Republic succumbed to wild swings of identity, rotating through a series of roles: self-sacrificing junior partner in the Soviet-led socialist world; self-reliant hermit completely divorced from and fighting both superpowers; the revolutionary vanguard of an alternative United Nations; self-styled third world champion of a New International Economic Order; status quo-maintaining "partner" of NATO and favored recipient of largesse at the World Bank; and now, lone socialist global power in a postcommunist world.

None of these identities has much to do with Asian regional identity. The vast gap between being and becoming in the drive for status—and the contradiction between being a regional power and having global aspirations—have introduced a fundamental paradox in the prioritization of China's multiple identities: China as a socialist country; China as an anti-imperialist actor taking a radical system-transforming approach to world order; China as a poor developing country entitled to maximum preferential treatment in trade, investment, aid, and technology transfers; China as an irredentist power flex-ing its military muscle power to defend its extensive territorial claims; China as a deft practitioner of zhoubian (good-neighbor) diplomacy; and China as a nuclear power, breaking the superpower nuclear duopoly....

REASSESSING CHINESE POWER

The Chinese concept of power is broad, dynamic, and shifting, fed by historical traditions and experiences. Reacting to the growth of the "decline" school in American studies of international relations, the new game nations now play is said to be a multidimensional notion of "comprehensive national strength" based on population, resources, economic power, science and technology, military affairs, culture, education, and diplomacy.

Of this list, science and technology have become the master key for China in its intense drive toward the promised land of modernity. If China is to become a global power, it must beef up its national power, especially in high-technology industries. There is no escape from this high-tech rat race if China is ever to regain its proper place—"global citizenship" (qiuji)—in the emerging world order.

The government claims that science and technology do not have a class character; indeed, they are rationalized as a kind of global collective goods. Such a realpolitik—nationalistic technocracy dressed in hard globalism—is what is meant by "global citizenship." It also bespeaks the persistence of the nineteenth-century "ti-yong" dilemma—how to strengthen Chinese essence by using foreign technology.

Whether or not the party-state controls the guns, such technocratic realism gives the military a comparative advantage in shaping national policy. Without sufficient military power, according to China's strategic analysts, it will be impossible to preserve and enhance the country's status as a world power or play a decisive role in global politics. In the wake of America's high-tech military victory in the 1991 Persian Gulf war, Beijing decided to reorder its vaunted four modernizations, making science and technology a top priority before agriculture, industry, and defense. At the same time the PLA [China's People's Liberation Army] has been called on to take up a new mission at variance with the Maoist doctrine of protracted struggle: limited war to achieve a quick, decisive high-tech military victory in only a few days.

IS CHINA A GLOBAL POWER?

The sudden diminution of China's global status and influence threatens to take away the party-state's last remaining source of and claim to legitimacy: restoring China's great-power status in the post–cold war and postcommunist world.

Of course, there is no "scientific" way of assessing Chinese national power. In a rapidly changing international environment the very notion of "regional power" or "global power" is subject to continuing redefinition and reassessment. Elsewhere I have constructed a typology of Chinese power, comparing it against Japan, Germany, the United States, and the former Soviet Union and giving China's global ranking in 15 specific categories. Since the United States, the Soviet Union/Russia, Japan, Germany, and China are generally regarded as the world's great powers, China would have to be included in the

top five global rankings to be regarded as a great power.

Not surprisingly, China easily ranks among the top five in population, strategic nuclear warheads, and global arms trade. The Chinese would be first to admit that the burgeoning population (now at 1.2 billion) is a liability rather than an asset in the enhancement of comprehensive national strength. Since 1978, China's population has grown by nearly 200 million people, and in the 1990s at least another 150 million to 180 million will be added. The implications of these enormous numbers wanting to become rich, and the accompanying social, political, and economic pressures, are staggering, especially when placed in the context of industrial modernization and shrinking ecological capacity. China has already become an environmental giant of sorts, contributing to global warming faster than any other major country (China now releases 9.3 percent of global greenhouse-gas emissions, following the United States and the former Soviet Union but ahead of Japan, India, and Brazil).

When Chinese military power is measured quantitatively in terms of the number of strategic nuclear warheads, global arms trade (including global nuclear technology proliferation), and military manpower, China comes out as one of the world's five-largest military powers. However, mere numbers say little about the quality of the PLA or its performance in armed conflict.

China's economic power is mixed. In aggregate gross national product China ranks ninth in the world, but it is projected to become the world's fifth-largest economy by the year 2000. Sheer demographic size left China's per capita GNP at only $350 in 1989 (104th in the world), and it is projected to reach about $800–$1,000 by 2000. Post-Mao China is a global economic power only in the sense of being a major source of cheap labor and a tempting cost-effective site for foreign toxic wastes and heavily polluting industries; indeed these are the defining features of China's place in the global economy. Although exports as a percentage of GNP increased from 4 percent to about 20 percent in the long Deng decade, China still has a long way to go to achieve the status of an important trading power.

Another category needs to be added in determining a country's global power position. East Asia emerged in the 1980s as the most dynamic region in the global economy with seemingly ever-expanding waves of regional economic integration. As the most important investor, trader, aid donor, and development model, Japan easily dominates the East Asian political economy. Japan's economic miracle demonstrates that a country's competitiveness in the global marketplace depends less and less on natural resource power and more and more on the brainpower needed for microelectronics, biotechnology, civilian aviation, telecommunications, robotics, computer hardware and software, and so forth.

China is extremely weak in this area. For example, China is not even included in the top fifteen in the category of issuing important patents. Revealingly, Chinese Foreign Economic Relations and Trade Minister Li Lanqing is reported to have proposed to Japanese Minister of International Trade and Industry Eiichi Nakao on March 22, 1991, a Sino-Japanese collaboration for the establishment of an "East Asian Economic-Cooperation Sphere." The prospect of China emerging as the world's second- or third-largest economy by 2010, which was prognosticated in 1988 by the Commission on Integrated Long-Term Strategy, is rather dubious.

Where does China rank among states when its international reputation, cultural and ideological appeal, development model, and diplomatic leadership in the shaping of international decisions, norms, and treaties in international organizations are considered? Advertised or not, Maoist China commanded such appeal as an antihegemonic third world champion of the establishment of the New International Economic Order, which led many *dependencia* theorists to embrace Beijing as a model of self-reliant development. Mao's China stood out as the only third world country that gave but never received any bilateral and multilateral aid. This alone vested Beijing with a measure of moral authority.

In 1978, all this changed when post-Mao China suddenly switched its national identity from a model of self-reliant socialist development to a poor global power actively seeking most-favored-nation trade treatment from the capitalist world. That same year also saw China's abrupt termination of its aid programs to Albania and Vietnam. The 1979 invasion of Vietnam was another reminder of the extent to which the post-Mao leadership was willing to bend the pledge never to act like a hegemonic power. These geopolitical and geoeconomic reversals, coupled with the harsh repression of the first wave of post-Mao democracy movements, began the decaying process of China's moral regime in global politics.

More than any event in modern Chinese history, the Tiananmen massacre, in a single stroke, dealt a severe blow to whatever credibility that was still retained by the make-believe moral regime. Almost overnight the People's Republic acquired a new national identity as an antipeople gerontocracy propped up by sheer repression. The worst was avoided because of a variety of geopolitical and geoeconomic reasons. Taking advantage of its permanent seat on the Security Council, Beijing once again demonstrated its negative power—and the Nixon/Kissinger/Haig/Bush line—that an engaged China is an irreducible prerequisite to any approach to world order. Beijing's bottom line seems clear enough: Ask not what China can do for a new world order; ask instead what every country, especially the lone superpower, can do to make China stable and strong in a sovereignty-centered international order.

The power China had as a "model" for the developing world has vanished in the post-Mao era. Not a single state in Asia or elsewhere looks up to Beijing as a development model. Nobody, not even the Chinese, knows what is meant by socialism with Chinese characteristics. That India and so many developing countries are now looking to Taiwan, not Russia, let alone China, as a model—or that this breakaway island country has recently surpassed Japan as the world's largest holder of foreign exchange reserves ($83 billion) must surely come as another blow to Beijing's national identity crisis. The born-again third world identity in the post-Tiananmen period seems hardly relevant to reestablishing a fit between tradition and modernity or for formulating the best strategies to make China the rich and powerful country that virtually all Chinese think is their due.

PERFORATED SOVEREIGNTY

Revolutionary power may grow from the barrels of guns, but no state—certainly not a huge multinational state—can be held together for long without a legitimizing value system, as was dramatically shown by the collapse of what was widely and wrongly perceived to be a strong state in the former Soviet Union. In at least one respect China is beyond compare. No country in our times has talked as much, launched as many ideological campaigns, succumbed to so many ideological mood swings, and accomplished so little in getting its ideological act together. Herein lies the ultimate tragedy of the Chinese Revolution.

To a startling degree, the post-Tiananmen government is paralyzed by a megacrisis—multiple and interlocking crises of authority, identity, motivation, and ideology. These have converged at a time when the center is fractured by another round of a deadly intraelite power struggle and is also facing challenges from an assertive civil society, peripheral but booming southern coastal provinces, and ethnonationalistic movements of non-Han minority peoples in the strategic borderlands of Tibet, Xinjiang, and Mongolia.

The extent to which China's legitimizing ideology has progressively decayed is captured in the common saying: "In the 1950s people helped people; in the 1960s people hurt people; in the 1970s people used people; in the 1980s and 1990s people eat people." For the majority of politically engaged intellectuals it is the Han Chinese nation, not the party-state, that has become the most significant referent for their individual and collective loyalty and identification, as found in the slogan,

"We love our country, but we hate our government."

Viewed against the longstanding state-society and state-nation concordance and the Chinese intellectual tradition of dedication to serving the state, this represents a radical change in the conceptual evolution of China's intellectual community. The defining and differentiating feature of a weak state such as China today is the high level of internal threats to the government's security. External events are seen primarily in terms of how they affect the state's internal stability. The idea of national security, which refers to the defense of core national values against external threats, becomes subverted to the extent that the Chinese government is itself insecure.

China no longer has a legitimizing and unifying ideology of sufficient strength to do away with the large-scale repressive use of force in domestic life. As noted earlier, the post-Tiananmen government increased its defense budget by 52 percent in the last three years while China enjoys the best external environment in history and when outside security threats seem to have all but vanished. A renewed emphasis on political indoctrination of PLA members is reported to have taken up 60 to 70 percent of training time. More tellingly, the People's Armed Police has experienced unprecedented growth in personnel and equipment as a way of coping with growing internal security threats.

The great irony is that the center no longer fully controls the peripheries; Chinese state sovereignty is highly perforated. Well over half of China's economy has already escaped the control of central planners in Beijing. The center has lost control of tax collection, and even profit remittances from many of the state enterprises it owns. Virtually all the gains China has enjoyed since the early 1980s have come from nonstate industries with their share of industrial output zooming from less than 15 percent to a little over half today.

At the same time, the contemporary global information revolution has broken down the exclusive control over information that the center once enjoyed. This revolution has facilitated the rapid mobilization of people's demands, frustrations, and intolerance—indeed, it is the second "revolution of people power." Although its actual speed and magnitude in post-Tiananmen China are difficult to assess, the information revolution nonetheless undergirds the critical social forces and movements for change that are weighed down by the full repressive force of the weak and insecure state.

State sovereignty thus no longer provides the center with security or control, since it is constantly perforated by the forces of supranational globalization and local and regional fragmentation. Against such trends and pressures Chinese state sovereignty is a paper tiger. China is a weak, if not yet disintegrating, state. How can the wobbly edifice of the Chinese state survive the multiple threats from within? Can a weak, oppressive state be expected to act as a responsible and peace-loving regional power? The once widely shared image of a China in disintegration and of a dragon rampant in Japan and Southeast Asia seems to be moving perilously close to reality.

POSTSCRIPT

Will China Become an Asian Superpower?

China has begun to assert itself slowly on the international stage. It has clashed with the United States, India, the Soviet Union, and Vietnam over border areas during the years since Mao took power. China will retake control of Hong Kong in 1997 and will reincorporate the Portuguese holding of Macao in 1999. Further, the government in Beijing continues to claim that Taiwan is a legal part of China.

There can be no doubt that China is powerful and growing more so yearly. One indication of that strength was the 1994 decision by President Bill Clinton to abandon his campaign pledge to withdraw China's most-favored-nation trade status with the United States unless Beijing adopted significant human rights reforms. China is not yet a superpower, but it could soon achieve that status.

The next few years are apt to be pivotal for China. One issue is who will take charge after Deng Xiaoping, born in 1904, dies or becomes so infirm that his behind-the-scenes control ends. President and Communist Party leader Jiang Zemin is widely regarded as a political lightweight, and Premier Li Peng reportedly has a troublesome heart condition. A growing number of analysts think that China might splinter into numerous, de facto, local and autonomous power centers akin to the "warlord" system that characterized China in the early part of this century. On this point see Edward A. McCord, *The Power of the Gun: The Emergence of Modern Chinese Warlordism* (University of California Press, 1993).

There are also important questions over how assertive China is likely to be in making claims to regain lost territory from Russia and others, to reincorporate Taiwan, or to secure a regional sphere of influence. The Spratly Islands are especially significant. They lie in the South China Sea in the middle of one of the world's busiest shipping lanes, and they may contain major petroleum deposits. The islands are claimed by China, Taiwan, Vietnam, the Philippines, Brunei, and Malaysia. China has also shown strong interest in developing military capabilities that would allow it to project its conventional, and perhaps tactical nuclear, forces far beyond its borders and immediate coastal region. These capabilities include efforts to enhance in-flight refueling capabilities for its warplanes and to purchase high-performance bombers and even an aircraft carrier from Russia or Ukraine. To explore the reasons behind China's growing aggressiveness, see Lowell Dittmer and Samuel S. Kim, eds., *China's Quest for National Identity* (Cornell University Press, 1993), and Robert A. Manning, "Beyond Human Rights," *Orbis* (Spring 1994).

ISSUE 7

Is Africa Heading Toward Disaster?

YES: Robert D. Kaplan, from "The Coming Anarchy," *The Atlantic Monthly* (February 1994)

NO: Michael Chege, from "What's Right With Africa?" *Current History* (May 1994)

ISSUE SUMMARY

YES: Robert D. Kaplan, a contributing editor of *The Atlantic Monthly,* focuses on Africa to explain how scarcity, crime, overpopulation, tribalism, and disease are rapidly destroying the social fabric of many African countries, and foreshadows what's in store for our planet.

NO: Michael Chege, a Kenyan who is a visiting scholar at the Center for International Affairs at Harvard University, acknowledges the extreme difficulties currently experienced by much of Africa, but he contends that a more balanced, less hysterical examination of Africa shows that there has been considerable social, economic, and political progress.

Of all the world's regions, the most distressed is sub-Saharan Africa, which is the area discussed in this debate between Robert Kaplan and Michael Chege. The sub-Saharan region is composed of those countries that lie to the south of the Arab countries in North Africa of Morocco, Algeria, Tunisia, Libya, and Egypt. The data on Africa is often depressing. In 1993, when world economic output increased by 1.8 percent, sub-Saharan Africa's output actually decreased by 0.2 percent. The data for some specific countries is even worse. Cameroon's gross domestic product (GDP) declined 5.2 percent in 1992, Madagascar's went down 6.3 percent, Malawi's dropped by 7.7 percent, and Zaire's GDP plunged 10.6 percent. Inflation is also a problem in many of these countries. Inflation in the industrialized countries during 1992 was 2.6 percent; it averaged 13.9 percent throughout the world, and stood at 36.1 percent in Africa. Global exports increased 5.7 percent between 1991 and 1992; Africa's exports were static. Africa's imports, however, rose 11.6 percent. This occurred in part because the price of manufactured goods, which Africa imports, rose 3.7 percent. The net result was to plunge the continent further into debt ($128.3 billion in 1992). Trying to pay its debts drained already impoverished sub-Saharan Africa, which accumulated a balance of payments deficit in 1992 of $8.8 billion.

Social statistics from Africa are often equally glum. Sub-Saharan Africa has over a half-billion people, and the population is growing at more than twice the world rate. The world's per capita wealth (measured in economic production) is about $4,200; sub-Saharan Africa's is $340. Disease rates are high. Life expectancy is 51 years for sub-Saharan Africans (world: 66 years).

Education is often lacking. Adult literacy in the region is 50 percent (world: 65 percent). Again, data from individual countries are even more alarming. The poverty rate in the United States is 14.5 percent; it is 82.5 percent in Zambia. The infant mortality rate in Malawi is 15 times higher than in the United States. Ninety-seven percent of adult Americans and Canadians are literate; only one in five adults in Sierra Leone can read.

Given these frequently dire economic and social statistics, it is not surprising that Africa has experienced political turmoil. Starvation in Ethiopia in the late 1980s and the bloody civil wars in Somalia and Rwanda have captured the headline news. There have been less widely known but also horrific recent civil wars in Liberia and the Sudan. Dictatorships, such as the one in Zaire, still persist in some countries.

For all of these problems, however, there are also positive signs in Africa. There are fewer authoritarian governments than there once were, and the ones that remain are under increasing pressure to surrender their power to the democratic process. Civil wars in Angola, Mozambique, and elsewhere have either abated or ended. An immense leap forward was achieved in South Africa when it ended apartheid, rewrote its constitution, and peacefully elected a black president, Nelson Mandela.

It is also important to note that many of Africa's problems are not of its own making. Long years of misrule by European colonial powers deprived these countries of the ability to attain normal economic development. Raw materials were extracted and exported, and few manufacturing plants were built. Most skilled and managerial jobs were reserved for Europeans. Education for the local population was generally limited. Colonial boundaries arbitrarily separated some tribes, while forcing others, who were sometimes hostile to one another, into the same political units. To make matters worse, the colonial powers often played one ethnic group off against another. The cold war was also waged in Africa by outsiders, usually to the detriment of the Africans. The long and terrible civil wars in Angola and Mozambique could not have persisted had it not been for the money and arms supplies by the rival superpower blocs. The prodigious amount of weaponry possessed by the Somali clans and others is the result of supplies given by East and West in an effort to win loyalty.

What does all this portend for sub-Saharan Africa? Robert Kaplan foresees coming anarchy amid which, to paraphrase English political philosopher Sir Thomas Hobbes, life is likely to be nasty, brutish, and short. Michael Chege believes that civil strife and famine receive more publicity than do the events and institutions that have enhanced the opportunity of sub-Saharan Africans to improve their lives in a peaceful environment.

YES

Robert D. Kaplan

THE COMING ANARCHY

The Minister's eyes were like egg yolks, an aftereffect of some of the many illnesses, malaria especially, endemic in his country. There was also an irrefutable sadness in his eyes. He spoke in a slow and creaking voice, the voice of hope about to expire. Flame trees, coconut palms, and a ballpoint-blue Atlantic composed the background. None of it seemed beautiful, though. "In forty-five years I have never seen things so bad. We did not manage ourselves well after the British departed. But what we have now is something worse— the revenge of the poor, of the social failures, of the people least able to bring up children in a modern society." Then he referred to the recent coup in the West African country Sierra Leone. "The boys who took power in Sierra Leone come from houses like this." The Minister jabbed his finger at a corrugated metal shack teeming with children. "In three months these boys confiscated all the official Mercedes, Volvos, BMWs and willfully wrecked them on the road." The Minister mentioned one of the coup's leaders, Solomon Anthony Joseph Musa, who shot the people who had paid for his schooling, "in order to erase the humiliation and mitigate the power his middle-class sponsors held over him."

Tyranny is nothing new in Sierra Leone or in the rest of West Africa. But it is now part and parcel of an increasing lawlessness that is far more significant than any coup, rebel incursion, or episodic experiment in democracy. Crime was what my friend—a top-ranking African official whose life would be threatened were I to identify him more precisely—really wanted to talk about. Crime is what makes West Africa a natural point of departure for my report on what the political character of our planet is likely to be in the twenty-first century.

The cities of West Africa at night are some of the unsafest places in the world. Streets are unlit; the police often lack gasoline for their vehicles; armed burglars, carjackers, and muggers proliferate.... Direct flights between the United States and the Murtala Muhammed Airport, in neighboring Nigeria's largest city, Lagos, have been suspended by order of the U.S. Secretary of Transportation because of ineffective security at the terminal and its environs. A State Department report cited the airport for "extortion by law-enforcement and immigration officials." This is one of the few times that the U.S. government has embargoed a foreign airport for reasons that are linked purely to crime. In Abidjan, effectively the capital of the Côte d'Ivoire, or Ivory Coast, restaurants have stick- and gun-wielding guards who walk you the fifteen feet or so between your car and the entrance, giving you an eerie taste of what American cities might be like in the future. An Italian ambassador was killed by gunfire when robbers invaded an Abidjan restaurant. The family of the Nigerian ambassador was tied up and robbed at gunpoint in the ambassador's residence. After university students in the Ivory Coast caught bandits who had been plaguing their dorms, they executed them by hanging tires around their necks and setting the tires on fire. In one instance Ivorian policemen stood by and watched the "necklacings," afraid to intervene. Each time I went to the Abidjan bus terminal, groups of young men with restless, scanning eyes surrounded my taxi, putting their hands all over the windows, demanding "tips" for carrying my luggage even though I had only a rucksack. In cities in six West African countries I saw similar young men everywhere —hordes of them. They were like loose molecules in a very unstable social fluid, a fluid that was clearly on the verge of igniting....

A PREMONITION OF THE FUTURE

West Africa is becoming *the* symbol of worldwide demographic, environmental, and societal stress, in which criminal anarchy emerges as the real "strategic" danger. Disease, overpopulation, unprovoked crime, scarcity of resources, refugee migrations, the increasing ero-

sion of nation-states and international borders, and the empowerment of private armies, security firms, and international drug cartels are now most tellingly demonstrated through a West African prism. West Africa provides an appropriate introduction to the issues, often extremely unpleasant to discuss, that will soon confront our civilization. To remap the political earth the way it will be a few decades hence—as I intend to do in this article—I find I must begin with West Africa.

There is no other place on the planet where political maps are so deceptive— where, in fact, they tell such lies—as in West Africa. Start with Sierra Leone. According to the map, it is a nation-state of defined borders, with a government in control of its territory. In truth the Sierra Leonian government, run by a twenty-seven-year-old army captain, Valentine Strasser, controls Freetown by day and by day also controls part of the rural interior. In the government's territory the national army is an unruly rabble threatening drivers and passengers at most checkpoints. In the other part of the country units of two separate armies from the war in Liberia have taken up residence, as has an army of Sierra Leonian rebels. The government force fighting the rebels is full of renegade commanders who have aligned themselves with disaffected village chiefs. A premodern formlessness governs the battlefield, evoking the wars in medieval Europe prior to the 1648 Peace of Westphalia, which ushered in the era of organized nation-states.

As a consequence, roughly 400,000 Sierra Leonians are internally displaced, 280,000 more have fled to neighboring Guinea, and another 100,000 have fled to Liberia, even as 400,000 Liberians have fled to Sierra Leone. The third largest city in Sierra Leone, Gondama, is a displaced-persons camp. With an additional 600,000 Liberians in Guinea and 250,000 in the Ivory Coast, the borders dividing these four countries have become largely meaningless. Even in quiet zones none of the governments except the Ivory Coast's maintains the schools, bridges, roads, and police forces in a manner necessary for functional sovereignty....

In Sierra Leone, as in Guinea, as in the Ivory Coast, as in Ghana, most of the primary rain forest and the secondary bush is being destroyed at an alarming rate. I saw convoys of trucks bearing majestic hardwood trunks to coastal ports. When Sierra Leone achieved its independence, in 1961, as much as 60 percent of the country was primary rain forest. Now six percent is. In the Ivory Coast the proportion has fallen from 38 percent to eight percent. The deforestation has led to soil erosion, which has led to more flooding and more mosquitos. Virtually everyone in the West African interior has some form of malaria.

Sierra Leone is a microcosm of what is occurring, albeit in a more tempered and gradual manner, throughout West Africa and much of the underdeveloped world: the withering away of central governments, the rise of tribal and regional domains, the unchecked spread of disease, and the growing pervasiveness of war. West Africa is reverting to the Africa of the Victorian atlas. It consists now of a series of coastal trading posts, such as Freetown and Conakry, and an interior that, owing to violence, volatility, and disease, is again becoming, as Graham Greene once observed, "blank" and "unexplored." However, whereas Greene's vision implies a certain romance, as in the somnolent and charmingly seedy Free-town of his celebrated novel *The Heart of the Matter*, it is Thomas Malthus, the philosopher of demographic doomsday, who is now the prophet of West Africa's future. And West Africa's future, eventually, will also be that of most of the rest of the world.

* * *

Consider "Chicago." I refer not to Chicago, Illinois, but to a slum district of Abidjan, which the young toughs in the area have named after the American city. ("Washington" is another poor section of Abidjan.) Although Sierra Leone is widely regarded as beyond salvage, the Ivory Coast has been considered an African success story, and Abidjan has been called "the Paris of West Africa." Success, however, was built on two artificial factors: the high price of cocoa, of which the Ivory Coast is the world's leading producer, and the talents of a French expatriate community, whose members have helped run the government and the private sector. The expanding cocoa economy made the Ivory Coast a magnet for migrant workers from all over West Africa: between a third and a half of the country's population is now non-Ivorian, and the figure could be as high as 75 percent in Abidjan. During the 1980s cocoa prices fell and the French began to leave. The skyscrapers of the Paris of West Africa are a façade. Perhaps 15 percent of Abidjan's population of three million people live in shantytowns like Chicago and Washington, and the vast majority live in places that are not much better. Not all of these places appear on any of the readily available maps. This is another indication of how political maps are the products of tired conventional wisdom and, in the Ivory Coast's case, of an elite that will ultimately be forced to re-linquish power.

Chicago, like more and more of Abidjan, is a slum in the bush: a checkerwork of corrugated zinc roofs and walls made of cardboard and black plastic wrap. It is located in a gully teeming with coconut palms and oil palms, and is ravaged by flooding. Few residents have easy access to electricity, a sewage system, or a clean water supply. The crumbly red laterite earth crawls with foot-long lizards both inside and outside the shacks. Children defecate in a stream filled with garbage and pigs, droning with malarial mosquitoes. In this stream women do the washing. Young unemployed men spend their time drinking beer, palm wine, and gin while gambling on pinball games constructed out of rotting wood and rusty nails. These are the same youths who rob houses in more prosperous Ivorian neighborhoods at night....

Fifty-five percent of the Ivory Coast's population is urban, and the proportion is expected to reach 62 percent by 2000. The yearly net population growth is 3.6 percent. This means that the Ivory Coast's 13.5 million people will become 39 million by 2025, when much of the population will consist of urbanized peasants like those of Chicago. But don't count on the Ivory Coast's still existing then. Chicago, which is more indicative of Africa's and the Third World's demographic present—and even more of the future—than any idyllic junglescape of women balancing earthen jugs on their heads, illustrates why the Ivory Coast, once a model of Third World success, is becoming a case study in Third World catastrophe.

President Félix Houphouët-Boigny, who died last December at the age of about ninety, left behind a weak cluster of political parties and a leaden bureaucracy that discourages foreign investment. Because the military is small and the non-Ivorian population large, there is neither an obvious force to maintain order nor a sense of nationhood that would lessen the need for such enforcement. The economy has been shrinking since the mid-1980s. Though the French are working assiduously to preserve stability, the Ivory Coast faces a possibility worse than a coup: an anarchic implosion of criminal violence —an urbanized version of what has already happened in Somalia. Or it may become an African Yugoslavia, but one without mini-states to replace the whole.

Because the demographic reality of West Africa is a countryside draining into dense slums by the coast, ultimately the region's rulers will come to reflect the values of these shantytowns. There are signs of this already in Sierra Leone—and in Togo, where the dictator Etienne Eyadema, in power since 1967, was nearly toppled in 1991, not by democrats but by thousands of youths whom the London-based magazine *West Africa* described as "Soweto-like stone-throwing adolescents." Their behavior may herald a regime more brutal than Eyadema's repressive one....

Ali A. Mazrui, the director of the Institute of Global Cultural Studies at the State University of New York at Binghamton, predicts that West Africa —indeed, the whole continent—is on the verge of large-scale border upheaval. Mazrui writes,

In the 21st century France will be withdrawing from West Africa as she gets increasingly involved in the affairs [of Europe]. France's West African sphere of influence will be filled by Nigeria—a more natural hegemonic power....It will be under those circumstances that Nigeria's own boundaries are likely to expand to incorporate the Republic of Niger (the Hausa link), the Republic of Benin (the Yoruba link) and conceivably Cameroon.

* * *

The future could be more tumultuous, and bloodier, than Mazrui dares to say. France *will* withdraw from former colonies like Benin, Togo, Niger, and the Ivory Coast, where it has been propping up local currencies. It will do so not only because its attention will be diverted to new challenges in Europe and Russia but also because younger French officials lack the older generation's emotional ties to the ex-colonies. However, even as Nigeria attempts to expand it, too, is likely to split into several pieces. The State Department's Bureau of Intelligence and Research recently made the following points in an analysis of Nigeria:

> Prospects for a transition to civilian rule and democratization are slim... The repressive apparatus of the state security service... will be difficult for any future civilian government to control.... The country is becoming increasingly ungovernable.... Ethnic and regional splits are deepening, a situation made worse by an increase in the number of states from 19 to 30 and a doubling in the number of local governing authorities; religious cleavages are more serious; Muslim fundamentalism and evangelical Christian militancy are on the rise; and northern Muslim anxiety over southern [Christian] control of the economy is intense... the will to keep Nigeria together is now very weak.

Given that oil-rich Nigeria is a bellwether for the region—its population of roughly 90 million equals the populations of all the other West African states combined—it is apparent that Africa faces cataclysms that could make the Ethiopian and Somalian famines pale in comparison. This is especially so because Nigeria's population, including that of its largest city, Lagos, whose crime, pollution, and overcrowding make it the cliché par excellence of Third World urban dysfunction, is set to double during the next twenty-five years, while the country continues to deplete its natural resources.

Part of West Africa's quandary is that although its population belts are horizontal [east-west], with habitation densities increasing as one travels south away from the Sahara and toward the tropical abundance of the Atlantic littoral, the borders erected by European colonialists are vertical [north-south], and therefore at cross-purposes with demography and topography.... [I]ndeed, the entire stretch of coast from Abidjan eastward to Lagos—is one burgeoning megalopolis that by any rational economic and geographical standard should constitute a single sovereignty, rather than the five (the Ivory Coast, Ghana, Togo, Benin, and Nigeria) into which it is currently divided.

As many internal African borders begin to crumble, a more impenetrable boundary is being erected that threatens to isolate the continent as a whole: the wall of disease. Merely to visit West Africa in some degree of safety, I spent about $500 for a hepatitis B vaccination series and other disease prophylaxis. Africa may today be more dangerous in this regard than it was in 1862, before antibiotics, when the explorer Sir Richard Francis Burton described the health situation on the continent as "deadly."... Of the approximately 12 million people worldwide whose blood is HIV-positive, 8 million are in Africa.

In the capital of the Ivory Coast, whose modern road system only helps spread the disease, 10 percent of the population is HIV-positive. And war and refugee movements help the virus break through to more-remote areas of Africa. Alan Greenberg, M.D., a representative of the Centers of Disease Control in Abidjan, explains that in Africa the HIV virus and tuberculosis are now "fast-forwarding each other." Of the approximately 4,000 newly diagnosed tuberculosis patients in Abidjan, 45 percent were also found to be HIV-positive. As African birth rates soar and slums proliferate, some experts worry that viral mutations and hybridizations might, just conceivably, result in a form of the AIDS virus that is easier to catch than the present strain.

It is malaria that is most responsible for the disease wall that threatens to separate Africa and other parts of the Third World from more-developed regions of the planet in the twenty-first century. Carried by mosquitoes, malaria, unlike AIDS, is easy to catch. Most people in sub-Saharan Africa have recurring bouts of the disease throughout their entire lives, and it is mutating into increasingly deadly forms. "The great gift of Malaria is utter apathy," wrote Sir Richard Burton, accurately portraying the situation in much of the Third World today. Visitors to malaria-afflicted parts of the planet are protected by a new drug, mefloquine, a side effect of which is vivid, even violent, dreams. But a strain of cerebral malaria resistant to mefloquine is now on the offensive....

And the cities keep growing. I got a general sense of the future while driving from the airport to downtown Conakry, the capital of Guinea. The forty-five-minute journey in heavy traffic was through one never-ending shantytown: a nightmarish Dickensian spectacle to which Dickens himself would never have given credence. The corrugated metal shacks and scabrous walls were coated with black slim. Stores were built out of rusted shipping containers, junked cars, and jumbles of wire mesh. The streets were one long puddle of floating garbage. Mosquitoes and flies were everywhere. Children, many of whom had protruding bellies, seemed as numerous as ants. When the tide went out, dead rats and the skeletons of cars were exposed on the mucky beach. In twenty-eight years Guinea's population will double if growth goes on at current rates. Hardwood logging continues at a madcap speed, and people flee the Guinean countryside for Conakry. It seemed to me that here, as elsewhere in Africa and the Third World, man is challenging nature far beyond its limits, and nature is now beginning to take its revenge.

* * *

Africa may be as relevant to the future character of world politics as the Balkans were a hundred years ago, prior to the two Balkan wars and the First World War. Then the threat was the collapse of empires and the birth of nations based solely on tribe. Now the threat is more elemental: *nature unchecked.* Africa's immediate future could be very bad. The coming upheaval, in which foreign embassies are shut down, states collapse, and contact with the outside world takes place through dangerous, disease-ridden coastal trading posts, will loom large in the century we are entering. (Nine of twenty-one U.S. foreign-aid missions to be closed over the next three years are in Africa—a prologue to a consolidation of U.S. embassies themselves.) Precisely because much of Africa is set to go over the edge at a time when the Cold War has ended, when environmental and demographic stress in other parts of the globe is becoming critical, and when the post–First World War system of nation-states—not just in the Balkans but perhaps also in the Middle East—is about to be toppled, Africa suggests what war, borders, and ethnic politics will be like a few decades hence. . . .

* * *

Returning from West Africa last fall was an illuminating ordeal. After leaving Abidjan, my Air Afrique flight landed in Dakar, Senegal, where all passengers had to disembark in order to go through another security check, this one demanded by U.S. authorities before they would permit the flight to set out for New York. Once we were in New York, despite the midnight hour, immigration officials at Kennedy Airport held up disembarkation by conducting quick interrogations of the aircraft's passengers—this was in addition to all the normal immigration and customs procedures. It was apparent that drug smuggling, disease, and other factors had contributed to the toughest security procedures I have ever encountered when returning from overseas.

Then, for the first time in over a month, I spotted businesspeople with attaché cases and laptop computers. When I had left New York for Abidjan, all the businesspeople were boarding planes for Seoul and Tokyo, which departed from gates near Air Afrique's. The only non-Africans off to West Africa had been relief workers in T-shirts and khakis. Although the borders within West Africa are increasingly unreal, those separating West Africa from the outside world are in various ways becoming more impenetrable.

But Afrocentrists are right in one respect: we ignore this dying region at our own risk. When the Berlin Wall was falling, in November of 1989, I happened to be in Kosovo, covering a riot between Serbs and Albanians. The future was in Kosovo, I told myself that night, not in Berlin. The same day that Yitzhak Rabin and Yasser Arafat clasped hands on the White House lawn, my Air Afrique plane was approaching Bamako, Mali, revealing corrugated-zinc shacks at the edge of an expanding desert. The real news wasn't at the White House, I realized. It was right below.

NO

Michael Chege

WHAT'S RIGHT WITH AFRICA?

Any objective account of success at the community and national level in sub-Saharan Africa must begin by acknowledging that the balance at the moment is overwhelmingly tilted in favor of disaster. It must also reckon with the hard fact that both in Africa and the Western world, the stories of civil strife and famine of unprecedented dimensions receive more publicity than those about events and institutions that have reversed social catastrophes and given ordinary citizens an opportunity to improve their lives in a peaceful environment.

Such a report must avoid the ultranationalist position now being voiced in African and some Western intellectual circles that the cascading tales of woe from sub-Saharan Africa are the latest racial assaults on the African peoples by the West and that, even assuming the stories are true, the real culprits are to be found in a conspiratorial European and American imperialist circle hell-bent on perpetuating a baleful "Afro-pessimism" on the continent's inhabitants. For most long-term residents of Africa, like this author, who have to watch and endure in agony the march of locally authored calamity as it ravages one country after another, such explanations seem outlandish and contrived.

A more balanced account must shun such positions with the same vigor with which it distances itself from those at the opposite end of the political spectrum that portray sub-Saharan Africa and its peoples as a lost cause, now and forever. One of the most widely read examples of the genre was the May 1993 *Reader's Digest* article apocalyptically entitled "A Continent's Slow Suicide." Drawing on a highly selective selection of African disaster cases—a method employed with equal success by advocates of a Western conspiracy theory out to prove perverse meddling by Europe and America—this article proceeded to demonstrate that even with the best intentions of donors and relief agencies, the chances of turning back the tide of continental tragedy were hardly worth rating.

Quite apart from the fact that it would not be difficult to invoke the prophecy of Cassandra for Eastern Europe, South Asia, urban America, Latin American, or any other region after running down a carefully biased list of intractable social and political problems there, the doomsayers' view of contemporary Africa ignores the old homily that every dark cloud has a silver lining. And this includes the political storms in overcast tropical Africa. The silver lining is as much a part of the story as the raging clouds, though not the only reality, as the romantic ultranationalists would have it. And for all their marginality—if indeed they are merely isolated exceptions—the rays of hope should be as scrutinized as the headline stories of collapse and national setback. For within the contours of the silver lining may lie the policy lessons that might realistically be applied toward improving the political and economic conditions under whose shadow a substantial proportion of Africans now live.

Such potential may not be immediately visible to the combatants at either extreme, which may explain why it is talked about only within a very narrow range of scholars, donors, and the many voluntary and nongovernmental agencies that concern themselves with Africa. But seeds for action may be found in case studies of African successes—even when the success is highly qualified—particularly in the high-priority areas of political stability, national governance, and economic development.

DEMOCRATIC GAINS

Beginning in 1990, a new wave of popular demands for democratic rule swept the continent. Yet as shown by events in Zaire, Malawi, Cameroon, Kenya, Guinea, Gabon, Rwanda, Sudan, and Togo, the war against dictatorships has hardly been won. In these and many other countries the heads of government have clung to power through a combination of brute force, manipulation of gullible opposition parties, bribery, crafty exploitation of ethnic loyalties, and cosmetic constitutional reforms to appease Western donors who demand "good governance" as a precondition for further development aid.

Still, there are solid gains that need to be recounted and built on in the quest for fully democratic and accountable government if the momentum is not to be lost. The courage of the independent press in Kenya, as represented by the *Nation* newspaper and the country's new magazines, as well as in Ghana, Nigeria, Malawi, Cameroon, Tanzania, and Ethiopia, marks a new departure. These periodicals run on shoestring budgets and the robust determination of their publishers never to be cowed by hostile authorities. Such spirit is what kept a group of Somali pressmen going —with little more than a mimeograph machine and rolls of paper—at the height of the brutal conflict in Mogadishu. On the whole, the horizons of freedom of speech have widened beyond all expectations at the start of the agitation for democracy.

Neither can the outcome of competitive multiparty elections since 1990 be dismissed as hopeless. Autocratic governments have given way to democratically elected administrations in Zambia, Cape Verde, São Tomé and Principe, Benin, Madagascar, Lesotho, and Burundi. French-style presidential elections have brought new faces to power in Niger, Mali, Central African Republic, and Congo. Whenever African voters have been given the chance to choose those who will govern them in genuinely free and fair circumstances, they have opted for accountable and more honest leadership than it has been their misfortune to have had in the past. And despite the undeniable attachment to ethnic loyalty, voters recognize leaders who transcend narrow provincial ambitions. Witness the trans-ethnic and cross-cultural backing for Moshood Abiola in the abrogated June 1993 elections in Nigeria, and the broad-based support for Etienne Tshisekedi, the foremost opposition leader in Zaire. That there has subsequently been violent conflict in Burundi, Congo, and Lesotho, and corruption in the government in Zambia, does not discount the progress made. The real test lies in developing the institutional capacity to resolve such political differences by due constitutional process.

Above all, the lesson is now sinking in: actions of rogue military units in countries like Burundi, Guinea, Lesotho, and Congo, no less than in Zaire, Togo, Cameroon, and Nigeria, demonstrate the need to bring the armed forces under civilian democratic control. The difficult process of doing so now needs to be discussed and implemented. A courageous start has been made with the unanimous warning in February 1993 from southern African government leaders, including President F. W. de Klerk of South Africa, to Lesotho's restive army to obey the democratically elected government, and with ongoing efforts by the Organization of African Unity (OAU) to monitor the army's neutrality in the tortured democratic transition in Burundi.

The vast majority of African countries, in fact, are in this sort of indeterminate transition from an authoritarian order rather than being home to the free-for-all violence of Angola, Somalia, and Liberia that the electronic media brings to Western living rooms so frequently. And the picture of a violent region leaves out the African countries that function normally on both the political and social planes.

Over the last 30 years, the southern African state of Botswana, for example, has been a working pluralistic democracy in which regular elections are held and human rights are respected. Though never a media favorite, the country has a grassroots democracy based on village councils (kgotla) and no history of large-scale corruption or civil strife. Next door, to the west, the Republic of Namibia, which gained independence in 1990 after a long war against colonial South Africa, has marched on to stability and administrative efficiency under one of the most liberal constitutions anywhere. Pragmatic and realistic, the governing South West African People's Organization (SWAPO) party ditched the doctrinaire socialist program it had espoused as a guerrilla organization and is busy courting local and international investors as it looks for sustainable policy alternatives that will bring the black majority into the mainstream of agricultural and industrial life. This February Namibia regained from South Africa the Walvis Bay enclave with its deep-water harbor after several years of conscientious diplomatic efforts. Doomsayers had said Walvis Bay was the powder keg that would set off armed confrontation between South Africa and Namibia.

To the east of Botswana, Zimbabwe, after a difficult political start, has developed a workable formula for ethnic and racial coexistence. All the while the country has maintained a comparatively efficient public service and a nationwide network of roads and telecommunications, water, power, and sanitation systems that stand out against the dereliction of infrastructure not just to the north of Zimbabwe on the continent but also in many richer nations in Europe, South America, and Asia.

Bold constitutional innovations have produced more decent governance and political stability in other parts of Africa. After years of internal warfare and a succession of brutally repressive regimes, Uganda has since 1986 settled into tranquility under President Yoweri Museveni. His administration has broken faith with the African mythological belief that ethnic loyalties can be replaced by a single national identity and enduring loyalty to an all-powerful head of state of a monolithic government. Museveni has permitted gradual decentralization that includes acceptance of once-outlawed provincial kingdoms such as Buganda, Toro, Bunyoro, and Ankole. Farther north, the regime of President Meles Zenawi in Ethiopia is pledged to a federalist structure that explicitly recognizes the nation's cultural diversity, but it must reckon with divisive movements that violate the human rights of non-natives in outlying areas, and must instill greater tolerance in its own ranks. The government's boldness is attested to by its acceptance of the 1993 referendum in favor of Eritrean independence—the first of its kind on the continent—ending 30 years of bloody separatist warfare.

The president of independent Eritrea, Isaias Afewerki, is representative of the new generation of epoch-making African reformers. At last year's OAU summit in Cairo, he broke tradition and criticized to their faces the incumbent gerontocracy of African dictators for violating civil liberties and ignoring the humanitarian plight of Eritreans during the war. His speech drew the spontaneous applause of the African press corps in the adjoining chamber.

Provided they can overcome daunting initial problems, the new liberal constitutional reformers will lead their countries into the small group of democracies in sub-Saharan Africa that include, in addition to Botswana, the Indian Ocean island of Mauritius, and Senegal and Gambia in West Africa. True, these are small states (as critics of political change on the continent are wont to point out), but it is important to note the swelling of their ranks and to see if this has an effect over time on reformist forces in the larger countries. What will happen on that score will most likely be settled by the leadership that emerges in the coming decade.

The catalog of benighted African autocrats leaves out what is right with many of the continent's local and national leaders. Consider Nelson Mandela, released after 27 years of incarceration under apartheid, offering the hand of reconciliation and a fresh partnership to the white community in South Africa, as Robert Mugabe had done in Zimbabwe and Jomo Kenyatta in Kenya years before. And Mandela did this while keeping hope alive in his constituents in the restive black majority and building bridges to the warmongering right-wingers of the Inkatha Freedom party and the Afrikaner Resistance Movement. How many leaders elsewhere in the world can claim to have paid such a high personal price, and to have accomplished so much in such difficult circumstances within such a brief period of time? How many could match the years of patient reconciliation efforts across races and communities carried off with graceful wit by Archbishop Desmond Tutu of Cape Town? And what of dozens of others who have acted as the nagging national conscience in their respective states, among them Wole Soyinka, the winner of the Nobel Prize for Literature, and the Kuti brothers in Nigeria: Archbishop Laurent Monsengwo Pasinya in Zaire; the late Jaramogi Oginga Odinga, the clergy, and the principled legal fraternity in Kenya; and honorably retired heads of government like Julius Nyerere of Tanzania, Leopold Senghor of Senegal, and Kenneth Kaunda of Zambia.

As the lessons of what has gone right with African governance sink in, supreme importance must increasingly be placed on high-quality, principled leadership committed to overhauling the ideas of monolithic rule. In the process, a premium must be placed on coming to constitutional terms with ethnic diversity as an enduring phenomenon—as is now happening in South Africa, Ethiopia, Uganda, and, one hopes, Rwanda and Burundi—without derogating from the principle of territorial integrity and the right to own property and live in peace anywhere in the country. The other challenge lies in regenerating economic growth and raising local incomes so as to give ordinary citizens a stake in the larger system.

PROFITABLE DEVELOPMENTS

Although the overall economic development record for Africa during the last 20 years has been discouraging, a different picture emerges when one disaggregates the figures to account for individual country performance. Per capita income in sub-Saharan Africa is said to have declined 1.2 percent annually over the period, but a small number of African countries did as well as if not better than the best in the rest of the world.

The economy in Botswana grew at a faster rate in the last two decades—between 7 percent and 8 percent a year—than the much-vaunted miracles in East Asia. With its emphasis on investment in human resources and sound macroeconomic management, Botswana's economy, centered around diamond production, is now branching out into tourism, manufactured exports, and regional banking services. Over the last 20 years Mauritius has transformed itself from a poor country dependent on the sugarcane crop into a full-employment society based on East Asian–style manufacturing and export of textiles and electronic goods. This was made possible by investment from Asia and Europe. As the country plans a second, deeper phase of economic development, it is moving into offshore banking and new branches of industry.

There are other successes. The region's premier source of development money, the African Development Bank, borrows from African and non-African governments and money markets. It carries a full triple-A rating—the highest possible —from Moody's, Standard and Poor's, and Japan's Credit Rating Agency. Most of its loans have gone into agriculture and public utilities. And in Ethiopia annual profits for the national airline have been good year after year, due to sound management and excellent service. Both the bank and Ethiopian Airlines have enjoyed protection from meddlesome state authorities and employed the skills of local technocrats—a lesson economic reformers must heed.

Despite the portrayal of sub-Saharan Africa as a land of perpetual hunger, some 10 countries—Chad, Cape Verde, Nigeria, Botswana, Guinea-Bissau, Uganda, Benin, Kenya, Tanzania, and Comoros —had what the World Bank termed good to excellent growth rates in agriculture, ranging from 3.5 percent to 20 percent, between 1980 and 1990. Farmers in Burkina Faso have pioneered cost-effective methods of reversing desertification and dispersing of new seeds. A recent study of the Machakos district in Kenya, reported on in the *Economist* [December 11, 1993], revealed that, contrary to the conventional wisdom on African development, high population growth rates had not led to overgrazing, soil degradation, and worsening poverty. On the contrary, as the population rose the smallholders of the district had switched from pastoralism to cultivation of neatly terraced farms that halted erosion and produced more for the Nairobi market and for export. To the extent that any outsiders can claim credit, the postindependence government can be cited for its introduction of individual titles for land, high-value cash crops like coffee, and better roads to the capital. In general, a thriving modern economic sector generated jobs, and the savings from those wages went back into agriculture. This has been demonstrated time and again whenever small-scale farming prospers, as in other parts of Kenya and in Ivory Coast and southern Cameroon in the 1950s and 1960s, and as was also the case in cocoa production in Ghana and Nigeria in previous decades.

On the whole, African countries that have a good record in cash crops for markets abroad, such as coffee, tea, and cocoa, have also done well in advancing toward the goal of food production to match the demands of a burgeoning population. And though African economies have been severely buffeted since the 1980s by falling global commodity prices, much has also depended on how they have managed export incomes and sustained farming incentives. Kenya and Malawi, for example, have increased their shares of the world tea

market in a relatively short period of time, principally because of an emphasis on high quality and lowering production costs. The private sector in Kenya has pioneered agricultural diversification into horticulture, while African trade diplomats engage in fruitless efforts to negotiate northern funding for it. Food production in Nigeria, which was in distress in the 1970s, has received a boost from exchange rate and price liberalization since the mid-1980s. Similar effects can be observed in Ethiopia even in the brief space of time after the 1991–1993 dismantling of rigid price controls for farm products and the abolition of the disastrous collectivization program undertaken by the Marxist-Leninist government of Mengistu Haile Mariam in the 1970s and 1980s.

As in the political arena, the lessons to be drawn from successful economic enterprises in Africa are the same as those from other rapidly growing areas of the developing world. Political stability and government committed to tangible results on the development transformation front are vital foundations for economic growth. It is in politically tranquil Mauritius and Botswana that decent governance (and macroeconomic stability) has been harnessed to market-based development policies to produce the best results. The same could be said of Kenya and Ivory Coast in their better days of rapid economic growth in the 1960s and 1970s.

What it takes for economic revival and poverty reduction in Africa is becoming clearer all the time. Once stability was restored in Uganda and Ghana in the 1980s and in Ethiopia after 1991, and accompanied by liberal economic policies and fiscal and monetary discipline, growth blossomed in the ruins. The beneficial impact, of course, will not quickly saturate all of society, but a positive beginning has been made. So long as such wisdom is accepted, and the limitations of current reforms are understood, there must be hope for the increasing number of African countries that are allocating markets a greater role in the national economy than ever before. This applies especially after the devaluation in mid-January of the subsidized African Financial Community (CFA) franc that is used in 13 francophone countries, which caused a wave of urban unrest but will in the longer run benefit the 13 economies.

AFRICAN RESPONSES TO AFRICAN PROBLEMS

The new setbacks in globally organized peacemaking in Somalia under United States leadership should not be allowed to overshadow promising local efforts in conflict resolution, even though, as in other areas of regional concern, there is still a long way to go. Pan-African peacemaking efforts have not received much publicity, but they continue to save lives and to restore confidence in local societies. Statesmen in the region must intensify these initiatives while consolidating gains thus far.

In Somalia, community elders and religious leaders have negotiated disarmament and political concord in areas of the northeast, the town of Kismayu, and in parts of the self-declared Republic of Somaliland. After three checkered years for the Economic Community of West African States (ECOWAS) force in war-torn Liberia, the warring factions agreed last year [1993] in Geneva to an elaborate peace pact. Despite repeated infringements, a provisional government was installed March 4 [1994]. Most of the diplomatic groundwork was under the auspices of the OAU and trusted African intermediaries, notably the Reverend Canaan Banana of Zimbabwe and Benin's president, Nicophole Soglo. But for a shortage of funds at both the UN and the OAU, a neutral African peacekeeping force would have been in Liberia at the beginning of the year, under the command of Kenya's Brigadier Daniel Opande, who served the UN with distinction in Namibia.

Further east, in Rwanda, the OAU played a critical role in bringing the government and the rebel Rwandese Patriotic Front to the conference table in Arusha, Tanzania, in 1992. Implementation of the peace agreement, scheduled to lead to internationally supervised elections last year, has had to be repeatedly postponed, and the process sustained severe setbacks because of the factional violence and assassination in Kigali, Rwanda's capital, in February. But the agreement presents the OAU in a new role, as a promoter of internal harmony, despite its very slim resource base. In other instances, African diplomats and statesmen have played pivotal parts in brokering the peace agreement that ended the bloody civil war in Mozambique in 1992, and in defusing border tensions like those between Nigeria and Cameroon in 1985 and again this year. They continue to work as representatives of the warring factions in the civil war in Angola and meet in Lusaka, Zambia. In eastern Africa, regional diplomatic initiatives attempt mediation of internal conflicts in Sudan and Somalia.

HOPE FROM BELOW

The brightest lights at the end of the tunnel in Africa must be those held aloft by ordinary citizens. Africans' resilience and stubborn refusal to cave in to despair against the odds of despotism at home and an increasingly hostile environment can be ignored only at great cost by those seriously concerned with the recovery of the region. The bravery and determination evident in the refugees returning to Mozambique and among the people of Somalia and Liberia, and the inventiveness that enables Africans to survive in ravaged Zaire and countless other places, demonstrate just how rapidly societies would rebuild themselves if political stability, the rule of law, and a hospitable economic environment were restored.

Although ruin and despair might seem pervasive, history is full of examples in which the turnaround from disaster came much sooner than observers, overwhelmed by gloom, had cared to notice. Revisionist history of the Middle Ages in Europe, for instance, holds that the Renaissance took too much credit for scientific and intellectual discoveries, some of which date back to the often-maligned medieval period. Likewise, as development specialists now celebrate the stunning economic achievements of China, Taiwan, South Korea, Singapore, and those following them, they tend to downplay the intellectual despondency that characterized development studies of Asia in the 1950s and through the Vietnam War. Terms like "dual economies" and "prismatic societies" employed to describe those societies dwelled on the intractability of local cultures faced with the need to accommodate modern development institutions and norms. Today the Confucian ethic and a rediscovered internal discipline can be advanced as the reasons East Asia and the Pacific Rim will economically challenge the West in the next century.

The prophecy of imminent doom in Africa cannot be dismissed, particularly considering the dreadful times the majority of the continent's people are now living through. But it would also be unwise to ignore the signs of hope, which could be amplified over time to allow the region to recover lost ground, should the leaders and thinkers of sub-Saharan Africa decide to do so. The right's current pessimism and the conspiracy theories of the left are inclined to throw the baby of hope out with the bathwater.

POSTSCRIPT

Is Africa Heading Toward Disaster?

Part of Africa's future will depend on the willingness of the outside world, especially the wealthy industrialized nations, to not forget Africa and, instead, to address its problems. The economically developed countries, for example, acted to help relieve many developing countries, especially those in Latin America, of their crushing foreign debt. Much less has been done for Africa, as is pointed out by E. Wayne Nafziger in *The Debt Crisis in Africa* (Johns Hopkins University Press, 1993). Moreover, many commentators complain that the assistance offered to Africa by such international institutions as the World Bank and the International Monetary Fund often come with strings attached that may even retard the economic growth of recipient countries. This view can be found in H. Brand, "The World Bank, the Monetary Fund, and Poverty," *Dissent* (Fall 1993).

Some critics argue that the industrialized nations, because of their responsibility for what has occurred in Africa, must extend more support. For a study of how colonialism has affected African societies and their politics, consult William S. Miles, *Hausaland Divided: Colonialism and Independence in Nigeria and Niger* (Cornell University Press, 1994). Another view that argues for support is the one that says that poverty breeds anger, creating an unstable world in which even the poorest nations are acquiring or will be able soon to acquire the military capability to present serious threats. On this point, Donald M. Snow, *Distant Thunder: Third World Conflict and the New International Order* (St. Martin's Press, 1993) is instructive.

It is also well to strike a balance between the overly rosy view that current problems will one day evaporate by themselves and the unduly gloomy view that whatever is currently a problem is permanent. Remember that part of the troubles in Africa may be short-term. The early 1990s have been especially troublesome for sub-Saharan Africa, marked by dropping commodity prices, lagging development, the violence that poverty so often breeds, and by unstable transitions from colonial rule, through more or less authoritarian self-government, to democracy. The volume *Economic Change and Political Liberalization in Sub-Saharan Africa* (Johns Hopkins University Press, 1994), edited by Jennifer A. Widner, includes a number of articles by various scholars who examine the progress toward democracy, within the context of poverty, that has occurred in Africa during the 1990s. This volume can be supplemented with a look at economic development in Africa in *Political Development and the New Realism in Sub-Saharan Africa* (University of Virginia Press, 1994), edited by David E. Apter and Carl G. Rosberg.

PART 2

Economics and International Affairs

International economic and trade issues have an immediate and personal effect on individuals in ways that few other international issues do. They influence the jobs we hold and the prices of the products we buy—in short, our lifestyles. In the worldwide competition for resources and markets, tensions arise between allies and adversaries alike. This section examines some of the prevailing economic tensions.

- Is the United States Unfairly Pressing Japan to Adopt Managed Trade?

- Should the Developed North Increase Aid to the Less Developed South?

- Is Free Trade a Desirable International Goal?

- Does Immigration Strain Society's Resources?

ISSUE 8

Is the United States Unfairly Pressing Japan to Adopt Managed Trade?

YES: Jagdish Bhagwati, from "Samurais No More," *Foreign Affairs* (May/June 1994)

NO: Roger C. Altman, from "Why Pressure Tokyo?" *Foreign Affairs* (May/June 1994)

ISSUE SUMMARY

YES: Jagdish Bhagwati, who is the Arthur Lehman Professor of Economics at Columbia University, argues that Japan's era of explosive growth is over and that Washington's attempts to institute managed trade are neither economically nor politically wise.

NO: Roger C. Altman, deputy secretary of the U.S. Department of the Treasury, maintains that the United States is not pressing Japan for managed trade. However, Japan must come to an agreement with the United States, he contends, about how to reduce Japan's merchandise trade surplus with the United States.

Two factors account for much of the current strain in the economic relations between the United States and Japan. Trade is one factor; the end of the cold war is the other. The trade data is indisputable, even if there are disagreements over how to interpret it. Japan runs a huge trade surplus with the United States and the rest of the world. Globally, Japan piled up a $140 billion merchandise trade surplus in 1993; the United States amassed a $137 billion trade deficit. For the global trade in services, there is an American surplus and a Japanese deficit of approximately equal amounts (about $42 billion). Within the context of Japan's overall trade surplus and the overall U.S. deficit, the bilateral trade relations between the two countries are particularly contentious. Japan has run a persistent surplus with the United States in what is called the "current accounts balance" (made up of three money flows: merchandise trade, services, and investment income). The merchandise trade between the two countries is the main issue of dispute, and in 1993 Japan accumulated a $60 billion surplus. This was offset somewhat by a $15 billion U.S. surplus for services and investment income combined, leaving the United States with a $45 billion current accounts balance deficit for 1993.

While these figures are stark, they are not particularly new. The U.S. trade deficit with Japan is long-standing. What has changed is the shape of the international system and U.S.–Japan relations within the post–cold war world. During the cold war, U.S.–Japan economic differences were suppressed in the interest of maintaining a united political front in the face of the opposing superpower bloc. With the disappearance of the Soviet Union, however, the political glue that held the Western alliance together has weakened considerably, and relations among the United States, Japan, and the European Union are more acrimonious.

Since the end of World War II, Japan has become an economic superpower. Meanwhile the United States has experienced a relative decline in its global economic position. The United States remains the world's largest economy; in 1993, the $6.38 trillion U.S. gross domestic product (GDP) was more than twice as large as Japan's $2.6 trillion GDP. Still, Japan's trade surplus with the United States has rankled many Americans and brought charges that Japan's economic tactics are predatory.

In addition to the unbalanced financial flow, there is American concern about the pattern of trade. The top 10 Japanese exports (measured in dollars) to the United States are high technology (such as computers, electronic components) and heavy industry (vehicles, vehicle parts and accessories). By contrast, only half of the top 10 U.S. exports to Japan are heavy industry (such as aircraft) or high technology (such as precision instruments), while the other half are primary products (wood, meat, corn, fish, tobacco) that are less stable in terms of price and market. Japan still dominates the U.S. auto market; Coca-Cola has 60 percent of Japan's soft drink market.

Since the late 1980s, ongoing discussions between the United States and Japan have not resolved trade disputes. Both governments have urged the other to take politically difficult moves. Americans, for example, want the Japanese to act like Americans; that is, for example, to spend more (go further into debt) and to allow superstore retailers to displace (and economically ruin) legions of small retailers. The Japanese in turn urge Americans to be a bit more Japanese in such ways as spending less and reducing the federal budget deficit. Neither government has made much headway in the face of strong domestic pressures.

One solution is the idea of managed trade. What this means is that the two sides would agree on specific targets for exports and imports and would use quotas and other mechanisms to ensure a more even relationship between exports and imports. When President Bill Clinton met with Prime Minister Kiichi Miyazawa in Tokyo in 1993, the president called for setting "objective criteria" to be used to measure progress. The Japanese rejected such quotas as a violation of free trade and license for Americans to say what and how much of U.S. products and services the Japanese had to buy.

In the following debate, economist Jagdish Bhagwati counsels that pressing Japan for a system of managed trade is unwise policy. Roger Altman, of the U.S. Treasury Department, argues that the United States is not really advocating managed trade but that criteria have to be set in order to evaluate Japan's seriousness about reducing the trade deficit.

YES

Jagdish Bhagwati

SAMURAIS NO MORE

The failure of the February 11 [1994] Hosokawa-Clinton summit in Washington to produce a trade agreement on U.S. terms was marked by theatrics on the American side. Deputy Treasury Secretary Roger Altman's banter was typical. He declared, with the bluntness that Wall Street breeds, that the United States would wait "until hell freezes over" for the Japanese to accept U.S. demands. When Prime Minister Hosokawa finally said no to them, the American anger was palpable.

U.S. Trade Representative Mickey Kantor brought to center stage the Motorola cellular phones dispute, which the administration had readied to coincide with the summit by speeding up ongoing negotiations. Amenable to manipulation as "proof" of Japan's perfidy, the dispute was also the one most likely to be settled at a low cost, financial and political, by the Hosokawa government to save U.S. face: a crumb thrown to the United States, it could be called a cake.

Indeed Japan ended the dispute by bribing Motorola with investment outlays while affirming the dispute's uniqueness and reiterating the policy of saying no. The Clinton administration, predictably, performed a war dance, celebrating a victory in a skirmish as if it had won the war, attributing the Motorola settlement to American resolve and threats, particularly to the president's revival in March of the "Super 301" weapon, which authorizes the administration to highlight countries it determines are trading unfairly and, if it chooses, to impose trade sanctions in retaliation.

BREAKING ITS OWN RULES

The Clinton administration, however, cannot conceal the reality that its policy is fatally flawed. The policy makes demands that are inconsistent with the very principles on which the United States has itself provided leadership in shaping the world trading system over half a century. As important, the policy fails to grasp the significant changes that make both the style and the substance of these demands unacceptable to the new Japan. American policy is thus both unworthy and unworkable.

From Jagdish Bhagwati, "Samurais No More," *Foreign Affairs*, vol. 73, no. 3 (May/June 1994). Copyright © 1994 by The Council on Foreign Relations, Inc. Reprinted by permission of *Foreign Affairs*.

The problems with that policy concern "quantities" and "process." The United States wants managed trade: specifically, it wants the Japanese government to accept numerical benchmarks and targets for increased imports in specific sectors. It is also pressing for one-way concessions from Japan in areas where the United States has judged Japan to be either closed to imports or in violation of treaty obligations, acting unilaterally instead of using impartial procedures to which Japan would also have recourse. In both respects, the United States has the double disadvantage of having been roundly condemned by other nations and of having not the remotest chance of acceptance by Japan.

Benchmarks are only a weasel word for targets (that is, quotas), and these import targets quickly turn into export protectionism: they work to guarantee for American firms a share of the foreign market just as conventional import protectionism gives firms a guaranteed share of the domestic market.

These targets will multiply because they are open to manipulation by domestic firms that seek assured export markets. When Japan unwisely accepted the Reagan administration's demand for a numerical benchmark (for the first time in U.S.-Japan trade negotiations), economists had forecast that other firms and industries would soon jump on the bandwagon. It was too rewarding a precedent not to exploit, and indeed that is exactly what has happened. Now a complaisant administration has become the agent for the lobbyists of industries such as autos, auto parts and medical equipment, seeking to impose many more such agreements on Japan.

The proliferation of such import targets to several sectors would also bring other countries onto the scene demanding their own guaranteed share of the Japanese market. The reason is plain enough: Japan must be fully aware that if it opens up to imports but those imports do not come from the United States, the pressure from Washington will continue. So Japan will have a powerful incentive to divert its imports from other nations to the United States, even if the United States pretends that its objective is to open the Japanese economy, not throw contracts the way of American firms. Hence, properly fearing trade diversion, the European Union [EU] has always said that if Japan concedes import targets to the United States, the EU will be right behind.

If numbers rather than rules are accepted as the way to conduct trade, the prospect is then certain that Japanese industry would soon be subject to heavy regulation and compelled to produce the politically agreed market shares. This would be bad enough for Japan. But it would also be a low blow to the rules-based world trading system that the United States has professed to uphold at the General Agreement on Tariffs and Trade.

In consequence, the United States, traditionally the leader on trade issues to the applause of economists, has found itself opposed by economists, whether Democrats or Republicans. There is also little support for America's Super 301-aided unilateralism. Washington is isolated when it wants to take the law in its own hands, especially now that the Uruguay Round has produced a binding settlement procedure. Even if Japan were guilty as charged, it is unacceptable that the United States should become complainant, judge and jury.

THE NEW JAPAN

Japan's resistance to U.S. demands was urged worldwide—from Europe in particular—undoubtedly strengthening Hosokawa's resolve to say no. But that resolve comes from within Japan itself, reflecting the nuanced yet remarkable changes that Japan is undergoing. The Clinton administration simply does not get it: the new Japan is trying to be like the old United States just as the new United States, with its flirtation with industrial policy, embrace of demands for managed trade, and (as in the president's announcement of the Saudi purchase of U.S. aircraft) unabashed use of political muscle rather than economic competitiveness to succeed in world markets, is trying to be like the old Japan.

Hosokawa, and the large numbers of reform-minded Japanese who voted the Liberal Democratic Party out of power, wish an end to old-fashioned regulation. Managed trade would turn the clock back when they want to push it forward. The reformers also believe in reciprocal rights and obligations; they reject unilateralism and want multilateralism; they want due process, not the peremptory judgments of the United States (which reflect the self-serving finger-pointing of individual U.S. companies).

Ironically, but predictably, these are American ideas. They have spread rapidly to Japan because, among other reasons, Japan has large numbers of its young citizens abroad. Over 40,000 Japanese students are in the United States today, learning to put their feet on the table in the classroom instead of meekly bowing to the *sensei* (the venerable teacher). With the dramatic shift in the 1980s in the share of Japanese direct foreign investment away from the poor countries to the rich, prompted in part by the outbreak of protectionism in the EU and in the United States, which restricted export access to these markets, great numbers of Japanese women and children also live in the West. They are a subversive, modernizing force. Increased numbers of Japanese academics can now be found on U.S. campuses, speaking English fluently and working with Americans at the frontiers of science when only a decade ago there were practically none.

The Japan that was so set on what the historian Henry Smith has aptly called "controlled openness"—drawing carefully on what it liked in other cultures rather than abandoning itself, like the United States, to free cultural influx and experimentation—is now beyond such control. The globalization of the Japanese economy and modern communications imposes its own logic on the nation. But the Clinton aides in charge of Japan policy, mainly Wall Street luminaries and high-profile lawyer-lobbyists with lifestyles that leave little room for reflection and put a premium on going for the jugular, appear to be ignorant of this historic transformation. These Clinton warriors think they are fighting the samurai when they are facing GIs....

In the end, the flaw in U.S. policy derives from the exaggeration of Japan's differences of yesterday as much as from an ignorance of its rapid convergence to the United States today. Washington is obsessed with the view that Japan is different and special, a predatory exporter and an exclusionary importer that must be dealt with as an outlaw, what Jonathan Rauch has called an "out-nation," with tough external *gaiatsu*

Figure 1
Import Penetration of Seven High-Tech Markets: 1981 and 1992

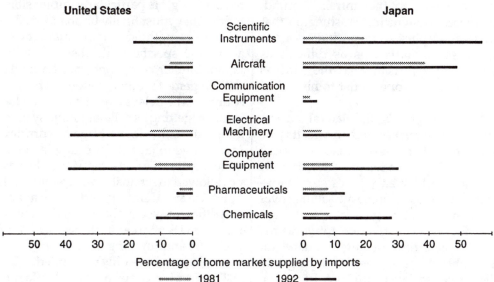

Percentage of home market supplied by imports

1981   1992

(foreign pressure) and targets to restrain exports and expand imports.

Economic analysis hardly supports such stereotypes. The simpleminded assertion coming from the Clinton administration that, because Japan's share of manufactured imports in GNP [gross national product] is below the average of the Group of Seven industrialized nations, Japan "underimports" and has a closed market requiring special measures is nonsense. By that token, since Canada's share is substantially higher than the United States', the United States should be judged closed relative to Canada. Sophisticated econometric studies of the question are badly divided; the better-crafted of these certainly do not support the thesis that Japan imports too little, nor do they indicate a special and extraordinary effect of informal trade barriers that make Japan a fit case for unusual treatment in the world trading system.

Even the imports by Japan of manufactured goods, a persistent source of complaint, have grown in the last decade to over half of its imports. Moreover, the foreign share in many of Japan's high-tech markets, so dear to Clintonites, is by no means static or small. [Figure 1], based on recently released data from the National Science Foundation, shows that in seven important high-tech markets, the U.S. and Japanese import shares look pretty similar, so much so that if the industries and the countries were blacked out, one could well mistake the U.S. chart for Japan's.

The notion of Japan's overwhelming difference nonetheless persists because it is reinforced by the egregious fallacy, often repeated by the president and his aides in public, that Japan's huge bilateral surplus with the United States is surefire proof that Japan's markets are closed, requiring a concentration of one's wrath and energy on Japan. Occasionally, counterintuitive economic sense will prevail for a moment, but then fallacy, so compelling to the untrained mind, resurfaces. Convincing Washington that bilateral surpluses are no index of the openness of markets is as difficult as convincing a peasant that the earth is round when it appears flat to his naked eye.

Nor does Japan's multilateral surplus set it apart as wicked and bizarre. Its persistence is shorter-lived than America's own surplus in the two decades after the Second World War. Japan's surplus reflects its excess of domestic savings over investment and is generally to be applauded as a contribution to world net savings at a time of huge demand for investible funds in the developing and the former socialist countries. In the immediate short run, Japan can certainly contribute to its own recovery and indirectly help the United States by undertaking the significant fiscal stimulus that Hosokawa had worked to get. But all macroeconomists agree that the spillover or "locomotive" effect of Japanese stimulus on U.S. prosperity will be small, making even this obsession of the Clinton administration seem strange. In short, nothing here requires that the United States think that Japan is "off the curve" in responsible macroeconomic management: its mistakes are no more gargantuan than those of the United States, for example, during the decade of fiscal irresponsibility from which it has just emerged.

COOPERATION, NOT CONFRONTATION

The cancer at the core of the U.S. policy then is the view that the United States needs a differential treatment of Japan and a special framework agreement. The justifications for that premise, never strong, are particularly implausible today. They must finally be abandoned.

There is nothing extraordinary even about the specific trade disputes with Japan. Similar complaints can be made with regard to other nations. The accounts of the delays experienced by Motorola in getting its cellular phone system adopted in the Tokyo-Nagoya corridor (one of two in Japan), for example, must be set against the facts that Motorola was not allowed to set up its own system at all in France and Germany and had to adapt to a different system there, and that entry into the U.S. market itself has been impeded by antidumping harassment. Such examples can be readily multiplied.

The time has come to admit that Japan must be allowed to trade by rules rather than quantities, and that the rules must include the adjudication of disputes by impartial procedures available to both parties. The notion that U.S.-Japan trade issues are so special that they must be dealt with bilaterally in a framework that permits the United States to impose one-way demands on Japan and to pronounce unilaterally its own verdicts that Japan has "failed to live up to its agreements" must finally be laid to rest.

Will the president, no stranger to principled and bold changes of course, rise to the occasion? It will not be easy: the failed trade policy toward Japan is most likely his own. After all, the North American Free Trade Agreement and the Uruguay Round were Republican initiatives; he needed one of his own. The Silicon Valley entrepreneurs were the first to swing to him during the campaign; he bought their view of Japan. He chose advisers that shared these jaundiced views. He chose a U.S. trade representative and a commerce secretary who proudly say that they disdain economic "theology" and want results; so they reflect interests, not principles, as they confront Japan.

The president may have fancied that he would have the glory of "opening Japan," as a sort of modern-day Commodore Perry. That historical parallel will not work. The tragedy is that, by persisting in the current policy, he may put two great nations on a course that may repeat history in less agreeable ways.

NO   Roger C. Altman

WHY PRESSURE TOKYO?

The strained relations between Japan and the United States cannot be explained by spurious charges that the Clinton administration is pushing managed trade, capitalizing on anti-Japanese sentiment to score domestic political points or needlessly bashing Japan over economically meaningless international surpluses. Rather, the tensions arise from two fundamental and related developments: changed American priorities and the pronounced drag of Japan's huge current account surplus on global demand, economic expansion and job creation.

The Clinton administration's drive to spur global economic growth and strengthen U.S. economic potential requires a new deal with Japan. For itself and all other nations, the United States is seeking to converge Japan's international accounts with the rest of the industrialized world and to open Japan's markets.

NO MORE FREE RIDE

The search for such convergence marks a transition in U.S.-Japan relations—the fourth such transition since World War II. First came the reconstruction period, running through the early 1950s, in which the United States consciously helped rebuild Japan's industrial capacity in order to make democracy permanent. The United States tolerated Japan's protection of home markets, its resurrection of certain prewar practices and the resulting *keiretsu* [interlocking companies] structure of industrial cross-share holdings, in which companies cooperate informally.

The second phase began with the 1952 Mutual Security Assistance pact, which ended U.S. occupation of Japan. The pact extended the U.S. nuclear umbrella over Japan and made Japan the Asian cornerstone of the Cold War containment strategy. Japan became vital to the defense of Pacific sea-lanes and host to the largest U.S. military base in the region. Although economic issues were steadily emerging, they remained secondary to security interests.

Japan's growing economic prowess ushered in the third phase, which lasted from the early 1970s until the end of the Cold War. During that period

From Roger C. Altman, "Why Pressure Tokyo?" *Foreign Affairs*, vol. 73, no. 3 (May/June 1994). Copyright © 1994 by The Council on Foreign Relations, Inc. Reprinted by permission of *Foreign Affairs*.

economic policy differences and trade frictions continually rose even while the security issue remained paramount. Japanese firms, assisted by Tokyo's administrative guidance and targeted industrial policies, became world-class producers and successful competitors for export markets. Aided by massive domestic savings and an undervalued yen, Japan ran growing trade and current account surpluses with the rest of the world, especially the United States. U.S. pressure on Japan to open its home market produced a pattern whereby the Japanese government engaged in protracted trade negotiations while opening its economy as little as possible. When agreements were finally reached, they were often vaguely worded and subject to conflicting interpretations.

Beginning in 1993, the U.S.-Japan relationship was jolted into its fourth phase by newly elected President Clinton, whose sense of post-Cold War priorities put economic matters first. Assessing the relationship, his administration found the security component to be solid and cooperation on global development and environmental issues to be in working order. But the economic dimension was badly in need of repair and required a new perspective on Japan. A diminished need for a bulwark against Soviet expansionism accompanied a rise of other viable economic partners in the Asia-Pacific region. Within the United States, public attention sharply shifted toward unmet domestic needs. The electorate wanted a leader whose primary focus was jobs and economic growth at home. And in trade competition, the public, business and Congress clamored for tough action to level the playing fields, particularly with Japan.

MEASURABLE RESULTS

The Clinton administration conceived its policy on three broad premises. The first premise was that ending stagnation at home required key initiatives, of which the first was congressional passage of the president's $500 billion deficit reduction plan. The second premise was that Japan's trade surplus of $130 billion ($50 billion with the United States) was too large to be sustained. Weak stimulus packages were inadequately addressing this surplus, despite Japan's structural budget surplus. The third premise was that continued recalcitrance explained why Japan's imports of manufactured goods represented only 3.1 percent of Japan's GNP [gross national product] compared to an average of 7.4 percent for other Group of Seven countries [G-7, which includes Canada, France, Germany, Great Britain, Italy, Japan, and the United States]....

Thus a fresh U.S. approach was needed. The new relationship required a framework encompassing both macroeconomic and trade policy. Stronger domestic demand-led growth in Japan would help facilitate import penetration. The trade component would focus on removing structural and sectoral barriers to raise the quantity of imports the Japanese will buy when their incomes increase and thereby reduce the current account imbalance. After tough negotiating, the framework agreement of July 1993 committed both parties to four basic commitments, two on each side.

The Clinton administration committed to further deficit reduction efforts and policies to raise savings and improve competitiveness. The administration also pledged a continued openness of U.S.

domestic markets provided that Japan holds up its end of the bargain.

For its part, Japan agreed to pursue policies that over the "medium term" would lead to a "highly significant" reduction in its global current account surpluses. The United States made clear that it interpreted "highly significant" to mean a fall in those surpluses from 3.5 percent of GDP [gross domestic product] to below 2 percent. Further, the United States defined the "medium term" to mean three to four years. Japan's second commitment was to pursue structural and sectoral policies that would lead to a significant increase in imports from all countries (not just the United States) over the same period. The American interpretation of "significant" was a one-third increase. In fairness, however, the U.S. interpretation in both cases was unilateral. Japan fiercely resisted quantifying these areas in the agreement and acknowledges only that the United States has such interpretations.

Nevertheless, in a significant departure from past agreements, a provision called for "qualitative or quantitative indicators" to measure progress. To the United States, this provision meant the two countries had finally agreed to a dialogue on measurable results. But the ink had barely dried on this provision before a fierce public relations campaign ensued against the use of such indicators. The Japanese claimed the agreement represented managed trade and that such a results-oriented approach is antithetical to liberalized trade. Indeed, they argued, the United States was demanding market-share targets in key sectors similar to those granted in the now-infamous 1986 semiconductor agreement.

The rhetorical campaign has been skillful, and many editorialists and econ-omists have joined the criticism. To be fair, the Clinton administration has occasionally compounded the problem by sending ambiguous signals. But Japan's rhetorical campaign does not withstand close scrutiny. The Japanese government that berates the United States on charges of managed trade has long been in the business of targeting market outcomes itself. Furthermore the same government agencies that make these pronouncements have tolerated a remarkable degree of collusion among private Japanese companies at the expense of foreign firms.

The reality is that the agreement does not mandate market-share targets, and the United States is not seeking targets. The issues are goals and measurability. In any particular sector, the U.S. aim is to negotiate a series of long-term goals and objective standards against which progress can be judged. The overall goal should be convergence toward international standards of market openness. Moreover, any particular sector can have several measurements. In the auto sector, for example, measurements might include increases in Japanese dealerships that sell both foreign and Japanese cars and domestic content levels in Japanese cars produced in the United States. The framework would measure progress against a series of these indicators of which no one measure would dominate.

The goal of market openness cannot be seriously disputed. It can be achieved almost entirely by deregulation, and that had been a central theme of Japanese Prime Minister Morihiro Hosokawa. And measurable results have no good argument to oppose them. If fair measures are chosen, the entire world can judge whether progress has occurred or not. Nor is the framework an attempt to reconstruct Japan in the U.S. image. The U.S. emphasis on results is precisely designed to shift the debate away from changing the nature of the Japanese economic system.

This new approach is not a bilateral deal for the United States and Japan. The U.S. goal is to open Japanese markets for the benefit of producers from all countries; reducing trade barriers is sought solely on a most-favored-nation basis. The new framework is not only consistent with the principles of the General Agreement on Tariffs and Trade [GATT], but, insofar as Japan's closed markets and unbalanced trade represent a major threat to the soundness of the multilateral trading system, the framework is essential to the viability of the GATT system.

The framework is also essential to maintaining support for further market-opening agreements around the world. For example, congressional support of the North American Free Trade Agreement or GATT cannot be obtained if Japan's import penetration problem is simply accepted. Those who say that the growth and job gains from opening Japanese markets are trivial and that the whole effort is misguided show no appreciation for this reality. In Washington, it is a matter of fairness.

The framework's objectives are consistent with the basic aspirations of people everywhere: lower prices, greater consumer choice and higher living standards, a reduction in international tensions and an improvement in their nation's standing. These principles have particular resonance today, given the new Japanese government's emphasis on improving the lot of the Japanese consumer.

IT'S JAPAN'S MOVE

Unfortunately, the two sides were unable to meet the framework's first six-month deadline for sub-agreements in the procurement, automotive and insurance sectors. Moreover, the macroeconomic developments were also disappointing. Tokyo announced a six trillion yen tax cut, ostensibly to boost domestic demand and work down the current account surplus. But the cut took the form of a rebate, with no assurance of lasting after one year. Such one-time tax cuts usually induce savings rather than spending and do not provide meaningful stimulus. Indeed, most analysts estimated that the tax cut would add only 0.7 percent to growth in 1994 and would cut the current account surplus by only $2 billion. The United States registered its disappointment with the tax package.

President Clinton and Prime Minister Hosokawa acknowledged these failures during their remarkably candid summit on February 11 [1994]. The president noted a particular disagreement over the issue of targets. He reaffirmed that the United States was not seeking guaranteed market outcomes, which is how most observers interpret the term "targets." He noted, however, that Japan feared that any goals would ultimately be interpreted as mandatory targets. As a result, therefore, Tokyo was unwilling to accept a combination of goals and measurements. For its part, Washington was adamant. "No agreement was better than an empty agreement," the president said.

Now the talks are suspended and both sides agree that the ball is in Japan's court. Discussions will only recommence if Tokyo develops a new proposal that responds to the framework criteria. After a cooling-off period, there is no reason why such an initiative should not come forward.

In the interim, the United States is taking some unilateral steps. The first has been to reexamine existing trade disputes and seek negotiated solutions or apply sanctions. An obvious example of this step was the cellular phone case and the finding that Japan was in violation. Almost all neutral observers agreed that Motorola had been denied a fair market opportunity. That is why Japan moved and a good agreement ensued, as had happened a few months earlier in the construction case. The second step involved the reimposition by executive order of the Super 301 trade tool. This tool requires identifying, every six months, "priority practices in priority countries" that violate Section 301 of the U.S. trade law. No such countries or practices will be designated before September 30. The administration carefully chose a flexible version of this tool, not the heavy-handed approach favored by some in Congress.

Other steps will be taken in a calm, deliberate manner. This is not a trade war, nor will it spin out of control. The United States will move only where the substance of a dispute is clear. Ultimately, the U.S.-Japan relationship will surmount this period of friction. These are the two largest economies in the world and they are highly interdependent. The security relationship remains strong and important, and the two nations share a vital agenda on global political cooperation.

The time has come for Japan to move toward global convergence in terms of its international accounts and the openness of its markets. On these points, industrialized nations concur even if some disagree with the particulars of the American approach. What issues and challenges will dominate the next century are unclear, but two things are certain: economics will be at the center of international affairs, and the U.S.-Japan partnership will play a key role in determining the course of global events. The Clinton administration is committed to charting a new course of relations with Japan that builds on these emerging realities.

POSTSCRIPT

Is the United States Unfairly Pressing Japan to Adopt Managed Trade?

During 1994 the strains between the United States and Japan have escalated. The approximately $60 billion U.S. deficit with Japan clearly indicates that little or no progress has been made. Several factors have created the stalemate. Both countries had been suffering economic woes, and those in Japan have persisted. The lagging economies have intensified pressures within each country to protect industries and workers. When Japan opened its rice market to wider foreign competition in 1993, Japanese rice farmers rose in stormy protest. Furthermore, both the American and Japanese governments have been unable to push through unpopular programs.

The bilateral meeting between President Bill Clinton and Prime Minister Morihiro Hosokawa in Washington during February 1994 was the least cordial meeting of American and Japanese heads of government in decades. Clinton was particularly stormy, publicly telling Hosokawa that Japan's markets "still remain less open to imports than any other [industrial country's markets]." Hosokawa rejected working toward managed trade, telling the audience at the joint press conference that "At the very end we were not able to clear the hurdle of numerical targets." For one look into the thinking of officials in the Clinton administration, consult *Who's Bashing Whom? Trade Conflict in High-Technology Industries* (International Institute for Economics, 1992) by Laura D'Andrea Tyson, who now heads the President's Council of Economic Advisers.

After the frustrating meeting, Clinton signed an executive order that would enable him to use Super 301 quickly to place sanctions on Japan if progress on trade issues was not made. The Japanese responded negatively to this clear threat. Japan also issued a 33-page report detailing alleged unfair U.S. trade practices.

For more on the causes and the chances of an equitable and amicable solution to U.S.–Japan trade relations, read C. Fred Bergsten and Marcus Noland, *Reconcilable Differences? United States–Japan Economic Conflict* (International Institute for Economics, 1993). At least part of the solution is for Americans to better understand Japan, its culture, and (like the United States) its domestic pressures. This process can be served by reading Steven R. Reed, *Making Sense of Japan* (University of Pittsburgh Press, 1994). It is also important to remember that trade conflict will almost inevitably spill over to affect U.S.–Japan political relations negatively. A discussion of these implications is available in David T. Mason and Abdul M. Turay, *U.S.–Japan Trade Friction: Its Impact on Security and Cooperation in the Pacific Basin* (Macmillan, 1994).

ISSUE 9

Should the Developed North Increase Aid to the Less Developed South?

YES: James P. Grant, from "Jumpstarting Development," *Foreign Policy* (Summer 1993)

NO: Editors of *The Economist*, from "The Kindness of Strangers," *The Economist* (May 7, 1994)

ISSUE SUMMARY

YES: United Nations executive James Grant contends that one way to jumpstart solutions to many of the world's problems is to extend more assistance to impoverished countries.

NO: The editors of *The Economist*, a well-known British publication, suggest that the usual ways in which international aid is distributed and spent make it a waste of resources and may even have a negative impact on the recipients.

One stark characteristic of the world system is that it is divided into two economic classes of countries. There is the North, which is industrialized and relatively prosperous. Then there is the South, which is mostly nonindustrial and relatively, and sometimes absolutely, impoverished. The countries that comprise the South are also called the Third World, or less developed countries, or developing countries. By whatever name they are known, however, Third World countries have conditions that are unacceptable. At a macroeconomic level, approximately three-quarters of the world's people live in the Third World, yet they possess only about one-seventh of the world's wealth (measured in gross national products, GNPs). On a more personal level, if you had been born in the South (compared to the North), your life would be almost 25 percent shorter; you would earn less than 8 percent of what you earn in the North; your children would be almost 8 times as likely to die before age 5; and it would be 11 times harder to find a physician.

Despite the rhetoric of the North about the Third World's plight, the countries of the North do relatively little to help. For example, U.S. economic foreign aid in 1991 was $11.3 billion, which amounted to only about half of what Americans spent in retail liquor stores. Canada's foreign aid in 1991 ($2.6 billion) was equivalent to only about a third of what its citizens spent on tobacco. Foreign investment in the Third World is also extremely limited, and while there has been an increase in recent years, it has been directed mostly at the relatively few countries—South Korea, for example—that have been able join the ranks of what are called newly industrializing countries (NICs). Furthermore, loans to the Third World have declined, and repayment of existing loans is draining capital away from many less developed countries. Trade earnings are another possible source of development capital, but the raw materials produced and exported by most Third World countries earn them little compared to the cost of importing the more expensive finished products manufactured by the North.

There are a number of ways of approaching this issue of greater aid by the North for the South. One approach focuses on morality. Are we morally obligated to help less fortunate humans? A second explores more aid as a means of promoting the North's own self-interest. Some analysts contend that a fully developed world would mean greater prosperity for everyone and would be more stable politically. A third avenue pursues the causes for the Third World's poverty and lack of development in order to assess who or what is responsible.

It is possible to divide views on the origins and continuance of the North-South gap into three groups. One believes that the uneven (but unintended) spread of the Industrial Revolution resulted in unequal economic development. A second group finds the Third World itself responsible for much of its continuing poverty. Advocates of this view charge the Third World with failure to control its population, with lack of political stability, with poor economic planning, and with a variety of other ill-conceived practices that impede development. This group believes that foreign aid is wasteful and destructive of the policies needed to spur economic development.

A third group maintains that the North bears much of the responsibility for the South's condition and, therefore, is obligated to help the Third World. Those who hold this view contend that the colonization of the Third World, especially during the 1800s when the Industrial Revolution rapidly took hold in the North, destroyed the indigenous economic, social, and political organizations needed for development. The colonial powers then kept their dependencies underdeveloped in order to ensure a supply of cheap raw materials. Even though virtually all former colonies are now independent, this view continues, and the developed countries continue to follow political and economic strategies designed to keep the Third World underdeveloped and dependent.

In the following debate, James P. Grant takes the position that, notwithstanding the poor media image of the Third World as a lost cause, there is real momentum for change. He believes that if the children of the Third World can be educated, kept healthy, and given other advantages, they can be the force for rapid positive change in the Third World. The editors of *The Economist*, in opposition, argue that aid is ill-managed today, and that even if aid were vastly increased and managed well, the question about whether or not the recipient countries would do much better can only be answered with a "maybe."

YES

James P. Grant

JUMPSTARTING DEVELOPMENT

Anyone who thought, amidst the euphoria of dizzying change starting in 1989, that the end of the Cold War would usher in an age of global harmony and easy solutions has long since been disabused of the notion. Every day we open our newspapers to dark headlines confirming that the world is still a very dangerous place—in some ways more dangerous than before. We are confronted with a host of problems, both old and new, that are reaching crisis proportions. Is there a way of "jumpstarting" solutions to many of those problems? In fact, there is.

To many, it may not seem so. Ethnic conflict, religious hatred, failed states, economic devastation in Eastern Europe and the former Soviet Union, AIDS, and environmental degradation all seem intractable problems. Meanwhile, the number of poor in the world continues to increase at about the same rate as the world's population. The World Bank put their number at 1.1 billion in 1990. A fifth of the world's population is living on less than one dollar a day, and during the 1980s the poor actually lost ground. The 1990s show little evidence that the world economy will return anytime soon to a high growth trajectory.

The negative trends have even begun to afflict the rich. In the last decade, poverty increased in a number of industrialized countries, most notably in the United States and the United Kingdom and, of course, in the former communist countries of Europe. In most of those countries, children bore the brunt of the reversal. In America today, one in five children is poor, the highest level of child poverty in a quarter century in the world's richest country. In both the United Kingdom and the United States, child poverty has nearly doubled in a decade.

Small wonder that the lead article in this journal's spring issue contended that "all the trends" are in the wrong direction and that the world "appears to be at the beginning, not of a new order, but of a new nightmare." Such pessimism, however, can be misplaced. The world is in fact on the threshold of being able to make vastly greater progress on many problems that have long seemed intractable. Rather than merely reacting to situations after they have become critical, as in Somalia, the world has an opportunity in the 1990s

From James P. Grant, "Jumpstarting Development," *Foreign Policy*, no. 91 (Summer 1993). Copyright © 1993 by The Carnegie Endowment for International Peace. Reprinted by permission of *Foreign Policy*.

to make an effective—and efficient— social investment to convert despair into hope and go a long way toward preventing future crises and building healthy societies.

The situation today may be analogous to that of Asia in the mid 1960s, when population growth seemed set to out- run the food supply. Many predicted widespread famine, chaos, and instabil- ity for the last third of this century. But then, quite suddenly, within four or five years, the Green Revolution took hold in Asia, extending from the Philippines through South Asia to Turkey. In country after country, wheat and rice production increased at annual rates unprecedented in the West. The immediate cause was not so much a scientific breakthrough— strains of the miracle wheats had been around for as many as 15 years—as a po- litical and organizational one. Only by the mid 1960s had fertilizer, pesticides, and controlled irrigation become widely used, thanks in large part to earlier aid programs. At the same time, the combi- nation of Asian drought and increasing awareness of the population explosion created the political will to drastically re- structure price levels for grains and agro- inputs, and to mobilize the multiple sec- tors of society—rural credit, marketing, transport, foreign exchange allocations, media—required for success. U.S. pres- ident Lyndon Johnson deserves credit for his leadership contribution to that effort, though his deep personal involvement remains a largely untold story.

We may be in a similar position today, but on a much broader front—poised for advances in primary health care, basic education, water supply and sanitation, family planning, and gender equity, as well as food production—and covering a much wider geographical area, including Africa and Latin America as well as Asia. With an earnest effort from the major powers, the 1990s could witness a second green revolution—extending, this time, beyond agriculture to human development.

Frequent illness, malnutrition, poor growth, illiteracy, high birth rates, and gender bias are among poverty's worst symptoms. They are also some of pov- erty's most fundamental causes. We could anticipate, therefore, that over- coming some of the worst symptoms and causes of poverty would have far- reaching repercussions on the national and global level. The recent experiences of such diverse societies as China, Costa Rica, the Indian state of Kerala, Sri Lanka, and the Asian newly industrial- izing countries (NICs) suggest that high population growth rates, which wrap the cycle of poverty ever tighter, can be re- duced dramatically. Reducing poverty would give a major boost to the fragile new efforts at democratization that will survive only if they tangibly improve the lives of the bottom half of society. As we know from the experience of Singapore, South Korea, Taiwan, and the other Asian NICs, such progress would in turn accel- erate economic growth. By breaking the "inner cycle" of poverty, we would in- crease the capacity of the development process to assault poverty's many exter- nal causes, rooted in such diverse factors as geography, climate, land tenure, debt, business cycles, governance, and unjust economic relations.

We are uniquely positioned to succeed in the 1990s. Recent scientific and techno- logical advances—and the revolutionary new capacity to communicate with and mobilize large numbers of people—have provided us with a host of new tools. The world's leaders can now use them together to produce dramatic, even unprecedented, results.

For example, the universal child immunization effort—the largest peacetime international collaboration in world history—has since the mid 1980s established systems that now reach virtually every hamlet in the developing world and are saving the lives of more than 8,000 children a day—some 3 million a year. Here, too, the technology was not new; vaccines had been available for some 20–30 years. Success has been the result of applying new communication and mobilization techniques to the immunization effort, often led personally by heads of state, making use of television and radio advertisements, and supported by a wide range of local leaders. School teachers, priests, imams, local government officials, nongovernmental organization (NGO) workers, and health personnel all joined the effort. By 1990, more than 80 per cent of the developing world's children were being brought in four or five times for vaccinations even before their first birthdays. As a result, Calcutta, Lagos, and Mexico City today have far higher levels of immunization of children at ages one and two than do New York City, Washington, D.C., or even the United States as a whole.

A similar effort is now being made to spread the use of oral rehydration therapy (ORT) to combat the single greatest historical killer of children, diarrhea, which takes the lives of some 8,000 children every day, down from 11,000 daily a decade ago. ORT was invented in the late 1960s, but only recently have leaders mobilized to use this lifesaver on a national scale. Every year it now saves the lives of more than 1 million children, a figure that could easily more than double by 1995 with increased national and international leadership.

The arsenal is now well stocked with other new technologies and rediscovered practices that can bring tremendous benefits with inspired leadership and only modest funding. Thus, the simple iodization of salt—at a cost of five cents annually per consumer—would prevent the world's single largest cause of mental retardation and of goiter, which affect more than 200 million people today as a result of iodine deficiency. Universal access to vitamin A through low-cost capsules or vegetables would remove the greatest single cause—about 700 cases per day—of blindness while reducing child deaths by up to a third in many parts of the developing world. The scientific rediscovery of the miracles of mother's milk means that more than a million children would not have died last year if only they had been effectively breast-fed for the first months of their lives, instead of being fed on more-costly infant formula. In such diverse countries as Bangladesh, Colombia, Senegal, and Zimbabwe, it has proven possible to get poor children, including girls, through primary education at very little cost. Recent advances have shown how to halve the costs of bringing sanitation and safe water to poor communities, to less than $30 per capita. New varieties of high-yield crops—from cassava to corn—are now ready to be promoted on a national scale in sub-Saharan Africa.

Meanwhile, with such tools in hand, the new capacity to communicate—to inform and motivate—empowers families, communities, and governments to give all children a better chance to lead productive lives. In short, we are now learning to "outsmart" poverty at the outset of each new life by providing a "bubble of protection" around a child's first vulnerable months and years. Strong international leadership and cooperation—facilitated enormously by the end of the Cold War and the expansion of democracy—could leverage that new capacity into wide-ranging social progress.

A CHILDREN'S REVOLUTION

Notwithstanding the media image of the Third World as a lost cause, there is real momentum there for change. In fact, for all the difficulties and setbacks, more progress has been made in developing countries in the last 40 years than was made in the previous 2,000, progress achieved while much of the world freed itself from colonialism and while respect for human and political rights expanded dramatically. Life expectancy has lengthened from 53 in 1960 to 65 today, and continues to increase at a rate of 9.5 hours per day. Thirty years ago, approximately three out of four children born in the developing countries survived to their fifth birthdays; today, some nine out of ten survive.

At the same time, the birth rates in countries as disparate as Brazil, China, Colombia, Cuba, Korea, Mexico, Sri Lanka, Thailand, and Tunisia have been more than halved, dramatically slowing population growth and the inherent strains it places on limited natural resources and social programs. Among the factors that have helped contain population growth, improving children's health is undoubtedly the least well-known and appreciated. As the United Nations Population Division puts it, "Improvements in child survival, which increase the predictability of the family building process, trigger the transition from natural to controlled fertility behavior. This in turn generates the need for family planning." While they are important priorities them-

selves, reductions in child mortality, basic education of women, and the availability of family planning make a strong synergistic contribution to solving what Yale historian Paul Kennedy calls, in *Preparing for the Twenty-First Century* (1992), the "impending demographic disaster." As population specialist Sharon Camp noted in the Spring 1993 issue of FOREIGN POLICY:

> Measures like quality reproductive health care, greater educational and economic opportunities for women, and reductions in infant and child death rates can and will bring about rapid birthrate declines. If all developing countries were to emulate the most effective policies and programs and if donor governments such as the United States were to provide adequate levels of assistance, the population problem could be resolved in the lifetime of today's children.

In fact, a children's revolution is already under way in the developing world, often led by those in power. Developing country leaders took the lead in seeking history's first truly global summit—the 1990 World Summit for Children—with an unprecedented 71 heads of state and government participating. They also pressed for early action on the Convention on the Rights of the Child, which was adopted by the [UN] General Assembly in November 1989 and which has since been signed or ratified in record time by more than 150 countries—with the United States now being the only major exception.

The experience of the past decade showed it possible—even during the darkest days of the Cold War and amid the Third World economic crisis of the 1980s—to mobilize societies and the international community around a package of low-cost interventions and services, building a sustainable momentum of human progress. The United Nations Children's Fund (UNICEF) and NGOs called it the Child Survival and Development Revolution, and as a result more than 20 million children are alive today who would not otherwise be; tens of millions are healthier, stronger, and less of a burden upon their mothers and families; and birth rates are falling.

Leaders are learning that productive things can be done for families and children at relatively low cost, and that it can be good politics for them to do so and bad politics to resist. More than 130 countries have issued or are actively working on National Programmes of Action to implement the goals set by the World Summit for Children, all of which were incorporated into Agenda 21 at the June 1992 Earth Summit in Rio de Janeiro. Those ambitious goals—to be met by the year 2000—include controlling the major childhood diseases; cutting child malnutrition in half; reducing death rates for children under five by one-third; cutting in half maternal mortality rates; providing safe water and sanitation for all communities; and making family planning services and basic education universally available. In 1992, most regions of the developing world took the process a step further by selecting a core of targets for 1995, when the first World Social Summit will review children's progress within the broader development process. For the first time since the dawn of history, humankind is making long-term plans for improving the lives of the young.

In part, that new concern has its roots in the communications revolution that brings daily pictures of large-scale famine or violence into our homes. At the same time, the new communications capacity has permitted deprived populations everywhere to see how much better people can live, firing grassroots movements for reform and democracy. But most of the Third World's suffering remains invisible. Of the 35,000 children under age five who die every day in the developing countries, more than 32,000 succumb to largely preventable hunger and illness. No earthquake, no flood, no war has taken the lives of a quarter million children in a single week; but that is the weekly death toll of the invisible emergencies resulting from poverty and underdevelopment In 1992, 500,000 children under the age of five died in the kind of dramatic emergencies that attract media attention, but that is a small portion of the nearly 13 million children under five who are killed every year by grinding poverty and gross underdevelopment. The tragic deaths of 1,000 children per day in Somalia last year captured far more public attention than those of the 8,000 children around the world who die every day from the dehydration caused by ordinary diarrhea, which is so easily treated and prevented.

As the international community assumes greater responsibility for proliferating civil strife and other emergencies, it must come to terms with the realities of limited resources. How many operations to rescue failed states like Somalia can the international community afford? It is estimated that the U.S. component of the Somalia operation alone will cost more than $750 million for just four months' involvement, nearly comparable to UNICEF's average annual global budget of recent years, much of which is used to prevent future crises. There are now 48 civil and ethnic conflicts in progress around the globe. The United Nations is involved in 14 peacekeeping operations on five continents. Last year, those operations cost more than $3 billion, about four times higher than the previous record. Those operations are the most expensive way to relieve suffering, and it is clearly time to invest far more in *preventing* emergencies and conflicts, and in buttressing the new democracies, even as we put out the world's fires. As U.N. secretary-general Boutros Boutros-Ghali argues in his *Agenda for Peace,* prevention can prove far less costly—and produce far greater results—than relying on expensive and sometimes ineffective rescue operations.

As the international community shifts toward prevention—as it must—it makes the most sense to focus on eradicating poverty's worst manifestations early in the lives of children, breaking the cycle of poverty from generation to generation. At the World Summit for Children, the international community identified the basic package of high-impact, low-cost interventions that can make a difference in the short and medium term, while helping to build long-term development. Now it has only to make them work, albeit on a massive scale.

The overall price tag for reaching all the year 2000 goals for children and women, which would overcome most of the worst aspects of poverty, would be an extra $25 billion per year. The developing countries themselves are trying to come up with two-thirds of that amount by reordering their domestic priorities and budgets, while the remaining third—slightly more than $8 billion per year—should come from the industrialized world in the form of increased or reallocated official development assistance (ODA) and debt relief. That is a small price for meeting the basic needs of virtually every man, woman, and child in the developing world in nutrition, basic health, basic education, water and sanitation, and family planning within this decade.

In Russia and the other former Soviet republics, such aid could produce rapid grassroots results at an affordable cost, easing pain and helping to buy time until democratic and macroeconomic reforms show concrete progress. Plans for restoring democracy to Cambodia, Haiti, and Mozambique will need to alleviate suffering among the poor quickly; and targeting the essential needs of children and women can produce the biggest impact at the lowest cost. International relief programs for Somalia must rapidly give way to assistance that constitutes an investment in human development, and no such investment has been found to be more cost-effective than primary health care, nutrition, and basic education for children and women. The road to power for many of the world's extremist movements—whether based in religion or political ideology—is paved with the unmet needs of the poor.

Sadly, the U.S. has stagnated or regressed over the past decade with respect to children, even while much of the developing world has been making impressive progress. The United States has provided little leadership for that progress, except for that provided by the bipartisanship of Congress, which actively encouraged U.S. support to child survival and development programs abroad. But by increasing investment in American children and strengthening American families, and by reordering foreign assistance to reflect that new priority, the United States, the world's sole superpower, could once more set the global standard and give a major boost to human development and economic growth.

First, few actions would have more immediate impact than the signature and ratification this year of the historic Convention on the Rights of the Child. President Bill Clinton's signature of the convention and its submission to the U.S. Senate for early ratification (as has been urged by bipartisan leadership) would send an important message to the world, bringing the rights of children close to becoming humanity's first universal law.

Second, the United States needs to demonstrate a new culture of caring for its own children. The much-needed reordering of priorities for American children, women, and families is already under way, with initiatives on Head Start, universal immunization, parental leave, family planning, and health services for all. A "Culture of Caring," the American plan in response to the World Summit for Children that was issued at the end of the Bush administration—in January 1993 —provides a useful base for bipartisan action.

Third, the United States needs "20/20 vision." It should support the May 1991 proposal of the United Nations Development Programme, which had two components: It called on developing countries to devote at least 20 per cent of their budgets to directly meeting the basic human needs of their people, roughly double current average levels. It also argued that 20 per cent of all international development aid should go to meet those same basic needs: primary health care, nutrition, basic education, family planning, and safe water and sanitation. Today, on average, less than 10 per cent of already inadequate levels of ODA are devoted to that purpose. Different ways of defining and reporting social sector allocations within national and ODA budgets make precise quantification of those proportions somewhat difficult, and efforts are therefore underway to achieve a common form of reporting. But even if subsequent research changes the target percentages, the "20/20 vision" concept underscores the importance of restructuring both sets of budgets in line with the priorities established at the World Summit for Children, which may require—on average—a doubling of existing allocations.

On the ODA side, the United States today devotes less than $1 billion to basic human needs. Of the projected $25 billion extra annually that will be required globally by mid-decade to meet the World Summit year 2000 goals, the U.S. share would be $2 billion. The roughly $3 billion total would then still be less than 20 per cent of all U.S. foreign and military assistance. It is a small price to pay for jumpstarting solutions to so many of the overwhelming problems of population, democracy, and the worst aspects of poverty, to say nothing about saving tens of millions of young lives this decade. The additional funds can be obtained from reductions in the military and security component of the U.S. international affairs budget.

Fourth, the new spirit of democratic change and economic reform in Africa will not survive if its creditors do not give it some debt relief: Together, the sub-Saharan African countries pay $1 billion in debt service to foreign creditors every month, and its debt is now proportionally three or four times heavier than that of Latin America. At the November 1992 Organization of African Unity–sponsored International Conference on Assistance to African Children, donor countries and lending agencies alike pledged to promote more debt relief while expanding or restructuring ODA in order to help Africa protect and nurture its children. Here again the

United States could help lead the way, preventing Africa from deteriorating into a continent of Somalias. The G-7 Summit in Tokyo in July 1993 should make a definitive commitment to debt relief, with much of the local currency proceeds going to accelerate programs for children, women, and the environment through a variety of debt-swapping mechanisms. With the right mixture of domestic and international support, and with apartheid ending in South Africa, we could see dramatic progress in most of Africa by the year 2000. That could include a food revolution every bit as green as Asia's—but African countries will need help. The alternative could be a return to authoritarian rule, corruption, and conflict throughout large parts of the continent.

Fifth, the United States must actively support multilateral cooperation. With human development and poverty alleviation increasingly accepted as the focus for development cooperation in the 1990s, the United States has an opportunity to transform rhetoric into reality. Active U.S. support and leadership along those lines in the World Bank, the International Monetary Fund, the regional banks, and throughout the U.N. system will go a long way toward overcoming, in our time, the worst aspects of poverty in the South, where it is most acute. Land-mark U.N. conferences have been scheduled on human rights (1993), population (1994), and women (1995); U.S. leadership at those conferences and at the U.N. summit on social development in 1995 will strengthen their impact. The U.S. role will also be critical in reducing poverty in the North and in the transitional societies of Eastern Europe and the former Soviet Union.

Finally, the United States must strengthen its commitment to the United Nations. The new administration's initiative to seek restoration of U.S. funding for the United Nations Population Fund is a welcome step—a step that Congress should rapidly implement. That and a decision to rejoin the United Nations Educational, Scientific, and Cultural Organization (UNESCO) would not only give an important boost to family planning and global education, but—together with full payment of its U.N. arrears—it would signal long-term U.S. commitment to the United Nations as the global village's central vehicle for development cooperation and safeguarding the peace.

Focusing on children as a means of attacking the worst aspects of poverty will not solve all the world's problems, but it would make a historic contribution—at this all-too-brief juncture of opportunity —to the better world we all seek. It could change the course of history.

NO

THE KINDNESS OF STRANGERS

The old jibe about aid—"poor people in rich countries helping rich people in poor countries"—has plenty of truth in it. Donors need to learn from past mistakes if they want to help poor countries grow.

Anybody who tried to see the case for aid by looking merely at the way it is allotted would quickly give up in despair. The richest 40% of the developing world gets about twice as much per head as the poorest 40%. Big military spenders get about twice as much per head as do the less belligerent. El Salvador gets five times as much aid as Bangladesh, even though Bangladesh has 24 times as many people and is five times poorer than El Salvador.

Since 1960, about $1.4 trillion (in 1988 dollars) has been transferred in aid from rich countries to poor ones. Yet relatively little is known about what that process has achieved. Has it relieved poverty? Has it stimulated growth in the recipient countries? Has it helped the countries which give it? Such questions become more pressing as donor governments try harder to curb public spending. This year, two of the biggest players in the international aid business are looking afresh at their aims and priorities.

Brian Atwood, appointed by the Clinton administration to run America's Agency for International Development (AID), inherited an organisation encumbered over the years with 33 official goals by a Congress that loved using aid money to buy third-world adherence to its pet ideas. Now, faced with a sharp budget cut, Mr Atwood is trying to pare down to just four goals: building democracy, protecting the environment, fostering sustainable economic development and encouraging population control. Not, however, anything as basic as the relief of poverty.

A few blocks away from Mr Atwood's Washington office, the World Bank is going through a similar exercise. Set up in 1946, the Bank has become the most powerful of all the multilateral development organisations. But a critical internal report recently accused the Bank of caring more about pushing out loans than about monitoring how well the money was spent. Now the Bank hopes to improve the quality of its lending. It is also wondering about its future. Some of its past borrowers in East Asia are now rich enough to turn lenders themselves. More should follow. The Bank is trying to move into new areas, such as cleaning up the environment and setting up social-welfare systems. But some people wonder how long it will really be needed.

AID and the World Bank are unusual (although their critics rarely admit as much) in their openness and in the rigour with which they try to evaluate what they do. But other donors will also have to think about which kinds of aid to abandon as their budgets stop expanding. In the 1980s the official development assistance[1] (ODA) disbursed by members of the OECD's [Organization for Economic Cooperation and Development's] Development Assistance Committee (DAC)—21 rich countries plus the European Commission—increased by about a quarter in real terms; but between 1991 and 1992, the DAC's disbursements rose by just 0.5%. Development Initiatives, an independent British ginger group [a driving force within a larger group], believes "the end of an era" may have come; it reckons that aid budgets around the world are ceasing to grow at all. Almost the only exception is Japan, which provides a fifth of DAC aid and plans a substantial increase over the next five years.

Most multilateral donors, such as the UN agencies, also have budgets frozen. A rare exception is the European Development Fund [EDF], the aid arm of the European Union, which is taking a rapidly rising share of member-states' aid budgets. The EDF's secrecy and its mediocre reputation with recipient countries make some bilateral donors unhappy. "British officials are concerned about having to devote increasing quantities of their aid, which they regard as successful, to the European programme," reports Robert Cassen, a British aid expert.

Figure 1

More from the Market: Net Resource Flows to Developing Countries [in] $bn, Constant 1991 Prices and Exchange Rates

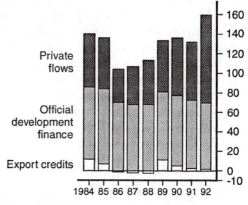

Source: OECD

NEEDED: A CASE FOR GIVING

Some developing countries—mainly the faster-growing ones perceived as "emerging markets"—have found the international capital markets to be increasingly willing suppliers of finance (see Figure 1). But demands for ODA are still appearing in new forms and from new sources. Astute third-world countries are giving old projects a green tinge to profit from fashionable enthusiasm for the environment. The countries of Eastern Europe and the former Soviet Union are competing with the third world for help. And the proportion of aid spent on relieving disasters has soared from 2% five years ago to around 7% today.

But with the clamour for more money goes increasing uncertainty about what aid is for and what it has achieved. The naive taxpayer might imagine that aid's main purpose was to relieve poverty. Yet only relatively small amounts of ODA go to the poorest of countries or to projects that benefit mainly the poorest of people. A study of America's aid programme conducted by the Overseas Development Council (ODC), a Washington, DC, think-tank, found that more than $250 per person went to relatively high-income countries, but less than $1 per person to very low-income countries. Mahbub ul Haq of the United Nations Development Programme (UNDP), a fierce critic of aid's failure to reach the poorest, points out that the ten countries that are home to two-thirds of the world's poorest people receive only one-third of world aid.

NOT HELPING THE POOR

Within poor countries, too, aid is rarely concentrated on the services that benefit the poorest. The World Bank reckons that, of all the aid going to low-income countries in 1988, a mere 2% went on primary health care and 1% on population programmes. Even the aid that is spent on health and education tends to go to services that benefit disproportionately the better-off. Aid for health care goes disproportionately to hospitals (in 1988–89, for instance, 33% of Japan's bilateral aid for health went on building hospitals); aid for education, to universities. In sub-Saharan Africa in the 1980s, only $1 of ODA went on each primary pupil; $11 on each secondary pupil; and $575 on each university student.

Such spending patterns often reflect the priorities of the recipient governments. Some donors have tried to persuade governments to distribute aid differently. They have had mixed success —not surprisingly, for their own motives in aid-giving often override the goal of poverty relief.

One such motive, powerful even since the end of the cold war, is the pursuit of national security. Most governments are coy about the role that national security plays in their aid budgets, but the biggest donor of all, the United States, is blatant: roughly a quarter of its $21 billion foreign-aid budget takes the form of military assistance, and roughly a quarter of the total budget goes to Israel and Egypt alone. "The United States has spent a lot less money on development than on advancing political and military goals," says John Sewell of the ODC. This year, America's aid budget protects the shares of Israel and Egypt. America also sees aid to Eastern Europe and to the countries of the former Soviet Union primarily in strategic terms.

"National security" is also now being used as an argument for giving more weight to all sorts of other goals in the drawing-up of aid budgets. Environmentalists claim that some types of environmental damage, such as global warming and the thinning of the ozone layer, may be worsened by poor-country growth, and they argue that rich-country aid donors should in their own interests take special care to minimise such risks. Others say aid should be used to parry the threats to rich countries posed by the trade in illegal drugs, by population growth and by third-world poverty.

If the goal of national security can conflict with that of poverty relief, then the commercial interests of aid donors can do so even more. Japan's approach has at least the merit of simplicity: its development assistance goes mainly to countries that are most likely to become its future customers. All DAC countries tie some aid—the average is about a quarter—to the purchase of their own goods and services. One problem with tying is that it forces countries to pay over the odds for imports: on average, some estimates suggest, recipients pay 15% more than prevailing prices. Another is that it often distorts development priorities. It is easier to tie aid to a large item of capital spending, such as a dam, road or hospital, than to a small rural project that may do more good. Not surprisingly, tying is especially common in transport, power generation and telecommunications projects.

Aid recorded as tied has been falling as a proportion of bilateral ODA, according to the OECD, which monitors the practice. That may be partly because of the rise in spending on disaster relief. It may also reflect an international agreement on guidelines for tied aid. But governments are clever at finding ways to use aid to promote exports. It has, for example, taken two official investigations to uncover some of the links between British aid to Malaysia and British arms sales to that country.

Some kinds of ODA are given in the sure knowledge that the money will be spent mainly in the donor country, but without explicit tying. One example is technical assistance. Of the $12 billion or so which goes each year to buy advice, training and project design, over 90% is spent on foreign consultants. Half of all technical assistance goes to Africa —which, observes UNDP's Mr Haq, "has perhaps received more bad advice per capita than any other continent". Most thoughtful people in the aid business regard technical assistance as one of the least effective ways to foster development.

Stung by the claims of their aid lobbies that too little help goes to the poor, some governments are trying to steer more money through voluntary bodies, such as charities and church groups. Such bodies, known in the trade as non-governmental organisations or NGOs, have proliferated at astonishing speed in both the rich and poor worlds. The OECD counted 2,542 NGOs in its 24 member countries in 1990, compared with 1,603 in 1980. The growth in the south may have been faster still. Roger Riddell, of the Overseas Development Institute in London, who has made a special study of NGOs and development, talks of a "veritable explosion" in their numbers; he mentions 25,000 grassroots organisations in the Indian state of Tamil Nadu alone. The public and private money dispensed by NGOs amounted to 13% of total net ODA flows in 1990, and the share has been creeping up.

NGOs may be better than central governments at handling small projects and more sensitive to what local people really need. But even NGOs, according to Mr Riddell, usually fail to help the very poorest. "If government and official aid programmes fail to reach the bottom 20% of income groups, most NGO interventions probably miss the bottom 5–10%," he guesses. And, as more aid is channelled through NGOs, some groups may find it harder to retain the element of local participation which is their most obvious strength. More searching questions might be asked about whether they are efficiently run, or achieve their purported goals: a study of projects supported by the Ford Foundation in Africa in the late 1980s found "very few successes to talk about, especially in terms of post-intervention sustainability".

AND WHAT ABOUT GROWTH?

When the modern panoply of official aid institutions grew up after the second world war, the intention was not to relieve poverty as such but to promote economic growth in poor countries. Aid was seen as a transitional device to help countries reach a point from which their economies would take off of their own accord. Its use was to remove shortages of capital and foreign exchange, boosting investment to a point at which growth could become self-sustaining.

In their baldest form, such views sit oddly beside the fact that, in many of the countries that have received the most aid and have the highest levels of capital investment, growth has been negligible. For at least 47 countries, aid represented more than 5% of GNP [gross national product] in 1988. Many of those countries were in sub-Saharan Africa, where GDP [gross domestic product] per head has been virtually flat for a quarter of a century. Yet, as David Lindauer and Michael Roemer of the Harvard Institute for International Development point out in a recent study, some of them were investing a share of GDP almost as large as that of much faster growing South-East Asian countries: Cameroon, Côte d'Ivoire, Kenya, Tanzania and Zambia all invested at least 20% of GDP, a figure comparable with that for Indonesia or Thailand.

Such rough comparisons may prove little, but they draw attention to an awkward point. Some third-world countries have enjoyed fast economic growth with relatively little aid per head. In particular, some Asian success stories, such as China and Vietnam, had little or no aid at a time when donors were pouring money into Africa (although China is now the World Bank's largest single customer). If some countries can achieve economic growth with little aid, while other countries which get a great deal of aid do not

grow at all, what if anything is aid good for?

One way to try to answer that question is to review the experience of individual countries and aid projects. In the late 1980s there were two valiant attempts to do just, this: one conducted by a team led by Mr Cassen, the other on a more modest scale by Mr Riddell. Mr Cassen's team argued that "the majority of aid is successful in terms of its own objectives", but added that "a significant proportion does not succeed." Aid had worked badly in Africa; better in South Asia. Where aid did not work, the reason was sometimes that donors failed to learn from their mistakes or the mistakes of other donors; and sometimes that a recipient country failed to make the most of what was offered to it.

As for the impact of aid on economic growth, Mr Cassen concluded cautiously that one could not say that aid failed to help. In some countries, indeed, he found evidence that it did increase growth. Mr Riddell was similarly tentative. Aid, he concluded, "can assist in the alleviation of poverty, directly and indirectly" and "the available evidence ... fails to convince that, as a general rule, alternative strategies which exclude aid lead in theory or have led in practice to more rapid improvements in the living standards of the poor than have been achieved with aid."

These are hardly ringing endorsements. But these evaluations of individual aid programmes and projects are more positive in their findings than attempts to establish broader links between aid and growth, which have usually failed entirely. Plenty of economists have picked holes in the original idea that aid would boost investment: why should it, some ask, when governments may simply use income from aid as an excuse to spend tax revenues in other, less productive ways?

Other economists, such as Howard White of the Institute of Social Studies at The Hague, who has reviewed many of the economic studies of the effects of aid on growth, point to the difficulties of generalising. Given the various transfers that count as "aid", the many conditions that donors attach, the differing importance of aid in national economies and the complexity of economic growth, there are simply too many variables to say much that is useful.

THIRD-WORLD DUTCH DISEASE

Since the start of the 1980s, many donors have come to believe that the quality of a country's economic management will do most to determine whether aid will do some good. Aid in the 1980s was frequently used, especially by the World Bank, as a prod to encourage countries to begin "structural adjustment" programmes. In some cases, the economic performance of these countries did improve—Ghana is one of the Bank's favourite examples. In other cases, it did not. A review by the IMF [International Monetary Fund] of 19 low-income countries which had undergone structural adjustment found that their current-account deficits averaged 12.3% of GDP before adjustment and 16.8% in the most recent year; and that their external debt had grown from 451% of exports to 482%.

Why was this? Were countries encouraged to adopt the wrong policies? Did they ignore the advice they were given? Or did the aid itself do some damage? Stefan de Vylder, a Swedish economist, argued for the last of these explanations at a conference in Stockholm in March.

Figure 2

Friends in Need: Aid* as % of GDP, 1992

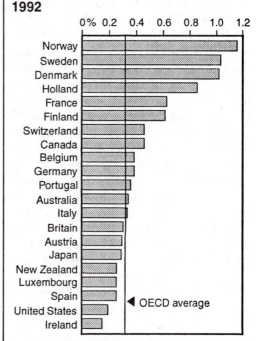

*Net official development assistance
Source: OECD

He argued that large volumes of aid (such as those associated with structural adjustment programmes) could damage an economy's international competitiveness; and countries where export performance was especially bad tended to be "rewarded" with low-interest loans and grants.

The damage to competitiveness, Mr de Vylder believes, is a version of "Dutch disease". This was the term coined in the 1970s to describe how Holland's exports of natural gas boosted its real exchange rate and thereby harmed its export competitiveness. Mr White thinks something similar happened in Sri Lanka between 1974 and 1988, when a sharp increase in aid contributed to a divergence between the nominal and real exchange rates; this hurt the growth of the country's manufactured exports.

Mr de Vylder also worries about the tendency of aid to compensate for failure rather than to reward success. Bilateral donors have increasingly found that much of the aid they give to some countries goes towards paying back money unwisely lent by international financial institutions. Take Zambia as an example. Between 1974 and 1987, Zambia had entered into seven stand-by or structural agreements with the IMF—one every two years. Each was broken by the Zambian government. When, in 1987, Mr de Vylder visited Zambia to assess the latest bout of economic disaster, he asked a minister how seriously the government was worried at being lambasted by every aid donor. "Concerned?" mused the minister, seeming somewhat surprised. Then: "Oh no. They always come back." The minister was right, says Mr de Vylder. Shortly afterwards, the international financial institutions were again knocking on the door, asking for a new agreement.

It is easy, with aid, to find examples of individual projects that do some good. Most of those who criticise aid argue that if the quality were better—if donors tried harder to learn from each other's mistakes, if they were less keen to reap commercial gain, if they concentrated harder on meeting basic human needs— then there would be far fewer failures. All that is true; but—other things being equal —there would also be much less aid. Will poor countries do worse, over the next 30 years, if rich countries decline to give or lend them another $1.4 trillion? At that price, the answer should be "Yes". Given the way that aid works at present, it is only "Maybe".

NOTES

1. Defined as aid administered with the promotion of economic development and welfare as the main objective; concessional in character; and with a grant element of at least 25%.

POSTSCRIPT

Should the Developed North Increase Aid to the Less Developed South?

There can be no argument that most of the people in most of the countries of the South live in circumstances that citizens in the developed countries of the North would find unacceptable. There is also no question that most of the Third World was subjugated and held in colonial bondage by the developed countries. In most cases, that colonialism lasted into the second half of this century. Apart from these points, there is little agreement on the causes and the solutions to the plight of the South.

Many Third World specialists blame colonialism for the Third World's lack of development, past and present. This view is held in much of the Third World and also is represented widely in Western scholarly opinion. Johan Galtung's "A Structural Theory of Imperialism," *Journal of Peace Research* (1971), is a classic statement from this perspective. This belief has led to the Third World's demand for a New International Economic Order (NIEO), in which there would be a greater sharing of wealth and economic power between North and South. It is also possible to argue that continued poverty in the Third World, especially amid the general prosperity of the economically developed countries, will increase anger among the people of the economically less developed countries, decrease global stability, and have a variety of other negative consequences for the people of all countries, wealthier and poorer alike. For discussions of this aspect, see Nicole Ball, "Militarized States in the Third World," in *World Security: Trends and Challenges at Century's End*, edited by Michael T. Klare and Daniel C. Thomas (St. Martin's Press, 1992).

Other analysts argue that colonialism actually benefited many dependencies by introducing modern economic techniques, and they say that those former colonies that have remained close to the industrialized countries have done the best. Still others have charged that some Third World countries have followed policies that have short-circuited their own development. This point of view sees calls for an NIEO as little more than an attempt by the South to reorder the international system to gain power. Steven D. Krasner's *Structural Conflict: The Third World Against Global Liberalism* (University of California Press, 1985) is written from this point of view.

There are also disagreements about how much the North should aid the South, irrespective of who has caused the problems. Humanitarian concerns, as well as a sense that all the world's people will eventually be more prosperous if the 80 percent who live in poverty in the South can develop, argue for greater aid, a view represented in David Aronson, "Why Africa Stays Poor and Why It Doesn't Have To," *The Humanist* (March/April 1993).

ISSUE 10

Is Free Trade a Desirable International Goal?

YES: Peter F. Drucker, from "Trade Lessons from the World Economy," *Foreign Affairs* (January/February 1994)

NO: Jeremy Brecher, from "Global Village or Global Pillage?" *The Nation* (December 6, 1993)

ISSUE SUMMARY

YES: Peter F. Drucker, a professor of social science and management at the Claremont Graduate School, contends that global economic integration is the only basis for an effective international trade policy, and the only way to rapidly revive a domestic economy.

NO: Historian Jeremy Brecher argues that unrestricted, unregulated trade has cost national governments much of their power to direct their own economies and is threatening the economic well-being of working people.

International trade has grown dramatically during this century, expanding from $13 billion (measured in exports) in 1913 to approximately $3.9 trillion in 1993. At the center of the effort to achieve worldwide free trade is the 1947 treaty known as GATT, the General Agreement on Tariffs and Trade, and the organization it created, now known as the the World Trade Organization (WTO). Trade has increased 65-fold in the 35 years since GATT, compared to an only 4-fold increase in trade during the 35 years before it was established.

This tremendous increase has many important ramifications. *Interdependence* is the term that is used to describe the reality that all countries are now part of a web of mutual economic dependence. National economic self-sufficiency is no longer possible. Both imports and exports are important to a country's economy, and domestic economies and standards of living have become much more enmeshed with foreign trade.

Exports, goods and services sold outside of a country, provide countries with jobs for their workers and with the revenue to buy needed or desired foreign products. Canadians, for example, are heavily dependent on exports for the economic health of their country. Exports accounted for 29.2 percent of Canada's 1993 gross domestic product (GDP), a measure of all the goods and services produced within a country. Even in a much more massive economy, such as that of the United States, exports are a key economic factor, accounting in 1993 for 10.4 percent of the U.S. GDP. Trade, it is important to mention, is a much broader concept than the tangible agricultural, mineral, and manufactured items often thought of as the whole of trade. The export and import of these items in particular is called *merchandise trade.*

A second, less well known part of trade is the export and import of services. When a Canadian engineer earns money by advising an African government on a dam project, or when Lloyds of London sells insurance policies to Japanese shipowners, the revenues each receives are from the export of services.

A third major factor in the flow of money between countries concerns investments. Direct investment and portfolio investment are two related terms that you will encounter in the article by Peter Drucker. Direct investment occurs when an investor (individual or corporation) builds and owns a facility (such as a factory) in another country or buys a controlling interest (usually 10 percent or more) in a foreign corporation or other economic enterprise. Portfolio investment is the buying or selling of stocks and bonds offered by foreign governments or economic enterprises in foreign countries without accumulating a controlling interest.

Imports are also a vital part of almost every country's well-being. They are the products and services that are unavailable, or are not available in sufficient quantity, or are less expensive to purchase from foreign producers. The United States, for example, cannot survive without imported oil. Imports also help control inflation and increase purchasing power by making relatively inexpensive foreign products available to consumers.

International trade also has its costs, however. For example, when products that were once bought from domestic manufacturers are imported, workers in the importing country often lose their jobs. Some people worry that interdependence means national vulnerability. If a foreign power were able to cut off U.S. oil imports or dramatically raise their price, the U.S. economy, and perhaps its national security, would be imperiled. Tariffs are also a source of revenue, and the latest round of tariff reductions under the most recent GATT revision is projected to cost the United States $13.9 billion in lost tariff revenue in the first five years. A problem with the theory of free trade is that there are many things that block it. All countries impose tariffs or non-tariff barriers (such as quotas) on imports. Social factors, such as buying preferences or savings rates, also affect trade. One reason that Americans are huge importers is that they save less of their disposable income than the citizens of virtually every other industrialized country.

In the following debate, Peter Drucker and Jeremy Brecher take up the wisdom of the continuing and expanding free trade and other forms of worldwide economic interchange. Drucker writes that the evidence is clear that prosperity for all is most likely to come from a global economy in which the marketplace governs the movement of goods, services, and capital. Jeremy Brecher disagrees strongly, contending that out-of-control globalization has had disastrous consequences.

YES

Peter F. Drucker

TRADE LESSONS FROM THE WORLD ECONOMY

In recent years the economies of all developed nations have been stagnant, yet the world economy has still expanded at a good clip. And it has been growing faster for the past 40 years than at any time since modern economies and the discipline of economics emerged in the eighteenth century. From this seeming paradox there are lessons to be learned, and they are quite different from what practically everyone asserts, whether they be free traders, managed traders or protectionists. Too many economists, politicians and segments of the public treat the external economy as something separate and safely ignored when they make policy for the domestic economy....

The segments that comprise the world economy—the flows of money and information on the one hand, and trade and investment on the other—are rapidly merging into one transaction. They increasingly represent different dimensions of cross-border alliances, the strongest integrating force of the world economy. Both of these segments are growing fast....

Today's money flows are vastly larger than traditional portfolio investments made for the sake of short-term income from dividends and interest. Portfolio money flows were once the stabilizers of the international economy, flowing from countries of low short-term returns to countries of higher short-term returns, thus maintaining an equilibrium. They reacted to a country's financial policy or economic condition. Driven by the expectation of speculative profits, today's world money flows have become the great destabilizers, forcing countries into precipitous interest rate hikes that throttle business activity, or into overnight devaluations that drag a currency below its trade parity or purchasing-power parity, thus generating inflationary pressures. These money flows are a pathological phenomenon. They underline the fact that neither fixed nor flexible foreign exchange rates (the only two known systems) really work. Contemporary money flows do not respond to attempted government restrictions such as taxes on money-flow profits; the trading just moves elsewhere. All that can be done as part of an effective trade policy is to build resistance into the economy against the impact of the flows.

From Peter F. Drucker, "Trade Lessons from the World Economy," *Foreign Affairs*, vol. 73, no. 1 (January/February 1994). Copyright © 1994 by The Council on Foreign Relations, Inc. Reprinted by permission of *Foreign Affairs*.

Information flows in the world economy are probably growing faster than any category of transactions in history. Consisting of meetings, software, magazines, books, movies, videos, telecommunications and a host of new technologies, information flows may already exceed money flows in the fees, royalties and profits they generate. Unlike money flows, information flows have benign economic impacts. In fact, few things so stimulate economic growth as the rapid development of information, whether telecommunications, computer data, computer networks or entertainment media. In the United States, information flows—and the goods needed to carry them—have become the largest single source of foreign currency income. But just as we do not view medieval cathedrals economically—although they were once Europe's biggest generators of economic activity next to farming, and its biggest nonmilitary employer—information flows have mostly social and cultural impacts. Economic factors like high costs restrain rather than motivate information flows.

The first lesson is that these two significant economic phenomena—money flows and information flows—do not fit into any theory or policy. They are not even transnational; they are nonnational.

WHAT TRADE DEFICIT?

For practically everyone international trade means merchandise trade, the import and export of manufactured goods, farm products and raw materials. But international trade is increasingly services trade—little reported and largely unnoticed. The United States has the largest share of the trade in services among developed countries, followed by the United Kingdom. Japan is at the bottom of the list. The services trade of all developed countries are growing fast, and it may equal or overtake their merchandise trade within ten years. Knowledge is the basis of most service exports and imports. As a result, most service trade is based on long-term commitments, which makes it —excluding tourism—impervious to foreign exchange fluctuations and changes in labor costs.

Even merchandise trade is no longer confined to the sale and purchase of individual goods. Increasingly it is a relationship in which a transaction is only a shipment and an accounting entry. More and more merchandise trade is becoming "structural" and thereby impervious to short-term (and even long-term) changes in the traditional economic factors. Automobile production is a good example. Plant location decisions by manufacturers and suppliers are made at the time of product design. Until the model is redesigned, say in ten years, the plants and the countries specified in the original design are locked in. There will be change only in the event of a catastrophe such as a war or fire that destroys a plant. Or take the case of a Swiss pharmaceutical company's Irish plant. Rather than sell a product, it ships chemical intermediates to the company's finished-product plants in 19 countries on both sides of the Atlantic. For this the company charges a "transfer" price, which is a pure accounting convention having as much to do with taxes as with production costs. The traditional factors of production are also largely irrelevant to what might be called "institutional" trade, in which businesses, whether manufacturers or large retailers, buy machinery, equipment and supplies for new plants or stores, wherever located, from the suppliers of their existing plants, that is, those in their home countries.

Markets and knowledge are important in these types of structural and institutional trade decisions; labor costs, capital costs and foreign exchange rates are restraints rather than determinants. More important, neither type of trade is foreign trade, except in a legal sense, even when it is trade across national boundaries. For the individual business—the automobile manufacturer, the Swiss pharmaceutical company, the retailer—these are transactions within its own system.

Accounting for these developments, U.S. trading activity is more or less in balance. The trade deficit bewailed in the media and by public and private officials is in merchandise trade, caused primarily by an appalling waste of petroleum and a steady decline in the volume and prices of farm exports. The services trade account has a large surplus. According to little-read official figures, published every three months, the services trade surplus amounts to two thirds of the merchandise trade deficit. Moreover, government statisticians acknowledge gross underreporting of service exports, perhaps by as much as 50 percent.

THE COMING OF ALLIANCES

... Alliances, formal and informal, are becoming the dominant form of economic integration in the world economy. Some major companies, such as Toshiba, the Japanese electronics giant, and Corning Glass, the world's leading maker of high-engineered glass, may each have more than 100 alliances all over the world. Integration in the [European] Common Market is proceeding far more through alliances than through mergers and acquisitions, especially among the middle-

sized companies that dominate most European economies. As with structural and institutional trade, businesses make little distinction between domestic and foreign partners in their alliances. An alliance creates a relationship in which it does not matter whether one partner speaks Japanese, another English and a third German or Finnish. And while alliances increasingly generate both trade and investment, they are based on neither. They pool knowledge.

THE VITAL LINK

For developed economies, the distinction between the domestic and international economy has ceased to be a reality, however much political, cultural or psychological strength remains in the idea. An unambiguous lesson of the last 40 years is that increased participation in the world economy has become the key to domestic economic growth and prosperity. Since 1950 there has been a close correlation between a country's domestic economic performance and its participation in the world economy. The two major countries whose economies have grown the fastest in the world economy, Japan and South Korea, are also the two countries whose domestic economies have grown the fastest. The same correlation applies to the two European countries that have done best in the world economy in the last 40 years, West Germany and Sweden. The countries that have retreated from the world economy (most notably the United Kingdom) have consistently done worse domestically. In the two major countries that have maintained their participation rate in the world economy within a fairly narrow range—the United States and France—the domestic economy has put in an average performance, neither doing exceptionally well nor suffering persistent malaise and crisis like the United Kingdom.

The same correlation holds true for major segments within a developed economy. In the United States, for instance, services have tremendously increased their world economy participation in the last 15 years; finance, higher education and information are examples. American agriculture, which has consistently shrunk in terms of world economy participation, has been in continual depression and crisis, masked only by ever-growing [government] subsidies.

Conversely, there is little correlation between economic performance and policies to stimulate the domestic economy. The record shows that a government can harm its domestic economy by driving up inflation. But there is not the slightest evidence that any government policy to stimulate the economy has an impact, whether it be Keynesian, monetarist, supply-side or neoclassical. Contrary to what some economists confidently promised 40 years ago, business cycles have not been abolished. They still operate pretty much the way they have for the past 150 years. No country has been able to escape them. When a government policy to stimulate the economy actually coincided with cyclical recovery (which has been rare), it was by pure coincidence. No one policy shows more such coincidences than any other. And no policy that "worked" in a given country in recession A showed any results when tried again in the same country in recession B or recession C. The evidence not only suggests that government policies to stimulate the economy in the short term are ineffectual but also something far

more surprising: they are largely irrelevant. Government, the evidence shows clearly, cannot control the economic weather.

The evidence of the past four decades does show convincingly that participation in the world economy has become the controlling factor in the domestic economic performance of developed countries. For example, a sharp increase in manufacturing and service exports kept the U.S. economy from slipping into deep recession in 1992, and unemployment rates for adult men and women never reached the highs of earlier post-World War II recessions. Similarly, Japan's sharply increased exports have kept its current recession from producing unemployment figures at European levels of eight to ten percent.

WHAT WORKS, WHAT DOES NOT

The evidence is crystal clear that both advocates of managed trade and conventional free traders are wrong in their prescriptions for economic growth. Japan's industrial policy of attempting to select and support "winning" business sectors is by now a well-known failure. Practically all the industries the Japanese Ministry of International Trade and Industry (MITI) picked—such as supercomputers and pharmaceuticals—have been at best also-rans. The Japanese businesses that succeeded, like Sony and the automobile companies, were opposed or ignored by MITI. Trying to pick winners requires a fortune-teller, and the world economy has become far too complex to be outguessed. Japan's economy benefited from a competency—an extraordinary ability to miniaturize products—that was virtually unknown to MITI. Pivotal economic events often take place long before we notice their occurrence. The available data simply do not report important developments such as the growth of the service trade, of structural and institutional trade, of alliances.

Still, the outstanding overall performance of Japan and other Asian countries cannot be explained away as merely a triumph of conventional free trade. Two common economic policies emerge from a recent World Bank study of eight East Asian "superstars"—Japan, South Korea, Hong Kong, Taiwan, Singapore, Malaysia, Thailand and Indonesia. First, they do not try to manage short-term fluctuations in their domestic economies; they do not try to control the economic weather. Moreover, not one of the East Asian economies took off until it had given up attempts to manage domestic short-term fluctuations. All eight countries focus instead on creating the right economic climate. They keep inflation low. They invest heavily in education and training. They reward savings and investment and penalize consumption. The eight started modernizing their economies at very different times, but once they got going, all have shown similar growth in both their domestic and international economies. Together they now account for 21 percent of the world's manufactured goods exports, versus nine percent 30 years ago. Five percent of their populations live below the poverty line, compared with about 40 percent in 1960, and four of them—Japan, Hong Kong, Taiwan and Singapore—rank among the world's richest countries. Yet the eight are totally different in their culture, history, political systems and tax policies. They range from laissez-faire Hong Kong to interventionist Singapore to statist Indonesia.

The second major finding of the World Bank study is that these eight countries pursue policies to enhance the competitiveness of their industries in the world economy with only secondary attention to domestic effect. These countries then foster and promote their proven successes in the world economy. Though MITI neither anticipated nor much encouraged Japan's world market successes, the whole Japanese system is geared to running with them. Japan offers its exporters substantial tax benefits and credits, which remain scarce and expensive for domestic businesses, and it deliberately keeps prices and profits high in a protected domestic market in order to generate cash for overseas investment and market penetration.

The same lessons were being taught until recently by the two countries in the West that showed similar growth: West Germany and Sweden. These countries, too, have very different domestic policies. But both created and maintained an economic growth climate, and through the same measures: control of inflation, high investment in education and training, a high savings rate obtained by high taxes on consumption and fairly low taxes on savings and investment. Both also gave priority to the world economy in governmental and business decisions. The moment they forgot this—when the trade unions a few years back began to subordinate Germany's competitive standing to their wage demands, and the Swedes subordinated their industries' competitive standing to ever-larger welfare spending—their domestic economies went into stagnation.

An additional lesson of the world economy is that investment abroad creates jobs at home. In both the 1960s and the 1980s, expanded U.S. business investments overseas spurred rapid domestic job creation. The same correlation held for Japan and Sweden, both of which invested heavily in overseas plants to produce goods for their home markets. In manufacturing—and in many services, such as retailing—investment per worker in the machinery, tools and equipment of a new facility is three to five times annual production. Most of this productive equipment comes from institutional trade (that is, from the home country of the investor), and most of it is produced by high-wage labor. The initial employment generated to get the new facility into production is substantially larger than the annual output and employment during its first few years of operation.

The last 40 years also teach that protection does not protect. In fact, the evidence shows quite clearly that protection hastens decline. Less-protected U.S. farm products—soybeans, fruit, beef and poultry—have fared a good deal better on world markets than have the more subsidized traditional crops, such as corn, wheat and cotton. Equally persuasive evidence suggests that the American automobile industry's share of its domestic market went into a precipitous decline as soon as the U.S. government forced the Japanese into "voluntary" export restraints. That protection breeds complacency, inefficiency and cartels has been known since before Adam Smith. The counterargument has always been that it protects jobs, but the evidence of the last 40 years strongly suggests that it does not even do that.

FREE TRADE IS NOT ENOUGH

The world economy has become too important for a country not to have a world-economy policy. Managed trade is a delusion of grandeur. Outright protectionism can only do harm, but simply trying to thwart protectionism is not enough. What is needed is a deliberate and active—indeed, aggressive—policy that gives the demands, opportunities and dynamics of the external economy priority over domestic policy demands and problems. For the United States and a number of other countries, it means abandoning ways of thinking that have dominated American economics perhaps since 1933, and certainly since 1945. We still see the demands and opportunities of the world economy as externalities. We usually do not ask whether domestic decisions will hurt American competitiveness, participation and standing in the world economy. The reverse must become the rule: will a proposed domestic move advance American competitiveness and participation in the world economy? The answer to this question determines what are the right domestic economic policy and business decisions. The lessons of the last 40 years teach us that integration is the only basis for an international trade policy that can work, the only way to rapidly revive a domestic economy in turbulence and chronic recession.

NO

Jeremy Brecher

GLOBAL VILLAGE OR GLOBAL PILLAGE?

For most of the world's people, the "New World Economy" is a disaster that has already happened. Those it hurts can't escape it. But neither can they afford to accept it. So many are now seeking ways to reshape it.

When I first started writing about the destructive effects of globalization three years ago, The North American Free Trade Agreement was widely regarded as a done deal. The near defeat of NAFTA reveals pervasive popular doubt about the wisdom of an unregulated international market. The struggle against NAFTA represented the first major effort by Americans who have been hurt by global economic integration to do something about it. Like many mass movements, it included contradictory forces, such as the Mexico-bashing bigotry of Pat Buchanan, the populist grandstanding of Ross Perot and the nationalistic protectionism of some in the labor movement.

But other elements of the struggle against NAFTA prefigure a movement that could radically reshape the New World Economy. Out of their own experiences and observations, millions of Americans have constructed a new paradigm for understanding the global economy. Poor and working people in large numbers have recognized that NAFTA is not primarily about trade; it is about the ability of capital to move without regard to national borders. Capital mobility, not trade, is bringing about the "giant sucking sound" of jobs going south.

For the first time in many years, substantial numbers of people mobilized to act on broad class interests. I haven't seen a movement for years in which so many people at the grass roots took their own initiative. Typical was the unexpectedly large, predominantly blue-collar anti-NAFTA rally in New Haven, where a labor leader told me, "We didn't turn these people out."

THE NEW GLOBAL PILLAGE

NAFTA became a symbol for an accumulation of fears and angers regarding the place of working people in the New World Economy. The North American economic integration that NAFTA was intended to facilitate is only one aspect of the rapid and momentous historical transformation from a system of national economies toward an integrated global economy. New information, communication, transportation and manufacturing technologies, combined with tariff reductions, have made it possible to coordinate production, commerce and finance on a world scale. Since 1983, the rate of world foreign direct investment has grown four times as fast as world output.

This transformation has had devastating consequences. They may be summarized as the "seven danger signals" of cancerous, out-of-control globalization:

Race to the Bottom. The recent quantum leap in the ability of transnational corporations to relocate their facilities around the world in effect makes all workers, communities and countries competitors for these corporations' favor. The consequence is a "race to the bottom" in which wages and social and environmental conditions tend to fall to the level of the most desperate. This dynamic underlies U.S. deindustrialization, declining real wages, eradication of job security, and downward pressure on social spending and investment; it is also largely responsible for the migration of low-wage, environmentally destructive industries to poor countries like Mexico and China.

Global Stagnation. As each work force, community or country seeks to become more competitive by reducing its wages and its social and environmental overheads, the result is a general downward spiral in incomes and social and material infrastructures. Lower wages and reduced public spending mean less buying power, leading to stagnation, recession and unemployment. This dynamic is aggravated by the accumulation of debt;

national economies in poor countries and even in the United States become geared to debt repayment at the expense of consumption, investment and development. The downward fall is reflected in the slowing of global GNP growth from almost 5 percent per year in the period 1948–1973 to only half that in the period 1974–89 and to a mere crawl since then.

Polarization of Haves and Have-Nots. As a result of globalization, the gap between rich and poor is increasing both within and between countries around the world. Poor U.S. communities boast world-class unemployment and infant mortality. Meanwhile, tens of billions of dollars a year flow from poor to rich regions of the world, in the form of debt repayment and capital flight.

Loss of Democratic Control. National governments have lost much of their power to direct their own economies. The ability of countries to apply socialist or even Keynesian techniques in pursuit of development, full employment or other national economic goals has been undermined by the power of capital to pick up and leave. Governmental economic power has been further weakened throughout the world by neoliberal political movements that have dismantled government institutions for regulating national economies. Globalization has reduced the power of individuals and communities to shape their destinies.

Walter Wriston, former chairman of Citicorp, recently boasted of how "200,000 monitors in trading rooms all over the world" now conduct "a kind of global plebiscite on the monetary and fiscal policies of the governments issuing currency.... There is no way for a nation to opt out." Wriston recalls the election of "ardent socialist" François Mitterrand as French President in 1981. "The market took one look at his policies and within six months the capital flight forced him to reverse course."

Unfettered Transnational Corporations. Transnationals have become the world's most powerful economic actors, yet there are no international equivalents to national antitrust, consumer protection and other laws that provide a degree of corporate accountability.

Unaccountable Global Institutions. The loss of national economic control has been accompanied by a growing concentration of unaccountable power in international institutions like the International Monetary Fund, the World Bank and the General Agreement on Tariffs and Trade (GATT). For poor countries, foreign control has been formalized in the World Bank's "structural adjustment plans," but I.M.F. decisions and GATT rules affect the economic growth rates of all countries. The decisions of these institutions also have an enormous impact on the global ecology.

Global Conflict. Economic globalization is producing chaotic and destructive rivalries. In a swirl of self-contradictory strategies, major powers and transnationals use global institutions like GATT to impose open markets on their rivals; they pursue trade wars against one another; and they try to construct competing regional blocs like the European Community and NAFTA. In past eras, such rivalries have ultimately led to world war.

In sum, the result of unregulated globalization has been the pillage of the planet and its peoples.

TRANSNATIONAL ECONOMIC PROGRAMS

What are the alternatives to destructive globalization? The right offers racism and nationalism. Conventional protectionism offers no solution. Globalization has also intellectually disarmed the left and rendered national left programs counterproductive. Jimmy Carter's sharp turn to the right in 1978; François Mitterrand's rapid abandonment of his radical program; the acceptance of deregulation, privatization and trade liberalization by poor countries from India to Mexico; and even the decision of Eastern European elites to abandon Communism—all reflect in part the failure of national left policies.

But the beginnings of a new approach emerged from the anti-NAFTA movement itself. Rather than advocate protectionism—keeping foreign products out—many NAFTA opponents urged policies that would raise environmental, labor and social standards in Mexico, so that those standards would not drag down those in the United States and Canada. This approach implied that people in different countries have common interests in raising the conditions of those at the bottom.

Indeed, the struggle against NAFTA generated new transnational networks based on such common interests. A North American Worker-to-Worker Network links grass-roots labor activists in Mexico, the United States and Canada via conferences, tours, solidarity support and a newsletter. Mujer a Mujer similarly links women's groups. The Highlander Center, Southerners for Economic Justice, the Tennessee Industrial Renewal Network and a number of unions have organized meetings and tours to bring together Mexican and U.S. workers. There are similar networks in other parts of the world, such as People's Plan 21 in the Asian-Pacific and Central American regions and the Third World Network in Malaysia.

These new networks are developing transnational programs to counter the effects of global economic restructuring. Representatives from environmental, labor, religious, consumer and farm groups from Mexico, the United States and Canada have drawn up "A Just and Sustainable Trade and Development Initiative for North America." A parallel synthesis, "From Global Pillage to Global Village," has been endorsed by more than sixty grass-roots organizations. Related proposals by the Third World Network have recently been published as "Towards a New North-South Economic Dialogue."

Differing in emphasis and details, these emerging alternative programs are important not only because of the solutions they propose but also because those solutions have emerged from a dialogue rooted in such a diversity of groups and experiences. Some require implementation by national policy; some by international agreement; some can be implemented by transnational citizen action. Taken together, they provide what might be described as "seven prescriptions" for the seven danger signals of the unregulated global economy:

International Rights and Standards. To prevent competition from resulting in a race to the bottom, several of these groups want to establish minimum human, labor and environmental rights and standards, as the European Community's "social charter" was designed to do. The International Metalworkers Federation recently proposed a ten-point "World So-cial Charter," which could be incorporated into GATT.

"A Just and Sustainable Trade and Development Initiative for North America" spells out in some detail an alternative to NAFTA that would protect human and worker rights, encourage workers' incomes to rise in step with productivity and establish continental environmental rights, such as the right to a toxics-free workplace and community. Enforcement agencies would be accessible to citizens and could levy fines against parties guilty of violations. The initiative especially emphasizes the rights of immigrants. Activists from nongovernmental organizations in all three countries have proposed a citizens' commission to monitor the human, labor and environmental effects of trade and investment.

Upward Spiral. In the past, government monetary and fiscal policy, combined with minimum wages, welfare state programs, collective bargaining and other means of raising the purchasing power of have-nots, did much to counter recession and stagnation within national economies. Similar measures are now required at international levels to counter the tendency toward a downward spiral of inadequate demand in the global economy. The Third World Network calls on the I.M.F. and World Bank to replace their ruinous structural adjustment plans with policies that "meet the broad goals of development... rather than the narrower goal of satisfying the needs of the creditors." It also demands a reduction of developing country debt. "A Just and Sustainable Trade and Development Initiative" proposes that the remaining debt service be paid in local currency into a democratically administered development fund. Reversing the downward spiral also ultimately requires a "global Keynesianism" in which international institutions support, rather than discourage, national full-employment policies.

An upward spiral also requires rising income for those at the bottom—something that can be encouraged by international labor solidarity. Experiments in cross-border organizing by U.S. unions like the Amalgamated Clothing and Textile Workers and the United Electrical Workers, in cooperation with independent unions in Mexico, aim to defeat transnationals' whipsawing by improving the wages and conditions of Mexican workers.

Redistribution from Haves to Havenots. "A Just and Sustainable Trade and Development Initiative" calls for "compensatory financing" to correct growing gaps between rich and poor. A model would be the European Community funds that promote development in its poorer members. The Third World Network calls for commodity agreements to correct the inequities in the South's terms of trade. It also stresses the need to continue preferential treatment for the South in GATT and in intellectual property protection rules.

Strengthened Democracy. NAFTA, GATT and similar agreements should not be used—as they now can be—to preempt the right of localities, states, provinces and countries to establish effective labor, health, safety and environmental standards that are higher than the guaranteed minimum in international agreements. Above all, democratization requires a new opportunity for people at the bottom to participate in shaping their destiny.

Codes of Conduct for Transnational Corporations. Several transnational grass-roots groups call for codes of conduct that would, for example, require corporations to report investment intentions; disclose the hazardous materials they import; ban employment of children; forbid discharge of pollutants; require advance notification and severance pay when operations are terminated; and prohibit company interference with union organizing. United Nations discussions of such a code, long stymied by U.S. hostility, should be revived.

While the ultimate goal is to have such codes implemented by agreements among governments, global public pressure and cross-border organizing can begin to enforce them. The Coalition for Justice in the Maquiladoras, for example, a group of religious, environmental, labor, Latino and women's organizations in Mexico and the United States, has issued a code of conduct for U.S. corporations in Mexico and has used "corporate campaign" techniques to pressure them to abide by its labor and environmental provisions.

Reform of International Institutions. Citizens should call on the U.N. to convene a second Earth Summit focusing on democratizing the I.M.F. and the World Bank, and consider formation of new institutions to promote equitable, sustainable and participatory development. International citizen campaigns, perhaps modeled on the Nestlé boycott and the campaign against World Bank-funded destruction of the Amazon, could spotlight these institutions.

Multiple-Level Regulation. In place of rivalry among countries and regions, such programs imply a system of democratically controlled public institutions at every level, from global to local.

AFTER NAFTA: GLOBALIZATION FROM BELOW

These proposals provide no short-term panacea; they are objectives to organize around. The New World Economy is not going to vanish from the political agenda. Neither will the passions and political forces aroused by the NAFTA debate. Many of the same issues will resurface in connection with the Asia-Pacific Economic Cooperation Forum and with GATT. As the fiftieth anniversaries of the I.M.F. and World Bank approach, calls for their reform are being sounded all over the world.

The struggle against NAFTA has shown that those harmed by the New World Economy need not be passive victims. So many politicians were so unprepared for the strength of the anti-NAFTA movement because it represented an eruption into the political arena of people who have long been demobilized. But to influence their economic destinies effectively, they need a movement that pro- vides an alternative to the Ross Perots and Pat Buchanans. Such a movement must act on the understanding that the unregulated globalization of capital is really a worldwide attack of the haves on the have-nots. And it must bring that understanding to bear on every affected issue, from local layoffs to the world environment. "From Global Pillage to Global Village" suggests a vision to guide such a movement:

The internationalization of capital, production and labor is now being followed by the internationalization of peoples' movements and organizations. Building peoples' international organizations and solidarity will be our revolution from within: a civil society without borders. This internationalism or "globalization from below" will be the foundation for turning the global pillage into a participatory and sustainable global village.

The organizations that have led the fight against NAFTA have a responsibility not to retreat to parochial concerns. They must regroup and begin addressing the broader impact of economic globalization on people and planet.

POSTSCRIPT

Is Free Trade a Desirable International Goal?

There can be little doubt that national sentiment in favor of protectionism has increased. Polls show that Americans rate protecting jobs as the top foreign policy goal. That feeling is shared by the citizens of several industrialized countries. For example, the Socialist party of French president François Mitterrand took a beating in the 1994 legislative elections, where 70 percent of all voters said that unemployment was one of the top two issues that determined their vote.

It is easy to favor stimulating employment; it is another thing to promote that by instituting protectionism. Prices will go up, and it is consumers, after all, who pay for tariffs in the end. Moreover, protectionism is a two-way street. Trade restrictions imposed by one country will almost certainly spark countermeasures by other countries. This retaliation will imperil the export-dependent jobs in the country that began the protectionist tit-for-tat process. The international political economy is a big subject to tackle, and a good start for further study would be to look at one of the several excellent texts in the field, such as Robert S. Walters and David H. Blake, *The Politics of Global Economic Relations* (Prentice Hall, 1992). One study that helps further explain political economy from the American perspective is Theodore Rueter, *The United States in the World Political Economy* (McGraw-Hill, 1994).

It must also be remembered that economic relations among countries do not exist in a vacuum. Instead, economic relations are part of a complex pattern of interchanges that make up the international system. Rising protectionism will thus also harm political relations. When, for example, President Clinton had to decide in 1994 whether or not to impose economic sanctions on China in retaliation for its alleged human rights abuses, the president also had to keep China's strategic importance in mind. Among other things, the United States wants China's cooperation in pressuring North Korea to open its nuclear facilities to international inspection; Washington wanted to avoid a Chinese veto in the UN Security Council on intervention in Haiti; and Americans were trying to persuade China not to sell weapons technology to Iran. For these reasons, in addition to the potential economic damage from a trade war, Clinton chose not to impose the sanctions.

There are many political and social factors that impede the flow of free trade, and that can disadvantage countries that are the most open. It is also the case, as Brecher points out, that there is a discontinuity between the global economic system and the system of national regulation. This view is argued by U.S. labor leader Gus Tyler in "The Nation-State vs. the Global Economy,"

Challenge (March/April 1993). It may well be that the growth of a true world economy means that a system of effective global controls administered by an international organization is needed.

ISSUE 11

Does Immigration Strain Society's Resources?

YES: Daniel James, from "Close the Borders to All Newcomers," *Insight* (November 22, 1993)

NO: Stephen Moore, from "Give Us Your Best, Your Brightest," *Insight* (November 22, 1993)

ISSUE SUMMARY

YES: Daniel James, an analyst and author who writes on social issues, contends that a tidal wave of immigration is hitting U.S. shores and is threatening the U.S. economy and sense of cultural cohesiveness. He says that it is time for a moratorium on immigration.

NO: Stephen Moore, an economist with the Cato Institute in Washington, D.C., maintains that the net gains that the country reaps from the contributions of immigrants far outweigh any social costs.

The world is awash in refugees and immigrants. For the most part, immigrants are people seeking a better standard of living, people seeking to escape restrictions on their human rights, or people seeking to flee violence in their native lands and find safety in a new country. Whatever their motivations, vast numbers of people have left their countries in search of new ones.

There are some 125 million people living outside their native homelands, according to a 1994 report by Population Action International, a private organization that studies population and mass migration issues. Displacement is particularly severe in sub-Saharan Africa, where some 6 million people, about 1 percent of that region's population, are refugees, according to the United Nations High Commission for Refugees.

Among the countries that in 1992 were housing refugees displaced by fighting, famine, and other calamities, Iran had the largest group at 4.2 million. Canada was eighth with 568,000 refugees, and the United States was eleventh with 479,000 refugees. With the end of the cold war, many political analysts fear that the world will embark on a new era of ethnic violence that will uproot additional millions of people from their homes.

Whether or not those who are seeking new homes are actual refugees who have unexpectedly had to leave their homelands or immigrants who had planned to leave their lands, migration has been a traditional path to seeking a new life in a new place. The difficulty is that many countries are reacting to the increase in immigration pressure by closing, not opening, their doors. The UN estimates that between 1980 and 1992 some 15 million people migrated to Western Europe. Three million of these asked for political asylum. In 1992 alone, Germany had 438,000 people apply for political asylum, and there are now an estimated 2.8 million people living illegally in the countries of Western Europe. Seven percent of France's population is foreign-born.

The reaction in Europe has been to tighten entry polices. Germany used to have one of the most liberal immigration policies, which was based on Article 16 of its constitution. Article 16 promised asylum to "people persecuted on political grounds." But Germany amended its constitution on July 1, 1993, and Germany's immigration policy is now among the most restrictive in Europe.

As in Europe, legal and illegal immigration has become the subject of heated debate in the United States. The case of the Haitians has been particularly important during the Clinton administration. As a candidate, Bill Clinton advocated allowing many more Haitians to enter the United States; as president, Clinton soon beat a retreat and followed essentially the same policy George Bush had when he was president. There are many causes for resistance to immigration in the United States. Many Americans believe that immigrants compete for jobs, a worrisome thought in an era of economic uncertainty. There is also the notion that immigrants often use expensive social services (such as education, housing, and health care) but pay little in taxes. Changes in attitude toward political asylum have also contributed to the recent increase in opposition to immigration. In the past, large refugee groups from communist countries were allowed into the United States: Czechoslovakians, Hungarians, Poles, Romanians, and Soviets made up the bulk of immigrants from Europe during the 1960s, 1970s, and 1980s. Cambodians, Laotians, and Vietnamese accounted for the vast majority of Asian immigrants, and Cubans were the largest single group from Latin America. Arthur Helton, head of the Lawyers Committee for Human Rights, made this observation about the change in attitude toward immigrants: "[It] raises the question—was asylum just a cold war luxury all along? It seems so."

Racism may also play a part in the current debate over immigration policy. A national poll on immigration conducted in 1993 revealed that, of those Americans surveyed, half thought that it should be easier for people from Eastern Europe to emigrate to the United States. By contrast, 73 percent of the poll respondents thought that it should be more difficult for Haitians to come to the United States, 59 percent favored making it more difficult for Africans to come to the United States, and 65 percent wanted to make it harder for Asians to seek residency and citizenship.

This is the issue taken up in the readings by Daniel James and Stephen Moore. James would declare a moratorium on immigration to avoid what he describes as "a crisis of incalculable magnitude." Moore believes that by pursuing liberal immigration policies the United States can ensure that the twenty-first century, like the twentieth century, will be the American century.

YES
Daniel James

CLOSE THE BORDERS TO ALL NEWCOMERS

Strip the rhetoric from the evolving immigration debate and the bottom line becomes crystal clear: We may desire more and more immigrants, but can we afford so many of them? In his recently published memoirs, *Around the Cragged Hill,* George F. Kennan, perhaps [America's] most eminent statesman, goes to the heart of the matter:

> "We are already, for better or for worse, very much a polyglot country; and nothing of that is now to be changed. What I have in mind here are sheer numbers. There *is* such a thing as overcrowding. It has its psychic effects as well as its physical ones. There *are* limits to what the environment can stand."

The sheer numbers are indeed mind-boggling:

- 10.5 million immigrants, including those arriving illegally, entered the U.S. in the 1980s. That topped the previous record of 8.8 million who came here from 1901 to 1910.
- 15 to 18 million more newcomers, both legal and illegal, are projected to reach America in the 1990s, assuming our present immigration policy remains unchanged. Already, the number arriving in this decade is greater than for the same period in the previous decade. And there were nearly 1.2 million immigrants in 1992, 20 percent more than in 1991.
- 30 million immigrants—perhaps as many as 36 million—are expected to arrive in the first two decades of the next century, according to demographic projections and extrapolation of 1991–92 Census Bureau data.

The last two projections indicate that between 45 million and 54 million people—almost equal to the population of Great Britain—will be entering the U.S. in little more than a generation.

Add the 20 million immigrants who arrived from 1965 to 1990, and the grand total who will have entered the U.S. in just over a half-century (1965–2020) will be 65 million to 74 million.

There is no precedent for these numbers anywhere in the world. They constitute the biggest wave of immigration ever to a single country. Called the "fourth wave" of immigration to the U.S., it is really a tidal wave.

Yet the numbers are conservative. Unforeseeable trends in countries that generate immigrants could swell the tidal wave even higher than projected. It is likely, for example, that the demise of Cuba's communist dictatorship would send a flood of refugees to Miami comparable to the 125,000 *Marielitos* who inundated it in 1980.

Mexico is an even bigger concern. In the 1980s, it sent the U.S. nearly 4 million immigrants, more than the total for all of Asia. Two great "push" factors will drive ever more of them northward: high population growth— Mexico's present 90 million inhabitants will become 110 million by 2000— and unemployment/underemployment levels of 40 to 50 percent.

The North American Free Trade Agreement [NAFTA] ... may generate a temporary upsurge in illegal border crossings. It would draw more Mexicans to the relatively affluent north and make entering the U.S. affordable. Meanwhile, an expected rise in imports of cheaper U.S. corn would bankrupt Mexico's peasant class, the *campesinos*, and drive them to seek work stateside. Only years from now would NAFTA create enough jobs to keep Mexicans at home.

The cost to U.S. taxpayers of accepting endless numbers of immigrants is intolerable. We learn from a new study, "The Costs of Immigration," by economist Donald Huddle, that the net 1992 public assistance cost of the 19.3 million immigrants who have settled here since 1970

was $42.5 billion, after subtracting $20.2 billion they paid in taxes.

Huddle examined costs in 22 categories of federal, state and local assistance available to immigrants, including a package of 10 county welfare and health services. The largest net costs for immigrants in 1992 were $16 billion for education (primary, secondary and bilingual), $10.6 billion for health and welfare services and $8.5 billion for Medicaid.

Criminal justice and corrections costs for immigrants were found by Huddle to total more than $2 billion in 1992. The social price was greater: A disproportionately large number of illegals were in prison for committing felonies. In California, they made up 11 percent of all inmates.

Huddle also found that immigrants in 1992 displaced—probably forever— 2.07 million American workers. This should answer the oft-debated question: Do immigrants take jobs away from Americans?

It is true that American workers frequently turn down tasks that immigrants willingly perform, such as picking fruit and vegetables under inhumane conditions or making garments in urban sweatshops. But that hardly explains the virtual elimination of blacks from jobs in entire industries. In Los Angeles, unionized blacks have been displaced by nonunion Hispanics in janitorial services, and in Washington, D.C., by Latino immigrants in hotels and restaurants.

The puzzling question is: Why does the U.S. continue to import competition for American workers at a time of high unemployment? The Labor Department reports that 8.5 million Americans, about 6.7 percent of our work force, are unemployed. Our two principal minorities suffer most from joblessness—12.6 percent of blacks and 9.7 percent of Latinos—and they are the most vulnerable to displacement.

Immigration costs will rise further in this decade, Huddle forecasts. He projects that from 1993 to 2002, 11.1 million legal and illegal immigrants will be added to the 19.3 million post-1970 immigrants already here, for a total of 30.4 million. Their net cost to taxpayers during the next decade would come to $668.5 billion, which is larger than the $496 billion of the national deficit that President Clinton and Congress have pledged to erase over five years.

Indeed, the savings from reducing immigration could be applied to cutting the deficit considerably, with less pain to the taxpayer than paring public services and raising taxes, as the administration proposes. Alternatively, Huddle suggests, such savings could be used to finance investment tax credits to create and maintain 4.1 million private sector jobs, or 1.4 million public works and service jobs, throughout the decade.

Impossible to quantify, but perhaps more devastating in the long run, is the cost of excessive immigration to the environment. As more and more people are added to our population—already excessive at 260 million—the greater the environmental degradation will be. The immigrants will contribute to increasing energy use, toxic waste, smog and urban crowding, all of which affect our mental and emotional health as well as the ecosystem.

Our population is increasing by 3 million a year, a rate faster than that of any other advanced country. California provides an example of what can happen to a nearly ideal environment when it is overwhelmed by too many people. Since 1980, its population has zoomed

from 23.7 million to more than 31 million, an increase of almost one-third. As a consequence, Los Angeles and its once pristine bay are all but hopelessly polluted, and San Diego and Orange counties are fast becoming sad miniatures of Los Angeles.

Equally alarming is the impetus that uncontrolled immigration provides to separatism and its obverse, multiculturism. Those living in areas where there are many other immigrants, such as Los Angeles and Texas's Rio Grande Valley, see no need to learn English and so live in virtual isolation from the general population. As long as these barrios are constantly replenished with newcomers from Mexico—virtually a stone's throw away—their inhabitants will feel less and less need or desire to assimilate. This process encourages a kind of natural separatism that could lead to political separatism.

Richard Estrada, a journalist and scholar, sees an ominous parallel with Quebec: "If Francophone Quebec can bring the Canadian confederation to the brink of disintegration even though France lies an ocean away, should there not at least arise a certain reflectiveness about our Southwest, which lies contiguous to an overpopulated Third World nation?"

A growing number of Americans of all classes and ethnic groups share these concerns about immigration and favor reducing it. For at least two decades, a majority of Americans have expressed in various polls their desire to stop or reduce immigration. In January 1992, a Gallup Poll found that 64 percent of registered voters would vote for a presidential candidate who favored tougher laws on immigration. In December, the Latino National Political Survey discovered that Hispanics overwhelmingly believed there is too much immigration.

* * *

Even politicians who previously shunned immigration as a taboo subject are jumping onto the immigration reform bandwagon. From President Clinton, a Democrat, to California's Gov. Pete Wilson, a Republican, most are clamoring to curb illegal immigration. We can hope that they soon will understand that the main problem, as the public generally has perceived, is legal immigration.

Serious though illegal immigration is, *legal* immigration poses a much graver problem. We receive more than three times as many legal immigrants, including refugees, as illegal ones. Their numbers are projected to grow exponentially, because under the 1990 Immigration Act they are permitted to bring in an endless procession of family members. In 1992, for example, family-related immigrants totaled 594,000, or 49 percent of the 1.2 million immigrants who entered the U.S. that year.

Legal immigrants account for almost three-quarters of the total costs calculated by the Huddle study. Thus, of the $668.5 billion projected net cost to taxpayers for all immigrants from 1993 to 2002, legal immigrants would account for $482 billion. Illegal aliens would cost $186.4 billion.

The most effective way to curb illegal immigration is to declare a moratorium on *all* immigration. Why? If the U.S. clamps down on illegals but permits legal immigration to continue uncontrolled, that tells the world we are not serious about solving either problem, for it is easier to reduce or halt the legal flow than to hunt down those who arrive undercover. To do so would require a mere stroke of the pen and wouldn't cost taxpayers extra—Congress could just reform the Immigration Act of 1990, which is directly responsible for the 40 percent increase to immigration. That would send the unequivocal message to anyone who plans to enter the U.S. that we cannot afford to receive them—at least for the time being.

The message would ring loud and clear to would-be illegal immigrants that we mean business. It must be backed up, however, by a whole range of law enforcement measures that are now on the books but are ignored or not used effectively. In addition, to smoke out illegals and also eliminate the racket in fraudulent documents, Congress should approve a universal ID, much like the health security card that President Clinton displayed when he presented his health plan.

The ID cards would identify those who are legally in the U.S. and entitled to work and receive benefits. Local and state authorities should be directed to share information on illegals with the Immigration and Naturalization Service to aid in apprehending them; at present, authorities deny such information to the INS, in effect protecting illegals.

Instead of sending the National Guard to patrol the border as advocated by some lawmakers. it would be more effective to give the Border Patrol sufficient personnel to do its job. At least 2,000 new agents should be added to the current force of about 4,000, as well as equipment such as better night sensors and new vehicles. The Customs Service will also require additional personnel, particularly if NAFTA is put into effect and vehicular traffic from Mexico increases as expected.

A vital component of any program to curb immigration must be the cooperation of the Mexican government. The White House should take advantage of our cordial relations with Mexico and our growing economic clout to request that our southern neighbor cease its traditional (though unwritten) policy of regarding the U.S. as a safety valve.

A U.S. moratorium on immigration would yield highly positive gains by allowing the 20 million immigrants now within our borders time to assimilate into the mainstream. It would remove the pressure of new millions crowding into inner-city barrios and encourage existing inhabitants to break out of them. This would mitigate the danger of separatism, counter multiculturalist trends, defuse interethnic tensions and reduce crime and violence.

If this prescription sounds like a pipe dream, let us recall that restrictive legislation in 1924 cut immigration to a trickle, allowing enough time for the masses of immigrants the U.S. had then to overcome the obstacles to assimilation. That literally saved America. For when the Japanese struck at Pearl Harbor in 1941 and the U.S. was confronted by their military might plus that of Ger-

many, which already had conquered Europe and had just invaded the Soviet Union, our nation stood united against them. Sadly, one doubts whether today's America, torn by an identity crisis spawned by divisive forces, would be capable of meeting a similar threat.

The United States is headed for a crisis of incalculable magnitude if mass immigration continues unchecked. The argument of those who favor an open border is that immigrants have always contributed to our society, and so they have. But we no longer can afford the world's "huddled masses" when our own are so often homeless and jobless. If we permit immigration to continue uncontrolled, it will explode in a full-blown crisis that will extend beyond the vociferous separatism/multiculturalism debate to engulf us in a violent civil conflict.

America is under siege. It is threatened from without by international terrorism and from within by centrifugal forces that already have revealed their capacity for destruction in bloody riots from Los Angeles to Miami, from Washington to Manhattan.

NO
Stephen Moore

GIVE US YOUR BEST, YOUR BRIGHTEST

For many Americans, the word "immigration" immediately conjures up an image of poor Mexicans scrambling across the border near San Diego to find minimum-wage work and perhaps collect government benefits. Recent public opinion polls confirm that the attitude of the American public toward immigration is highly unfavorable. Central Americans are perceived as welfare abusers who stubbornly refuse to learn English, Haitians are seen as AIDS carriers, Russian Jews are considered to be mafiosi, and Asians are seen as international terrorists. The media reinforce these stereotypes by battering the public with negative depictions of immigrants.

The conception of immigrants as tired, poor, huddled masses seems permanently sketched into the mind of the public, just as the words are sketched irrevocably at the feet of the Statue of Liberty. But the Emma Lazarus poem simply does not describe the hundreds of thousands of people who are building new lives here in the 1990s. It would be more appropriate if the words at the base of the statue read: "Give us your best, your brightest, your most energetic and talented." Why? Because in large part those are the people who come to the United States each year.

Before we start slamming shut the golden door, it might be worthwhile to find out who the newcomers are and how they truly affect our lives.

Anyone who believes that immigrants are a drain on the U.S. economy has never visited the Silicon Valley in California. Here and in other corridors of high-tech entrepreneurship, immigrants are literally the lifeblood of many of the nation's most prosperous industries. In virtually every field in which the United States asserted global leadership in the 1980s—industries such as computer design and softwear, pharmaceuticals, bioengineering, electronics, superconductivity, robotics and aerospace engineering—one finds immigrants. In many ways these high-growth industries are the modern version of the American melting pot in action.

Consider Intel Corp. With profits of $1.1 billion in 1992, it is one of the most prolific and fast-expanding companies in the United States, employing tens of thousands of American workers. It is constantly developing exciting, cutting-edge technologies that will define the computer industry in the 21st century.

And it is doing all of this largely with the talents of America's newest immigrants. Three members of Intel's top management, including Chief Executive Officer Andrew S. Grove, from Hungary, are immigrants. Some of its most successful and revolutionary computer technologies were pioneered by immigrants, such as the 8080 microprocessor (an expanded-power computer chip), invented by a Japanese, and polysilicon FET gates (the basic unit of memory storage on modern computer chips), invented by an Italian. Dick Ward, manager of employee information systems at Intel, says: "Our whole business is predicated on inventing the next generation of computer technologies. The engine that drives that quest is brainpower. And here at Intel, much of that brainpower comes from immigrants."

Or consider Du Pont-Merck Pharmaceutical Co., an $800 million-a-year health care products company based in Wilmington, Del., which reports that immigrants are responsible for many of its most promising new product innovations. For example, losartan, an antihypertensive drug, was developed by a team of scientists that included two Chinese and a Lithuanian. Joseph Mollica, Chief Executive Officer of Du Pont-Merck, says that bringing together such diverse talent "lets you look at problems and opportunities from a slightly different point of view."

Intel and Du Pont-Merck are not alone in relying on immigrants. Robert Kelley Jr., president of SO/CAL/TEN, an association of nearly 200 high-tech California companies, insists: "Without the influx of Asians in the 1980s, we would not have had the entrepreneurial explosion we've seen in California." David N. K. Wang, vice president for worldwide business operations at Applied Materials Inc., a computer-technology company in California, adds that because of immigration, "Silicon Valley is one of the most international business centers in the world."

Take away the immigrants, and you take away the talent base that makes such centers operate. Indeed, it is frightening to think what would happen to America's global competitiveness if the immigrants stopped coming. Even scarier is the more realistic prospect that U.S. policymakers will enact laws to prevent them from coming.

New research has begun to quantify the contributions of immigrants to American industry. The highly respected National Research Council reported in 1988 that "a large fraction of the technological output of the United States [is] dependent upon foreign talent and that such dependency is growing." Noting that well over half of all scientists graduating with doctorate degrees from American universities and one in three engineers working in the United States are immigrants, the report states emphatically: "It is clear... that these foreign-born engineers enrich our culture and make substantial contributions to the U.S. economic well-being and competitiveness."

The United States' competitive edge over the Japanese, Germans, Koreans and much of Europe is linked closely to its continued ability to attract and retain highly talented workers from other countries. A 1990 study by the national Science Foundation says, "Very significant, positive aspects arise from the presence of foreign-born engineers in our society."

For example, superconductivity, a technology that is expected to spawn hundreds of vital new commercial applications in the next century, was discovered by a physicist at the University of Houston, Paul C. W. Chu. He was born in China and came to the U.S. in 1972. His brilliance and inventiveness have made him a top contender for a Nobel Prize.

Of course, if Chu does win a Nobel, he will join a long list of winners who were immigrants in America. In the 20th century, between 20 percent and 50 percent of the Nobel Prize winners, depending on the discipline involved, have been immigrants to the United States. Today there are more Russian Nobel Prize winners living in the U.S. than there are living in Russia.

Public opinion polls consistently reveal that a major worry is that immigrants take jobs from American workers. The fear is understandable but misplaced. Immigrants don't just take jobs, they create jobs. One way is by starting new businesses. Today, America's immigrants, even those who come with relatively low skill levels, are highly entrepreneurial.

Take Koreans, for example. According to sociologists Alendro Portes and Ruben Rumbaut, "In Los Angeles, the propensity for self-employment is three times greater for Koreans than among the population as a whole. Grocery stores, restaurants, gas stations, liquor stores and real estate offices are typical Korean businesses." Cubans also are prodigious creators of new businesses. The number of Cuban-owned businesses in Miami has expanded from 919 in 1967 to 8,000 in 1976 to 28,000 in 1990. On Jefferson Boulevard in Dallas, more than 800 businesses operate, three-quarters of them owned by first- and second-generation Hispanic immigrants. Just 10 years ago, before the influx of Mexicans and other Central Americans, the neighborhood was in

decay, with many vacant storefronts displaying "for sale" signs in the windows. Today it is a thriving ethnic neighborhood.

To be sure, few immigrant-owned businesses mature into an Intel. In fact, many fail completely. Like most new businesses in America, most immigrant establishments are small and only marginally profitable. The average immigrant business employs two to four workers and records roughly $200,000 in annual sales. However, such small businesses, as President Clinton often correctly emphasizes, are a significant source of jobs.

It should not be too surprising that immigrants are far more likely than average U.S. citizens to take business risks. After all, uprooting oneself, traveling to a foreign culture and making it requires more than the usual amount of courage, ambition, resourcefulness and even bravado. Indeed, this is part of the self-selection process that makes immigrants so particularly desirable. Immigrants are not just people—they are a very special group of people. By coming, they impart productive energies on the rest of us.

This is not just romanticism. It is well-grounded in fact. Countless studies have documented that immigrants to the United States tend to be more skilled, more highly educated and wealthier than the average citizen of their native countries.

Thomas Sowell, an economist and senior fellow at the Hoover Institution in Stanford, Calif., reports in his seminal study on immigration, "Ethnic America," that black immigrants from the West Indies have far higher skill levels than their countrymen at home. He also finds that the income levels of West Indies immigrants are higher than those of

West Indies natives, American blacks and native-born white Americans.

Surprisingly, even illegal immigrants are not the poverty-stricken and least skilled from their native countries. Surveys of undocumented immigrants from Mexico to the United States show that only about 5 percent were unemployed in Mexico, whereas the average unemployment rate there was about three times that level, and that a relatively high percentage of them worked in white-collar jobs in Mexico. In addition, surveys have found that illiteracy among undocumented Mexicans in the U.S. is about 10 percent, whereas illiteracy in Mexico is about 22 percent.

Perhaps the greatest asset of immigrants is their children, who tend to be remarkably successful in the U.S. Recently, the city of Boston reported that an incredible 13 of the 17 valedictorians in its public high schools were foreign-born—from China, Vietnam, Portugal, El Salvador, France, Italy, Jamaica and the former Czechoslovakia. Many could not speak a word of English when they arrived. Public high schools in Washington, Chicago and Los Angeles also report remarkably disproportionate numbers of immigrant children at the top of the class. Similarly, Westinghouse reports that over the past 12 years, about one-third of its prestigious National Science Talent Search winners have been Asians. Out of this group might emerge America's next Albert Einstein, who himself was an immigrant.

So one hidden cost of restricting immigration is the loss of immigrants' talented and motivated children.

In the past century, America has admitted roughly 50 million immigrants. This has been one of the largest migrations in the history of the world. Despite this infusion of people—no, because of it

—the United States became by the middle of the 20th century the wealthiest nation in the world. Real wages in America have grown more than eightfold over this period. The U.S. economy employed less than 40 million people in 1900; today it employs nearly 120 million people. The U.S. job machine had not the slightest problem expanding and absorbing the 8 million legal immigrants who came to this country in the 1980s. Eighteen million jobs were created.

But what about those frightening headlines? "Immigration Bankrupting Nation." "Immigrants Displacing U.S. Workers." "Foreigners Lured to U.S. by Welfare."

Here are the facts. The 1990s census reveals that roughly 6 percent of native-born Americans are on public assistance, versus 7 percent of the foreign-born, with less than 5 percent of illegal immigrants collecting welfare. Not much reason for alarm. Because immigrants tend to come to the United States when they are young and working, over their lifetimes they each pay about $20,000 more in taxes than they use in services, according to economist Julian Simon of the University of Maryland. With 1 million immigrants per year, the nation gains about $20 billion more than cost. Rather than fiscal burdens, immigrants are huge bargains.

Nor do immigrants harm the U.S. labor market. A comprehensive 1989 study by the U.S. Department of Labor concluded: "Neither U.S. workers nor most minority workers appear to be adversely affected by immigration—especially during periods of economic expansion." In the 1980s, the top 10 immigrant-receiving states —including California, Florida, Massachusetts and Texas—recorded rates of unemployment 2 percentage points below the U.S. average, according to the

Alexis de Tocqueville Institution in Arlington, Va. So where's the job displacement?

We are now witnessing in America what might be described as the return of the nativists. They are selling fear and bigotry. But if any of their allegations against immigrants are accurate, then America could not have emerged as the economic superpower it is today.

In fact, most Americans do accept that immigration in the past has contributed greatly to the nation's economic growth. But they are not so sanguine in their assessment of present and future immigrants. It is strangely inconsistent that Americans believe that so long-standing and crucial a benefit is now a source of cultural and economic demise.

Shortly before his death, Winston Churchill wrote, "The empires of the future are the empires of the mind." America is confronted with one of the most awesome opportunities in world history to build those empires by attracting highly skilled, highly educated and entrepreneurial people from all over the globe. The Andrew Groves and the Paul Chus of the world do not want to go to Japan, Israel, Germany, France or Canada. Almost universally they want to come to the United States. We can be selective. By expanding immigration but orienting our admission policies toward gaining the best and the brightest, America would enjoy a significant comparative advantage over its geopolitical rivals.

By pursuing a liberal and strategic policy on immigration, America can ensure that the 21st century, like the 20th, will be the American century.

POSTSCRIPT

Does Immigration Strain Society's Resources?

In New York Bay on Liberty Island stands the Statue of Liberty, who greets those entering the bay from the Atlantic Ocean. Her torch is meant to symbolically light the way of immigrants to nearby Ellis Island, which served as the chief point of entry for immigrants to the United States from 1892 to 1943. Both the statue and Ellis Island are now part of the Statue of Liberty National Monument, which honors the important role that immigrants, famous and forgotten, have played in American history.

To raise money in 1883 to build a pedestal for Frédéric-Auguste Bartholdi's Statue of Liberty, a citizens' committee invited authors to write appropriate words of commemoration and to donate their manuscripts to the committee for a fund-raising auction. One author, Emma Lazarus, penned a sonnet, "The New Colossus," whose most famous lines read:

> Give me your tired, your poor,
> Your huddled masses yearning to breathe free,
> The wretched refuse of your teeming shore.
> Send these, the homeless, temptest-tost to me,
> I lift my lamp beside the golden door.

These words are on a plaque on the pedestal of the Statue of Liberty. The central question of this debate is whether or not this sentiment should still govern U.S. policy.

In reality, the open door to immigration ended long ago. The decade 1911–1920 was the last with an average annual rate of over 5 immigrants per 1,000 Americans. Since then the rates have fluctuated, with the 1931–1940 rate at 0.4 immigrants per 1,000, the lowest in history. It may well be that Stephen Moore is right and that immigration should be encouraged, but those who argue this case need to account for the changing circumstances of immigrants. By the same token, those who oppose immigration need to be careful of their arguments also. To total up numbers of immigrants and to quote unemployment statistics is an easy exercise in data collection. To say that A (immigration) caused B (unemployment) is another matter. They may not be related at all. Indeed, in a low-birth-rate, graying America, it may be that immigrants provide new sources of labor for both high-skill jobs and those that many Americans disdain.

For more pro and con discussion of the economic contributions of immigrants to the United States, read George Borjas, *Friends or Strangers* (Basic Books, 1990) and Julian L. Simon, *The Economic Consequences of Immigration*

(Basil Blackwell, 1989). Then there are those, such as Lawrence E. Harrison, "America and Its Immigrants," *National Interest* (Summer 1992), who favor selective immigration—only those with desirable skills should be permitted into the United States. *Time* magazine's special issue "The New Face of America: How Immigrants Are Shaping the World's First Multicultural Society" (Fall 1993) is worth consulting, despite its arguable assertion that the United States is the first multicultural society.

PART 3

THEY SHALL BEAT THEIR SWORDS INTO PLOWSHARES. AND THEIR SPEARS INTO PRUNING HOOKS. NATION SHALL NOT LIFT UP SWORD AGAINST NATION. NEITHER SHALL THEY LEARN WAR ANY MORE

International Security and World Politics

Whatever we may wish, war, terrorism, and other forms of physical coercion are still important elements of international politics. Countries calculate both how to use the instruments of force and how to implement national security. There can be little doubt, however, that significant changes are under way in this realm as part of the changing world system. Strong pressures exist to expand the mission and strengthen the security capabilities of international organizations, to reduce or eliminate nuclear weapons worldwide, and to reevaluate the utility of intelligence agencies in the post–cold war era. This section examines how countries in the international system are addressing these issues.

■ Should a Permanent UN Military
   Force Be Established?

■ Should the United States Forcefully
   Oppose North Korea's Nuclear
   Weapons Program?

■ Is It Time to Terminate the CIA?

■ Does the World Have to Have Nuclear
   Weapons at All?

ISSUE 12

Should a Permanent UN Military Force Be Established?

YES: Boutros Boutros-Ghali, from *An Agenda for Peace: Preventive Diplomacy, Peacemaking and Peacekeeping* (United Nations, 1992)

NO: John F. Hillen III, from "Policing the New World Order: The Operational Utility of a Permanent U.N. Army," *Strategic Review* (Spring 1994)

ISSUE SUMMARY

YES: United Nations Secretary-General Boutros Boutros-Ghali contends that both the scope of the United Nations' security mission and the extent of the UN's military capabilities should be expanded significantly in the interest of world peace.

NO: John F. Hillen III, a lieutenant in the U.S. Army and a doctoral student in international relations at Oxford University, criticizes the idea of a permanent UN army in general and the specific recommendations of Boutros-Ghali. He argues that such a force is unworkable.

More than any single purpose, the United Nations was established with the hope that it could help save "succeeding generations from the scourge of war which . . . has brought untold sorrow to mankind." These opening words of the UN Charter (its constitution) reflect a realization born of World War I, World War II, and the advent of the atomic age that, whatever the horrendous past toll of warfare, the future cost could be far, far worse.

The UN seeks to maintain and restore peace through a variety of methods. These include creating norms against violence, providing a forum to debate questions as an alternative to war, efforts to prevent the proliferation of weapons, diplomatic intervention (such as mediation), and the establishment of diplomatic and economic sanctions. Additionally, and at the heart of the issue here, the UN can dispatch troops under its banner or authorize member countries to use their forces to carry out UN mandates.

United Nations forces involving a substantial number of military or police personnel have been used more than two dozen times in the organization's nearly half-century history and have involved troops and police from more than 75 countries. UN forces have helped maintain or restore the peace in many locations; almost 1,000 blue-helmeted UN soldiers have died in the quest for international peace; and those who have served received the Nobel

Peace Prize in 1988. Nevertheless, recent events and attitude changes have renewed the debate over the military role of the UN.

Of all UN operations, 18 total, about half are currently active. Several of these, including the UN presence in Bosnia and Herzegovina, Cambodia, and Somalia, include large numbers of troops and collectively cost approximately $2 billion annually. Often UN forces have played an important part in the peace process; other times they have been unsuccessful. The limited mandate (role, instructions) and strength (personnel, armaments) of UN forces have frequently left them helpless bystanders. The change in the international system has also added to the controversy over the UN's role. The cold war has ended; some people hope for and are trying to promote a new world order. They want countries to live up to the UN charter, which requires countries to use force unilaterally *only* for immediate self-defense, unless they are authorized to use force by the UN or a regional organization. This means that collective action under UN auspices is becoming more the accepted practice; unilateral action by a country more the exception.

United Nations forces have served in two capacities: to provide *collective security* and to act as *peacekeepers*. Collective security is the idea that aggression against anyone is a threat to everyone. Therefore, the collective body should cooperate to prevent and, if necessary, defeat aggression. The second, long-standing role of peacekeeper usually involves UN forces acting as a buffer between two sides to provide an atmosphere that will allow them to settle their differences, or at least not to fight. Neither collective security nor peacekeeping, however, precisely apply to situations such as domestic civil wars (Bosnia and Herzegovina, Cambodia, Rwanda, Somalia) where there is no (a) international aggressor and/or (b) clearly identifiable aggressor. Some people consider this a gap in what the UN does to prevent the scourge of war and, therefore, would expand the UN's role to include *peacemaking*. This would involve intervening in either international or civil wars, with or without the consent of any of the participants, to *make* the warring parties stop fighting.

Another proposed change for the United Nations is to create a standing UN army, or at least a ready reserve of troops. These troops would remain with the forces of their home countries but would train for UN operations and would be available to the UN at all times.

The immediate debate in this issue was touched off by a January 1992 summit meeting of the leaders of the 15 countries with seats on the UN Security Council. Leaders called on the UN secretary-general to report on ways to enhance the UN's ability "for preventative diplomacy, for peacemaking, and for peacekeeping." The response of Secretary-General Boutros Boutros-Ghali is the first of the two following selections. In it, Boutros-Ghali makes far-reaching recommendations to strengthen and expand the UN's role in promoting, maintaining, and restoring peace. John Hillen III argues that the secretary-general's recommendations and other such proposals are mostly ill-conceived and should not be supported.

YES

Boutros Boutros-Ghali

AN AGENDA FOR PEACE: PREVENTIVE DIPLOMACY, PEACEMAKING AND PEACEKEEPING

INTRODUCTION

In its statement of 31 January 1992, adopted at the conclusion of the first meeting held by the Security Council at the level of Heads of State and Government, I was invited to prepare, for circulation to the Members of the United Nations by 1 July 1992, an "analysis and recommendations on ways of strengthening and making more efficient, within the framework and provisions of the Charter, the capacity of the United Nations for preventive diplomacy, for peacemaking and for peacekeeping."

The United Nations is a gathering of sovereign States and what it can do depends on the common ground that they create between them. The adversarial decades of the Cold War made the original promise of the Organization impossible to fulfill. The January 1992 Summit therefore represented an unprecedented recommitment, at the highest political level, to the Purposes and Principles of the Charter.

In these past months a conviction has grown, among nations large and small, that an opportunity has been regained to achieve [one of] the great objectives of the Charter—a United Nations capable of maintaining international peace and security.... This opportunity must not be squandered. The Organization must never again be crippled as it was in the era that has now passed.

I welcome the invitation of the Security Council, ... to prepare this report. It draws upon ideas and proposals transmitted to me by Governments, regional agencies, nongovernmental organizations, and institutions and individuals from many countries.... [But] the responsibility for this report is my own.

The sources of conflict and war are pervasive and deep. To reach them will require our utmost effort to enhance respect for human rights and fundamental freedoms, to promote sustainable economic and social development for wider prosperity, to alleviate distress and to curtail the existence and use of massively destructive weapons.... I bear them all in mind as, in the present report, I turn to the problems that the Council has specifically requested I consider: preventive diplomacy, peacemaking and peacekeeping—to which I have added a closely related concept, post-conflict peace-building.

The manifest desire of the membership to work together is a new source of strength in our common endeavor. Success is far from certain, however. While my report deals with ways to improve the Organization's capacity to pursue and preserve peace, it is crucial for all Member States to bear in mind that the search for improved mechanisms and techniques will be of little significance unless this new spirit of commonality is propelled by the will to take the hard decisions demanded by this time of opportunity....

THE CHANGING CONTEXT

In the course of the past few years the immense ideological barrier that for decades gave rise to distrust and hostility —and the terrible tools of destruction that were their inseparable companions—has collapsed. Even as the issues between States north and south grow more acute, and call for attention at the highest levels of government, the improvement in relations between States east and west affords new possibilities, some already realized, to meet successfully threats to common security.

Authoritarian regimes have given way to more democratic forces and responsive Governments. The form, scope and intensity of these processes differ from Latin America to Africa to Europe to Asia, but they are sufficiently similar to indicate a global phenomenon. Parallel to these political changes, many States are seeking more open forms of economic policy, creating a worldwide sense of dynamism and movement.

To the hundreds of millions who gained their independence in the surge of decolonization following the creation of the United Nations, have been added millions more who have recently gained freedom. Once again new States are taking their seats in the General Assembly. Their arrival reconfirms the importance and indispensability of the sovereign State as the fundamental entity of the international community.

We have entered a time of global transition marked by uniquely contradictory trends. Regional and continental associations of States are evolving ways to deepen cooperation and ease some of the contentious characteristics of sovereign and nationalistic rivalries. National boundaries are blurred by advanced communications and global commerce.... At the same time, however, fierce new assertions of nationalism and sovereignty spring up, and the cohesion of States is threatened by brutal ethnic, religious, social, cultural or linguistic strife....

The concept of peace is easy to grasp; that of international security is more complex, for a pattern of contradictions has arisen here as well. As major nuclear Powers have begun to negotiate arms reduction agreements, the proliferation of weapons of mass destruction threatens to increase and conventional arms continue to be amassed in many parts of the world. As racism becomes recognized for the destructive force it is and as apartheid is being dismantled, new racial tensions are rising and finding expression in violence. Technological advances are altering the nature and the expectation of life all over the globe. The revolution in communications has united the world in awareness, in aspiration and in greater solidarity against injustice. But progress also brings new risks for stability: ecological damage, disruption of family and community life, greater intrusion into the lives and rights of individuals. ...

So at this moment of renewed opportunity, the efforts of the Organization to build peace, stability and security must encompass matters beyond military threats in order to break the fetters of strife and warfare that have characterized the past. But armed conflicts today, as they have throughout history, continue to bring fear and horror to humanity, requiring our urgent involvement to try to prevent, contain and bring them to an end.

Since the creation of the United Nations in 1945, over 100 major conflicts around the world have left some 20 million dead. The United Nations was rendered powerless to deal with many of these crises because of the vetoes—279 of them —cast in the Security Council, which were a vivid expression of the divisions of that period.

With the end of the Cold War there have been no such vetoes since 31 May 1990,* and demands on the United Nations have surged. Its security arm, once disabled by circumstances it was not created or equipped to control, has emerged as a central instrument for the prevention and resolution of conflicts and for the preservation of peace. Our aims must be:

- To seek to identify at the earliest possible stage situations that could produce conflict, and to try through diplomacy to remove the sources of danger before violence results;

- Where conflict erupts, to engage in peacemaking aimed at resolving the issues that have led to conflict;

- Through peacekeeping, to work to preserve peace, however fragile, where fighting has been halted and to assist in implementing agreements achieved by the peacemakers;

- To stand ready to assist in peacebuilding in its differing contexts: rebuilding the institutions and infrastructures of nations torn by civil war and strife; and building bonds of peaceful mutual benefit among nations formerly at war;

- And in the largest sense, to address the deepest causes of conflict: economic despair, social injustice and political oppression....

The Security Council has been assigned by all Member States the primary responsibility for the maintenance of international peace and security under the Charter. In its broadest sense this responsibility must be shared by the General Assembly and by all the functional elements of the world Organization....

The foundation-stone of this work is and must remain the State. Respect for its fundamental sovereignty and integrity are crucial to any common international progress. The time of absolute and exclusive sovereignty, however, has passed; its theory was never matched by reality. ... The United Nations has not closed its door. Yet if every ethnic, religious or linguistic group claimed statehood, there would be no limit to fragmentation, and peace, security and economic well-being for all would become ever more difficult to achieve.

One requirement for solutions to these problems lies in commitment to human rights with a special sensitivity to those of

*[This is no longer true.—Ed.]

minorities, whether ethnic, religious, social or linguistic.... The General Assembly soon will have before it a declaration on the rights of minorities. That instrument, together with the increasingly effective machinery of the United Nations dealing with human rights, should enhance the situation of minorities as well as the stability of States.

... The sovereignty, territorial integrity and independence of States within the established international system, and the principle of self-determination for peoples, both of great value and importance, must not be permitted to work against each other in the period ahead.... Our constant duty should be to maintain the integrity of each while finding a balanced design for all.

DEFINITIONS

The terms preventive diplomacy, peacemaking and peacekeeping are integrally related and as used in this report are defined as follows:

Preventive diplomacy is action to prevent disputes from arising between parties, to prevent existing disputes from escalating into conflicts and to limit the spread of the latter when they occur.

Peacemaking is action to bring hostile parties to agreement, essentially through such peaceful means as those foreseen in Chapter VI of the Charter of the United Nations.

Peacekeeping is the deployment of a United Nations presence in the field, hitherto with the consent of all the parties concerned, normally involving United Nations military and/or policy personnel and frequently civilians as well. Peacekeeping is a technique that expands the possibilities for both the prevention of conflict and the making of peace.

The present report in addition will address the critically related concept of post-conflict peace-building—action to identify and support structures which will tend to strengthen and solidify peace in order to avoid a relapse into conflict....

These four areas for action, taken together, and carried out with the backing of all Members, offer a coherent contribution towards securing peace in the spirit of the Charter. The United Nations has extensive experience not only in these fields, but in the wider realm of work for peace in which these four fields are set.... The world has often been rent by conflict and plagued by massive human suffering and deprivation. Yet it would have been far more so without the continuing efforts of the United Nations. This wide experience must be taken into account in assessing the potential of the United Nations in maintaining international security not only in its traditional sense, but in the new dimensions presented by the era ahead.

PREVENTIVE DIPLOMACY

The most desirable and efficient employment of diplomacy is to ease tensions before they result in conflict—or, if conflict breaks out, to act swiftly to contain it and resolve its underlying causes. Preventive diplomacy may be performed by the Secretary-General personally or through senior staff or specialized agencies and programs, by the Security Council or the General Assembly, and by regional organizations in cooperation with the United Nations. Preventive diplomacy requires measures to create confidence; it needs early warning based on information gathering and informal or formal fact-finding;

it may also involve preventive deployment and, in some situations, demilitarized zones....

Preventive Deployment

United Nations operations in areas of crisis have generally been established after conflict has occurred. The time has come to plan for circumstances warranting preventive deployment [of UN forces], which could take place in a variety of instances and ways. For example, in conditions of national crisis there could be preventive deployment at the request of the Government or all parties concerned, or with their consent; in inter-State disputes such deployment could take place when two countries feel that a United Nations presence on both sides of their border can discourage hostilities; furthermore, preventive deployment could take place when a country feels threatened and requests the deployment of an appropriate United Nations presence along its side of the border alone. In each situation, the mandate and composition of the United Nations presence would need to be carefully devised and be clear to all.

In conditions of crisis within a country, when the Government requests all parties consent, preventive deployment could help in a number of ways to alleviate suffering and to limit or control violence. Humanitarian assistance, impartially provided, could be critical importance; assistance in maintaining security, whether through military, police or civilian personnel, could save lives and develop conditions of safety in which negotiations can be held....

In these situations of internal crisis the United Nations will need to respect the sovereignty of the State; to do otherwise would not be in accordance with the understanding of Member States in accepting the principles of the Charter....

In this context, humanitarian assistance should be provided with the consent of the affected country and, in principle, on the basis of an appeal by that country....

In inter-State disputes, when both parties agree, I recommend that if the Security Council concludes that the likelihood of hostilities between neighboring countries could be removed by the preventive deployment of a United Nations presence on the territory of each State, such action should be taken....

In cases where one nation fears a cross-border attack, if the Security Council concludes that a United Nations presence on one side of the border, with the consent only of the requesting economy, would serve to deter conflict, I recommend that preventive deployment take place....

Demilitarized Zones

In the past, demilitarized zones have been established by agreement of the parties at the conclusion of a conflict. In addition to the deployment of United Nations personnel in such zones as part of peacekeeping operations, consideration should now be given to the usefulness of such zones as a form of preventive deployment, on both sides of a border, with the agreement of the two parties, as a means of separating potential belligerents, or on one side of the line, at the request of one party, for the purpose of removing any pretext for attack. Demilitarized zones would serve as symbols of the international community's concern that conflict be prevented.

PEACEMAKING

Between the tasks of seeking to prevent conflict and keeping the peace lies the responsibility to try to bring hostile parties to agreement by peaceful means. Chapter VI of the Charter sets forth a comprehensive list of such means for the resolution of conflict. These have been amplified in various declarations.... The United Nations has had wide experience in the application of these peaceful means. If conflicts have gone unresolved, it is not because techniques [for a] peaceful settlement were unknown or inadequate. The fault lies first in the lack of political will of parties to seek a solution to their differences through such means as are suggested in the Charter, and second, in the lack of leverage at the disposal of a third party if this is the procedure chosen. The indifference of the internal community to a problem, or the marginalization of it, can also thwart the possibilities of solution. We must look primarily to these areas if we hope to enhance the capacity of the Organization in achieving peaceful settlements....

Use of Military Force

It is the essence of the concept of collective security as contained in the Charter that if peaceful means fail, the measures provided in Chapter VII should be used, on the decision of the Security Council, to maintain or restore international peace and security in the face of a "threat to the peace, breach of the peace, or act of aggression." The Security Council has not so far made use of the most coercive of these measures—the action by military forces foreseen in Article 42. In the situation between Iraq and Kuwait, the Council chose to authorize Member States to take measures on its behalf. The Charter, however, provides a detailed approach which now merits the attention of all Member States.

Under Article 42 of the Charter, the Security Council has the authority to take military action to maintain or restore international peace and security. While such action should only be taken when all peaceful means have failed, the option of taking it is essential to the credibility of the United Nations as a guarantor of international security. This will require bringing into being, through negotiations, the special agreements foreseen in Article 43 of the Charter, whereby Member States undertake to make armed forces, assistance and facilities available to the Security Council for the purposes stated in Article 42, not only on an ad hoc basis but on a permanent basis. Under the political circumstances that now exist for the first time since the Charter was adopted, the long-standing obstacles to the conclusion of such special agreements should no longer prevail. The ready availability of armed forces on call could serve, in itself, as a means of deterring breaches of the peace since a potential aggressor would know that the Council had at its disposal a means of response. Forces under Article 43 may perhaps never be sufficiently large or well enough equipped to deal with a threat from a major army equipped with sophisticated weapons. They would be useful, however, in meeting any threat posed by a military force of a lesser order. I recommend that the Security Council initiate negotiations in accordance with Article 43, supported by the Military Staff Committee, which may be augmented if necessary by others in accordance with Article 47, paragraph 2, of the Charter. It is my view that the role of the Military Staff Committee should be seen in the context of Chapter VII, and not that of the planning or conduct of peacekeeping operations.

Peace-Enforcement Units

The mission of forces under Article 43 would be to respond to outright aggression, imminent or actual. Such forces are not likely to be available for some time to come. Cease-fires have often been agreed to but not complied with, and the United Nations has sometimes been called upon to send forces to restore and maintain the cease-fire. This task can on occasion exceed the mission of peacekeeping forces and the expectations of peacekeeping force contributors. I recommend that the Council consider the utilization of peace-enforcement units in clearly defined circumstances and with their terms of reference specified in advance. Such units from Member States would be available on call and would consist of troops that have volunteered for such service. They would have to be more heavily armed than peacekeeping forces and would need to undergo extensive preparatory training within their national forces. Deployment and operation of such forces would be under the authorization of the Security Council and would, as in the case of peacekeeping forces, be under the command of the Secretary-General. I consider such peace-enforcement units to be warranted as a provisional measure under Article 40 of the Charter. Such peace-enforcement units should not be confused with the forces that may eventually be constituted under Article 43 to deal with acts of aggression or with the military personnel which Governments may agree to keep on standby for possible contribution to peacekeeping operations.

Just as diplomacy will continue across the span of all the activities dealt with in the present report, so there may not be a dividing line between peacemaking and peacekeeping. Peacemaking is often a prelude to peacekeeping—just as the deployment of a United Nations presence in the field may expand possibilities for the prevention of conflict, facilitate the work of peacemaking and in many cases serve as a prerequisite for peace-building.

PEACEKEEPING

Peacekeeping can rightly be called the invention of the United Nations. It has brought a degree of stability to numerous areas of tension around the world.

Increasing Demands

Thirteen peacekeeping operations were established between the years 1945 and 1987; 13 others since then. An estimated 528,000 military, police and civilian personnel had served under the flag of the United Nations until January 1992. Over 800 of them from 43 countries have died in the service of the Organization. The costs of these operations have aggregated some $8.3 billion till 1992. The unpaid arrears towards them stand at over $800 million, which represent a debt owed by the Organization to the troop-contributing countries. Peacekeeping operations approved at present are estimated to cost close to $3 billion in the current 12-month period, while patterns of payment are unacceptably slow. Against this, global defense expenditures at the end of the last decade had approached $1 trillion a year, or $2 million per minute.

The contrast between the costs of United Nations peacekeeping and the costs of the alternative, war—between the demands of the Organization and the means provided to meet them—would be farcical were the consequences not so damaging to global stability and to the credibility of the Organization. At a time when nations and peoples increasingly are looking to the United Nations for assistance in keeping the peace—and holding it responsible when this cannot be so —fundamental decisions must be taken to enhance the capacity of the Organization in this innovative and productive exercise of its function. I am conscious that the present volume and unpredictability of peacekeeping assessments poses real problems for some Member States. For this reason, I strongly support proposals in some Member States for their peacekeeping contributions to be financed from [countries' national] defense, rather than foreign affairs, budgets and I recommend such action to others....

New Departures in Peacekeeping

The nature of peacekeeping operations has evolved rapidly in recent years. The established principles and practices of peacekeeping have responded flexibly to new demands of recent years, and the basic conditions for success remain unchanged: a clear and practicable mandate; the cooperation of the parties in implementing that mandate; the continuing support of the Security Council; the readiness of Member States to contribute the military, police and civilian personnel, including specialists, required; effective United Nations command at Headquarters and in the field; and adequate financial and logistic support. As the international climate has changed and peacekeeping operations are increasingly fielded to help implement settlements that have been negotiated by peacemakers, a new array of demands and problems has emerged regarding logistics, equipment, personnel and finance, all of which could be corrected if Member States so wished and were ready to make the necessary resources available.

Personnel

Member States are keen to participate in peacekeeping operations. Military observers and infantry are invariably available in the required numbers, but logistic units present a greater problem, as few armies can afford to spare such units for an extended period. Member States were requested in 1990 to state what military personnel they were in principle prepared to make available; few replied. I reiterate that request to all Member States to reply frankly and promptly. Standby arrangements should be confirmed, ... concerning the kind and number of skilled personnel they will be prepared to offer the United Nations as the needs of new operations arise.

Increasingly, peacekeeping requires that civilian political officers, human rights monitors, electoral officials, refugee and humanitarian aid specialists and police play as central a role as the military. Police personnel have proved increasingly difficult to obtain in the numbers required. I recommend that arrangements be reviewed and improved for training peacekeeping personnel—civilian, police, or military—using the varied capabilities of Member State Governments, or nongovernmental organizations and the facilities of the Secretariat....

Logistics

Not all Governments can provide their battalions with the equipment they need for service abroad. While some equipment is provided by troop-contributing countries, a great deal has to come from the United Nations, including equipment to fill gaps in underequipped national units. The United Nations has no standing stock of such equipment. Orders must be placed with manufacturers, which creates a number of difficulties. A pre-positioned stock of basic peacekeeping equipment should be established, so that at least some vehicles, communications equipment, generators, etc. would be immediately available at the start of an operation. Alternatively, Governments should commit themselves to keeping certain equipment, specified by the Secretary-General, on standby for immediate sale, loan or donation to the United Nations when required.

Member States in a position to do so should make air- and sea-lift capacity available to the United Nations free of cost or at lower than commercial rates, as was the practice until recently.

POST-CONFLICT PEACE-BUILDING

Peacemaking and peacekeeping operations, to be truly successful, must come to include comprehensive efforts to identify and support structures which will tend to consolidate peace and advance a sense of confidence and well-being among people. Through agreements ending civil strife, these may include disarming the previously warring parties and the restoration of order, the custody and possible destruction of weapons, repatriating refugees, advisory and training support for security personnel, monitoring elections, advancing efforts to protect human rights, reforming or strengthening governmental institutions and promoting formal and informal processes of political participation....

COOPERATION WITH REGIONAL ARRANGEMENTS AND ORGANIZATIONS

The Covenant of the League of Nations, in its Article 21, noted the validity of regional understandings for securing the maintenance of peace. The Charter devotes Chapter VIII to regional arrangements or agencies for dealing with such matters relating to the maintenance of international peace and security as are appropriate for regional action and consistent with the Purposes and Principles of the United Nations. The cold war impaired the proper use of Chapter VIII and indeed, in that era, regional arrangements worked on occasion against resolving disputes in the manner foreseen in the Charter....

SAFETY OF PERSONNEL

When United Nations personnel are deployed in conditions of strife, whether for preventive diplomacy, peacemaking, peacekeeping, peace-building or humanitarian purposes, the need arises to ensure their safety. There has been an unconscionable increase in the number of fatalities. Following the conclusion of a cease-fire and in order to prevent further outbreaks of violence, United Nations guards were called upon to assist in volatile conditions in Iraq. Their presence afforded a measure of security to United Nations personnel and supplies and, in addition, introduced an element of reassurance and stability that helped to prevent renewed conflict. Depending upon the nature of the situation, different configurations and compositions of security deployments will need to be considered. As the variety and scale of threat widens, innovative measures will be required to deal with the dangers facing United Nations personnel.

Experience has demonstrated that the presence of a United Nations operation has not always been sufficient to deter hostile action. Duty in areas of danger can never be risk-free; United Nations personnel must expect to go in harm's way at times. The courage, commitment and idealism shown by United Nations personnel should be respected by the entire international community. These men and women deserve to be properly recognized and rewarded for the perilous tasks they undertake. Their interests and those of their families must be given due regard and protected.

Given the pressing need to afford adequate protection to United Nations personnel engaged in life-endangering circumstances, I recommend that the Security Council, unless it elects immediately to withdraw the United Nations presence in order to preserve the credibility of the Organization, gravely consider what action should be taken towards those who put United Nations personnel in danger. Before deployment takes place, the Council should keep open the option of considering in advance collective measures, possibly including those under Chapter VII when a threat to international peace and security is also involved, to come into effect should the purpose of the United Nations operation systematically be frustrated and hostilities occur.

FINANCING

A chasm has developed between the tasks entrusted to this Organization and the financial means provided to it. The truth of the matter is that our vision cannot really extend to the prospect opening before us as long as our financing remains myopic....

To remedy the financial situation of the United Nations in all its aspects, my distinguished predecessor repeatedly drew the attention of Member States to the increasingly impossible situation that has arisen and, during the forty-sixth session of the General Assembly, made a number of proposals... with which I am in broad agreement.... [One] suggested the adoption of a set of measures to deal with the cash flow problems caused by the exceptionally high level of unpaid contributions as well as with the problem of inadequate working capital reserves:

1. Charging interest on the amounts of assessed contributions that are not paid on time;
2. Suspending certain financial regulations of the United Nations to permit the retention of budgetary surpluses;
3. Increasing the Working Capital Fund to a level of $250 million and endorsing the principle that the level of the Fund should be approximately 25 percent of the annual assessment under the regular budget;
4. Establishment of a temporary Peacekeeping Reserve Fund, at a level of $50 million, to meet initial expenses of peacekeeping operations pending receipt of assessed contributions.
5. Authorization to the Secretary-General to borrow commercially, should other sources of cash be inadequate....

In addition..., others have been added in recent months in the course of public discussion. These ideas include: a levy on arms sales that could be related to maintaining an Arms Register by the United Nations; a levy on international air travel, which is dependent on the maintenance of peace; authorization for the United Nations to borrow from the World Bank and the International Monetary Fund, for peace and development are interdependent; general tax exemption for contributions made to the United Nations by foundations, businesses and individuals;

and changes in the formula for calculating the scale of assessments for peacekeeping operations.

As such ideas are debated, a stark fact remains: the financial foundations of the Organization daily grow weaker, debilitating its political will and practical capacity to undertake new and essential activities. This state of affairs must not continue. Whether decisions are taken on financing the Organization, there is one inescapable necessity: Member States must pay their assessed contributions in full and on time. Failure to do so puts them in breach of their obligations under the Charter....

AN AGENDA FOR PEACE

The nations and peoples of the United Nations are fortunate in a way that those of the League of Nations were not. We have been given a second chance to create the world of our Charter that they were denied. With the cold war ended we have drawn back from the brink of a confrontation that threatened the world and, too often, paralyzed our Organization.

Even as we celebrate our restored possibilities, there is a need to ensure that the lessons of the past four decades are learned and that the errors, or variations of them, are not repeated. For there may not be a third opportunity for our planet which, now for different reasons, remains endangered....

Never again must the Security Council lose the collegiality that is essential to its proper functioning, an attribute that it has gained after such trial. A genuine sense of consensus deriving from shared interests must govern its work, not the threat of the veto or the power of any group of nations....

Power brings special responsibilities, and temptations. The powerful must resist the dual but opposite calls of unilateralism and isolationism if the United Nations is to succeed. For just as unilateralism at the global or regional level can shake the confidence of others, so can isolationism, whether it results from political choice or constitutional circumstance, enfeeble the global undertaking....

Reform is a continuing process, and improvement can have no limit. Yet there is an expectation, which I wish to see fulfilled, that the present phase in the renewal of this Organization should be complete by 1995, its fiftieth anniversary. The pace set must therefore be increased if the United Nations is to keep ahead of the acceleration of history that characterizes this age. We must be guided not by precedents alone, however wise these may be, but by the needs of the future and by the shape and content that we wish to give it.

... The United Nations was created with a great and courageous vision. Now is the time, for its nations and peoples, and the men and women who serve it, to seize the moment for the sake of the future.

NO

John F. Hillen III

POLICING THE NEW WORLD ORDER: THE OPERATIONAL UTILITY OF A PERMANENT U.N. ARMY

Proposals to create a U.N. Army are not new. They are designed to provide a mechanism and structure that will allow the U.N. to exercise its mandate while circumventing the problem that usually hobbles U.N. operations: the lack of a common political will. Political obstacles aside, there are operational reasons for rejecting a standing U.N. Army. The most important reason for this rejection is that such a force is redundant if employed at the lower end of the U.N. military operations spectrum (observation missions and first generation peacekeeping) but incapable of having any real impact at the upper end (second generation peacekeeping and enforcement).

In the three years immediately following the end of the Cold War, there was a heady optimism about the renewed capacity of the United Nations to enforce resolutions concerning international peace and security. Now, due to the apparent impotency of United Nations forces in Bosnia and Somalia, the mood has swung back toward the pessimism characteristic of the Cold War era. This has not stopped debate about mechanisms that the U.N. can use to enforce its resolutions, including an idea that never quite seems to go away for long: a permanent U.N. Army. Proponents say that such a force could rise above the ebb and flow of national interests and provide a genuinely useful security tool for the United Nations. However, what many of these observers fail to realize is that the limited operational capabilities of a permanent U.N. Army would rarely allow it to influence situations like Bosnia and Somalia. In some respects, it is a worthwhile idea, but it is self-defeating in that the force could make little impact on the very problems it was created to alleviate....

A RECURRING THEME

The idea of a permanent force for the U.N. is not envisaged by the U.N. Charter: it is in fact a concept that seeks to rectify a weakness in the Charter.

From John F. Hillen III, "Policing the New World Order: The Operational Utility of a Permanent U.N. Army," *Strategic Review* (Spring 1994). Copyright © 1994 by The United States Strategic Institute. Reprinted by permission. Notes omitted.

Article 43 of the U.N. Charter was intended to create for the U.N. continued access to the massive forces of the victorious World War II alliance. Even the most modest of proposals for U.N. forces constituted under Article 43 visualized 12 Army divisions, 900 combat aircraft, and almost 50 capital warships. The charter structure for using these forces visualized a fairly consistent process. The Security Council could determine a threat to international peace and security (Article 39), order action to redress such a threat by land, sea, and air forces under U.N. authority (Article 42), and call said forces to its service through the agreements reached according to Article 43. However, this security structure was doomed from the start because the critical agreements of Article 43 never materialized.

Thus, all proposals for a permanent U.N. Army have a common goal: to provide the U.N. with the mechanism and structure necessary to exercise its mandate: to maintain international peace and security....

[C]urrent proposals for a permanent U.N. Army are fueled by the desire for a tool that the U.N. can employ without being buffeted by the tides of a fickle international community. This most recent revival of the call for a permanent U.N. force does not seek to harness international consensus for the United Nations... but to institutionalize a security mechanism for the U.N. that does not rely on that consensus. The contemporary rationale for a permanent U.N. force is that it can circumvent the lack of political resolve in such situations as Bosnia.

THE SPECTRUM OF U.N. MILITARY OPERATIONS

Operations involving military personnel conducted under the auspices of the United Nations or its mandates span a broad operational spectrum. This spectrum ranges from unarmed peace observation missions to the conduct of war against an intransigent state. The operational nature of a U.N. military mission can be determined by many different factors, most of which can be subsumed under two categories: 1) the environment in which the force operates; and 2) the level of military effort or force used.

The environment in which the operation takes place could range from completely benign to very hostile. This important factor in the planning of U.N. military missions largely determines the size, nature, and composition of the U.N. force and its tasks. The level of military effort and the force employed reflects the environment and/or opposing forces as well as the nature of the tasks to be performed. By measuring these factors in all U.N. military operations, one can actually plot the spectrum of operations. While it is a continuous spectrum, there are discernible mission subsets: 1) Observation Missions; 2) First Generation Peacekeeping; 3) Second Generation Peacekeeping; and 4) Enforcement Actions.

The first two sets of U.N. military operations share many of the same operational characteristics. These are largely derived from the "principles of peacekeeping" which were recently articulated by the Under Secretary-General for peacekeeping operations.

1. They are United Nations operations. The forces are formed by the U.N. at the outset, commanded in the field

by a U.N.-appointed general, under the ultimate authority of the U.N. Secretary-General, and financed by member states collectively.

2. Peacekeeping forces are deployed with the consent of all the parties involved and only after a political settlement had been reached between warring factions.

3. The forces are committed to strict impartiality. Military observers and peacekeepers can in no way take sides with or against a party to the conflict.

4. Troops are provided by member states on a voluntary basis. During the Cold War era, the superpowers or even "big five" [the permanent members of the Security Council—China, France, Great Britain, the Soviet Union (now Russia), and the United States] rarely participated in these missions, and the majority of troops were supplied by the so-called "middle nations" to reinforce the concept of neutrality.

5. These units operate under rules of engagement that stress the absolute minimum use of force in accomplishing their objectives. This is usually limited to the use of force in self-defense only, but some missions have used force in "situations in which peacekeepers were being prevented by armed persons from fulfilling their mandate."

These five principles are especially applied in earnest in *observation missions.* There have been fifteen of these missions to date, and they represent the low end of the operational spectrum....

FIRST GENERATION PEACEKEEPING

Another class of U.N. military operations guided by the "principles of peacekeep-ing" are first generation peacekeeping missions. These operations were all initiated during the Cold War era, as an improvised response to "the failure of collective security and the success of early U.N. peace observation missions." There were seven operations of this kind.... Three are still operational: Cyprus, the Golan Heights, and Lebanon, in their 29th, 19th and 15th years respectively. These operations share the salient feature of observation missions. Because peacekeeping forces are deployed after a political settlement and because they must remain strictly neutral, they rely on the goodwill and cooperation of the belligerents to accomplish their mission.

These forces differ from observation missions in that they are made up of entire military units from U.N. member states. These units are organically equipped, organized, trained, and armed (albeit lightly) for combat. They therefore possess some modicum of offensive capability and a credible defensive capacity. First generation peacekeeping forces have usually been deployed in a "buffer" role, physically occupying and controlling neutral territory between belligerents. These missions have focused primarily on ensuring the continued separation of the previously warring factions.

First generation peacekeeping missions do not generally have ambitious tasks: missions are derived from political objectives. The main objective is to contain the armed conflict in order to provide a stable atmosphere in which the conflict can be politically resolved. First generation peacekeeping missions (with the exception of parts of the U.N. intervention in the Congo) have no mandate or capacity to impose a political solution on the belligerents. After all, if deployed in accordance with the "principles of peacekeeping" there should be no need for forceful action in an atmosphere of cooperation. However, the operational environment has generally been more bellicose than that experienced by observation missions and there have been over 750 U.N. peacekeepers killed in these seven missions. That environment, and the more complicated military tasks involved for these combat units place these operations higher on the operational spectrum.

SECOND GENERATION PEACEKEEPING

Second generation peacekeeping missions share some operational characteristics with their Cold War predecessors but transcend the "principles of peacekeeping." The U.N. has initiated five of these operations since the relaxation of the superpower confrontation in 1987–1989: in Namibia, Cambodia, the former Yugoslavia, Somalia and Mozambique. In the main these operations are far more ambitious in their objectives, which include disarming the warring factions, maintaining law and order, restoring civil government and its associated functions, setting up and supervising elections, and delivering humanitarian aid. What makes these second generation tasks so challenging is that they very often take place in an atmosphere of continued fighting between factions, civil turmoil, and general chaos. The rate of U.N. fatalities in these missions is climbing.

There are considerable differences between these missions and those of the first two classes. While second generation peacekeeping forces are formed and deployed with unprecedented Security Council consensus, the warring parties

often do not want them. Unlike first generation peacekeeping, a cease-fire is not a *sine qua non* [essential] for U.N. deployment. The U.N. forces involved in these operations face the prospect of having little or no cooperation from the factions on the ground, since second generation peacekeeping missions often consist of heavily armed combat units possessing considerable offensive capability, frequently contributed by the major powers.

The large and combat-heavy force structure of second generation peacekeeping forces means that they are able not only to protect themselves and other U.N. personnel, but also to attempt to impose an agreement on unwilling belligerents. The risks inherent in this have been most graphically portrayed in Bosnia and Somalia. In each case, military force has been employed against particular parties in the conflict. In Bosnia, it has mainly consisted of an enforced flight ban against the Serbs and the low level use of force to protect the delivery of humanitarian aid and keep supply lines open. In Somalia, the U.N. authorized the capture by force of Mohammed Aideed, again clearly taking sides in the attempt to impose a political solution. The offensive use of military force in these missions has not produced great dividends for the "peacekeepers" as yet.

The operational characteristics of most second generation peacekeeping missions bear little resemblance to the five "principles of peacekeeping." 1) While they are U.N. operations, they sometimes must rely nonetheless on other organizations or member states for complex operational capabilities that the U.N. does not possess. The use of NATO to enforce the Bosnian flight ban and a U.S. military task force to initially intervene in Somalia are two examples of this. 2) There has been no concrete political settlement in some cases and there is hardly an environment of consent for a U.N. presence. 3) As mentioned above, the doctrine of strict neutrality has not been followed. 4) The forces of the permanent members of the Security Council are often heavily involved. 5) The rules of engagement have been enlarged substantially to allow second generation peacekeepers the capacity to impose a solution on the local parties through the use of force.

In most respects, these missions are only one step short of full-scale enforcement operations. The U.N. has recognized that, considering the innocuous forces and methods employed, traditional peacekeeping can only succeed under favorable political conditions. But second generation peacekeeping military forces are caught on the horns of a prickly dilemma. While lesser operations are governed by the principles of peacekeeping and higher operations are governed by the principles of war, second generation peacekeeping operations are quite simply ungoverned by doctrine of any kind.

ENFORCEMENT

Enforcement actions represent the high end of the operational spectrum, taking place in a bellicose and adversarial environment that necessitates the use of large-scale military force. The operational characteristics of these campaigns are those of war. The role of military forces in this enterprise is obviously more clear cut than the somewhat ambiguous parameters of action in peacekeeping missions. There is no cooperation from the enemy and therefore no need for impartiality. The forces can use purely military doctrine to calculate the force needed to impose the dictates of the U.N. resolution on the aggressor. From a military point of view, this is the only type of U.N. operation where the force can actually create the environment it needs to guarantee success. The only two examples of U.N. collective security operations of this type are Korea in 1950–1953 and Kuwait in 1990–1991.

Each of these situations presented a unique set of circumstances for the exercise of collective security under the auspices of the U.N. In each case the command and control of the operation and the majority of forces were provided by the United States, leading many to dismiss these operations as American wars. However, both were multinational operations authorized by the legislative bodies of the U.N. The fact that the U.N. was essentially following the U.S. lead in both cases illustrates an important characteristic of large-scale enforcement actions. They must have the wholesale participation of a great power in order to bring about the huge resources, sacrifices, and political will required to wage modern war against an intransigent state. Only a few states or groups of states can provide the complex infrastructure and large forces necessary to undertake complicated military enterprises like Operation Desert Storm.

THE PERMANENT U.N. ARMY

Having described the types of military operations in which a U.N. force operates, we must now briefly address the different types of permanent U.N. force proposed. This paper will not consider Article 43-type proposals which would create, on paper, a huge force available to the U.N. for any operation up to major enforcement actions. The main reason for this is that there appears to be no chance that an Article 43 agreement will be signed in the foreseeable future. This is the main reason that [U.N. Secretary-General Boutros] Boutros-Ghali's *An Agenda for Peace* calls for the mobilization of a large force separate from Article 43 agreements. It is an effort to bypass the perpetual deadlock surrounding that luckless article.

Boutros-Ghali proposes "units that would be available on call and would consist of troops that have volunteered for such service." This plan would identify units from member states that could be called upon to build a U.N. force "package" when the Security Council authorizes a mission. Communications units, logistics units, transportation units, medical units, and other expensive sophisticated support elements would be earmarked by member states for U.N. service as well as the traditional light infantry units. These units would have to concentrate the majority of their training on U.N. duties and it has been recommended that their deployments be financed through national defense budgets. Needless to say, the response to these proposals from member states has been tepid at best. "Such modeling assumes that there will be major cuts in national armies as a result of diminishing East-West tensions and that this reduction could be matched by a growth in U.N. military capabilities." That assumption has proved to be naive in the extreme.

The proposal addressed here calls for a supra-national force of U.N. volunteers. Much like the civilian bureaucrats and officials employed by the U.N., these soldiers would be international civil (military) servants. They would be volunteers for international service and would not be under military obligation to any member state: only to the United Nations. They would be recruited, trained, equipped, and paid by the United Nations. The force proposed is usually infantry brigade-size, five to six thousand troops, with organic support and transportation capabilities. There are countless practical difficulties associated with forming such a force, but let us for the moment assume that it can be formed, trained, and deployed by the U.N.

THE UTILITY OF A U.N. ARMY

Naturally, even the most enthusiastic proponents of this small U.N. force recognize that its utility is limited by its size and capabilities. The most important advantage of this force is its rapid reaction capability. Since it is not drawn from member states, with all the attendant difficulties of that process, it can be deployed at the discretion of the Secretary-General on very short notice. The key element contributing to its success would be timeliness. "Clearly, a timely intervention by a relatively small but highly trained force, willing and authorized to take combat risks and representing the will of the international community, could make a decisive difference in the early stages of a crisis." This force would be akin to a small kitchen fire extinguisher, whose greatest utility is in the very earliest stages of a possible fire.

But operationally, we must ask where such a force could really enhance the credibility of the U.N. It is not needed for observation missions, as they are composed of experienced individual military observers. In addition, these missions are formed to observe a previously concluded political settlement. An unarmed observation mission would never be undertaken in a situation where dangerous tensions are at the boiling point and the rapid deployment of combat troops is needed.

Would timely and rapid intervention by such a small force make any difference in first generation peacekeeping missions? As these are also only initiated in response to a completed political agreement, would a rapid deployment force greatly increase the efficiency of the peacekeepers on the ground? "Even a full contingent of peacekeeping troops cannot prevent renewal of hostilities by a determined party. Maintenance of the cease-fire ultimately depends on the willingness of the parties to refrain from fighting." On the other hand, rapid deployment can have a favorable impact. In the case of Cyprus, "Canadian troops arrived... within twenty-four hours of UNFICYP's [U.N. force in Cyprus's] approval. A symbolic presence is perhaps all that is needed in the first days of a cease-fire anyway."

Surprisingly, it is in the conduct of second generation peacekeeping missions that U.N. Army enthusiasts foresee the greatest utility for such a permanent force, despite the bellicose environment frequently associated with these missions. To use this force in such a mission would mean that the U.N. would continue its selective abandonment of its "principles of peacekeeping" which it articulated to define success. In fact, the force is targeted for these difficult missions because "few, if any, governments are willing to commit their own troops to a forceful ground role in a situation which does not threaten their own security and which may well prove to be both violent and open ended."

Thus the paradox of using a permanent U.N. force in these operations is exposed. On the one hand it is proposed as a mechanism to circumvent the unwillingness of member states to get involved in difficult missions such as those of the second generation of peacekeeping. It will replace the ground troops which were never committed by reluctant member states. On the other hand, it is acknowledged that this small and symbolic force would be deployed to impose a solution on an armed party which has not accepted a solution through diplomatic channels. It is genuinely hard to imagine how the timely intervention of such a force could have forced a different outcome in Bosnia or Somalia.

In Bosnia, without the conclusion of a political settlement, any U.N. force in limited numbers operating under peacekeeping rather than enforcement rules of engagement is bound to be hostage to its environment. Because the lack of consensus among member states keeps the mandate and size of the force small and innocuous, any U.N. force is powerless to influence the environment in which it operates. Therefore, dozens of U.N. resolutions on the conflict go unenforced. Rapid reaction by a U.N. military force would not have changed this. Neither unarmed observers nor light infantry with soft-skinned armored vehicles can impose or enforce action in a bellicose combat environment. In both cases, the force is merely a tripwire and its operating imperative is almost solely based on its moral strength as a symbol.

In Somalia, the dilemma stems from the fact that "the basic distinction between peacekeeping and enforcement action... has been blurred. The forceful measures taken by U.S. troops to disarm warring factions, while fully within the mandate of UNOSOM II [U.N. force in Somalia], have highlighted the particular risks of attempting to combine the coercive use of force with peacekeeping objectives." Once again, the basic question is how to use the force to effect the political objectives. Any permanent U.N. force would be faced with exactly the same question no matter when it arrived. Only it might get to face that dilemma a bit sooner.

Naturally, a small, permanent U.N. force would have no great utility in enforcement action either. The fact that large-scale enforcement actions are taking place means that diplomacy or previous intervention has failed. The only scenario in which a permanent U.N. force could be involved at this end of the spectrum was if it was deployed, came under heavy attack, or suffered a similar failure to pacify a volatile environment, and withdrew prior to large scale intervention authorized by an Article 42 resolution.

The only outstanding use of such a force would be in preventative deployments, of which Macedonia is the only current example. In this case, the force does not seek to exercise any sort of operational capability other than limited observation and patrolling. It is a human tripwire, a symbol of the will of the international community. Any violent actions directed against this force (or the peace it seeks to keep) will have to be met with a U.N. response that transcends the organic capacity of this very small and lightly armed force. The soldiers involved are in an unenviable position, as they are powerless to influence their own environment. Their fate rests on the goodwill of the belligerents and the credibility of the United Nations in the eyes of the opposing factions. That bluff has been called in the past and the casualty lists are fast approaching 1000.

OPERATIONAL QUESTIONS

In short, preventative deployment by a permanent U.N. force begs a whole series of operational questions:

1. Under what circumstances will the force be deployed? Guidelines for intervention must be clearly defined. After all, "demand for U.N. peacekeeping since early 1992 has begun to outstrip the supply, whether that supply is measured in money or in national political will." Resources ultimately come from the member states, and are limited no matter what form they take. It is easy to imagine the small force being called upon for almost every potential conflict.

2. Will the U.N. force be governed by the "principles of peacekeeping" or will it be expected to enforce or impose solutions on belligerent factions? If the time-consuming negotiations necessary to obtain the consent of all parties are still underway, the rapid deployment capabilities of this force will have little utility.

3. What explicit mechanisms would be needed to determine the composition and missions of follow-on forces to relieve the rapid reaction force? There must be an organized process by which the crisis is evaluated, and intervention is either continued, upgraded, or abandoned. The involvement of a permanent U.N. force in an open-ended commitment would completely negate its utility.

While such guidelines are necessary, in some cases they will be inadequate to address the *sui generis* [unique] conflicts of the post–Cold War era. On the one hand, doctrine governing the use of a U.N. force must be stringent enough to provide real direction. On the other hand, that same doctrine will rule out intervention in many pressing crises. The doctrine guiding the use of U.N. force must cover a bewildering myriad of crises. It must also have a mechanism which forces decisionmakers to evaluate its immediate utility in a timely manner.

The deployment of a permanent U.N. rapid reaction force would catapult issues onto the U.N. agenda which member states are not ready to address. It could quite easily upset a natural control measure in an organization made up of nation-states. "States may well prefer a situation in which the provision of military force for U.N. activities is managed in an *ad hoc* manner, thereby giving them a greater degree of control over events."

There have been situations where the U.N. Security Council has called for troops to staff operations and the member states have simply failed to comply (Somalia 1992, Georgia 1993). It is reasonable to assume that these same member states would not support the deployment of a force controlled by the Secretary-General, which would require them to provide quick reinforcements. The reaction of member states to calls for collective operations are an important barometer of their willingness to act in common with others. A mechanism which forces or circumvents that common ground could backfire.

CONCLUSION

Even when one completely ignores these attendant political difficulties discussed briefly, it is still obvious that the operational utility of a permanent U.N. force is extremely limited. The value of such a force lies in its preventative role. Other

than that role, it does not fit naturally into the spectrum of U.N. military operations conducted since 1948. Even in a preventative role, its small size, limited operational capabilities, and constrained mandate would limit its effectiveness to operations at the low end of the spectrum.

And at this end of the spectrum, there is not only little need for rapid deployments, but little need for forces other than those constituted by traditional means. When acting as a tripwire and in a symbolic role, an *ad hoc* blue-helmet force or an expensive permanent U.N. Army are scarcely different in terms of operational effectiveness or political viability. The past approach to staffing U.N. operations at the low end of the spectrum has always been adequate, has never been seen as responsible for mission failures, and is an important mechanism for involving states in the maintenance of international peace and security. The strategic utility of such a force is marginal when compared with the current system for staffing U.N. operations at the low end of the spectrum.

Many supporters want the U.N. force to solve problems in operations at the upper end of the operational spectrum. This force could never have the complex operational infrastructure and capabilities to make a difference in missions which entail even modest enforcement operations. The whole issue of staffing and directing U.N. operations at the high end of the spectrum needs much greater attention. Second generation peacekeeping and enforcement missions are quite obviously much more reliant on the vigorous political backing of powerful member states. Beyond the politics involved, these missions require the leadership of a major power for two reasons: 1) large-scale enforcement against an intransigent party is an immensely complicated and expensive enterprise; and 2) only a very few member states have the actual military capability to command and control such a campaign. A small force only under the control of the Secretary-General cannot affect these types of situations.

This dilemma stems from the nature of the post–Cold War world and the attendant difficulties of military intervention. It cannot be solved by the implementation of a single mechanism whose operational utility is very limited.

POSTSCRIPT

Should a Permanent UN Military Force Be Established?

The idea of creating what could be the beginnings of a permanent international police force, or even an army, is being debated seriously in many forums. For the cautious view that military solutions are only possible amid common political efforts, see Canadian general Dan G. Loomis's "Prospects for UN Peacekeeping," *Global Affairs* (Winter 1993). For a skeptical view, see Eugene V. Rostow, "Should UN Charter Article 43 Be Raised from the Dead?" *Global Affairs* (Winter 1993). For an outright negative opinion, see Doug Bandow, "Avoiding War," *Foreign Policy* (Winter 1992/1993).

One reason for the current debate on UN military operations is the increased use of the UN to intervene in all sorts of international and domestic clashes. During 1993 the UN spent approximately $3.8 billion on peacekeeping, nearly quintuple its 1991 budget. In mid-1994, more than 69,000 troops from 71 countries were deployed under the UN flag. A second reason for the current debate is that some critics charge that it is difficult to field one, unified, successful military force cobbled together from many armies. Many observers do not believe that the multinational armies now deployed by the UN can ever be effective. Multinational armies suffer from lack of training and differences in communications, weapons, and logistics. Fractured command structures and even basic language difficulties are additional complications.

President Bill Clinton's ambassador to the UN, Madeleine Albright, has commented that "ad hoc approaches dominate what should be a far more efficient and regularized system of peacekeeping operations.... I do think a standby [UN] force is the way to go." More recently, however, and after U.S. experiences in Somalia, President Clinton and Ambassador Albright have become much more cautious about U.S. involvement in UN operations or the idea of a permanent UN force. For an exchange on the idea of an all-volunteer force, see Brian Urquhart, "For a UN Volunteer Military Force," and Robert Oakley, "A UN Volunteer Force—The Prospect," *The New York Review of Books* (June 10, 1993).

A related matter involves the constitutional processes by which the United States and other countries go to war. If the UN can authorize a war and can require countries to supply forces, then those countries might be forced to fight a war in which they would otherwise not wish to participate. Could countries be forced to do so without going through the legal processes required by their own legal systems?

ISSUE 13

Should the United States Forcefully Oppose North Korea's Nuclear Weapons Program?

YES: John McCain, from "United States Policy With Respect to the North Korean Nuclear Program," *Congressional Record* (February 1, 1994)

NO: Doug Bandow, from "Can Anything Be Done About North Korea's Nuclear Threat?" *USA Today Magazine,* a publication of the Society for the Advancement of Education (January 1994)

ISSUE SUMMARY

YES: U.S. Senator John McCain (R-Arizona) advocates taking strong action to persuade and, if necessary, force North Korea to open itself to international inspection and to give up its nuclear weapons program.

NO: Doug Bandow, a senior fellow at the Cato Institute in Washington, D.C., argues that there is little clear information available about the nuclear capability or intentions of North Korea and no immediate threat to U.S. national security. Therefore, he concludes, it would be wise for the United States to avoid taking drastic measures.

When it comes to nuclear weapons, there are two contradictory trends occurring in the world today. Although the United States and Russia and the other former Soviet republics (FSRs) have significantly reduced their nuclear arsenals, there is an increasing number of countries with nuclear weapons or nuclear weapons ambitions.

Most analysts believe that nuclear proliferation is dangerous. They believe that the more nuclear countries and nuclear weapons there are, the greater the chance of either a nuclear weapons accident or of rebels, terrorists, or an unstable military commander gaining control of and using a nuclear weapon. In some ways this concern has been heightened by the end of the cold war and the restraint that the superpowers could exercise over other countries: "I think it is fair to say that there is somewhat more disarray in the system, by which not only nuclear but other weapons of mass destruction are capable of being produced and distributed, than there was [during the cold war]," President Bill Clinton recently observed. "In other words, the bipolar world had a little more discipline, certainly on the nuclear side."

Proliferation is also a concern because it may have a ripple effect, like a stone dropped in water. Each country that acquires nuclear weapons creates pressure on other countries to do the same. There are many industrialized countries that could build nuclear weapons quickly. If North Korea has weapons, can South Korea remain without them? If the two Koreas were to have them, and with China, Russia, and the United States all having nuclear weapons, wouldn't the pressure on Japan to acquire nuclear arms be intense?

Some experts also believe that the lead time required even for less developed countries to build a nuclear weapon is decreasing. Leonard Spector, an expert with the Carnegie Endowment for International Peace, notes, "In the old days it took 10 years from the time a country wanted a bomb to when they could actually get a bomb. Now countries may be able to suddenly jump ahead."

What are some of the factors promoting nuclear proliferation? One is that it has become simpler to acquire weapons because of the spread of nuclear-power plants and other relevant forms of technology. National security is a second factor that promotes nuclear proliferation. What seems to be a threat to some may appear to be protection to the country developing the weapons. A third factor prompting proliferation is insecurity. Some non-nuclear countries suspect that the pressure on them to shun nuclear weapons is mostly designed to ensure that a few countries retain a nuclear monopoly to lord it over small countries.

For all of these pressures, it is also possible to say that non-proliferation efforts have largely been a success. The heart of this effort is the nuclear Non-Proliferation Treaty (NPT) of 1968. The NPT prohibits its signatories that have nuclear weapons from aiding others to develop them and countries without nuclear weapons from acquiring them. A related international effort is conducted through the UN's International Atomic Energy Agency (IAEA), which conducts inspections under NPT.

It is against this background that North Korea's alleged nuclear weapons program and the following debate between John McCain and Doug Bandow are set. The current confrontation began amid growing reports that NPT member North Korea was reprocessing fuel from its nuclear power plants for weapons-grade plutonium. In early 1993 the IAEA asked to inspect North Korea's nuclear sites. The North Koreans refused and threatened to withdraw from the NPT. The West, led by the United States, brought pressure on North Korea. A series of threats, concessions, and other diplomatic maneuvers have continued. At the time that Republican senator John McCain made his presentation to Congress and conservative analyst Doug Bandow wrote his selection, in early 1994, a year of moves and countermoves had gone by with no resolution to the simmering crisis. McCain believes that the North Koreans will continue to stall and build weapons unless very forceful action is taken. Bandow rejects the idea of escalating the crisis and argues for continued negotiations to find out North Korea's intent and capabilities.

YES

John McCain

UNITED STATES POLICY WITH RESPECT TO THE NORTH KOREAN NUCLEAR PROGRAM

I rise... to offer this amendment regarding the United States policy with respect to the North Korean nuclear program.

... [T]his amendment expresses the sense of Congress regarding the continued intransigence of North Korea in refusing to comply with the terms of the Nuclear Non-Proliferation Treaty. For nearly a year, North Korea has refused to allow access to its nuclear-related facilities, as required under its safeguard agreements with the International Atomic Energy Agency.

The International Atomic Energy Agency has not formally declared a break in the continuity of safeguards on nuclear-related facilities in North Korea, but inspections have not been permitted since last January. This raises serious questions as to the possibility of diversion of nuclear material to a weapons development program—a situation which cannot be permitted to stand unchallenged and unexplored.

The [Clinton] administration has been unsuccessful in resolving this issue, and this amendment sets forth a firm new policy approach designed to demonstrate United States resolve and to encourage North Korea's agreement to permit inspections at all of its nuclear-related sites.

In general, this amendment urges the President to use strong measures to accomplish the primary objective—halting the North Korean nuclear weapons program and implementing the full-scope safeguards agreement between North Korea and the International Atomic Energy Agency.

Let me briefly explain the most significant points of the policy which this amendment urges the President to adopt:

First, the amendment urges the President to seek international consensus to impose sanctions and other measures to isolate North Korea economically until IAEA [International Atomic Energy Agency] inspections resume. While the administration has threatened to impose sanctions through the U.N. Security Council, they have effectively left the decision to seek such sanctions to the IAEA. Unless the International Atomic Energy Agency admits defeat in

From John McCain, "United States Policy With Respect to the North Korean Nuclear Program," *Congressional Record* (February 1, 1994).

its efforts to gain North Korea's agreement to resume inspections, the United States will not press for U.N. action to impose economic sanctions. Instead, the administration should take the lead now in seeking a multilateral economic embargo on North Korea in order to compel them to agree to inspections and stop building nuclear weapons....

Second, the President is urged to support United States–South Korea joint military exercises as a demonstration of our commitment to our South Korean allies. The amendment rejects the administration's ill-advised linkage of these exercises with North Korea's willingness to live up to its international commitments.

Third, the amendment calls on the President to ensure that sufficient United States forces, including Patriot missiles, are deployed in South Korea to adequately defend our ally against any aggressive action by the North. General Luck, commander of United States forces in Korea, has requested Patriot systems in order to counter Scud missiles from the North. The administration should immediately approve the deployment of these systems to better defend our troops against possible attack.

This amendment does not specifically authorize the President to use military force to compel North Korea's compliance with the NPT [Nuclear Nonproliferation Treaty]. The President should, however, use all means necessary to achieve that goal, and there are many such options available to him. In addition to continued diplomatic pressure, the President should seek multilateral support for an economic embargo against North Korea. He should urge Japan to stop the flow of hard currency from resident North Koreans to their homeland. He should seek full cooperation from the Chinese in any

multilateral sanctions on North Korea, by making clear to China that renewal of most-favored-nation status will be conditioned upon China's demonstrated efforts to compel North Korea to comply with the NPT.

This amendment states that resolving the stalemate on nuclear inspections in North Korea is a matter of the highest national security priority. I believe that the President should very seriously consider the use of all necessary means, including military force, in the event that all other measures fail to achieve the desired result of halting the North Korean nuclear weapons program. I do not say this lightly, and I do not advocate the use of force at this time. But I believe that it must be made very clear to the North that their refusal to comply with their freely undertaken international obligations will not be tolerated by the United States.

THE NORTH KOREAN THREAT

... [T]he greatest challenge to U.S. security and world stability today is the proliferation of weapons of mass destruction. The most dangerous and immediate expression of that global threat now confronts American forces across the Korean DMZ [demilitarized zone].

There can be no serious doubt that our vital national interests are imperiled by North Korea's nuclear program and the war they have threatened to protect it. If North Korea possesses or soon obtains nuclear weapons, the threat it poses to the region will multiply exponentially, as will proliferation in Asia.

Every action taken in Washington should reaffirm to Kim Il Sung that the price of North Korea's lawlessness and belligerency is too great for even the most inhuman regime to endure. [Kim died in the summer of 1994; his son succeeded him.] So far, the administration has signaled an accommodationist mentality that will only embolden North Korea and encourage other nations to engage in proliferation.

CIA Director Woolsey has stated publicly that United States intelligence indicates that North Korea has extracted enough plutonium from its reactors to build two bombs. There are some estimates that they possess 12 kilograms of plutonium. Yet, the administration seems not to recognize the urgency of a situation wherein North Korea may possess nuclear weapons and may be purposely delaying resumed inspections in an effort to extract additional plutonium and produce additional nuclear bombs.

My colleagues should also know that North Korea's Scud missiles are capable of carrying primitive nuclear warheads to Seoul. North Korea is continuing to develop its No Dong series of missiles which could carry nuclear warheads to Japan.

The administration's efforts have been aimed at securing North Korea's agreement to allow the IAEA to resume inspections under the safeguards agreement, including maintaining recording devices at Yongbyon that will reduce the likelihood that the plutonium will be diverted to weapons production. The administration has yet to address the possibility that North Korea may have other means to obtain weapons-grade nuclear material beyond those currently in question, such as centrifuges, calutrons, or chemical separation. As we belatedly discovered in Iraq, these means of producing fissionable material are harder to detect. It is also unclear whether the IAEA can provide absolute assurances that the Yongbyon reactor does not have concealed chambers to produce additional small amounts of plutonium in ways that normal inspections will not detect.

Another important consideration is the military threat to our allies in South Korea.

Canceling military exercises with our South Korean allies is quite possibly the worst signal the United States could send to an increasingly bellicose North Korea, indicating in advance to North Korea the profits to be realized in proliferation and saber rattling. By canceling Team Spirit exercises, the administration has taught would-be aggressors throughout the world that, if you want American military exercises canceled, violate an international treaty.

According to the International Institute for Strategic Studies, the North Korean Army has increased its tank force by 40 percent and its artillery pieces by 50 percent. Much of the North's 1.2 million-man army is massed on the border, with combat ready units poised for attack at strategic locations.

Experts have estimated North Korea's current stockpile of biological and chemical weapons at 250 tons, with 13,000 North Korean troops trained to use them. North Korea has reportedly armed its Scud missiles with chemical warheads, and we do not yet have Patriot batteries in place to protect our forces from their use.

Unfortunately, the administration has shown a willingness to bargain with North Korea separately from South Korea. It has issued vague promises about normal relations and economic assistance, while broadly hinting at our willingness to cancel military training exercises with our South Korea allies.

Initially, President Clinton responded to this crisis by emphatically stating that the United States would not allow North Korea to possess nuclear weapons. After CIA Director Woolsey indicated North Korea's probable possession of weapons-grade plutonium, the administration then seemed content to oppose the North's emergence as a serious nuclear power. This dangerous vacillation by the Clinton administration will only encourage North Korea to dismiss the President's latest opposition as quickly as it dismissed his original pronouncement.

THE NEW POLICY

Now is the time for the administration to reverse its image abroad as vacillating and insecure. There is nothing to be gained and much to be lost by being frightened into appeasement for the sake of a single concession which in the end may not matter very much. North Korea is testing our resolve. Let us make certain they understand how grave are the consequences of their unlawful ambitions.

We should emphatically make clear that we do not rule out any potential response to North Korea's continued intransigence, including a military response. We should insist that North Korea discontinue its nuclear weapons program immediately and that it open all of its nuclear-related facilities to international inspection.

The United States should begin devoting its energies to building an international consensus to further economically isolate North Korea. Our diplomacy should be conducted with forceful representations of our seriousness. We should make it as difficult as possible for other nations to resist our efforts.

To make sanctions effective against the insular economy of North Korea, President Clinton must insist on full cooperation from China—now. Secretary of State Warren Christopher dismissed China's repeated opposition to sanctions as something less than China's final word on the subject. The Secretary should focus his immediate efforts on making certain that China's next pronouncement on the subject proves his current optimism to be well-founded.

We should put the case plainly to China: all benefits derived from their relationship with the United States—from most-favored-nation trade status to licenses for the transfer of supercomputers and satellite technology—will be directly connected to China's full implementation of sanctions, should they prove necessary, and its central involvement in efforts to prevent North Korean proliferation and aggression. Currently, United States policy toward China is primarily focused on human rights and trade disputes. These are appropriate concerns for United States diplomacy, but proliferation, and more specifically, Chinese aid and comfort to North Korean proliferation, should be treated by the administration as the most urgent problem in our relations.

The United States should begin making all the force improvements necessary to enhance our conventional and rapid deployment capabilities in South Korea, including the immediate deployment of Patriot batteries to protect United States soldiers. Our forces should be fully ready to repel aggression irrespective of whether North Korea's bellicosity is real or contrived to intimidate American diplomacy. Joint military exercises are a necessary determinant of our readiness. Finally, we should make unambiguously clear to Pyongyang [the capitol of North Korea] that any use of weapons of mass destruction against South Korea will be met with greater retaliation in kind.

URGENCY

Almost a month ago, Under Secretary of State Lynn Davis announced triumphantly that North Korea had agreed to discuss with the IAEA the resumption of inspections, despite well-founded fears that North Korea would permit only one-time inspection of its seven declared nuclear sites. Further, North Korea steadfastly refused access to its nuclear waste sites. Now these discussions with the IAEA have apparently run into another intentional roadblock set up by the North Koreans, and they are refusing inspections of even the declared sites.

On February 21, [1994,] the IAEA board of governors will meet, and if an agreement with North Korea has not been reached at that time, the IAEA may vote to refer this issue to the United Nations to seek economic sanctions or other measures to compel North Korea to comply with the NPT.

How much longer can we tolerate North Korean intransigence on this vital national security issue? Every day that North Korea stalls inspections is another day's advance toward acquiring additional nuclear weapons. This amendment recognizes the need for decisive action now, to prevent any increase in the North Korean threat.

CONCLUSION

... I urge my colleagues to vote for this important amendment. I have worked with my colleagues on the other side to craft this amendment so that it would have broad bipartisan support. Although my remarks have been critical of administration policy to date, they were not made, nor was this amendment offered, to score partisan political points. I feel very strongly that U.S. policy on this question is in urgent need of revision. I sincerely hope the administration recognizes the weakness of its previous response to this crisis, and takes immediate action to recover the advantage in our test of wills with North Korea.

The clear and present danger which a nuclear North Korea poses to the United States and our allies does not automatically confer on North Korea a position of greater strength in this contest with us. Only a failure of nerve on the part of U.S. policymakers can do that.

North Korea's economy is tottering on the verge of total collapse. Pyongyang desperately needs to open its economy to the West to forestall complete economic ruin and the political changes that will likely accompany it. And despite their bellicose posturing, North Korea's military leaders must recognize that they are unlikely to win a war with South Korea and the United States or even emerge from the conflict with their regime intact.

The United States and our South Korean allies still occupy the better ground in this crisis. But we are squandering that advantage every day we allow North Korea to believe that it can extract from us military, diplomatic, and economic concessions without abandoning its nuclear program entirely. ...

By our reluctance to aggressively challenge North Korea's nuclear program—a reluctance which can be fairly criticized as a failure of nerve—we have gone a long way to build the confidence of North Korean leaders that they can intimidate the United States into tolerating their nuclear power pretensions while allowing economic lifelines to be thrown to their dys-functional economy. We may have gone a long way as well toward reinforcing their suspicions that the United States no longer has the will to defend our interests in Korea and the rest of Asia by whatever means necessary.

Despite the ground we have already conceded, we can recover some of it by immediately returning to a zero tolerance policy. Yes, Seoul is uniquely vulnerable. It is within reach not only of North Korean artillery, but quite possibly within reach of its nuclear weapons. However, Pyongyang is well within reach of ours.

We should make abundantly clear... that as economic ruin and political collapse will accompany their continued intransigence on this issue, utter destruction will accompany their resort to force. We have served up enough carrots to North Korea. The time has come to show them the stick.

To paraphrase Churchill, let it not be said one day that in a definite crisis, the United States faced a choice between accommodation and the prospect of war; that we chose accommodation first and got war later.

NO

Doug Bandow

CAN ANYTHING BE DONE ABOUT NORTH KOREA'S NUCLEAR THREAT?

After rejecting demands from the International Atomic Energy Agency (IAEA) to allow inspection of two suspected nuclear facilities, the Democratic People's Republic of Korea (DPRK) threatened to withdraw from the Nuclear Nonproliferation Treaty (NPT). Fears of a North Korean nuclear bomb, which had receded as Pyongyang [the capitol of North Korea] allowed a half-dozen IAEA [International Atomic Energy Agency] inspections over the past year, have risen to a fever pitch.... [D]emands for a military response are growing. There is no easy solution to the threat of a nuclear DPRK, but precipitous U.S. action could spark a new war that would endanger not only the 36,000 American service personnel presently stationed on the Korean peninsula, but millions of South Koreans as well.

The Korean War during 1950–53 was followed by a bitter mini–Cold War that lasted nearly four decades. By the end of the 1980s, the North found itself increasingly isolated internationally and falling ever further behind the Republic of Korea (ROK) economically. The violent collapse of ... communism in ... Romania and [in Eastern Europe] had proved particularly unsettling for the retrograde Stalinist regime in Pyongyang. With the cutoff of subsidized trade by China and the Soviet Union, officials of the DPRK no longer could deny their nation's economic distress. By December, 1991, officials of the two Koreas had held several meetings; South Korean businessmen were heading north to invest; and the two governments had approved a nonaggression pact and agreed to allow mutual inspections for nuclear weapons. The Korean political winter, it seemed, was over.

However, extensive saber rattling occurred in the North during the 1993 joint U.S.–ROK Team Spirit military exercises, and the Central Intelligence Agency warns that the North may have enough plutonium to develop one or two nuclear weapons. The ROK has suspended economic activities in the DPRK; Japan and the U.S. temporarily suspended discussions about improving relations with Pyongyang; and some Western analysts are calling for war —immediately.

From Doug Bandow, "Can Anything Be Done About North Korea's Nuclear Threat?" *USA Today Magazine* (January 1994). Copyright © 1994 by The Society for the Advancement of Education. Reprinted by permission.

Since their separation following World War II, the two Koreas have competed bitterly in the economic, military, and political arena.... By the 1980s, the game between the two states essentially was over—the South was twice as populous, dramatically more prosperous, a serious player in the international economic and technological markets, and one of the globe's leading trading nations. Only on the military front did Pyongyang retain a lead, largely reflecting the fact that America's security guarantee, then backed by a 43,000-man tripwire, made additional defense spending by the ROK unnecessary. As early as the 1980s, there was little justification for maintaining the so-called mutual defense treaty. South Korea was capable of overtaking the North's military capabilities with only modest increases in defense expenditures —had Seoul chosen to do so.

Today, the gap between the two nations is even wider. The South's gross national product is estimated to be 12 times that of its northern rival.... Pyongyang lacks the hard currency necessary to buy spare parts for its tanks and other weapons.... The readiness and training of the DPRK forces is questionable.... The North's domestic transportation infrastructure is primitive and in disrepair; many military personnel spend their time performing public-works tasks; and the DPRK apparently never has conducted a combined arms exercise. Although a sudden onslaught by the North might succeed in capturing or destroying Seoul, which lies just 30 miles south of the demilitarized zone (DMZ), even many South Korean analysts discount the likelihood of an invasion.

Given Pyongyang's mounting economic and diplomatic failures and the looming prospect of the South's reaching parity in conventional military capability, North Korea's only potential trump card is the development of a nuclear weapon. Pyongyang apparently has had a program under way for some time. Since the DPRK began its efforts when the U.S. still maintained tactical nuclear weapons in the South—they were withdrawn only in late 1991—it is possible that Pyongyang wanted the bomb primarily as a defensive weapon, although the goal of nuclear blackmail of neighboring countries can not be ruled out. As the North's allies, the former U.S.S.R. and, more recently, China, have recognized Seoul over the DPRK's objections, dictator Kim Il Sung and his son Kim Jong Il, the anointed successor, probably have come to believe even more strongly that an atomic bomb is perhaps the only means of ensuring the regime's survival, whether against a military attack by the South or more general political pressure. As defector Ko Young Hwan explained in 1991, a nuclear weapon was viewed by officials in the North "as the last means they can resort to to protect their system."

That perception is quite plausible. After all, only the threat of a North Korean bomb has caused such powers as Japan and the U.S. to treat the DPRK seriously. The mere whisper of a project, no matter how limited, has allowed the North to manipulate not only its antagonists, but also its allies, including China, that do not want Pyongyang to possess a bomb. The well-publicized, almost hysterical fear of Pyongyang's nuclear efforts probably has encouraged the regime to push ahead.

North Korea's nuclear-weapons program appears to be centered at Yongbyon, 60 miles north of Pyongyang. At that site are a 30-megawatt reactor and reprocessing facility. The North also is constructing a 200-megawatt reactor that could produce an estimated 100 pounds of plutonium a year once it is operational. More worrisome is the possibility that the DPRK also has underground nuclear facilities, as alleged by Ko Young Hwan.

While South Korean defense officials and American newspaper columnists were calling for a preemptive military strike in the summer and fall of 1991, Pyongyang finalized an inspection agreement under the NPT, which it had signed in 1985. The North seemed prepared to go even further in December, 1991, signing a bilateral agreement with the ROK that provided for more extensive examinations in both North and South. Hope for a real détente between the two bitter enemies blossomed.

Even though the two Koreas subsequently deadlocked over inspection procedures, progress was made on other fronts. In particular, the IAEA made its first visit to the North in early 1992 and subsequently conducted six examinations of North Korean nuclear facilities. The agency's conclusions were encouraging, if not definitive—the DPRK had produced some plutonium, but did not seem to have an effective ongoing nuclear program. Although the IAEA was skeptical of some of the Pyongyang's explanations of the purpose of its apparent reprocessing facility, the North took IAEA investigators to sites not on the formal inspection lists and offered to allow the agency to make special visits on demand. As a result, in November, 1992, Ronald Lehman, head of the Arms Control and Disarmament Agency, reversed his earlier pessimistic assessment of the North's nuclear efforts when he stated that international pressure had "stopped" the DPRK's program. While the future nevertheless remained uncertain, Pyongyang had moved closer to normal participation in international affairs in two years than it had in the previous 40. Equally important, economic pressure for reform continued to mount with China's announcement that it was ending its barter trade with the North.

On the IAEA's visit to North Korea in January, 1993, however, the DPRK refused access to two possible nuclear-waste depositories. North Korea tied this stand to the ongoing Team Spirit military exercises in the South; they since have ceased. When the IAEA made an unprecedented demand for a special inspection of the two sites, Pyongyang threatened to withdraw from the NPT and abrogated the inspection agreement. Secretary of State Warren Christopher told a House appropriations subcommittee, "There will be enforcement action taken within the UN Security Council." He focused on economic sanctions, though there was no guarantee that such measures would have much effect on the DPRK's already isolated economy. Moreover, UN action requires the acquiescence of China, long the North's closest ally, which says that it will not endorse coercive measures against Pyongyang. "We support patient consultations to reach an appropriate solution," explained Chinese foreign minister Qian Qichen in March. "If the matter goes before the Security Council, that will only complicate things."

More ominous, discussions of military remedies are being heard. ... Frank Gaffney of the Center for Security Policy ... contends that "the choice—as with Iraq ... is not between possibly going to war with North Korea and not going to war. Rather, it is a question of risking going to war *now*, when U.S. military capabilities are relatively strong and

North Korean nuclear forces are minimal (or not yet completed), rather than later when such advantageous conditions will almost surely not exist." House Defense Appropriations Subcommittee chairman John Murtha (D.-Pa.) has called for destroying the North Korean facilities, even though, he admits, "There is no question we would have to be prepared to go to war."

ASSESSING NORTH KOREAN INTENTIONS

What makes the present situation so difficult is that Washington knows neither the North's capabilities nor its intentions. Pyongyang's official explanation is that it was forced into its present course by the U.S. and that the DPRK merely is defending its "socialist system."

In private conversations, DPRK diplomats argue that the facilities at issue are conventional military, not nuclear, and therefore are exempt from the inspection regime, and that, in making its demands, the IAEA is yielding to pressure from Washington. Would America have opened its bases under similar circumstances? they ask. Their government, they maintain, remains committed to three-way talks with the U.S. and the ROK about nuclear inspections on the peninsula and is willing to abide by the NPT if such negotiations get under way. North Korean diplomats also say they are ready to discuss the two sites with the IAEA if it acts independently, not under U.S. pressure, though they do not guarantee that Pyongyang ultimately will allow inspections of those facilities.

What is really going on? In February, 1993, CIA Director R. James Woolsey indicated "an obvious reason for the standoff is that North Korea has something sig-nificant to hide." While certainly plausible, that is not the only interpretation. There are at least four possible causes of Pyongyang's present course. The first and most threatening is the Woolsey thesis that the North has a nuclear-development program under way and is, and always has been, committed to building a bomb. According to that scenario, Kim Il Sung thought he could gain the diplomatic benefits of accepting IAEA inspections while shielding his nuclear efforts from the agency's scrutiny. When the inspectors got too close, he threatened to withdraw from the NPT.

There are other possibilities, however, which presumably explain why China is predicting that the North will abide by the NPT. For instance, the DPRK may have had a nuclear program under way, but decided to drop it in exchange for expected benefits: diplomatic recognition by Japan and the U.S.; aid from the ROK and Japan; and investment from and trade with Seoul and the U.S. In a move perhaps triggered by the 1993 Team Spirit exercises, however, more hard-line elements may have demanded a change in policy, contending that all the DPRK had received for its more conciliatory course were ever-escalating demands. Such a scenario differs significantly from the first in that it suggests the North may yet be convinced to eschew a nuclear capability.

A third possibility is that a frustrated North is playing the "nuclear card," irrespective of the actual state of its program, in an attempt to wring more concessions from the U.S., the ROK, and Japan. Since those nations have shown that nothing else gets their attention, the DPRK may believe that it has to revive the nuclear threat from time to time.

Finally, the fourth scenario is that North Korea's new intransigence reflects an effort by heir apparent Kim Jong Il to shore up his rather thin military credentials by proving that he will protect the defense establishment's, and his nation's, interests. If he gains foreign concessions as a result, he could be assured of a strengthened political position.

It is impossible to know for sure which of those scenarios is accurate. The ultrasecretive nature of Kim's totalitarian political system makes any evaluation purely speculative. The critical point is that only the first scenario represents a serious dilemma to which there is no diplomatic solution. The situations presented by the other three scenarios, at least theoretically, are solvable by negotiation, no matter how much today's enthusiasts of the "start bombing" school may hate that course.

Although a matter of great concern, the North's withdrawal from the NPT would pose no immediate crisis. There is no credible evidence that the DPRK currently possesses a bomb. U.S. officials acknowledge that the North, assuming that it is committed to building a bomb, still may lack enough plutonium to produce even one weapon, let alone several. In the longer term, the possibility that Pyongyang might use nuclear arms to blackmail the ROK and other East Asian neighbors is worrisome. Nevertheless, a small arsenal would be more useful as a guarantee of the survival of the North Korean state and as political leverage than as offensive weapons against the ROK and other states in the region. The most important impact of a North Korean bomb ultimately might be to drive both the ROK and Japan to obtain their own nuclear arsenals.

That is an unpleasant prospect, certainly, but not one that warrants war now, especially without any serious attempt to resolve the issue before beginning bombing. Proposals to strike militarily are foolhardy. An attack would be unlikely to eliminate the North's nuclear program; the two sites from which the DPRK has barred inspectors are suspected waste sites, not production facilities. If the latter exist, they probably are buried deep underground somewhere, and there is no way of destroying them unless Washington is willing to use nuclear weapons. A meaningless strike at unimportant installations actually might encourage the regime to persevere with its presumed program, since American or ROK attacks would strengthen the argument of those who believe that only an atomic bomb can guarantee the security of the North, which lacks a serious air defense.

The odds are long against Washington and Seoul's successfully taking out unknown facilities at unknown locations. Equally dubious is the assumption of some that Pyongyang, long considered one of the most bizarre and unpredictable regimes on Earth, would acquiesce quietly to such a devastating, and very public, international humiliation. At a minimum, the North probably would restart a terror campaign that once blew commercial airliners out of the sky and massacred South Korean politicians visiting other nations. This time, though, Americans almost certainly would become targets as well.

Far worse is the possible ignition of what remains perhaps the world's most dangerous flashpoint: 1,500,000 soldiers currently sit astride the 155-mile DMZ and within a short drive of Seoul and its population of 12,000,000. A new war in Korea would be ruinous to all concerned.

Even the hawkish Richard Fisher of the Heritage Foundation acknowledges that "War against North Korea would devastate the Korean peninsula and must be avoided at every reasonable cost."

Any rational calculation by the North's leadership would cause Pyongyang to restraining itself, since it ultimately would lose any general conflict. That realization has helped to keep the peace for 40 years. Air strikes by the U.S. or a commando operation by the South, however, would be an act of war that Pyongyang could not ignore easily. Even small-scale reprisals by the DPRK could lead to counterattacks by Seoul and soon escalate out of control. Or, Kim Il Sung might adopt Frank Gaffney's analysis as his own: if the U.S. and the ROK appear dedicated to the destruction of his regime, it might be better to have war now rather than later, when his nation will be weaker and the South stronger. A few weeks or months into such a conflict, American soldiers probably would occupy Pyongyang, but Seoul, too, might lie in ruins, and tens of thousands of Koreans—and hundreds or thousands of Americans—probably would have died.

CIRCUMSPECTION NEEDED

A different course is called for. First, the U.S. should avoid taking precipitous action. If there is a crisis involving American security interests, it will occur in the future, not today. Washington should look for evidence that will help it decide whether North Korea irrevocably is committed to the acquisition of nuclear weapons or might be willing to trade away that capability. As long as Washington believes the latter may be the case

and that negotiations could be fruitful, the diplomatic option should be pursued.

That strategy should start with a U.S. commitment to establish diplomatic relations with and end the economic embargo against Pyongyang if the DPRK remains within the NPT and fulfills its obligations to the IAEA. That overture would provide the North with an immediate, positive reason to remain in the NPT. Is that a "concession," something some hard-line Western analysts do not want to give to North Korea? Of course, but it is a minimal one that would offer some small benefits to the U.S. as well—access to DPRK mineral exports, for instance, as well as a larger window into the secretive "hermit kingdom." It certainly is better to offer some cheap carrots to Pyongyang than to risk driving two nations of more than 60,000,000 people into war.

More significant, the diplomatic option should include a commitment to three-way talks to implement the two Koreas' independent inspection agreement signed in late 1991. South Korean and American officials argue that such talks would allow the DPRK to divide the allies, but Pyongyang has little leverage with which to promote a split. Another complaint is that engaging in the talks would be yielding to Northern extortion, but negotiations are a very cheap price to pay for the possibility of finding a way to avoid war and denuclearize the peninsula. As the nation that first introduced nuclear weapons to the region, the U.S. voluntarily should join discussions about a nuclear-inspection regime that would satisfy both the North and the South.

The ultimate objective of such talks should be a willingness on all sides to allow an investigation of any suspected facility. Washington should offer to open several American bases in the South where it once deployed nuclear weapons in return for IAEA access to the two disputed facilities and South Korean inspection of the Yongbyon complex. In time, additional bases and facilities could be opened to view.

The U.S. also should offer to help jumpstart talks between South and North through the Joint Military Committee in order to promote inspections of conventional facilities. As part of that process, the ROK and America should announce cancellation of future joint military exercises and a phased withdrawal of the 36,000 U.S. soldiers stationed in the South. In addition, Seoul should invite the North to respond by demobilizing some of its forces and pulling others back from their advanced, threatening positions in the DMZ. A refusal by Pyongyang to respond positively would provide evidence of its aggressive intentions and should cause the South to engage in a serious military buildup. With its enormous economic, political, and technological edge, the ROK can not maintain seriously that it is unable to raise the forces needed to defend itself.

What should happen to the U.S. military presence if the North refuses to choose peace? Under no circumstances should Washington leave U.S. troops on the peninsula, especially if the North acquires a bomb. America's original security commitment grew out of guilt at having left Seoul militarily unprepared for the DPRK onslaught in 1950. Moreover, during the Cold War, South Korea was viewed as an important surrogate in the strategy of containment. The world has changed, however. Not only has the U.S.S.R. dissolved, but the ROK now vastly outstrips its rival. American troops remain in the South out of habit, not need.

It is bad enough that 36,000 Americans continue to act as a living tripwire between the DMZ and Seoul in the event of a conventional war. To leave them as nuclear hostages if the North acquires an atomic bomb would be unforgivable. Nowhere else on Earth would so many Americans be at such great risk. The possibility that the DPRK may become a nuclear power should increase, not decrease, incentives for a prompt U.S. military withdrawal from Korea.

For similar reasons, the U.S. should not maintain, let alone strengthen, nuclear guarantees to South Korea and Japan. America's past conventional interventions on behalf of tangential interests— in Vietnam, for instance—proved costly, but the risks that could accompany a nuclear contest between small American allies and their antagonists is far worse. Washington already finds itself dangerously entangled in the affairs of India and Pakistan, which repeatedly have fought each other and now possess nuclear capabilities. There are disturbing reports, albeit discounted by some U.S. officials, that those two states approached the nuclear brink in 1990 over Kashmir. There is no reason for the U.S. to risk nuclear exposure in East Asia as well.

If the North forges ahead with its nuclear program, America should inform Pyongyang that Washington no longer will block Seoul from developing nuclear weapons. Indeed, if necessary, the U.S. will provide the South with a small nuclear inventory, sufficient to cancel the DPRK's advantage, as well as anti-missile technology. The North then would find itself further behind its southern rival. North Korea's position also would deteriorate further if Japan acquired nuclear weapons in a spreading regional arms race. In contrast, if Pyongyang fulfilled its obligations to the IAEA, foreign investment, recognition, and trade would be forthcoming.

The thought of expanding the world's nuclear club may seem unsettling—especially because Japan, too, ultimately might seek a limited arsenal, given the tensions between that nation and both Koreas. Still, for a variety of reasons, an increasing number of nations are likely to acquire atomic weapons in the years ahead, despite the NPT. To the extent that the treaty works, it bears a disturbing resemblance to gun control—the law-abiding submit while the criminals arm themselves. As a result, more analysts are proposing coercive nonproliferation, particularly through the use of military force. However, the problems with such a strategy are manifold, including the difficulty of destroying the most important sites, the danger posed to nearby nations as well as local civilian populations by radioactive leaks, the risk of terrorist retaliation, and the significant political difficulties of mounting a pre-emptive strike. In the case of North Korea, full-scale war also is a serious possibility.

Consequently, it would be better to begin discussing how the U.S. can adjust best to a world in which nuclear weapons do proliferate. That does not mean there is no value in attempting to slow some programs and stop other countries from acquiring nuclear weapons. A mixture of strategies—including development of anti-missile technologies, expansion of anti-aircraft capabilities, maintenance of a sufficient U.S. nuclear deterrent, and a judicious acceptance of the acquisition of independent deterrent forces by friendly nations—needs to replace today's all-or-nothing approach, under which Washington either prevents a country from acquiring weapons or simply extends America's nuclear umbrella. As Ted Galen Carpenter observed in *National Interest* (Summer, 1992), "Without the threat posed by a would-be hegemon, it is difficult to imagine what interest could be important enough for the United States to risk the consequences of a nuclear war to defend Turkey from a nuclear-armed Iran or to defend South Korea from a nuclearized North Korea."

POSTSCRIPT

Should the United States Forcefully Oppose North Korea's Nuclear Weapons Program?

There will no doubt be a good-sized book written to detail the complex maneuvering over North Korea's nuclear weapons program that occurred during 1993 and 1994, and that continues as of this writing. Several factors have made matters on this issue extremely complicated and often confusing. One is that there has been some disarray in the U.S. position. Initially, in late 1993, President Clinton made a "very firm" declaration that "North Korea cannot be allowed to develop a nuclear bomb." He soon retreated from that statement in light of disclosures that the CIA estimated that North Korea already had one or two bombs. North Korea denies this. Since then, the administration has taken the stance of opening North Korea to IAEA inspection and, perhaps, dismantling the program. American action was also limited by public opinion. A December 1993 poll found that to resolve the crisis, 46 percent of the respondents favored a continuation of working through diplomatic channels, 34 percent wanted a UN trade embargo, and only 11 percent favored military action. Eight percent were unsure. Another poll that asked what the United States should do if North Korea invaded South Korea as a result of the confrontation found that only a minority, 44 percent, favored using U.S. troops (including the ones already stationed there) to defend the country. Some 40 percent favored supplying South Korea with weapons, 15 percent were unsure, and 1 percent refused to even answer the question.

Possible strong action was also hampered by international opinion, especially the process of taking action through the UN Security Council. China, which has a veto on the Security Council, almost certainly does not want North Korea to have nuclear arms. Yet North Korea and China are longstanding allies, they are two of the few remaining communist countries, and China has repeatedly demonstrated that it is disinclined to interfere in what it considers other countries' sovereign prerogatives. The potential for war has also made South Korea and Japan reluctant to press too hard. The North Koreans tried to promote these fears by making loud threats. "If Japan should join forces in any sanctions against us," a North Korean official warned, "we would regard it as a decision of war and Japan would be unable to avoid a deserving punishment for it."

North Korea's stand also seemed to move back and forth; sometimes the North Koreans seemed willing to allow inspections, other times they rejected them. At times the North seemed to reject any outside effort to control its nuclear program, at other times it seemed willing to bargain its program away for some combination of presidential-level negotiations with South Korea and the United States, full diplomatic recognition, and extensive foreign aid. Whether these shifts were the result of clever maneuvering or whether they represented uncertainty in the North is unclear. If all that was not enough, the picture became even muddier in July 1994 when Kim Il Sung, North Korea's only leader since World War II, died suddenly of a heart attack. His place was taken by his son, Kim Jong Il. Almost nothing specific is known about him, or his views, or how firm his control is.

A hopeful sign was that the North Korean delegation, which was negotiating with the United States and others in Geneva, Switzerland, agreed to continue talks after a period of mourning for the deceased, senior Kim. Then in early August 1994, the government in Pyongyang indicated a willingness to halt the production of plutonium and allow inspections in return for a package that included full diplomatic recognition by the United States, South Korea, and others, a sizable foreign aid package, and the billions of dollars and technical help needed to build a huge light-water nuclear reactor. This would free North Korea from obtaining hard-to-secure heavy water for its nuclear reactor.

In the last analysis, the debate, then, is not about North Korea, as such. It is about nuclear proliferation. More on this can be found in Peter Van Ham, *Managing Non-Proliferation Regimes in the 1990s* (Council on Foreign Relations, 1994) and Mitchell Reiss and Robert S. Litwak, *Nuclear Proliferation After the Cold War* (Johns Hopkins University Press, 1994).

ISSUE 14

Is It Time to Terminate the CIA?

YES: Marcus Raskin, from "Let's Terminate the C.I.A.," *The Nation* (June 8, 1992)

NO: R. James Woolsey, from "Threats to the U.S. and Its Interests Abroad: Intelligence and Security," *Vital Speeches of the Day* (March 1, 1994)

ISSUE SUMMARY

YES: Marcus Raskin, cofounder of the Institute for Policy Studies, argues that in the post–cold war world the CIA and other intelligence agencies of the United States should be dismantled or transformed, not merely reorganized.

NO: R. James Woolsey, U.S. Director of Central Intelligence, contends that the end of the cold war has not brought an end to security threats to the United States and American interests abroad. Therefore, the country continues to need an effective intelligence capability.

The Central Intelligence Agency (CIA), is a product of the cold war. It was established in 1947 as a successor to the Office of Strategic Services (OSS), the World War II intelligence agency, and was intended primarily to combat the activities of the Soviet Union and its intelligence services (the KGB in particular), as well as the spy and subversive operations of other communist countries.

Of the U.S. intelligence agencies, the CIA is the best known and the most problematic because of its extensive ability to carry out covert operations. Other U.S. intelligence organizations include the National Security Agency (which specializes in electronic intelligence gathering and is even larger than the CIA), the National Reconnaissance Office, the National Imagery Office, the Defense Intelligence Agency, the State Department's Bureau of Intelligence and Research, and the intelligence services attached to each of the military services.

The CIA has two distinct divisions: one is information gathering and analysis, the other is operations. Over the years, the operations side has dominated the agency. Several directors of the CIA have progressed up the agency's chain of command on the operations side before reaching the top of the organization.

Critics of the CIA argue that its origins and mission have created a culture of suspicion and secrecy that is dangerous to a democractic society because the agency feels justified in hiding its activities from public comment and control.

They charge that the CIA often ignores the law and undertakes questionable activities in the name of the greater good or the national interest, as defined solely by the CIA. At the height of the cold war tension, in the grip of the near-hysteria of the late 1940s and early 1950s, one government report argued that, through the CIA, "we must learn to subvert, sabotage, and destroy our enemies by more clever, more sophisticated, and more effective methods than those used against us." "The world isn't Beverly Hills," one CIA official later told an audience, "it's a bad neighborhood at 2:00 in the morning." This imagery led, as another former CIA official has suggested, to a belief within the agency that it must not be "expected to respond like a man in a barroom brawl who will fight only according to the Marquis of Queensberry rules." Such an orientation worried Dean Acheson, who was undersecretary of state at the time of the CIA's creation. As he later recalled, "I have the gravest foreboding about this organization and warned the President [Truman] that as set up, neither he, the National Security Council, nor anyone else would be in a position to know what it [the CIA] was doing or [be in a position] to control it."

Beginning in 1974, under pressure because of changes in public attitudes that grew out of the country's experiences with the Vietnam War, Congress has attempted to beef up its oversight of covert operations. Congress launched several investigations into the CIA and other intelligence operations and in 1980 enacted the Intelligence Oversight Act, which created two committees, the House and Senate Intelligence Committees, to oversee the intelligence community.

These efforts improved oversight, but many critics allege that continued CIA attempts to cloak its activities from outside scrutiny rendered oversight superficial, at best. As one member of Congress noted, "If you do not know that an operation is under way to begin with, then you have to be pretty smart to know what the question is that will get you the answer you are seeking." On one occasion, for example, a congressional committee member asked Reagan administration CIA director William Casey if the CIA was mining Nicaraguan harbors. "No," Casey replied, thinking that he was telling the technical truth because the CIA was planting mines on the docks in the harbors but not in the harbors themselves.

As long as the cold war lasted, and recall that that was what spawned the CIA in the first place, there was greater consensus among the American public and federal officials for support for the CIA. The "clear and present danger" of international communism backed by Soviet power made it unlikely that the CIA and the rest of the intelligence agencies would face any real political threat to their existence or mission. That has changed somewhat with the end of the cold war. In the following debate, Marcus Raskin argues that the CIA should become as extinct as the Soviet Union. CIA director R. James Woolsey argues that the demise of one enemy does not mean safety for the United States and that the CIA is needed for the future.

YES
Marcus Raskin

LET'S TERMINATE THE C.I.A.

The end of the cold war and the collapse of our chief adversary in that conflict challenges the very existence of the national security state, which has dominated American society for almost a half-century. A pillar of that apparatus is the nation's intelligence community—the Central Intelligence Agency, the National Security Agency and related agencies.[1] With an annual secret budget estimated at between $30 billion and $40 billion, these agencies, led by the C.I.A., have been in the forefront of the "secret war" for forty-five years. Aside from rare official inquiries such as the Church committee's investigations in 1975 and periodic exposés in the media, they have operated virtually exempt from public scrutiny. Only when the not uncommon disaster —such as Iran/*contra*—breaks into the headlines do Americans get a glimmer of what is being done in their name by the secret services.

Now that the cold war is over, it's time for a far-reaching public debate on the future role of the intelligence agencies. In my view they should be dismantled or transformed, not merely reorganized.... In... debates in the Senate, the question of the C.I.A.'s future has been raised, but only a few legislators, most notably Senator Daniel Patrick Moynihan, have challenged its cold war premises or questioned its future usefulness. Rather, the approach has been to try to think up new jobs for the C.I.A. The Senate Select Committee on Intelligence entertained such ideas as using the agency to help multinational corporations compete in the global economy or to wage stepped-up antiterrorist campaigns or to collect environmental intelligence.

On February 5, [1992,] the chairmen of the Senate and House Intelligence Committees, David Boren and Dave McCurdy, respectively, introduced parallel bills on reorganizing the "intelligence community." But these legislative efforts merely sanctify into law the cold war traditions of U.S. intelligence— covert operations, a threat mentality, a presumption for military intervention and the continuing need for the intelligence community.... As Senator Ernest Hollings said in committee, the intelligence community should maintain the capacity "to keep policy-makers abreast of the great variety of threats the nation faces... proliferation of high-technology weapons, regional threats, terrorism, drug trafficking, economic and business developments among our trade rivals, and environmental change."

... [S]eeking to increase Congressional control over the C.I.A., Senator John Glenn introduced a bill requiring that top officials of the agency, in addition to the director, be confirmed by the Senate, but this bill, which was tacked onto the Intelligence Authorization Act of 1991, was voted down by the Senate, 59 to 38. Opponents of Glenn's amendment argued that secrecy and czarlike power for the director were still necessary. The Senate's main concerns were about waste and duplication of effort. By April 1992 the Senate Intelligence Committee returned to its traditional role of covering for the C.I.A., even though the agency lied at least twice to the committee about the transfer of intelligence information to Iraq. After the end of the Gulf War, the C.I.A. told the Intelligence Committee that the agency had stopped giving intelligence to the Iraqis two years before Iraq's August 1990 invasion of Kuwait. During the Gates nomination hearings the agency changed its tune and said it had ceased cooperating with the Iraqis in early 1990. After the nomination was approved, the C.I.A. said it gave intelligence for another three to four months beyond early 1990. Then further information was released that suggested that the agency continued to give information until August 1990. Senator Boren did not seem bothered by these contradictions.

Reform efforts in Congress have been timid and marginal and will remain dormant until another intelligence scandal surfaces. The opportunity to restructure U.S. intelligence for the post–cold war world has been temporarily lost. Nevertheless, transforming the cold war in-telligence apparatus should be a topic of public debate for the rest of this century, just as U.S. national defense assumptions must be continually re-examined and revised in the light of realities of the post–cold war world. The debate over American and world security has just begun. The purpose of this symposium is to contribute to that debate by reconsidering the root assumptions and policy alternatives of national security.

In my view, such a reappraisal will show that the cold war mission of the intelligence community has ended and that it should be dismantled, along with the atmosphere of paranoia and conflict that it fed and propagated at home and abroad. The history of U.S. intelligence over the past forty-five years teaches us what needs to be done if it is to serve democratic ends.

I.

During the cold war years, U.S. intelligence operations were carried out according to a conflict/threat model of international relations. Within that model, American policy-makers assumed that the United States is under continuous siege from enemies real or potential, but mostly conjured. It assumed that America's place in the world is primarily achieved through military and covert means. And it assumed that the United States can never be at peace, that it must always be involved in some kind of military or paramilitary activity that it initiates and controls.

American leaders believed that the state required an extensive covert intelligence operation that would assure the nation's superiority in the conflict with its chief enemy, the Soviet Union. Also needed were internal security controls to insure a compliant citizenry. The role of the intelligence community was to perceive the world through the lens of distrust. Institutionalized paranoia was the prescription for the American people, not only against enemies abroad but against their fellow Americans as well.

In addition to exaggerated fears of Soviet power and intentions, the conflict/threat model presumed a world inhabited by Enemy Others. America's competitive spirit accepted cooperation in military alliances only when the United States was the leading partner. The Soviet Union was portrayed as the archrival, an enduring, pervasive threat that was behind all mischief in the world. To combat it, the United States had to engage in a variety of dirty tricks in the "back alleys" of the world, in Secretary of State Dean Rusk's phrase.

As a recent Pentagon working paper ("Defense Planning Guidance: 1994–1999") indicates, the conflict/threat model is far from dead. Under this Defense Department proposal the United States would preside over a Pax Americana and "discourage" advanced industrial nations from "challenging our leadership," as well as deter "potential competitors from even aspiring to a larger or global role." This country, the Pentagon said, "will retain the preeminent responsibility for addressing selectively those wrongs which threaten not only our interests, but those of our allies or friends, or which could seriously unsettle international relations." ...

We tend to forget that there is an alternative to the conflict/threat model —the cooperation model. It calls for international cooperation, with nations working through international bodies, adhering to international norms and settling disputes peacefully. The coopera-

tion model gives high priority to finding solutions to the difficult problem of squaring national sovereignty with a code of international human rights, eschewing unilateral intervention and pursuing a comprehensive disarmament program while establishing an international security arrangement through the Military Staff Committee of the United Nations.

During World War II and immediately after, the cooperation model enjoyed a brief ascendancy, reflecting the U.S.-Soviet alliance, the hopes for the newly formed U.N., the people's yearning for peace. But with the defeat of Henry Wallace's Progressive Party in the 1948 election; the death of two-time G.O.P. presidential candidate Wendell L. Willkie, whose internationalist ideas dominated the liberal wing of the Republican Party; the rise of McCarthyism; the victory of the Maoists in China; the economic recession of 1949; and the escalation of border skirmishes between the forces of North and South Korea into full-scale war the following year, the cooperation model died, eclipsed by the cold war. The conflict/threat model dominated government policy and other institutions as well —cultural, educational, economic.

The bureaucratic rationale for the C.I.A. emerged from fears of officials in the Office of Strategic Services ([O.S.S.,] the wartime precursor to the C.I.A.) that the United States was too dependent on British intelligence, that the Soviet Union was seeking control over Eastern Europe and that adequate information was needed to counterbalance Soviet attempts at expansion.... Congress disbanded the O.S.S., and under the terms of the National Security Act of 1947 set up a new organization to supersede it.... The major civil liberties safeguard imposed on the C.I.A. was that it was barred from carrying out internal police functions. Those functions were left to the noted civil libertarian J. Edgar Hoover. Soon enough, the C.I.A.—and other intelligence units within the armed forces as well—would compete with the F.B.I. in domestic spying by infiltrating political groups, often for disruptive purposes. The classic cases of such C.I.A. and N.S.A. [National Security Agency] activities were Operations Chaos and Minaret, which were illegal spying programs against Americans that used warrantless electronic surveillance and human intelligence.

A Game Without Rules

In 1954, a commission appointed by President Eisenhower and chaired by Lieut. Gen. James Doolittle formulated an official rationale to justify intelligence activities already under way. In a key statement, the commission said: "It is now clear that we are facing an implacable enemy whose avowed objective is world domination by whatever means and at whatever cost. There are no rules in such a game. Hitherto acceptable norms of human conduct do not apply. If the United States is to survive, long-standing American concepts of 'fair play' must be reconsidered. We must . . . learn to subvert, sabotage and destroy our enemies by more clever, more sophisticated and more effective methods than those used against us." It also concluded, "Another important requirement is an aggressive covert psychological, political and paramilitary organization more effective, more unique and, if necessary, more ruthless than that employed by the enemy. No one should be permitted to stand in the way of the prompt, efficient and secure accomplishment of this mission."

Spying was indeed a dirty business. The operations of the C.I.A. and other agencies were often immoral, unconstitutional and criminal. Such activities would have made the public uneasy, so they had to be shrouded by the arts of secrecy and plausible denial. Since the C.I.A. often operated as the President's private army, the executive branch became a kind of front for illegal covert actions. The President gave them a patina of legitimacy, thereby turning the office into a switching point between criminal and lawful activities. Sometimes, of course, Presidents or their subordinates were caught flatfooted participating in criminal activities, as when Howard Hunt, a former C.I.A. agent working for the White House, used the agency to help him break into the office of Daniel Ellsberg's psychiatrist.

Secrecy also served to shield the intelligence establishment (and its hefty budgets) from Congressional and media scrutiny. It insulated the C.I.A. from public examination that might have prevented it from launching disastrous operations like the Bay of Pigs invasion or Operation Phoenix in Vietnam, in which some 20,000 innocent people and suspected Vietcong supporters were murdered. Without outside criticism of its past mistakes, the C.I.A. was doomed to repeat them.

And so for decades it conducted interventions worldwide, subverting governments, arming insurgencies, spreading black propaganda. Often these actions produced harmful consequences. The "victorious coup" in Iran that expelled Mossadegh brought back the Shah, whose misrule paved the way for the Ayatollah Khomeini. The 1954 coup that overthrew Guatemala's democratically elected government produced decades of cruel dictatorship. The glorious putsch that expelled Sukarno in Indonesia brought in its wake the murder or imprisonment of hundreds of thousands of Indonesians. Back in Washington, the exaggerations of Soviet capabilities and intentions by various elements of the intelligence community fed and sustained the arms race.

'Scholars and Spies'

The benign view of itself the C.I.A. projected—as a mere gatherer and dispenser of information to the President from its "campus" at Langley, Virginia, where strolled professorial, pipe-smoking types —was gradually eroded by belated revelations that some of these men had conducted experiments on unwilling subjects with mind-altering drugs, had used germ warfare agents against poor nations and had planned and executed coups.

... "[S]cholars and spies" were hardly dedicated to independent inquiry. Often their analyses were slanted to pander to the desires of the policy-makers and the predilections of the national security curia. To advance their careers, junior analysts skewed their reports to harmonize with what the "hierarchic other," or superiors in the organization, wanted.

Secrecy invariably assumes a priesthood dealing in fixed truths and essences. It is the antithesis of the spirit of free inquiry. . . .

A secret bureaucracy, a policy of secrets within secrets, disclosed only to those with "a need to know," by its very nature engenders paranoia, institutional ignorance and control by a handful of executives, especially in the context of the conflict/threat mindset. The career of James Jesus Angleton, the . . . former head of C.I.A. counterintelligence, exemplified this tendency toward paranoia at the highest levels. Angleton apparently concluded that William Colby, a former Director of Central Intelligence and the head of Operation Phoenix, was a mole for the Soviet Union. Angleton's malign suspicions, fed by a Soviet defector, rocked the agency for more than a decade.

Angleton's case is perhaps extreme. In the closed society of the intelligence community, what the analyst concludes may be distorted by institutional pressures and a deep-seated policy that goes unquestioned but that distorts analysts' structuring of the data. In an intelligence agency millions of pieces of data are processed daily. As in any scientific inquiry, this flux must be arranged into some order, and the task of the analyst is to make an existential judgment of what he or she believes to be true or authentic. But what is found to be authentic in the closed society of intelligence may derive from a desire or a vested interest simply to please the boss. Undeniably, these factors are at work in other, nonsecret agencies of government. But there is an important difference: "Open" governmental agencies operate with some degree of accountability to Congress, the courts and, through the media, the public.

Covert Wars

But intelligence collection and analysis sometimes seemed the least of the C.I.A.'s purposes. The agency has generally been more interested in carrying out direct paramilitary interventions with the sanction of Congress or the President or, sometimes, on its own motion. In September 1970 President Nixon ordered C.I.A. Director Richard Helms to take measures to make the Chilean economy "scream" in order to destabilize the government of socialist President Salvador Allende. Assassination attempts were made against unwanted foreign leaders, usually leftists like Patrice Lumumba in the Congo. Cuba's Fidel Castro has been a favorite bête noire [source of fear] since the Eisenhower Administration. But rightists were not immune. In the Dominican Republic, Rafael Trujillo, a right-wing dictator who had lost the confidence of Washington, was assassinated in 1961. C.I.A. "assets" who became leaders of their country and showed some independence, like Panama's Manuel Noriega, were cut down to size. Under the Reagan Administration C.I.A.-backed surrogates, or "freedom fighters," waged wars in Nicaragua, El Salvador, Afghanistan, Angola, Cambodia and Chad. Covert support to diverse elements in Eastern Europe was stepped up, sometimes with the help of Pope John Paul II.

C.I.A. Director William Casey served as the field marshal of a worldwide system of covert wars. No area of the world was immune from intervention by the C.I.A., N.S.A. and other agencies. All of these escapades flowed from what Frank Wisner, former Deputy Director of the C.I.A., once called "the mighty Wurlitzer"—the ten aspects of intelligence work. Each activity is inextricably linked to the others; like an onion, peel away one layer and you reach another, more dangerous layer. The ten are:

1. The gathering of information by overt or covert means (if the information is gathered by covert means, then as likely as not, another nation's laws are violated).

2. Evaluating, analyzing and storing information; finding assets (covert sources) and establishing proprietaries (dummy companies) to undertake specific tasks.

3. Advising and disseminating information that is often false and self-deceiving; getting U.S. government consumers to use the information, developing a market for it and fashioning information and facts that are custom-made for particular clients in the government. The market may want truthful information or lies.

4. Persuading government consumers to use information they may not ordinarily be interested in (an organization dependent on the whim of a President must provide him with what he wants, but he may bore easily, and so irrelevant or tabloidlike information has to be generated to keep presidential interest).

5. Organizing more covert activities to obtain information, verify conclusions and answer new requests of policy-makers....

6. Organizing clandestine activities to obtain classified information of other nations as well as undertaking disinformation campaigns in which material is manufactured to promote either the position of the C.I.A., the official policies of the United States, the agendas of specific groups within the intelligence community or policies that are contrary to those stated to Congress or that violate American law....

7. Organizing black operations of a complex nature such as economic and political destabilization, mining harbors, [and] funding third-party nations to do the bidding of the United States....

8. Employing scientific and technological means to undercut the development or abort or inhibit the activities of an adversary nation; developing technical intelligence capacity, cryp-

tography and topographic analysis through satellites.

9. Recruiting local armies and guerrilla groups and developing and guiding them so they can be used for the national objectives of the United States. Covertly sponsoring labor unions, women's groups and paying for crowds and demonstrators.

10. Using force—assassination teams when necessary—to assert the considered (or ill-considered) policy. Fighting small wars that are kept out of the U.S. media. Shielding the President by offering plausible denial and cover for illegal and criminal actions he ordered.

These activities form the foundation stones of the intelligence community. The entire project of this community helped to make the government of the United States into an Orwellian nightmare, in which "intelligence" became synonymous with massive self-deception and treachery. Force and fraud had found a home base in the intelligence community and in the cold war conception of intelligence.

II.

The United States is now at a turning point: It must decide what sort of nation it wants to be. The future role of the intelligence community will have a direct bearing on the character of our nation, for the intelligence community helps determine the policy-makers' perception of the world. It can sustain myths, generate and authenticate "threats," and give the color of rationality to force and fraud.

The struggles now smoldering in Eastern Europe and the former Soviet Union, the clan animosities raging from Angola to Croatia, the endemic tensions in the Middle East and elsewhere in the world provide plenty of potential stages for future intelligence actions should we decide to continue playing the dirty game of back-alley wars.

But there is an alternative: adopting the cooperation model. This would mean dismantling the present intelligence community, abandoning those functions that served the cold war state and reassigning to other agencies the functions that can be integrated into the cooperation model of international relations. In this scheme, intelligence analysis would be used as a communications bridge among nations rather than as a tool for power and control.

The cooperation model would be based on the premise that the problems of our world at the close of the twentieth century cannot be resolved by a single nation, the United States, pursuing its own ends. The environment, immigration, disarmament, economic justice and health, as well as the need for mediating regional and international disputes, are matters of world concern requiring the public exchange of ideas and information among a wide array of very different national cultures. A shift away from the conflict/threat paradigm, which means demilitarization and the shift of budget expenditures away from militarized national security policies, would free badly needed resources to deal with this country's pressing domestic problems.

The United States is in the best position to lead the shift to the cooperation model because its military security problems can be dealt with through a worldwide general disarmament process in tandem with the strengthening of U.N. peacekeeping functions.

Under the cooperation model, intelligence would of course cease to be a clandestine enterprise. Instead it would operate as an international social project, in tandem with a new foreign policy agenda dedicated to environmental protection, scientific understanding, improved communications and information dispersal, worldwide economic development, health improvement and military disarmament.

Steps to an Open Society

What changes should be made in the intelligence community so that it could serve a nation that acts within the cooperation model of international politics? I would propose the following steps:

Step One. There should be a comprehensive revision of the National Security Act of 1947 to insure that the United States pursues policies of cooperation with the U.N. and respect for international law and human rights.... The language of a revised National Security Act would emphasize global disarmament, stimulation of international communication, reinvestment in the U.S. infrastructure, preservation of the environment, protection of human rights and cooperation on common problems among nations in the post–cold war world. Intelligence activities would be harnessed to achieving those ends.

Step Two. There should be a review of all laws and executive orders that give the intelligence community special status. The most relevant examples are laws that exempt various agencies from systematic review of their operations, from the federal pay scale and from federal labor-management relations statutes....

Several other cold war laws should be repealed or revised, including those making intelligence agencies only vaguely accountable for how they spend their money....

Step Three. The C.I.A.'s analytic functions should be transferred to non-covert agencies of government. This would affect some nongovernmental sectors of society as well—the universities, international corporations, labor unions and media that have maintained a symbiotic relationship with the national security state, including the intelligence agencies, since World War II.

The idea that knowledge and information know no boundaries, which dominated the scientific community before World War II, should be revived. The data-collection and analysis functions of the C.I.A. and N.S.A. should be internationalized much in the manner that medical information is now exchanged internationally and publicly. The information could be made available as part of an international information agency that would establish regional centers. The United States, with the assent of the U.N. Security Council and General Assembly, could form a worldwide consortium of intelligence agencies, served by a worldwide community of scholars and analysts whose researches would be made public and distributed widely through regional centers. It would be understood that this consortium would operate under the U.N. Just as no nation can afford not to trade internationally, so no nation or society can afford not to share information for the common good.

The specific areas on which this consortium would concentrate are scientific data gathering and dissemination;

economic justice reporting; conflict resolution/environmental enhancement; the state of human rights; and the state of international agreements, especially in this disarmament area.

Step Four. The paramilitary functions that the C.I.A. performed during the cold war should be placed under the control of the uniformed military services, where they would be subjected to public scrutiny and civilian control.... C.I.A. covert actions under the military would be publicly accountable. To underscore this point, the laws on mercenaries should be amended so that they apply directly to government officials or their agents.... Throughout the cold war, covert activities, many of them unauthorized, took place under the color of bureaucratic legality. In the future, rogue operators or those who otherwise transgress legal authority would be subject to criminal prosecution.

In other words, military interventions, economic destabilization and other covert actions would be deemed criminal offenses....

Step Five. The Secretary of State should set forth a needs and requirements report to Congress in order to improve the political reporting of the State Department. The secretary would make clear that the department will absorb analysts from the C.I.A., but that it will not countenance being used as a cover for covert and clandestine activities.

Step Six. A Protection of Records Act should be crafted to insured that no records of the C.I.A. or other intelligence agencies are destroyed. In this way a true account of the history of the cold war period could be written. These records should be made public as quickly as possible after being transferred to the Archivist of the United States. Substantial penalties should apply to those government officials who attempt to forge or rewrite the record.

Step Seven. Except for that part of the National Security Agency that would be given over to the Arms Control and Disarmament Agency and, for specific and narrowly defined purposes, the Defense Department, the N.S.A. would become an international public library under the control of the Librarian of Congress and secondarily the Archivist of the United States.

Any residual activities of the N.S.A. should be subjected to rigorous public scrutiny by Congress in order to assure that its information be made publicly available, and to assure that its various activities are in fact constitutionally sanctioned. (For example, monitoring telephone calls is an invasion of privacy when those on the phone are not informed and have not given their permission.)...

Step Eight. Throughout the cold war, security procedures and surveillance of government officials have been used as an *in terrorem* [intimidation] policy to protect secrets and enforce loyalty. These secrets, as often as not, have reflected two types of material. The first broad category is related to technical scientific matters and military plans. The second is related to operations that were in violation of American law or the law of other nations and international law. Security procedures that in fact have been thinly veiled cover-up schemes (for example, Iran/*contra*) should now be forbidden by executive order.

Matters that pertain to the defense of the United States would continue to be secret. Such secrecy is warranted so long as classification is carried out by the Defense Department as part of its constitutional mandate and pertains to defensive measures permitted by the U.N. Charter, international law and the laws of the United States. However, the entire system of classifying documents would require comprehensive revision so that it would conform to the revised National Security Act described in Step One....

Step Nine. The end of the cold war is the right time to restore a rule that is clearly contemplated by the Constitution, namely, that secrecy in government is the exception and not the normal way of doing business. Congress itself should now revise its own organizational structure on national security matters. It should re-examine its own assumptions regarding secrecy and the harm caused by its failure to be an independent and disinterested public guardian over the intelligence agencies....

* * *

The United States is a protean organism; it can change its shape and purpose. And it can assist in giving birth to a cooperative world civilization that recognizes the importance of cultures and nations outside Europe. If American leaders attempt to control a messy, recalcitrant reality through military and covert means, if the nation does not take stock of itself and initiate its own internal reconstruction, then we will indeed live a nightmare of decline and continuous war, with the covert agencies leading the way. We will mistake paranoia for intelligence, and American leaders will be seeking new Enemy Others to justify the national security state. Without substantial changes in attitudes and direction, the intelligence community will be a willing accomplice, supplying or inventing new threats to an insecure leadership and nation. This year the threat could be the Japanese and next year the Germans, or perhaps it is Iraq or Iran or Libya, or Croatians, North Koreans, African-Americans or immigrants, that justify covert operations.

It is time for the executive and Congress to come in from the cold. It is time for knowledge workers inside and outside governments to work together and fashion a world cooperation model that could help humanity transcend the horrible follies of the twentieth century.

NOTES

1. The U.S. "intelligence community" properly includes the intelligence units in each branch of the armed services, as well as those in the State Department, the Energy Department, the Drug Enforcement Administration, the Justice and Treasury Departments and the National Imaging Agency.

NO

R. James Woolsey

THREATS TO THE U.S. AND ITS INTERESTS ABROAD: INTELLIGENCE AND SECURITY

Delivered before the United States Senate Select Committee on Intelligence, Washington, D.C., January 25, 1994.

I welcome the opportunity to testify before this committee on the threats to the United States and its interests abroad. Much has transpired since I addressed your Senate colleagues on the Armed Services Committee on this same topic last March. Let me highlight a few of these historic events.

- In East Asia, North Korea's attempt to develop a clandestine nuclear capability, together with its military preparations and arms transfers to other countries, threatens its neighbors and our fundamental national security interests.
- In Russia and the rest of the former Soviet Union the struggle for democracy and economic reform has been intense and—as witnessed last fall in Moscow—at times, violent. Progress is occurring, but it is spotty.
- Local strife in Somalia and Haiti, and the tragedy in Bosnia, continue to threaten stability in those countries and nearby regions.

    On the positive side, Mr. Chairman, in the Asia/Pacific region, Latin America, and Europe—while there are some specific difficulties, including those mentioned above—the political, security, and economic pictures are generally in the range from light gray to bright.
- In Kiev and Moscow, the President brokered an agreement with Russia and Ukraine on the disposition of the nuclear weapons stationed on Ukrainian soil. Implementation will take substantial effort, but the agreement is a step toward removing not only an obstacle to better relations between those two countries but also a source of critical concern to U.S. and Western security interests.
- On the international economic front, the GATT [General Agreement on Tariffs and Trade] agreement, bringing the Uruguay Round to a successful conclusion, paves the way for a significant boost in world trade.

- Two conflicts, both of which preceded the onset of the cold war, have shown movement toward resolution, although in neither case are we yet home free. In South Africa, apartheid is being dismantled, and an historic agreement was reached last July paving the way for the first multi-racial, national, democratic election this spring. In the Middle East, Israel and the PLO [Palestine Liberation Organization] concluded their famous agreement in the Rose Garden. Implementation awaits further negotiation, but here and elsewhere in the Mid-East there has been positive movement to reduce tensions between Israel and its neighbors.

The lesson that I draw from my first year as Director of Central Intelligence is that hope coexists with uncertainty, promise with danger. We had one central threat which dominated our work for nearly half a century. That threat is gone, and we gladly leave the cold war with the communist U.S.S.R. to historians and scholars.

But the end of the cold war does not mean the end of conflict, nor the end to threats to our security and to that of our friends and allies. Indeed, your invitation to me to address this committee listed no fewer than ten major issues, ranging from developments in the former Soviet Union to countering the proliferation of weapons of mass destruction. As we know, that list is by no means exhaustive.

The conflicts today may have different names and may be grouped under different banners; at times, the question which could determine war or peace may not be where you stand, politically, but who you are, ethnically. I might add that these types of conflicts are not new to U.S.

intelligence: half of the stars etched into the marble wall at CIA are dedicated to those officers who lost their lives to such conflicts. And today I wear a black ribbon to honor all of those at CIA who have lost their lives in defense of their country, and particularly to commemorate the sad anniversary of the slaying of two Agency officers at our door, only five miles from where we sit today.

The task for intelligence in the post cold war era is clear:

- First, we must support policymakers working hard to nurture promise and hope, to protect the gains of the past five remarkable—indeed revolutionary—years.
- Second, we must remain vigilant against North Korea, Iran, Iraq, Libya and others throughout the globe who want to make a mockery of our goal of a more peaceful world.
- Third, we must provide the early warning and the information systems needed to keep our reduced defense forces up to the tasks they may face in an uncertain future.
- Fourth, we must be prepared for the unknown. Next year might bring a different set of headlines, and a new set of problems which can threaten our interests, task our resources, and challenge our resolve.

This afternoon I would like to highlight the critical challenges we face in the intelligence community, and the efforts underway to help counter the threats to our interests.

I want to begin my presentation on regional issues: East Asia, focusing first on North Korea and then on China; developments in Russia and in the former Soviet Union; [and] the Middle East.... I will then turn to transnational issues:

proliferation, terrorism, drug trafficking, and international economics.

I take this approach for ease of presentation only. As we know, in the real world regional and transnational problems are often intertwined, whether we speak of international economic trends constraining the ability of key nations to maintain defense capabilities, or of proliferation fueled by—and exacerbating—regional conflicts.

REGIONAL ISSUES

The Far East: North Korea and China
Let me begin with North Korea. Mr. Chairman, in recent months North Korea has vaulted to the top of our agenda in the intelligence community. North Korea presents us and our friends and allies with three critical challenges.

First is its effort to develop its nuclear capability. As I testified publicly before the Congress on July 28 of last year, we believe that North Korea could already have produced enough plutonium for at least one nuclear weapon. Moreover, their Yongbyon reactor may be shut down soon, enabling them to extract fuel, reprocess, recover the plutonium, and use it to produce weapons. In addition, North Korea is building a larger reactor which could be completed by the mid 1990s, expanding its capability to produce even more plutonium. Even with NPT [Non-Proliferation Treaty] and full IAEA [International Atomic Energy Agency] safeguards, North Korea will not be barred from producing, reprocessing, and stockpiling significant amounts of plutonium. We will continue to provide support to policymakers as they press for full implementation of IAEA safeguards and the 1991 North-South Non-Nuclear

Agreement, which is intended to prevent the further production of fissile material on the peninsula.

We are also providing analytical support to policymakers working to resolve through diplomatic means the serious concerns raised by North Korean actions. At the same time, I have asked the intelligence community to undertake additional specific steps, in cooperation with the defense community, to ensure strong intelligence support to our military forces.

A second challenges is what North Korea calls its war preparations program, including both improvements in military capabilities and continuing efforts to bring their economy and society to a heightened state of military readiness. North Korea's deployment of rocket launchers and artillery to protected sites close to the DMZ [demilitarized zone], from which it is possible to target Seoul and South Korean defenses, is just the most recent manifestation of their steady allocation, over the last several years, of resources to the military at the expense of the needs of the North Korean people. Despite remaining readiness inadequacies affecting some North Korean forces, we are concerned with their military preparations and, as in the case of monitoring North Korea's nuclear program, here too we will continue to assign high priority to intelligence coverage.

The third challenge stems from North Korean export of missiles, including those in the 1,000 kilometer range, which can be made capable of carrying nuclear, chemical or biological weapons. Deployment and sale of such missiles provides a qualitative increase in the capabilities of both North Korea and its customers in the Mid-East. Potentially at risk is most of North East Asia as well as potential targets of North Korea's customers in the Mid-East, such as Israel, Turkey, Saudi Arabia, and other states.

Turning to China, because of its enormous population, growing economy and military strength, China will continue to play a key role in the stability not only of Asia but of much of the rest of the world as well. We are focusing our efforts on the political, economic and military evolution in China.

Politically, at some point there will of course be a change in China's leadership. Deng Xiaoping, the last of the original communist revolutionaries to serve as China's top leader, will turn 90 this August. Although formally in retirement, he is still consulted by other leaders who depend on him for cohesion, legitimacy and guidance. When Deng departs we will face a potentially unsettled period, when prospective leaders jockey for position.

Turning to economics, we see China's economy as one of the fastest growing in the world, after two years of back-to-back 13 percent real growth. Increased inflation is one concern. China's rediscovered entrepreneurial spirit has also been accompanied by unfair trading practices to which the U.S. Government has recently responded, with some success. We will continue to monitor China's trade, although decreasing central control makes some of these practices even more difficult to expose. The stakes, however, for American products—and American jobs —are enormous: we estimate that the China market will exceed $220 billion by the year 2000. At $23 billion, our bilateral trade deficit with China is already nearly half our deficit with Japan, and this deficit's size depends in part on whether the playing field is level or not.

The pace and scope of China's economic growth affect not only bilateral and world trade, but social and political life in China itself. Prosperity has not dampened the calls for reform and political freedom in China's essentially closed political system; if anything, the continued contact with outsiders, along with the freedom of the market place, has spawned a greater desire for a loosening of political controls. We have seen some evidence of small-scale social unrest in several provinces as decentralization proceeds, although certainly not on the scale we saw in Tiananmen Square in 1989. And we will continue to assist in monitoring violations of human rights. The world's ecology and fuel consumption can also be affected by China's rapid growth.

Finally, we are closely monitoring China's military modernization, as well as its attempts to export extremely potent weapons technology into some of the more unstable regions of the world such as the Middle East. The cooperation of China is essential if we are to succeed in curbing proliferation of these technologies and weapons.

Russia and the Former Soviet Union

In Russia, last December's parliamentary election reflected, to a large degree, the ambivalence of the Russian people. The Parliament which they elected— and which opened two weeks ago— contains several elements united more in their opposition to past reforms than in their interest in presenting credible alternatives to those reforms. At the same time, the Russian people gave President Yeltsin enhanced constitutional powers which he can use to help secure Russia's course. President Yeltsin and his advisors are aware that many Russians across the political spectrum believe both that the social safety net must be expanded and that the fabric of public order has frayed to an unacceptable degree.

There are four broad areas to which we have devoted our efforts.

First, we are providing critical—and sometimes unique—political and economic analysis to policymakers to warn them of potential risks facing Russia's uncertain future and to help them sort out the myriad confusing and conflicting aspects of the Russian economy....

Second, we continue to monitor the disposition and status of Russia's 27,000 or so nuclear warheads, as well as the strategic systems still deployed to deliver these weapons.

The combination of declining morale in the military, increased organized crime, and efforts by states like Iran seeking to purchase nuclear material or expertise will make these matters a major concern for us throughout this decade and beyond. We investigate every report or claim of the illegal transfer of weapons or weapons-grade material. To date, reports of illegal transfers of weapons do not appear credible. As for weapons-grade material, we are not aware of any illegal transfers in quantities sufficient to produce a nuclear weapon. In addition to our monitoring efforts, we will continue to provide support to policymakers working with Russian officials on ways to improve the physical security of nuclear weapons and fissile material.

Third, the intelligence community continues to monitor the state of Russia's general purpose forces. As I reported last year, these forces are suffering from a host of ills: inadequate housing, erratic pay, and declining morale. Russia's military has not been immune from the vicissi-

tudes of the country's economic, political and social transformations.

Fourth, we are closely monitoring Russia's relations with its newly independent neighbors—the other former Soviet Republics. The presence of some 25 million ethnic Russians in those states, as well as the complex legacy of economic linkages, will be key factors in the evolution of policies toward those states.

In sum, Mr. Chairman, the long existence of a system encrusted by decades of inefficiency, coupled with the stresses in an empire once held together by force and one-party rule, have had a profound impact on the Russian people. Thus, it should come as a surprise to no one that the road ahead will continue to be a long and difficult one, and that these problems will exist in some form for years to come. In the meantime, crises can occur at any point along the political, social, and regional fault lines in Russia and the rest of the former Soviet Union.

Mr. Chairman, there are other conflicts raging in the states of the former Soviet Union, including the ongoing war over Nagorno-Karabakh involving Armenia and Azerbaijan. But I want to take a few minutes to highlight a potential crisis in Ukraine. The celebration of Ukrainian independence has given way to disillusionment as a result of economic mismanagement and political drift. Reform has been nonexistent, energy shortages have become a way of life, the inflation rate for December was 90 percent, and nearly half of Ukraine's citizens are living below the poverty level. Parliamentary elections in March and a Presidential election in June could serve as barometers of how well or poorly Ukrainians are facing up to their multiple serious problems....

Along with our interest in seeing a viable, stable Ukraine, our interests are focused on the nuclear weapons still on Ukrainian soil. Mr. Chairman, Ukraine is not the only state to have inherited nuclear weapons when the U.S.S.R. dissolved in December 1991; we are also tracking the nuclear weapons in Kazakhstan, and Belarus. But, of these three states, Ukraine has the largest number of these weapons, and their disposition has been a thorny issue in Russian-Ukrainian relations and a key concern for us.

The President's efforts recently helped bring Ukraine and Russia together to resolve the dispute over the final disposition of nuclear warheads in Ukraine. We provided direct analytical support to Administration officials who worked closely with Russian and Ukrainian officials to reach the Trilateral Accord, and will continue to do so in the months ahead as the U.S. continues its engagement in the trilateral discussions on implementing the agreements that we have reached.

The accord is being heavily criticized by hardliners and nationalist in Ukraine, and is currently being examined by the Rada—the Ukrainian Parliament. The intelligence community will continue to assign high priority to tracking the debate in Ukraine over these weapons.

The Middle East

Let me turn now to the Middle East, beginning first with the peace process. American resolve over the years in standing up to extremists and opponents of the peace process, willingness to explore any avenue to advance that process, and persistence in encouraging the parties themselves to work directly together for peace, have helped to bring about this step toward an end to the Arab-Israeli conflict.

Still, much needs to be done. The road to the signing of the Israeli-PLO accord was tortuous and dramatic; the road to a comprehensive settlement will be no less arduous, and will require determination and vision. It will also require help from the United States, including help from the intelligence community. There are four ways we are assisting this process.

First, we are providing daily, intense intelligence support to our negotiators involved in the peace process.

Second, we are continuing our liaison efforts with intelligence services throughout the region to help nurture an atmosphere of confidence and trust.

Third, as we have for twenty years, we are continuing to use our unique intelligence capabilities to monitor existing peace agreements in the Sinai and Golan. If there is a breakthrough leading to a comprehensive settlement on the Golan Heights—a goal of the President's discussion earlier this month with President Assad in Geneva—we stand ready to do all we can to help monitor any agreement.

Fourth, we are continuing vigorous counter-terrorism intelligence efforts to help keep the opponents of the peace process at bay. The decades of hot war and cold peace have come at too high a price for us to allow terrorist groups and nations which support them to strangle our hopes for peace in the Middle East.

Mr. Chairman, there are other dangers in the region, especially those stemming from Iran and Iraq and their efforts to obtain weapons of mass destruction and to support terrorism.

On Iran, I wish I could tell this committee that 15 years after the triumph of the extremists, the voices of hate have given way to the policies of moderation. But there is no basis for such a view. Iran remains determined to maintain its implacable hostility, to eliminate any opposition to its rule, and to undermine our security interests and those of our friends and allies in the region. Terrorism remains a central tool for Iran's leaders in seeking to accomplish these objectives, and Iranian support for Hizballah and other such groups from Algeria to Tajikistan has not abated.

We are especially concerned that Iran continues to develop its ambitious multibillion dollar military modernization program and to pursue development of weapons of mass destruction. The intelligence community estimates that left to its own devices Iran will take at least 8–10 years to build its own nuclear weapons, but that it will try to shortcut this process by buying nuclear material and ballistic missiles.

Over the past year the intelligence community has been instrumental in the ongoing, intensive, dialogue with our European allies to outline for them the continued threats posed by Iran. The Administration intends to expand these consultations with our friends and allies in the Far East as well, and we will play a key role in these discussions.

Turning to Iraq, let us be clear: without U.N. sanctions and inspections Saddam Hussein would have been well on his way by now toward rebuilding his programs for weapons of mass destruction. The importance of sanctions and monitoring cannot be overstated. Because of the unprecedented information the intelligence community has given to the U.N. Special Commission since 1991 to track down and eliminate Iraq's weapons of mass destruction, we have destroyed a far larger share of Iraq's capability in this area than was destroyed during the war itself.

Mr. Chairman, there are no easy or quick solutions to the threats posed by these two rogue regimes. For years to come, the intelligence community will continue to require the necessary resources to monitor their military programs, to uncover their attempts to establish clandestine procurement networks aimed at obtaining material and expertise for development of weapons of mass destruction, and to support terrorist activity. It was less than a year ago that Saddam attempted an audacious and outrageous crime—the assassination of a former American President. We cannot relax our guard against such governments. . . .

TRANSNATIONAL ISSUES

Proliferation

Mr. Chairman, I would like to move now to transnational issues, beginning with the problem of proliferation. The proliferation of weapons of mass destruction —and the means to deliver them—is not a new problem, but it is a growing one. Whether it be North Korea, Iran, Iraq, Libya or other nations throughout the globe aspiring to acquire these weapons, all of them will be paying close attention to how we handle each individual crisis to see whether we are wavering in our commitment to nonproliferation.

I have addressed the problem of proliferation in many meetings and briefings with members of Congress. Let me reaffirm several sobering points:

Ballistic missiles are becoming the weapon of choice for nations otherwise unable to strike their enemies at long ranges.

Today there are 25 countries—many hostile to our interests, some of whom I have already mentioned—that are developing nuclear, biological, or chemical weapons. More than two dozen countries alone have research programs underway on chemical weapons.

Moreover, some of these countries may place little stock in the classic theory of deterrence which kept the cold war from becoming a hot one between the United States and the Soviet Union.

Biological weapons are a particular concern, especially given the ease of setting up a laboratory, and the difficulty in distinguishing between dual-use products. It is hard to get international consensus to condemn a supplier or user of such dual-use material or technology.

We have supported efforts by the Administration, in cooperation with other countries, to prevent the acquisition of materials and equipment by nations bent on developing weapons of mass destruction. To cite several examples of successful interdictions which occurred last year:

- Egyptian authorities impounded a shipment of anhydrous hydrofloric acid enroute to Iraq for the processing of nuclear-related materials. The acid also is a known nerve agent precursor.
- The Italian Government prevented shipment of equipment to Iran which could be used in the production of chemical warfare materials. Italian officials also blocked the delivery of excavation equipment enroute to Libya for possible use in construction of an underground chemical warfare agent production facility.
- Polish Government authorities stopped the sale by Polish firms of nuclear power plant equipment and components to Iran.

Nevertheless, the task for the intelligence community will remain daunting. We need to decipher an intricate web of suppliers and end-users; we need to distinguish between legitimate and illicit purposes, particularly for dual-use technology or products; and we must help track the activities of others and work with them to see that the flow of material, technology, and know-how is interdicted. These tasks will continue to demand substantial allocation of resources and personnel for years to come.

Terrorism

Mr. Chairman, turning now to the issue of terrorism, I noted earlier particularly Iranian support for terrorism. Unfortunately, as we know, terrorism does not come from one isolated regime. This year, for example, the State Department added Sudan to its list of countries which support terrorism. Nor is terrorism confined to the Middle East; it is still being used in Latin America and in Western Europe.

Terrorism has not abated: there were 427 terrorist incidents world-wide last year compared to 362 in 1992. Indeed, terrorist incidents could increase as a result of growing ethnic, religious, and regional conflicts throughout the globe.

The intelligence community will continue to support the FBI and the Justice Department here at home, as well as foreign intelligence organizations abroad, in combating terrorism. Our work must often be done out of the glare of publicity —and you will rarely find us speaking out about the successes we have had in disrupting or foiling terrorist plots. This is because we need to protect those who would provide us with vital information, and to protect methods critical to us if we are to continue to keep Americans out of harm's way.

There are several cases, however, which I feel can be mentioned here today, beginning with the investigation on the attempted assassination of former President Bush in Kuwait.

- CIA used its substantial analytic capability and its technical analysis of the forensic evidence, in cooperation with the FBI and Department of Justice, to establish that the assassination attempt operation was ordered by Saddam Hussein's regime.
- One example of a terrorist brought to justice was the FBI's recent arrest of Umar Muhammed Ali Rizaq, responsible for hijacking and murder in November 1985. His crime includes shooting three Americans, killing one and leaving another suffering permanent brain damage.
- We are working closely with FBI and local law enforcement officials in the investigations surrounding last years' bombing of the World Trade Center.
- We are using our resources to provide whatever information we can to help locate and bring to justice Mir Aimal Kansi, accused of the brutal murders which occurred just one year ago outside CIA headquarters. On this day in particular, we want to let Mr. Kansi know that, as Muhammed Ali Rizaq discovered eight years after his crime, we do not forget, and we do not give up.

Drug Trafficking
Mr. Chairman, on the subject of drug trafficking, we play a constructive role around the world in countering the flow of illegal drugs into this country. We provided essential intelligence support to Colombia's Pablo Escobar Task Force.

We are focusing our efforts on obtaining the information necessary for disrupting and dismantling the entire chain of drug trafficking—transportation, finances and chain of command. We do this against traffickers both in Latin America and in the Far East. The challenge can-

not be met by targeting one sector alone; nor can it be accomplished by one agency alone. Our intelligence work in support of law enforcement efforts by the DEA and FBI will continue, because we believe that only through coordinated efforts can we hope to defeat this cancer on our society.

But in this field we can never guarantee to you that we and the other U.S. agencies involved will never be betrayed by those who assist us in Latin America or Asia. Part of the unfortunate reality of the counternarcotics business is that local foreign officials sometimes succumb to the lure of drug money. Moreover, American officials—ours and those of other agencies—are not always correct in the difficult judgments that must be made in this complex area. One risk that U.S. Government employees run is sensationalist distortions in some media reports about this complex subject. We work too hard and consider this problem too important to ignore such distortions. So, let me say simply and categorically that the recent allegation made in a television report that CIA officers intentionally smuggled narcotics into the United States for distribution is flat wrong.

International Economics
In closing, Mr. Chairman, although the topic of international economics was not specifically mentioned in your invitation to me, I'd like to take the opportunity of this hearing to highlight this area of critical importance to the work of the intelligence community.

For nearly half a century, international economic issues took a back seat to our struggle against the Soviet Union and its allies. That has changed. As the President said last fall, "More than

ever, our security is tied to economics."
Interest rates, trade policies, and currency
fluctuations all can have an immediate
and significant impact on our economic
well-being. Moreover, as industrialized
nations pull themselves out of the longest
recession since the depression of the
1930s, they are discovering that their
economic recoveries are not accompanied
by a growth in jobs, thus making the
competition on the world market that
much sharper.

The intelligence community is being
asked to provide a strong supporting role
in this new international economic arena.
Let me briefly describe our tasks.

First, we are providing policymakers
analytical support on world economic
trends and on key international trade issues. This support includes evaluating
the economic plans, intentions and strategies of foreign governments and their
impact on U.S. interests and initiatives.
It also includes analytical assistance to
American negotiators involved in foreign
trade discussions—such as GATT.

Second, we are providing analytical
road maps on how well or poorly the
nations in the former Soviet Union and
in Eastern and Central Europe are faring
with their economic reform efforts. How
these nations perform economically can
determine how well they do politically
and whether regional and global stability
will be enhanced or threatened.

Third, we are providing our expertise
in trade, finance and energy to help the
Administration thwart efforts by countries such as Iraq, Libya, and Serbia from
circumventing United Nations sanctions.

Fourth, we are assessing how some
governments violate the rules of the game
in international trade. This doe not mean
that the CIA is in the business of economic

espionage—for example, trying to learn
the business plans of foreign companies
in order to give such information to
American firms. It does mean, however,
that we are paying careful attention to
those countries or businesses who are
spying on our firms, to the disadvantage
of American businesses and American
workers, and to those governments and
foreign companies that try to bribe their
way into obtaining contracts that they
cannot win on the merits. Frequently we
are able to help the U.S. government
obtain quick redress when such foreign
bribery occurs or is about to occur,
to the benefit, measured in billions of
dollars, of American companies. Most
such companies never realize that they
have received our assistance and even
state publicly that they do not need it.
This is fine with us. It is the nature of the
intelligence business.

Mr. Chairman, what I have outlined
today for you and for your colleagues on
the committee is far from being the sum
total of our work. Nor should intelligence
be viewed as an end in itself. When we try
to penetrate a closed society like North
Korea, when we verify dismantlement of
nuclear weapons in Russia and Ukraine,
or peace agreements in the Middle East,
when we work to help defeat terrorists
or the ambitions of Saddam Hussein,
when we try to answer the "why" the
"where" and the "when" of global ethnic
and nationalist conflict, we do so as part
of our contribution to the overall safety
and security of the United States and the
American people.

My year as Director of Central Intelligence has made it clear to me how critical
intelligence will continue to be in helping
our leaders to chart a course for our nation, to protect our interests and to keep
our citizens safe.

POSTSCRIPT

Is It Time to Terminate the CIA?

The CIA has not experienced so much criticism since the days after the war in Vietnam, when many unsavory practices were disclosed. What is different now is that without the existence of a superpower enemy of the United States, the CIA is having trouble justifying its existence.

During the Bush administration, the nomination of Robert Gates to be the director of the CIA provoked unparalleled criticism, not only by liberal critics on the outside (on the grounds that Gates had been involved in the Iran-Contra affair), but also by some former CIA insiders. One of these, Melvin Goodman, a CIA Sovietologist from 1966 to 1986, charged that, as a high-ranking official, Gates had manipulated agency information to promote ends that he and director William Casey favored. Goodman, who now teaches at the National War College, has recently written an op-ed piece in the *New York Times* (July 21, 1994) entitled "We Need Two C.I.A.'s." Goodman thinks that Congress should recast the CIA along the British model, which divides operations and intelligence gathering and analysis into two organizations.

Other critics have been even stronger. New York State's Democratic senator Patrick Daniel Moynihan has called for the outright abolishment of the CIA, which would please Marcus Raskin. For a critical perspective on the fit, or lack thereof, of CIA operations and a democratic society, see Rhodri Jeffreys-Jones, *The CIA and American Democracy* (Yale University Press, 1989). Restraining the CIA is also taken up by Loch K. Johnson in "On Drawing a Bright Line for Covert Operations," *American Journal of International Law* (Spring 1992). The pressure on the agency and other intelligence services has also escalated because of their costs. Their budgets are secret, part of the so-called black budget, but their sum total is what the *New York Times* has called "the worst-kept secret in the capital." It amounts to about $28 billion for fiscal year 1995. That amount is about twice the entire U.S. foreign aid budget and about five times the annual operating expenses of the entire United Nations, including its peacekeeping operations.

CIA fortunes were further cast into a shadow by the spectacular disclosure in 1994 that Aldrich H. Ames, a ranking CIA official, had long been a double agent, a mole, spying on the CIA for the Soviet Union's KGB. Ames had served in such posts as chief of the counterintelligence branch within the CIA's Soviet division. The information he sold to the Soviets led to the execution of at least a dozen secret agents working for the United States in Moscow and elsewhere, among other things. It seems that Ames was able to operate for so long in part because of the cozy, "old boy" network within the operations directorate of the CIA, which made it hard for operational officers to question one of their own. Director Woolsey admitted that "camaraderie within the [spy] fraternity can smack of elitism and arrogance" and that the American people have "the right to ask where the CIA is going after the cold war and after, for that matter, Aldrich Ames." The debate, then, is not settled and you, the reader, can begin to play a role in the CIA's tomorrow by joining today in deciding whether you agree with Marcus Raskin or R. James Woolsey. Or perhaps you have an entirely different view. If so, so much the better! You might also wish to consult Michael W. Reisman and James E. Baker, *Regulating Covert Action* (Yale University Press, 1992).

ISSUE 15

Does the World Have to Have Nuclear Weapons at All?

YES: Michael Quinlan, from "The Future of Nuclear Weapons: Policy for Western Possessors," *International Affairs* (July 1993)

NO: Lincoln Wolfenstein, from "End Nuclear Addiction," *The Bulletin of the Atomic Scientists* (May 1991)

ISSUE SUMMARY

YES: Sir Michael Quinlan, director of the Ditchley Foundation in England and former permanent under-secretary of state at the British Ministry of Defense, contends that, in light of the current world situation, a good case can be made to support the maintenance of nuclear weapons capability by the United States and others.

NO: Lincoln Wolfenstein, a member of the U.S. National Academy of Sciences and a professor of physics at Carnegie-Mellon University, argues that the collapse of the former Soviet Union and other destabilizing changes in world politics, and the continuing danger of nuclear weapons, makes now the right time to pursue complete nuclear disarmament.

Two pivotal events occurred in 1945. One was the detonation of city-smashing atomic bombs over Hiroshima and Nagasaki, Japan, which signaled the onset of the nuclear-weapons era. The second was the start of the bipolar cold war between the United States and the Soviet Union in the aftermath of World War II. And for 50-plus years, the number of nuclear weapons escalated, the cold war heated up and cooled down, and the two seemed inextricably linked. With the dissolution of the Soviet Union in 1991, the cold war was over, a new era begun. Where did that leave nuclear arms control?

Efforts to control weapons go back to near the beginning of written history. During the nineteenth century the destructive capacity of weapons grew exponentially. The first, albeit ineffective, multilateral arms negotiations were the Hague Conferences (1899 and 1907). The awful toll and fearsome weapons of World War I prompted renewed arms control efforts. There were conferences in Washington, D.C., and London, England, that set limits on battleship tonnage among the world's leading naval powers. There were other arms negotiations and agreements in the 1920s and 1930s, and in 1928 some 23 countries signed the Kellogg-Briand Treaty and forswore resorting to war.

The outbreak of World War II was evidence that these various efforts failed to either keep the peace or reduce the devastation of war.

Arms control efforts were spurred yet again by the horror of World War II and by the existence—and use of—potentially civilization-ending atomic weapons. In January 1946 the United Nations established the International Atomic Energy Agency to try to limit the use of nuclear technology to peaceful purposes. Later that year, the UN also called for the "general regulation and reduction of armaments and armed forces" and established a Commission for Conventional Armaments.

Still, for almost 20 years nuclear weapons building and testing continued unimpeded. In 1963, however, the first major nuclear weapons agreement was signed, and the countries that signed it agreed to cease testing nuclear weapons in the atmosphere. Arms control efforts strengthened in the 1970s and continued to gain wider acceptance in the 1980s. The cost of weaponry; the fact that each superpower had over 10,000 long-range nuclear weapons and hundreds of shorter-range systems; the ever-increasing speed, power, and accuracy of those weapons; and then the end of the cold war all prompted the acceleration of arms control efforts.

As background to this debate, it is worth noting several of the arms control agreements: there are two Strategic Arms Limitation Talks treaties (known as SALT I and SALT II, 1972 and 1979); the Intermediate-range Nuclear Forces (INF) Treaty (1987), and two Strategic Arms Reduction Talks treaties (START I and START II, 1991 and 1993). The SALT treaties limited the number of weapons systems each superpower could possess. The INF Treaty eliminated an entire type of missile—those missiles with an intermediate range (of 500–5,500 kilometers). The START treaties addressed intercontinental-range missiles (those that could travel beyond 5,500 kilometers) belonging to the United States and the Soviet Union. It later covered those former Soviet republics that inherited Soviet nuclear arms (Belarus, Kazakhstan, Russia, and Ukraine).

The question before us here is this: If the United States and the Soviet Union have been able to slim down their nuclear system by approximately 75 percent, then why not reduce the number to zero? Before moving to that debate, it is important to note that the closer one comes to zero, the more important the nuclear arsenals belonging to countries other than the United States and the former Soviet Union become. Three countries that have substantial arsenals (and the number of weapons they possess) are China (284), France (534), and Great Britain (200). Israel, India, Pakistan, and perhaps North Korea also have nuclear weapons.

The following two readings carry the debate on nuclear weapons into the future. Michael Quinlan outlines a number of reasons that, he suggests, lead to the conclusion that it would not be wise to eliminate nuclear weapons in the foreseeable future. Lincoln Wolfenstein finds the arguments of nuclear abolitionists wanting, and he contends that a nuclear-free world is attainable and desirable.

YES

Michael Quinlan

THE FUTURE OF NUCLEAR WEAPONS: POLICY FOR WESTERN POSSESSORS

For over 40 years since 1945, Western countries in possession of nuclear weapons have justified their retention and development of this capability with reference to the context of a bipolar confrontation between the Atlantic alliance and the Soviet superpower. Now that the Soviet Union no longer exists, the arguments relating to the Western nuclear capability require reconsideration and reconstruction in the light of new existing and potential circumstances. Michael Quinlan reviews the current situation and suggests that there may still be reasons for the maintenance of a nuclear military capability by the West.

For nearly the entire period since nuclear weapons first burst upon the world's attention at Hiroshima the development of Western nuclear weapons, doctrines and policies has taken place almost entirely within the context of a bipolar confrontation with a huge totalitarian power, in close and harsh proximity to much of the Western community, with a disquieting history, an alien and hostile political ideology and a massive military armoury of all sorts.... Now, however, the Soviet Union has spectactularly fallen apart. Its political structure has vanished. Among the fragmented components, economies are in deep disarray; security frontiers have receded eastwards by several hundreds of kilometres; the military establishment is reduced, disheartened and dislocated; the old ideology has been utterly discredited; and international behaviour has been transformed for the better. There remains room for debate about whether or how far particular elements of this new picture may be reversible; but a return of the old construction in its totality is so enormously unlikely, that Western policy need no longer cater for that eventuality.

A confrontational bipolar world was, in a perverse way, distinctly convenient for security policy, at least in intellectual terms; and that convenience was particularly marked in the nuclear field. The world was able to do most of its thinking and learning about the significance of nuclear weapons and their effect upon international order in an environment that was relatively

From Michael Quinlan, "The Future of Nuclear Weapons: Policy for Western Possessors," *International Affairs*, vol. 69, no. 3 (July 1993). Copyright © 1993 by The Royal Institute of International Affairs. Reprinted by permission.

simple, as being dominated by two power groupings vastly stronger than any others; and in which, moreover, the fact of mortal danger was unmistakable, because of the political severity and, in Europe, the geographical proximity of the confrontation. The freshness in memory of how appalling any major war could be was doubtless another useful element in the earlier years. All in all, we might well have managed the nuclear revolution a good deal less successfully—and 48 years of complete non-use is notable success—in a less tidy and less stark environment.

However that may be, we now have to think about nuclear weapons in a radically altered framework; and it is arguable, given the human revulsion that rightly attaches to instruments of such appalling potential, that an initial onus of proof rests upon anyone still disposed to answer 'yes' to the basic questions: Does the world have to have nuclear weapons at all? Are there adequate reasons for not adopting a firm and serious policy goal of a nuclear-free world? The disposition towards continuing to say 'yes' is inevitably influenced, for many, by habit and perhaps by an element of institutional preference; and the argument therefore needs to be tested firmly.

THE SHORT-TERM AND LONG-TERM CASES FOR CONTINUED CAPABILITY

For the short and medium term the case for continued Western policies accepting the possession of nuclear arms seems clear. Huge nuclear armouries—several thousands of warheads on each main side —still exist and will do so for a long time yet; the sweeping reductions which the US and Russian presidents have announced will take a decade to carry out, and even thereafter numbers of warheads in the planned armouries will remain in four figures. Their total destruction, even if (improbably) it were not readily agreed, would be an enormous technical and resource-consuming task of a kind never before attempted, let alone achieved. It could scarcely be completed until well into the next century at best; and the existence of the weapons meanwhile requires some system of political and strategic management.

Further and more particular considerations underline this general argument. First, the still massive ex-Soviet capability, during its unavoidable years of continued existence, will be in the hands of one or perhaps more states grappling with an aggregate of huge and unfamiliar political, economic and social problems, both internally and externally. However well we wish these possessors in the resolution of their problems, responsible prudence compels the West to reckon still with the possibility that, under all the stresses, regimes of more unpleasant character and less cooperative behaviour may come again—perhaps quite suddenly—to power, and so to control over very large forces, including the nuclear armouries. Second, not all the world's current nuclear-weapon capability or potential relates solely to the crumbling East–West confrontation. China is a nuclear power. Even if its leadership stood by its long-professed willingness to give up that status if others did, assured divestment would take time. There is moreover a group of near-possessors, varying a good deal in character and international responsiveness; and one other evident though unavowed possessor, Israel, which has acquired nuclear capability quite aside from East–West context. (The fact that a further such possessor, in

South Africa, has emerged into clear sight only through a welcome declaration of completed renunciation is indirectly another cautionary reminder.)

For such reasons as these, Western thinkers and planners must, on any view, deal with a nuclear world for at least 10–15 years ahead; and their concepts and policies have to be concerned accordingly, not just with a technical task of running down and dismantling armouries, but with a continuing strategic need for disciplining and sealing off risks. There are however arguments, at a deeper and more lasting level, which suggest that the need for some war-preventing Western nuclear possession, with concepts and policies to frame it, stretches beyond the impossibility of rapid escape from present circumstances.

It is a truism that the scientific and technical knowledge of how to make nuclear weapons cannot now be forgotten. We simply do not have the option of returning to a condition of pre-nuclear innocence (if innocence is an apt way of describing the mindsets and conditions which produced the two world wars). For the rest of history humanity has to live with the reality that almost any substantial and reasonably advanced independent state could eventually, if it so chose and was not forcibly prevented by others, construct a nuclear armoury to support its external goals, be they offensive or defensive. The case for building such an armoury might be especially compelling if the state found itself engaged in, or imminently facing, military conflict where the stakes were of an order it was minded to regard as vital. No such conflict situation has however arisen between major developed states for several decades past. That is very remarkable in relation to the record of history, especially when ideological hostility has been as sharp as in the East–West confrontation. The main reason is that such states have become increasingly, and by now immensely, careful to avoid situations in which military conflict between them could seem appropriate. Some of that care may reflect the vivid general memory of the world wars; but though the point is unprovable either way, the most distinctive pressure which has made the last forty years so unlike most earlier epochs in this regard is the very existence of nuclear weapons. There has been a deepening recognition that these weapons create and express a *reductio ad absurdum* in warfare, making serious war between major developed states no longer an option for the conduct of business or the pursuit of interest.

There would always be a latent menace, even if nuclear weapons were no longer in existence at all, implicit simply in the fact that they could be rebuilt; and it is formally conceivable that awareness of this menace could come in itself to be enough to maintain the recognition of the 'no war' imperative and the priceless caution it engenders among advanced states. Alternatively, international behaviour might become so securely accustomed to the 'no war' assumption that it could always and everywhere be relied upon, even amid severe stresses. Such possibilities, however, are at best far too remote to be a dependable basis for security policy now. If we want nuclear weapons to help deter war —or limit its incidence and severity— in a world like ours today, they have to have some physical actuality. If we further judge (as we reasonably now can) that fears of nuclear war arising purely by accident, just from the existence of any nuclear weapons at all, can be discounted as far-fetched, there then remains a strong fundamental case of a general kind for maintaining in being some properly controlled military nuclear capability.

The more particular fact that the world faces a phase of highly uncertain political development reinforces the general argument. Put another way, that argument is that the world community need not and should not allow circumstances to arise in which there could be any temptation to revert to the illusion that major war could be dependably held to tolerable levels of destructiveness and so could again be an option for settling serious differences among advanced military powers. Nor do we want circumstances to arise in which a state with a risk-taking leadership (or one feeling under especial threat) might be tempted to gamble on a clandestine dash to seize advantage through a period of sole nuclear possession. We cannot tell precisely how high such risks are; our concern must be to avoid ever having to find out the hard way. The point is further reinforced by the tacit value of nuclear weapons as an underlying element of deterrence to intolerable use of force in other ways, for example with chemical or biological weapons. (The 'negative security assurances' whereby the Western nuclear powers in the late 1970s formally renounced the option of nuclear use against non-nuclear powers theoretically excludes that last argument. But Saddam Hussein is unlikely to have felt confident in 1991 of relying upon the exclusion; and that lack of confidence seems both realistic and healthy.) In brief, a purportedly non-nuclear world would be likely to be a more dangerous world, even if the formidable problems of transition from our present state could be effectively managed.

THE UNITED STATES AS PRIMARY POSSESSOR

The argument having been taken thus far, no elaborate discussion is needed to bring out the facts that the United Nations is nowhere near the state of assured political development where a general-purpose nuclear armoury could be created and sustained entirely under truly supranational control; that Europe as an entity is, likewise, nowhere near the point at which it could command and demonstrate a united cohesion and will to wield any such armoury; and that accordingly the United States is the inescapable primary holder of any such role, from the Western standpoint. (The argument could not reasonably reject a desire on the part of Russia—especially if, as must still be our hope and aim, the smaller political fragments of the ex-Soviet armoury are eventually properly dissolved—then to retain some counter-vailing nuclear power.) To recognize the United States as inescapable possessor is not to propose its establishment as global nuclear policeman with specific rights and duties beyond those of others, or as some kind of protecting nuclear mother-figure for us all. It is simply to recognize the absence today of any other credible candidate, in terms of global reach, influence and acceptance—in world-wide pervasiveness—to be the prime possessor of nuclear weapons, for the purposes outlined above, in a long-term international system. If the United States were to refuse such a role, the risk would grow that new nuclear possessors, with less experience and narrower stakes in international order, might seek to fill the need in a more fragmented and more precarious way....

A concept envisaging, as the main line of this argument suggests, a role for nuclear capability extending in scope and perhaps in timescale beyond the classic central task of providing a secure counterbalance to Eastern military power can and should be a low-key one. It ought not to be understood, still less presented, as seeking merely to substitute a new North versus South or Rich versus Poor framework of deterrence for the old East versus West one.... The concept need not, and should not, rest on an assumption that any particular state or class of state, whether defined ideologically, politically or otherwise, is the adversary to be fended off. It would genuinely reflect a non-specific concept of helping to underpin world order in whatever context it might be threatened, and to reduce the risk of major war wherever it might arise. In addition, it ought wherever possible to be seen, along with other instruments of security policy in the hands of nations, in a wider context of anchoring the contribution which its possessors make to the effective working of international structures, especially the UN, which should increasingly hold primacy and define legitimacy in security-related action....

AVOIDING PROLIFERATION

Alongside all this it must remain a major Western interest—indeed, in the long view, a general global interest—that the number of additional nuclear powers beyond those acknowledged in the Non-Proliferation Treaty (NPT) should be kept to a minimum, and preferably to zero. That approach is open to the easy charge that it enshrines nuclear elitism; but the realistic arguments in favour are clear. The present group (aside from the special and unacknowledged case of Israel) is a long-established and well-understood feature of the international system, legitimated moreover by a long-standing treaty to which the vast majority of UN members are party. Any addition now would be a perturbation of this settled situation, with likely repercussions; it is, to put the point mildly, not easy to be confident that if there were one addition the increment would stop at one....

Non-proliferation strategy over the past quarter-century has been generally successful, through a combination of instruments which are without doubt individually imperfect but have proved on the whole notably powerful when woven together: formal arms control agreements, material safeguard arrangements, export controls, direct political influence and pressure, general world expectations, security assurances and the like. It is important not to take this strategy for granted—improvement remains possible within it, for example in the breadth, solidity and policing of safeguards, which are bound to gain in prominence if nuclear energy spreads, as seems still more likely than not; and the need to sustain improvement is reinforced by the fact that, despite successes in South Africa and South America, the pressures against the non-proliferation bulwark look, in various ways, stronger today than for a long time past....

The useful scope for further formal measures of nuclear arms control by now relates almost exclusively to non-proliferation concerns. The task of improving stability and reducing cost and friction in the 'central balance,' so far as that concept remains relevant, is well on course in the START [Strategic Arms Reduction Talks] process and in the increasing readiness of the two main powers to take unilateral or informally agreed steps of reduction or restraint. The West may however now face delicate choices over a

Comprehensive Test Ban Treaty (CTBT). The true operational significance of such a measure within non-proliferation strategy has usually been greatly overstated by its advocates; testing has in practice been neither a necessary nor a customary stage on the road towards proliferation in the past three decades. A CTBT has, however, progressively become a touchstone and totem for non-nuclear opinion, and that has by now to be reckoned with as an important political fact, however poorly we may think of its logical basis. The nuclear powers, and those others who understand and support their responsibilities, clearly have to look afresh at the balance of advantage between pleasing those who hold this viewpoint and retaining whatever distinctive benefits further testing may confer in making weapons safer or more discriminate, or keeping them reliable. . . .

POSSIBLE DEVELOPMENTS IN EUROPE

It is natural to consider a wider European perspective. Given an assumption that British and French nuclear forces will continue to exist, should they progressively be embraced, perhaps through WEU [Western European Union], in some formal and systematic structure of collective European control, doctrine-shaping and participation, to reflect the developing unity or at least convergence of European defence and security policy? The realism of anything so ambitious seems slight, especially on any early timescale. Even if there were a basic inclination in both London and Paris to move down such a path (and that is at best questionable) it is most unlikely that other European nations—notably EC entry candidates—would welcome the addition of

nuclear matters, with all their domestic and international sensitivities and divisive potential, to the already difficult and heavily laden agenda of European unification. There would moreover be a significant risk of creating a new strand of tension within the North Atlantic alliance, for the relationship of any new joint arrangements to NATO would have to be defined; and it is hard to believe that in this of all fields debate could develop far without opening up yet another ground of dispute between those Europeans who aspire to create an all-purpose European superpower sharply differentiated from, and even in substitution for, the United States, and those others who regard that aspiration as a sentimental yet dangerous delusion.

Most modest lines of advance, however, seem worth exploring. Even if, on the analysis offered earlier, either France or the United Kingdom were to conclude against cooperation soon in the procurement of a new delivery system, the current quiet dialogue on aspects of operational coordination, like waterspace management for submarines, might be extended further, for example into submarine patrol scheduling or contingency targeting; and even if preferences from past history continued, though in logic they need not, to keep France out of the Nuclear Planning Group, Anglo-French exchanges about concepts, doctrines and planning could be deepened, with important involvement of Germany in particular from among other allies. All this could progressively yield a valuable dividend in political cohesion and mutual support, and indirectly therefore in the robustness and perhaps the economy of the European contribution to general war prevention.

* * *

In summary, the particular East–West conditions to which nuclear weapon provision in the free world has for 40 years been mainly geared have changed dramatically, and in many respects irreversibly. But there remains in physical existence enough of the military force that was to be deterred, together with enough possibility of adverse political change in its control, to warrant continued provision, on a slimmer but still significant scale, for a long time to come. Beyond that there will remain—probably for longer still, if not indefinitely—a cogent case for the free world to maintain and support some nuclear weapon capability to underpin war prevention, to close off nuclear adventurism and to serve as a low-key element of insurance, not directed against specific adversaries, in support of world order. The United States is, now and for the foreseeable future, the unavoidable prime holder of such a role, and will need and deserve the political and practical support of others. British and French capabilities can remain a useful supplement, but their scale and future development will merit rigorous scrutiny. General non-proliferation strategy will need continued care, refinement and political energy from the international community; and decisions by the nuclear powers on their own future capabilities must be increasingly sensitive to political impact in that direction. In short, the aim should be not a non-nuclear world, but a world of much less nuclear salience.

NO

Lincoln Wolfenstein

END NUCLEAR ADDICTION

The world of [today] is far different from that of 1980. The rising ethnic conflicts and the... war in the [Persian Gulf] suggest that [the fragmented world of today] resembles 1917 more than it does [the bipolar world of] 1980.... If nuclear weapons continue to be accepted as a significant part of military arsenals, the collapse of Soviet central power and the inevitable disintegration of NATO will lead to a world of many nuclear powers, with the instability that implies.

At the same time, these are days of hope, not despair. The Berlin wall is a bad memory, and we can watch Soviets and Americans destroying their intermediate-range missiles.

But little of this change is reflected in the thinking of professional strategists. Even those who advocate drastic reductions in... nuclear arsenals feel compelled to defend their proposals in terms of traditional concepts of bipolar strategic stability. However, these arguments are almost irrelevant to the current situation.

It is time to strip away the complex and arcane strategic theory of the Cold War and start from scratch. A good place to begin is the proposition that no nation should have nuclear weapons in its military arsenal. This idea stems from the work of J. Robert Oppenheimer as formulated in the Acheson-Lilienthal report of March 1946. Although the Cold War doomed the proposal, particularly as it was put forth by Bernard Baruch, the end of the Cold War means that it can now be revived.

Oppenheimer's scheme was founded on the control of fissionable material —plutonium or highly enriched uranium—needed for any bomb. This concept plays a major role in the 1970 Non-Proliferation Treaty. But that treaty's discriminatory character, dividing the world into nuclear "haves" and "have-nots," is intrinsically destabilizing. The only satisfactory solution is a world of have-nots.

* * *

The main reason to abolish nuclear weapons is to eliminate the danger of a great nuclear disaster. Even "extreme" proposals that would allow "each

From Lincoln Wolfenstein, "End Nuclear Addiction," *The Bulletin of the Atomic Scientists* (May 1991). Copyright © 1991 by The Educational Foundation for Nuclear Science, 6042 South Kimbark, Chicago, IL 60637 USA. Notes omitted. A one-year subscription is $30.

side" a thousand warheads leave this danger in place. As long as military establishments retain large nuclear stockpiles, they will plan for the use of these weapons in war; and as long as such plans exist, one cannot rule out the possibility of a deliberate decision to carry them out.

Strategists try hard to configure nuclear forces to increase stability so that no conceivable disturbance could lead to a rational decision to use them. But in the real world those in power often make decisions from a mixture of political and emotional considerations bearing little relation to strategists' calculations. Indeed, those in power may not be rational at all. One need only recall Richard Nixon's last months in power, or ponder the [fate] of the Soviet Union and its many republics—or reflect on the U.S. submarine officers who spend months in virtual isolation and yet maintain ultimate control over 192 nuclear warheads per submarine. In a related area, much has been done to reduce the possibility of accidentally launching nuclear weapons. But the history of false alarms leading to nuclear alerts is not reassuring, and most of that history is still secret.

So far only five major powers have large nuclear arsenals, but Israel is known to be able to stockpile a hundred or more nuclear weapons, and a number of other countries are believed to be on the nuclear weapons threshold. The Non-Proliferation Treaty has had a certain success, but most potential nuclear weapon states have refused to sign it. This refusal is in many cases more a protest against the treaty's discriminatory character than an indication of a desire to obtain nuclear weapons. No more signatures are likely, and the future of the treaty may be in danger, unless the nuclear powers take seriously Article VI—a "pledge to work toward universal nuclear disarmament."

* * *

The well-known arguments against abolition are generally considered overwhelming:

- *Because it is impossible to verify total nuclear disarmament, the nation that cheats gains enormous advantage.* If "each side" has 1,000 or more weapons, the argument goes, there is little to be gained from cheating.
- *The nuclear powers could guarantee a new peaceful world order in the wake of the Cold War.* If the major powers do not have nuclear weapons, even a second-rate country could obtain a small number of nuclear weapons and gain an inordinate amount of power, which would threaten world peace.
- *Nuclear weapons have prevented the outbreak of world war for 45 years.* Without them, the probability of a terrible conventional world war will greatly increase.

The essence of these arguments is the belief that if one country has nuclear weapons while others have none, that country has enormous political power and can gain its goals by nuclear blackmail. This belief probably originated in World War II, when the United States had only two nuclear weapons and apparently defeated Japan by dropping them. The problem with this is that Japan was already defeated, and nuclear weapons were at most the straw that broke the camel's back. Other cases of conflict in which one side had a nuclear monopoly point to different conclusions.

A striking example is the Korean War. The United States suffered two dramatic defeats in the first year of the war: the initial retreat to the southern tip of the Korean peninsula and the later retreat from the Yalu River in the face of the Chinese onslaught. The U.S. nuclear arsenal consisted of a few hundred atomic bombs while the Soviet side had essentially none. But nuclear weapons played no role in the war's outcome. There is no evidence that President Harry Truman's vague threats to use nuclear weapons or the transfer of bombers to forward bases significantly influenced the North Koreans or the Chinese.

A number of reasons are cited for the irrelevance of nuclear weapons in the Korean War. One is that nuclear weapons might have totally destroyed North Korea, but that would not have served any military purpose. Another was that U.S. leaders were reluctant to waste a limited arsenal of nuclear weapons on an area of secondary importance, when a major confrontation might still occur in Europe.

A second case is the recent Persian Gulf War. By standard logic, it was inconceivable that Iraq should have defied all the nuclear powers aligned against it. But nuclear weapons proved totally irrelevant: they neither deterred Iraq nor aided the war effort. The total destruction of Iraq and the spread of radioactive fallout in the region would have been pointless as well as horrifying.

An interesting exercise is to suppose that nuclear weapons are banned and dream up scenarios in which one country cheats and obtains nuclear weapons: would any such situation threaten U.S. security or lead to a drastic shift in power? The above examples suggest that this may be as difficult as imagining scenarios in which the present "stable" nuclear balance fails and general nuclear war breaks out.

A common fear is that a Third World country with a crazy ruler—until its defeat, Iraq was the most recent favorite —would obtain several nuclear weapons. This does not seem as dangerous as the possibility that a First World country with a huge number of nuclear weapons would obtain a crazy ruler, but it is a threat to be considered. The important question is whether the danger is greater, less, or the same if the great powers give up their nuclear weapons.

The nuclear weapons of all the powers in the world do not reduce the damage that one country's nuclear weapons could do. As to deterrence, if the large powers are aligned against a small power the latter is sure of enormous retribution if it dares to use nuclear weapons, even if the others have none. The standard concepts of big-power nuclear deterrence seem inappropriate.

A related problem is the possibility of nuclear terrorism by a small group—and the great powers' nuclear weapons are obviously useless against this threat. The only way to prevent nuclear terrorism is to safeguard all nuclear weapons, and the best way to do this is to destroy them.

A cooperative hegemony of the big powers creates the possibility of using preemptive military force to prevent nuclear proliferation. Whether this is desirable can be debated, but such preemption does not require nuclear weapons, as the recent war shows. The best way to prevent nuclear proliferation, however, is to strengthen the non-proliferation regime, not by military methods but by broadening the existing treaty to apply equally to all countries— that is, to abolish nuclear weapons.

The argument that nuclear weapons have prevented global conventional wars is open to serious question. Two of the five deadliest wars in U.S. history [took place during the Cold War]. The fact that there [was] no major war in Europe is a result of the cleancut division into two blocs, neither with any real reason to start a war. The contribution of nuclear weapons to this stability is a subject of continuing debate....

* * *

The first step toward eliminating nuclear weapons is eliminating ballistic missiles. For a brief moment at Reykjavik [Iceland] in 1986, Mikhail Gorbachev and Ronald Reagan agreed on the idea of destroying all ballistic missiles within 10 years. Although it lasted only a day, this agreement at the highest levels may have been the most promising of the nuclear age. The dramatic destruction of intermediate-range missiles now underway makes the Reykjavik vision seem possible. Apart from leading to nuclear abolition, eliminating huge intercontinental ballistic missiles would lengthen the fuse on a nuclear war and decrease possibilities of nuclear accidents. In the post–Cold War world, these nuclear behemoths are totally anachronistic.

Nuclear warheads should be eliminated as well as missiles, unlike in the Intermediate-Range Nuclear Forces Treaty which permits warheads to be recycled into other weapons. The possibility of verifying the elimination of nuclear warheads has been the subject of recent studies related to a second strategic arms reduction treaty. This subject should also be studied in the context of nuclear abolition, especially estimating how many nuclear weapons might be concealed and considering inspection methods that might deter concealment.

Why has a treaty banning nuclear weapons been considered impossible, while treaties banning chemical and biological weapons are widely supported? Verification and control are simpler for nuclear weapons than for chemical and biological weapons: nuclear weapons require either enriched uranium or plutonium, while a large range of substances can arm chemical and biological weapons. Despite the horrors of chemical and biological warfare, the potential long-term dangers of large-scale nuclear warfare are even greater. It is often argued that the knowledge of how to make nuclear weapons will always exist, but the same is true of chemical and biological weapons.

A key to the difference between these weapons is that we have become addicted to nuclear weapons; we have integrated them into our military forces, and getting rid of an addiction is painful. The uses planned for nuclear weapons are similar to those planned for other types of bombs and missiles, and banning nuclear weapons comes close to the idea of banning other types of high-explosive weapons.

The U.S. Air Force may feel most threatened by a nuclear weapons ban. When various strategic bombing surveys after World War II discredited the idea that strategic bombing could be decisive in war, the discovery of nuclear weapons came as a godsend to the air force. The decisiveness of air power in the Iraq war should prompt air force strategists to reconsider their support for nuclear weapons, although they are not likely to do so. One could even argue that the greatest threat to the continuing superiority of the high-tech U.S. Air Force might be the proliferation of "low-tech" nuclear weapons.

Advocating the abolition of nuclear weapons has been unrespectable, an indication of hopeless naïveté, among professional strategists. In the past this was partly because Soviet leaders gave lip service to nuclear disarmament but opposed adequate verification. But now the Soviets at times seem more eager for inspection than do the Americans.

The numerous steps on the road to nuclear disarmament will provide a learning process, but there is no obvious barrier to going all the way to zero. Strategists should now take this goal seriously, studying its implications and how it can be implemented. Most of the books on nuclear strategy over 40 years have become obsolete in the last four; it is time to go back to the drawing board.

POSTSCRIPT

Does the World Have to Have Nuclear Weapons at All?

Do arms, nuclear or otherwise, provoke war or provide security? There is no doubt that arms make war possible and also sometimes help create the tensions that are fertile ground for war. But the relationship is complex. Arms may be amassed *because* of war-producing tension. Many analysts argue that weapons are necessary for survival in a predatory world. As political scientist Hans Morgenthau once put it, "Men do not fight because they have arms. They have arms because they ... fight." If this is true, then arms are both inevitable and necessary, even for those of good will. This logic suspects that disarmament would actually increase the likelihood of war or domination by tempting aggressors to cheat and spring their weapons on an unsuspecting and defenseless victim. One recent study of the relationship between arms control and political tension is Vally Koubi, "International Tensions and Arms Control Agreements," *American Journal of Political Science* (February 1993).

Nuclear weapons makes the relationship between weapons and war particularly important. The contention that nuclear arms are dangerous and that they decrease security is the prevailing view among political leaders, scholars, and analysts. But it is not a universally accepted view. As British prime minister Winston Churchill once suggested, "It may be that we shall by a process of sublime irony [come to a point] where safety will be the sturdy child of terror and survival the twin brother of annihilation." Churchill's thought was that nuclear weapons may have rendered both nuclear war and large-scale conventional war between nuclear powers too dangerous to fight. This view was not just an idiosyncrasy of Churchill's. Some would point to the lack of a U.S.–U.S.S.R war during decades of confrontation as proof that nuclear arms do provide security. Secretary of State James A. Baker III made this point in 1991 when he rejected total nuclear disarmament on the grounds that he was "not prepared to walk away from the concept of nuclear deterrence that has kept the peace for more than 40 years." Indeed, there are a few commentators who have suggested that the way to end war is to arm all countries with invulnerable nuclear retaliatory forces. This, the logic goes, would create a nuclear checkmate system in which aggression would mean the aggressor's fiery destruction. The matter of deterrence in the post–cold war world is taken up by George Quester in "The Future of Nuclear Deterrence," *Survival* (January 1992).

The catch in such arguments, of course, is that nuclear weapons are extremely powerful, and if deterrence does not work, then the apocalypse is possible. Even a handful of nuclear weapons launched, say, at New York,

Chicago, Los Angles, and other major cities would kill tens of millions of people in an instant. Thus, the decision whether or not to eliminate all nuclear weapons is a cosmic roll of the dice. If, as Chruchill and Baker suggest, nuclear weapons have eliminated war between major powers, then they are a force for peace, however scary they may be. If Churchill and Baker are wrong, and war has not occurred for other reasons, and if nuclear war is possible by accident or conscious decision, then people who subscribe to their view are living in a fool's paradise by advocating keeping the vehicles of Armageddon. For more on this issue, read Regina Cowen Karp, ed., *Security Without Nuclear Weapons? Different Perspectives on Non-nuclear Security* (Oxford University Press, 1992).

PART 4

Values and International Relations

In this era of increasing global interdependence, the state of relations among countries will become an ever more vital concern to all the world's people. This section examines issues of global concern and issues related to the values that affect relations and policy making among nations.

- Should Morality and Human Rights Strongly Influence Foreign Policy Making?

- Is There a Global Environmental Crisis?

- Is the United Nations Advocating Objectionable Policies to Control World Population Growth?

- Is Self-Determination a Right of All Nationalities?

- Are U.S. Efforts to Promote Human Rights Culturally Biased and Self-Serving?

ISSUE 16

Should Morality and Human Rights Strongly Influence Foreign Policy Making?

YES: Cyrus R. Vance, from "The Human Rights Imperative," *Foreign Policy* (Summer 1986)

NO: George Shultz, from "Morality and Realism in American Foreign Policy," *Department of State Bulletin* (December 1985)

ISSUE SUMMARY

YES: Former U.S. secretary of state Cyrus R. Vance contends that a commitment to human rights must be a central principle of foreign policy.

NO: Former U.S. secretary of state George Shultz asserts that foreign policy must avoid idealism if it conflicts with the national interest.

One of the classic debates among academics and policymakers is the debate over the degree to which morality should be a factor in formulating foreign policy. As the following articles by two U.S. secretaries of state show, few argue for either absolute *idealism,* adhering to morality and ignoring other aspects of the national interest, or absolute disregard of morality in pursuit of *realism,* or "realpolitik" national interest. The debate, then, is one of priority, or of emphasis.

Academically, the founder of the realist school was Hans Morgenthau, and Shultz's speech was occasioned by his acceptance of the Hans J. Morgenthau Memorial Prize awarded by the National Committee on American Foreign Policy. Most foreign policy practitioners have also followed the realist approach; President Richard Nixon and his secretary of state, Henry Kissinger, are especially good examples, as is President George Bush. As Shultz notes, realists do not reject morality. Instead, they argue that a country faced with enemies in an armed and dangerous world cannot always afford to be idealist if doing so threatens the national interest.

The realist approach is rejected by those who believe that foreign policy must be founded on moral principles. This approach is often labeled idealism. President Jimmy Carter and his secretary of state, Cyrus Vance, are the most recent notable idealists to have guided U.S. foreign policy. Idealists reject the idea that morality and national interest are incompatible. Instead, they argue that the United States and others are best served by setting high standards of international conduct. Such a policy, idealists maintain, is most likely to show the contrast between the United States and oppressive countries, such as China, and make U.S. leadership attractive to the people of the world.

Throughout most of history, realism has governed foreign policy. When Hitler's Nazi Germany invaded Stalin's communist Soviet Union, democratic Great Britain's Winston Churchill offered Stalin aid. When Churchill's decision was challenged in Parliament, he replied: "If Hitler had invaded Hell, ... [I would] make favorable reference to the devil." Churchill's American contemporary, President Franklin D. Roosevelt, was also a realist. When, for example, critics objected to U.S. support of Dominican Republic dictator Rafael Trujillo, FDR answered that "[Trujillo] may be an SOB, but he is our SOB."

The end of World War II and the founding of the United Nations marked the beginning of increased idealist influence on international conduct. The world was appalled by the war, the Holocaust, and other wartime tragedies, and countries pledged in the UN Charter to promote human rights, and abandon violence except to defeat aggression. Other affirmations of human rights, such as the Universal Declaration of Human Rights (1948), the International Covenant on Civil and Political Rights (1966), and the European-focused Helsinki Agreements (1975), followed. Thus, most of the world's countries have pledged to live in peace and to respect the civil rights and liberties of both their own citizens and those in other countries. It has become more difficult for countries to ignore their public pledges.

Modern communications, especially television, have also promoted concern with morality. Now, acts of oppression, such as those inflicted by the South African government on its black citizens or by China on its dissenters, are rapidly and graphically transmitted to the living rooms and consciences of the world. This has prompted debate on relations with those governments. Similarly, the use or support of violence is often vividly portrayed, spurring moral objection by idealists and counterarguments by realists. Whether or not to support rebels against governments the United States opposes is a related moral issue, and it is discussed by both Cyrus R. Vance and George Shultz in the following pieces.

YES

Cyrus R. Vance

THE HUMAN RIGHTS IMPERATIVE

The last 5 years have not been easy for those who believe that a commitment to human rights must be a central tenet of American foreign policy. The concept and definition of human rights have been twisted almost beyond recognition. Long-standing principles of international law and practice have been chipped away. Doublespeak has too often been the order of the day. Yet the time may be coming when Americans will be able to sweep aside the illusions and myths that have been used, often deliberately, to fog the human rights debate. The time may be coming when the opportunities presented by a strong human rights policy can again be seized.

These signs do not presage merely a belated recognition that former President Jimmy Carter was correct in committing U.S. foreign policy to human dignity and freedom. One can sense a rising desire among Americans to see a return to the fundamental beliefs on which their country's human rights policy must rest and from which it draws its strength. If so, and if their leaders will respond to this desire, Americans will be able again to pursue their ideals without sacrificing their traditional pragmatism.

[Former] President Ronald Reagan is fond of calling America a "city upon a hill." But the Puritan leader John Winthrop, who first uttered those words in the 17th century, intended them as a warning about the importance of adhering to the values that eventually shaped America's founding and development—particularly those later reflected in the U.S. Constitution in the Bill of Rights—not as a boast about military or economic power. As a country, America cannot be, as Reagan suggests, the "last, best hope of man on earth" unless it is prepared to restore to its rightful place in American national life respect for and protection of human rights at home and abroad.

Let me define what I mean by human rights. The most important human rights are those that protect the security of the person. Violations of such rights include genocide; slavery; torture; cruel, inhuman, and degrading treatment or punishment; arbitrary arrest or imprisonment; denial of fair trial; and invasion of the home. . . .

Second is that bundle of rights affecting the fulfillment of such vital needs as food, clothing, shelter, health care, and education—in the scheme of President

From Cyrus R. Vance, "The Human Rights Imperative," *Foreign Policy,* no. 63 (Summer 1986). Copyright © 1986 by The Carnegie Endowment for International Peace. Reprinted by permission of *Foreign Policy.*

Franklin Roosevelt's four freedoms, the freedom from want. Americans recognize that fulfilling these rights depends largely on the stage of a country's economic development. [T]he United States can and should help others attain these basic rights....

Third, there is the right to enjoy civil and political liberties. These include not only freedom of speech, freedom of the press, freedom of religion, and freedom to assemble and to petition the government to redress grievances,... but also the right that most Americans take for granted—the freedom to move freely within and to and from one's own country.

Civil and political rights also must include the liberty to take part in government;... the only just powers of a government are those derived from the consent of the governed. By exercising this freedom, citizens may insist that their government protect and promote their individual rights.

Finally, there is a basic human right to freedom from discrimination because of race, religion, color, or gender.

Almost all of these rights are recognized in the United Nations Universal Declaration of Human Rights, a document... that draws heavily on the American Bill of Rights, the British Magna Carta, and the French Declaration of the Rights of Man and of the Citizen. Each of these documents has played a vital role in the historical evolution of respect for human rights. But after World War II, the world witnessed an unprecedented human rights revolution, including measures to institutionalize the international enforcement of human rights.

Until then, the idea that a regime could be held accountable to international standards and to the world for the treatment of its people was regarded largely as an idiosyncrasy of the democratic West, invoked only when it served a Western power's interests. A sovereign government, tradition held, could rule its people or its territory as it saw fit....

[A]ttitudes changed radically after World War II, principally because of the horror felt around the world when the Holocaust was exposed and when the full extent of Joseph Stalin's purges became clear. Individuals and countries suddenly realized that without standards, there were also no limits. The war also revealed that the far-flung colonial systems were bankrupt. Great powers could no longer hold sway over peoples they had for so long considered, in the English writer Rudyard Kipling's words, "lesser breeds without the Law."

Against this historical background, substantial progress has been made over the last 40 years. Since 1945, the world has codified a wide range of human rights. That process is in itself an enormous achievement. The power of these codes is demonstrated when movements like Poland's outlawed independent trade union Solidarity cite international norms to justify population demands for greater liberty. Even countries that show little respect for human rights feel a need to pay lip service to them. But codes alone are not enough. It also has been necessary to develop international institutions to implement them.

First, in 1945, the United Nations Charter was adopted, enshrining human rights both as a basic objective of the newly created body and as a universal obligation....

In 1946, the Commission on Human Rights was established in the United Nations.... In 1948 came the Universal Declaration of Human Rights, a basic though nonbinding declaration of principles of human rights and freedoms. The 1940s and 1950s also saw the drafting of the Convention on the Prevention and Punishment of the Crime of Genocide and the preparation of two separate human rights covenants—one on political and civil rights and the other covering economic, social, and cultural rights.

During much of the 1950s, Washington stood aloof from treaties furthering those rights and limited itself to supporting U.N. studies and advisory services. But during the 1960s, America resumed its leadership, and in 1965–1966, the two covenants were finally adopted by the United Nations and presented for ratification by member states.

Largely in response to American pressure, the world moved to implement these codes more effectively. To this end, Western Europe, the Americas, and later, Africa, established their own human rights institutions. On another front, the U.N. system for several years confined its public human rights activities to only three cases: Chile, Israel, and South Africa. But beginning in the Carter years, further U.S. prodding led the international community to broaden its concern to include the examination of human rights violations in many countries, including communist countries. Progress, though sometimes halting, has been made in a process that has no precedent.

DANGEROUS ILLUSIONS

Many opportunities and obstacles lie ahead. But first the illusions that cloud, and fallacies that subvert, American human rights policy must be dispelled. Only then can a coherent and determined course be charted.

The first and most dangerous illusion holds that pursuing values such as human rights in U.S. foreign policy is incompatible with pursuing U.S. national interests. This is nonsense. As Reagan stated in March 1986: "A foreign policy that ignored the fate of millions in the world who seek freedom would be a betrayal of our national heritage. Our own freedom, and that of our allies, could never be secure in a world where freedom was threatened everywhere else."

Moreover, no foreign policy can gain the American people's support unless it reflects their deeper values. Carter understood this when, as president, he championed human rights. In addition to enabling millions of people to live better lives, this commitment helped redeem U.S. foreign policy from the bitterness and divisions of the Vietnam War. It reassured the American people that the U.S. role abroad can have a purpose that they could all support.

Human rights policy also requires practical judgments. Americans must continually weigh how best to encourage progress while maintaining their ability to conduct necessary business with countries in which they have important security interests. But the United States must always bear in mind that the demand for individual freedom and human dignity cannot be quelled without sowing the seeds of discontent and violent convulsion. Thus supporting constructive change that enhances individual freedom is both morally right and in America's national interest.

Freedom is a universal right of all human beings.... In a profound sense, America's ideals and interests coincide, for the United States has a stake in the stability that comes when people can express their hopes and build their futures freely. In the long run, no system is as solid as that built on the rock of freedom. But it is not enough simply to proclaim such general principles. The more difficult question remains: What means of support should be provided to those whose rights are denied or endangered? And to answer this question, two underlying groups of questions must be addressed.

First, what are the facts? What violations or deprivations are taking place? How extensive are they? Do they demonstrate a consistent pattern of gross violations of human rights? What is the degree of control and responsibility of the government involved? Will that government permit independent outside investigation?

Second, what can be done? Will U.S. actions help promote the overall cause of human rights? Can U.S. actions improve the specific conditions at hand, or could they make matters worse? Will other countries work with the United States? Does America's sense of values and decency demand that the country speak out or take action even where there is only a remote chance of making its influence felt?

If the United States is determined to act, many tools are available. They range from quiet diplomacy, to public pronouncements, to withholding economic or military assistance from the incumbent regime. In some cases, Washington may need to provide economic assistance to oppressed peoples and, in rare instances like Afghanistan, limited military aid. Where appropriate, the United States should take positive steps to encourage compliance with basic human rights norms. And America should strive to act in concert with other countries when possible.

A second illusion that must be exposed is one pushed by many critics of Carter's human rights focus. Wrapping themselves in a rhetorical cloak of democracy and freedom, these critics pursue a curious logic that leads them to support governments and groups that deny democracy and abuse freedom. They insist on drawing a distinction for foreign-policy purposes between "authoritarian" countries that are seen as friendly toward the United States and "totalitarian" states seen as hostile. Authoritarian governments, the argument continues, are less repressive than revolutionary autocracies, more susceptible to liberalization, and more compatible with U.S. interests. Generally speaking, it is said, anticommunist autocracies tolerate social inequities, brutality, and poverty while revolutionary autocracies create them.

Sadly, this specious distinction, rooted in America's former U.N. representative Jeane Kirkpatrick's November 1979 *Commentary* article "Dictatorships and Double Standards," became a central element of the new human rights policy set forth at the start of the Reagan administration. Kirkpatrick's thesis damaged America's image as a beacon of freedom and a wise and humane champion of human rights. If it were simply an academic exercise, this version of the authoritarian-totalitarian distinction might cause little mischief. But it has a deeper political purpose. The implication that such a distinction provides a basis for condoning terror and brutality if committed by authoritarian governments friendly to the United States is mind-boggling.

The suggestion that America should turn a blind eye to human rights violations by autocrats of any stripe is unacceptable. Such thinking is morally bankrupt and badly serves U.S. national interests. To the individual on the rack it makes no difference whether the torturer is right- or left-handed—it remains the rack. In short, a sound and balanced human rights policy requires condemnation of such conduct, no matter who the perpetrator is....

A third human rights illusion, deriving from the second, is the fallacy inherent in the so-called Reagan Doctrine enunciated in the president's 1985 State of the Union address. Speaking about U.S. policy toward armed insurgencies against communist regimes, he declared: "We must not break faith with those who are risking their lives—on every continent, from Afghanistan to Nicaragua—to defy Soviet-supported aggression and secure rights which have been ours from birth.... Support for freedom fighters is self-defense."

No doubt there will be situations in which the United States should aid insurgencies—as in Afghanistan, where such aid promotes human rights and clearly serves American interests. There, the Soviet Union invaded a small neighboring country with overpowering military force, deposed the existing government, and imposed its own hand-picked government that, with the support of massive Soviet firepower, slaughtered tens of thousands of Afghans and turned millions more into refugees. It is critical to note that in supporting the Afghan rebels, Americans are not merely supporting an anticommunist rebellion. The United States is vindicating universal principles of international law and helping the Afghan people to determine their own future.

Yet the Reagan Doctrine, taking shelter under the banner of human rights, commits America to supporting anticommunist revolution wherever it arises. By implication, the doctrine offers no such assistance to opponents of other tyrannies. As the case of Nicaragua shows, the support the doctrine promises can include American arms....

This policy is both wrong and potentially dangerous to America's interests and its standing in the world. As with virtually all doctrines, it is automatic and inflexible by nature. That inflexibility blinds policymakers in a double sense. It blinds them to the realities and available alternatives in individual situations, and it blinds them to the principles of respect for national territorial sovereignty and nonintervention—cornerstones of international order.

The Reagan Doctrine's evident bias toward military options could easily prompt Washington to overlook better ways to achieve worthy goals. Even where economic incentives or restrictions may be sufficient, and even where U.S. policy may lack regional support and might work against broader U.S. interests, the Reagan Doctrine suggests that, at a minimum, America should fund military forces.

Beyond this strategic misconception, the Reagan Doctrine obscures the hard but essential questions of means and consequences. To avoid self-delusion, Americans must recognize that anticommunism cannot always be equated with democracy. Nor is anticommunism a shield against the consequences of unrealistic and imprudent action. At the very least, the United States must ask whom it intends to support. Do they believe in democratic values? Can they attract sufficient support in their country and region to govern if they take power? How would such a change affect the citizens of their country? Does America risk raising hopes or expectations that it cannot or will not fulfill? Can America deliver enough aid to decisively affect the outcome? Finally, will such a policy have the domestic support needed to sustain Washington's chosen course of action?

Ironically, many champions of the Reagan Doctrine call themselves realists. Yet any policy that tempts the country to ignore these basic questions cannot be called hardheaded or realistic. The doctrine's dogmatism and seductive ideological beckoning to leap before looking, are, in fact, strikingly unrealistic. So systematically ignoring the principles of sovereignty and nonintervention is not in America's national interest.

NEW HOPE FOR PROGRESS

A key strength of this country has always been its respect for law and moral values. To follow the Reagan Doctrine would undermine America's moral authority. What the United States and the Soviet Union have to offer the world must be distinguished by more than the simple declaration that, by definition, whatever Washington does is right and whatever Moscow does is wrong.

President John Kennedy once said that the United States is engaged in a "long, twilight struggle" in world affairs. But if that is so, America's principles and interests both are more likely to thrive if the country keeps faith with the ideals for which it struggles.

Principle must be the foundation of America's course for the future, but policy will be sustained only if it is also pragmatic. That must not mean that pragmatism should dominate. U.S. foreign policy must never become realpolitik unconnected with principle. Yet promoting ideals that have no chance of being put into practice risks becoming mere posturing. Nor should Americans

focus simply on the great issues and ignore the fact that, at heart, human rights concern individual human beings. Indeed, it matters greatly what America can do in concrete cases, in individual countries, for any one person to live a better life.

The charge to U.S. human rights policy has rarely been put more clearly than by Felice Gaer, executive director of the International League for Human Rights. Testifying before a subcommittee of the House Committee on Foreign Affairs in February 1986, she said: "The United States needs to do more than make declarations and to provide free transport for fleeing dictators.... The U.S. Government has leverage to use—if it chooses to use it. It has the power to persuade governments."

The United States has many opportunities, and faces many problems, in trying to advance human rights abroad. In a few countries, there is reason to give thanks for recent progress. In others, recent shifts in stated U.S. policy provide hope for future progress....

Encouraging news recently has come from the Philippines and Haiti as well. In Haiti, the heir to one of the world's worst traditions of government finally was driven from power. This island country remains desperately poor and faces a difficult future. But at least its destiny is being determined largely by men and women who seek a better life for all Haitians. America can and must help, beginning with immediate emergency food aid, while it urgently assesses Haiti's longer-term needs. In the Philippines, the problems are even more complex, but the victory achieved is even more inspiring. All Americans have marveled at the magnificent commitment of the Filipino people to freedom, at the physical and moral courage of President Corazon Aquino, at the support of the Roman Catholic church under the leadership of Jaime Cardinal Sin, and at the unforgettable sight of peaceful, unarmed men and women facing down tanks and guns with their "prayers and presence." The United States should offer whatever support it can as that country seeks to rebuild both politically and economically.

One of the most striking developments of the 1980s has been the answer to Stalin's question concerning how many divisions the pope has. From Poland to the Philippines, the world has heard the answer. Quite a few. Much remains to be done in the Philippines, and the doing will not be easy. But what has been shown in Buenos Aires, in Port-au-Prince, and in Manila is that peaceful, democratic change is possible in today's world, that such change carries with it great promise, and that there is much that American human rights policies can do to promote it.

In many other countries the pace of change has been maddeningly slow, and in some, nonexistent. Both opportunities and pitfalls abound. This is particularly true in Central America, and nowhere more so than in Nicaragua. Furnishing military aid to the *contras* is a disastrous mistake. The United States should listen to the virtually unanimous advice of its Latin American neighbors who urge it not to give such aid and to give its full support instead to the Contadora process. Despite temporary setbacks, this regional peace effort provides a framework for ending Central America's agony while safeguarding the hemisphere's security interests. But whatever their viewpoint, Americans all should be able to agree that human rights are denied and abused

in Nicaragua, and have been for decades —by the late dictator Anastasio Somoza Debayle and his supporters and by the Sandinistas. Americans must continue to demand an end to all such abuses....

[Then] there is South Africa. The United States has maintained diplomatic relations with South Africa for many years.... South Africa is a source of important raw materials, occupying a strategic position along the sea routes running from the Indian Ocean and the Middle East into the Atlantic Ocean. Yet productive relations with South Africa are impossible because of sharp differences over apartheid, over the right of South Africa's blacks to live decent lives, and over their right to participate as full citizens in governing their country.

South Africa has institutionalized discrimination of the most vicious sort and resists fundamental change of this abhorrent system. What the United States seeks in the near term is clear: the dismantling of apartheid, root and branch, and the sharing of political power among whites, blacks, mixed-blood "Coloreds," and Asians alike.

The United States should make unmistakably clear to President P. W. Botha [South Africa's former president] and all South Africans that Americans are committed to the total abolition of apartheid and to genuine power sharing. The U.S. government must underscore that South Africa cannot adopt one policy for worldwide public consumption and a second, less stringent policy for private discussion in Pretoria. America must make unmistakably clear that time is running out and that major steps must be taken now.

The South African government also must be told that, without prompt action, the United States will impose more stringent economic restrictions.... And

America should work with like-minded countries to pressure South Africa to make those decisions that are necessary now to stop further repression and a bloody civil war later.

The world has a long agenda in the pursuit of human rights. There will be, I fear, no final victory over tyranny, no end to the challenge of helping people to live decent lives, free from oppression and indignity. But this generation has set the highest standards for human rights in human history. It has achieved much; it has proved repeatedly that no idea is so compelling as the idea of human freedom. America was "conceived in Liberty, and dedicated to the proposition that all men are created equal." It is America's task, a century and a quarter after Abraham Lincoln spoke, to do its utmost to help redeem that promise for men and women everywhere.

NO

George Shultz

MORALITY AND REALISM IN AMERICAN FOREIGN POLICY

HANS MORGENTHAU'S LEGACY

Hans Morgenthau was a pioneer in the study of international relations. He, perhaps more than anyone else, gave it intellectual respectability as an academic discipline. His work transformed our thinking about international relations and about America's role in the postwar world. In fundamental ways, he set the terms of the modern debate, and it is hard to imagine what our policies would be like today had we not had the benefit of his wisdom and the clarity of his thinking.

As a professor of the University of Chicago, . . . in 1948 he published the first edition of his epoch-making text, *Politics Among Nations.* Its impact was immediate—and alarming to many. It focused on the reality of so-called power politics and the balance of power—the evils of the Old World conflicts that immigrants had come to this country to escape and which Wilsonian idealism had sought to eradicate.

Morgenthau's critics, however, tended to miss what he was really saying about international morality and ethics. The choice, he insisted, is not between moral principles and the national interest, devoid of moral dignity, but between moral principles divorced from political reality and moral principles derived from political reality. And he called on Americans to relearn the principles of statecraft and political morality that had guided the Founding Fathers.

Hans Morgenthau was right in this. Our Declaration of Independence set forth principles, after all, that we believed to be universal. And throughout our history, Americans as individuals—and, sometimes, as a nation—have frequently expressed our hopes for a world based on those principles. The very nature of our society makes us a people with a moral vision, not only for ourselves but for the world.

At the same time, however, we Americans have had to accept that our passionate commitment to moral principles could be no substitute for a sound

From George Shultz, "Morality and Realism in American Foreign Policy," *Department of State Bulletin* (December 1985).

foreign policy in a world of hard realities and complex choices. Our Founding Fathers, in fact, understood this very well.

Hans Morgenthau wrote that "the intoxication with moral abstractions... is one of the great sources of weakness and failure in American foreign policy." He was assailing the tendency among Americans at many periods in our later history to hold ourselves above power politics and to believe that moral principles alone could guide us in our relations with the rest of the world. He correctly worried that our moral impulse, noble as it might be, could lead either to futile and perhaps dangerous global crusades, on the one hand, or to escapism and isolationism, equally dangerous, on the other.

The challenge we have always faced has been to forge policies that could combine morality and realism that would be in keeping with our ideals without doing damage to our national interests. Hans Morgenthau's work shaped our national debate about this challenge with an unprecedented intensity and clarity.

IDEALS AND INTERESTS TODAY

That debate still continues today. But today there is a new reality.

The reality today is that our moral principles and our national interests may be converging, by necessity, more than ever before. The revolutions in communications and transportation have made the world a smaller place. Events in one part of the world have a more far-reaching impact than ever before on the international environment and on our national security. Even individual acts of violence by terrorists can affect us in

ways never possible before the advent of international electronic media....

In our world, our ideals and our interests thus are intimately connected. In the long run, the survival of America and American democracy is essential if freedom itself is to survive. No one who cherishes freedom and democracy could argue that these ideals can be gained through policies that weaken this nation.

We are the strongest free nation on earth. Our closest allies are democracies and depend on us for their security. And our security and well-being are enhanced in a world where democracy flourishes and where the global economic system is open and free. We could not hope to survive long if our fellow democracies succumbed to totalitarianism. Thus, we have a vital stake in the direction the world takes—whether it be toward greater freedom or toward dictatorship.

All of this requires that we engage ourselves in the politics of the real world, for both moral and strategic reasons. And the more we engage ourselves in the world, the more we must grapple with the difficult moral choices that the real world presents to us.

We have friends and allies who do not always live up to our standards of freedom and democratic government, yet we cannot abandon them. Our adversaries are the worst offenders of the principles we cherish, yet in the nuclear age, we have no choice but to seek solutions by political means. We are vulnerable to terrorism because we are a free and law-abiding society, yet we must find a way to respond that is consistent with our ideals as a free and law-abiding society.

The challenge of pursuing policies that reflect our ideals and yet protect our national interests is, for all the difficulties, one that we must meet. The political reality of our time is that America's strategic interests require that we support our ideals abroad.

Consider the example of Nicaragua. We oppose the efforts of the communist leaders in Nicaragua to consolidate a totalitarian regime on the mainland of Central America—on both moral and strategic grounds. Few in the United States would deny today that the Managua regime is a moral disaster. The communists have brutally repressed the Nicaraguan people's yearning for freedom and self-government, the same yearning that had earlier made possible the overthrow of the Somoza tyranny. But there are some in this country who would deny that America has a strategic stake in the outcome of the ideological struggle underway in Nicaragua today. Can we not, they ask, accept the existence of this regime in our hemisphere even if we find its ideology abhorrent? Must we oppose it simply because it is communist?

The answer is we must oppose the Nicaraguan dictators not simply because they are communists but because they are communists who serve the interests of the Soviet Union and its Cuban client and who threaten peace in this hemisphere. The facts are indisputable. Had the communists adopted even a neutral international posture after their revolution; had they not threatened their neighbors, our friends and allies in the region, with subversion and aggression; had they not lent logistical and material support to the Marxist-Leninist guerrillas in El Salvador—in short, had they not become instruments of Soviet global strategy, the United States would have had a less clear strategic interest in opposing them.

Our relations with China and Yugoslavia show that we are prepared for constructive relations with communist countries regardless of ideological differences. Yet, as a general principle in the postwar world, the United States has and does oppose communist expansionism, most particularly as practiced by the Soviet Union and its surrogates. We do so not because we are crusaders in the grip of ideological or messianic fervor, but because our strategic interests, by any cool and rational analysis, require us to do so.

Our interests, however, also require something more. It is not enough to know only what we are against. We must also know what we are for. And in the modern world, our national interests require us to be on the side of freedom and democratic change everywhere—and no less in such areas of strategic importance to us as Central America, South Africa, the Philippines, and South Korea.

We understood this important lesson in Western Europe almost 40 years ago, with the Truman Doctrine, the Marshall Plan, and NATO; and we learned the lesson again in just the last 4 years in El Salvador: the best defense against the threat of communist takeover is the strengthening of freedom and democracy. The most stable friends and allies of the United States are invariably the democratic nations. They are stable because they exist to serve the needs of the people and because they give every segment of society a chance to influence, peacefully and legally, the course their nation takes. They are stable because no one can question their fundamental legitimacy. No would-be revolutionary can claim to represent the people against some ruling oligarchy because the people can speak for themselves. And the people never "choose" communism.

One of the most difficult challenges we face today is in South Africa. Americans naturally find apartheid totally reprehensible. It must go. But how shall it go? Our influence is limited. Shall we try to undermine the South African economy in an effort to topple the white regime, even if that would hurt the very people we are trying to help as well as neighboring black countries whose economies are heavily dependent on South Africa? Do we want to see the country become so unstable that there is a violent revolution? History teaches that the black majority might likely wind up exchanging one set of oppressors for another and, yes, could be worse off.

The premise of the President's policy is that we cannot wash our hands of the problem or strike moralistic poses. The only course consistent with American principles is to stay engaged as a force for peaceful change. Our interests and our values are parallel because the present system is doomed, and the only alternative to a radical, violent outcome is a political accommodation now, before it is too late.

The moral—and the practical—policy is to use our influence to encourage a peaceful transition to a just society. It is not our job to cheer on, from the sidelines, a race war in southern Africa or to accelerate trends that will inexorably produce the same result.

Therefore, the centerpiece of our policy is a call for political dialogue and negotiation between the government and representative black leaders. Such an effort requires that we keep in contact with all parties, black and white; it means encouraging the South African Government to go further and faster on a course on which it has already haltingly embarked. The President's Executive order a month ago, therefore, was directed against the machinery of apartheid, but in a way that

did not magnify the hardship of the victims of apartheid. This approach may suffer the obloquy of the moral absolutists— of those opposed to change and of those demanding violent change. But we will stick to this course because it is right.

THE IMPORTANCE OF REALISM

A foreign policy based on realism, therefore, cannot ignore the importance of either ideology or morality. But realism *does* require that we avoid foreign policies based exclusively on moral absolutes divorced from political reality. Hans Morgenthau was right to warn against the dangers of such moral crusades or escapism.

We know that the spread of communism is inimical to our interests, but we also know that we are not omnipotent and that we must set priorities. We cannot send American troops to every region of the world threatened by Soviet-backed communist insurgents, though there may be times when that is the right choice and the only choice.... The wide range of challenges we face requires that we choose from an equally wide range of responses: from economic and security assistance to aid for freedom fighters to direct military action when necessary. We must discriminate; we must be prudent; we must use all the tools at our disposal and respond in ways appropriate to the challenge. Realism, as Hans Morgenthau understood it, is also a counsel of restraint and healthy common sense.

We also know that supporting democratic progress is a difficult task. Our influence in fostering democracy is often limited in those nations where it has never before taken root, where rulers are reluctant to give up their privileged status, where civil strife is rampant, where extreme poverty and inequality pose obstacles to social and political progress.

Moral posturing is no substitute for effective policies. Nor can we afford to distance ourselves from all the difficult and ambiguous moral choices of the real world. We may often have to accept the reality that advances toward democracy and greater freedom in some important pro-Western nations may be slow and will require patience.

If we use our power to push our nondemocratic allies too far and too fast, we may, in fact, destroy the hope for greater freedom; and we may also find that the regimes we inadvertently bring into power are the worst of both worlds: they may be both hostile to our interests *and* more repressive and dictatorial than those we sought to change. We need only remember what happened in Iran and Nicaragua. The fall of a strategically located, friendly country can strengthen Soviet power and, thus, set back the cause of freedom regionally and globally.

But we must also remember what happened in El Salvador and throughout Latin America in the past 5 years—and, for that matter, what is happening today in Nicaragua, Cambodia, Afghanistan, and Angola, where people are fighting and dying for independence and freedom. What we do in each case must vary according to the circumstances, but there should not be any doubt of whose side we are on.

... [The Carter] administration took the position that our fear of communism was inordinate and emphasized that there were severe limits to America's ability or right to influence world events. I believe this was a council of despair, a sign that we had lost faith in ourselves and in our values.

...Our ideals must be a source of strength—not paralysis—in our struggle against aggression, international lawlessness, and terrorism. We have learned that our moral convictions must be tempered and tested in daily grappling with the realities of the modern world. But we have also learned that our ideals have value and relevance, that the idea of freedom is a powerful force. Our ideals have a concrete, practical meaning today. They not only point the way to a better world, they reflect some of the most powerful currents at work in the contemporary world. The striving for justice, freedom, progress, and peace is an ever-present reality that is today, more than ever, impressing itself on international politics.

As Hans Morgenthau understood, the conduct of a realistic and principled foreign policy is an honorable endeavor and an inescapable responsibility. We draw strength from our ideals and principles, and we and our friends among the free nations will not shrink from using our strength to defend and further the values and principles that have made us great.

POSTSCRIPT

Should Morality and Human Rights Strongly Influence Foreign Policy Making?

There are times when morality and realpolitik national interest support the same policy choice. Defeating dangerously militaristic and unconscionably evil Nazi Germany is a clear example. Usually, though, the choice is not that easy and presents a troubling dilemma. If you ignore morality and support oppression, even in the most indirect fashion by befriending those who practice it, you leave yourself open to the charge of guilt by inaction or association. Yet most people also have qualms about self-sacrificing morality.

To study the divergent realist and idealist approaches, review Hans Morgenthau's *Politics Among Nations* (Alfred A. Knopf, 1985) along with leading idealist Stanley Hoffmann's review of the book in the *Atlantic Monthly* (November 1985). From the practitioner point of view, the realists are well represented by George Shultz, *From Turmoil and Triumph* (Charles Scribner's Sons, 1993). Cyrus Vance's memoirs *Hard Choices* (Simon & Schuster, 1982) is an idealist counterpart.

Even if we try to apply realpolitik or morality, the choices are not always certain. If we take the realist approach, what is the "real" national interest? In the short term, supporting the white South African government may be in the amoral national interest because they are "our SOBs." But, in the long run, the blacks will probably prevail, and perhaps, morality aside, the smarter choice is to get on the winning side now. Similarly, what is moral is often uncertain. Should we, for one, intervene in the internal affairs of another sovereign country, be it South Africa or China? Also, is there really a universal morality on which we all can agree, or, by applying our own standards, are we practicing "cultural imperialism"? Finally, if we withdraw support from a friendly dictator or topple an unfriendly one, what is our responsibility for what happens next? The Shah of Iran was certainly a despot, but were the people of Iran better off under the Ayatollah Khomeini, who replaced him?

Further readings on this topic include: Robert W. McElroy, *Morality and American Foreign Policy* (Princeton University Press, 1992); Henry A. Kissinger, *Diplomacy* (Simon & Schuster, 1994); and Kenneth Waltz, "The Emerging Structure of International Politics," *International Security* (Fall 1993).

ISSUE 17

Is There a Global Environmental Crisis?

YES: Hilary F. French, from "Can the Environment Survive Industrial Demands?" *USA Today Magazine,* a publication of the Society for the Advancement of Education (January 1994)

NO: Julian L. Simon, from *More People, Greater Wealth, More Resources, Healthier Environment* (1994)

ISSUE SUMMARY

YES: Hilary F. French, a senior researcher at the Worldwatch Institute in
Washington, D.C., warns that countries cannot continue to strip the planet's
resources and pollute the air and water in the name of doing business as
usual without dire consequences.

NO: Julian L. Simon, a professor of economic and business administration at
the University of Maryland, asserts that the current gloom and doom about
the "crisis" of our environment is not supported by scientific facts.

We live in an era of almost incomprehensible technological boom. In a very
short time—less than a long lifetime in many cases— technology has brought
about some amazing things. If you talked to a 100-year-old person, he or
she would remember a time before airplanes, before automobiles were common, before air conditioning, and before medicines were available that could
control polio and a host of other deadly diseases. And 100 years ago, the
world's population was 25 percent of what it is today, uranium (crucial for
making nuclear reactors and bombs) was considered to be useless, and ozone
depletion, acid rain, and global warming were unthought of.

There are three points to bear in mind here. One is that technology and economic development have been a proverbial two-edged sword. Most people
in the economically developed countries (EDCs) and even many people in the
less developed countries (LDCs) have benefited mightily from modern technology. For these people, life is longer, easier, and filled with material riches
that were the stuff of science fiction not long ago. Yet we are also endangered
by the by-products of progress: the world's population now stands at about
5.5 billion people, and resources are being consumed at an exponential rate.
Cities have smog alerts and mountainous piles of trash in overused landfills,
which leak their effluent into the groundwater. Acid rain is damaging forests,
and extinction is the fate of an alarming array of species of flora and fauna.

The second notable point is that most of this has occurred so rapidly. It is
probable that between 80 and 90 percent of all technological advancement has

occurred within the last 100 years. The speed of change is important because it says that if there is a critical problem, as Hilary French argues there is, then it must be addressed quickly. From French's point of view, the globe cannot stand a hundred more years of progress that emulate the last century.

But not everyone is worried. There are those, like Julian Simon, who contend that worries about population, the environment, and resources are overwrought. They suggest that a number of factors, especially advancing technology, will enable humankind to meet and resolve such concerns.

The issue turns on whether or not environmental safety requires us to alter drastically some of our consumption patterns; to pay more in taxes and prices for technologies to clean the environment; to use substitutes (which are perhaps more expensive or less satisfactory) for products that threaten the environment or resources that are scarce; and to alter (some might say reduce) our lifestyles by conserving energy and taking other such measures.

Sustainability is one term that is important to this debate. Sustainable development means progress that occurs without further damaging the ecosystem. *Carrying capacity* is another key term. The question is whether or not there is some finite limit to the number of people that the Earth can accommodate. Carrying capacity is about more than just numbers. It also involves how carefully people manage the planet's resources—the lifestyles they develop. If you live to be 100 years old, you may well share the Earth with a world population of 10 billion, twice what it is today. Can the world carry 10 billion people who consume resources as rapaciously as we do today? Can 10 billion environmentally careful people survive?

This leads to the third notable point, which is that individual countries and the global community collectively have begun to try to figure out how to protect the environment, while maintaining—indeed increasing and spreading —economic prosperity as well. In June 1992 most of the world's countries and a huge array of private organizations gathered in Rio de Janeiro, Brazil, to attend the United Nations Conference on Environment and Development (UNCED). The conference represented a major international effort under the auspices of the UN to address sustainability. Among other things, UNCED reached two agreements: a convention to cut down emissions that create global warming and a convention to protect biodiversity. Many developed countries resisted strong language in the two treaties. The EDCs, for example, rejected LDC demands that a strict timetable be set for the reduction of the emission of carbon dioxide and other gases that promote global warming.

For Hilary French and others, UNCED represented only a beginning. In the following selections, she argues that governments must struggle to reconcile antiquated trade rules with present-day environmental realities, while Julian Simon maintains that we should not overreact. His central assertion is that almost every economic and social change or trend has been positive, as long as we view the matter over a reasonably long period of time.

YES

Hilary F. French

CAN THE ENVIRONMENT SURVIVE
INDUSTRIAL DEMANDS?

Low-cost tropical timber that is harvested from the rain forest in Malaysia is shipped to Japan, where it is processed into plywood that becomes shuttering used in construction that could have been made from plantation-growth softwoods. Lead car batteries are exported from the U.S. to a recycling plant on the outskirts of São Paulo, Brazil, which has health and environmental controls so inadequate that 86% of workers tested have lead concentrations in the blood that exceed the American recommended limit, some by as much as two to three times. A dam built on the La Grande River in northern Quebec to generate electricity for export to New England floods an area half the size of Belgium, displacing the Cree Indians who called the land home and poisoning their fishing grounds with the release of naturally occurring mercury. In these and thousands of other cases, international trade is spurring environmental degradation and transferring it around the globe.

Yet, the growing integration of the world economy has some positive environmental effects. For instance, fuel-efficient Japanese cars reduced air emissions in the U.S. and forced American manufacturers to develop comparable models.

International merchandise trade, now about 3.5 million dollars, has grown 5.5% annually since 1950, regularly outpacing the expansion of global output as a whole. This includes primary goods such as food, raw materials, minerals, and energy, as well as manufactured products. Trade in services, running at more than $800,000,000,000, also is growing fast, as is direct investment in foreign countries. These trends mean that international commerce is shaping worldwide environmental practices in various ways each day.

Trade magnifies the ecological effects of production by expanding the market for commodities beyond national boundaries. Second, it allows nations that have depleted their resource bases or passed strict laws protecting them to reach past their borders for desired products, effectively shifting the environmental impacts of consumption to someone else's backyard. Finally, national environmental laws and even some international treaties are coming under attack as "nontariff barriers to trade," jeopardizing efforts to restore

From Hilary F. French, "Can the Environment Survive Industrial Demands?" *USA Today Magazine* (January 1994). Copyright © 1994 by The Society for the Advancement of Education and Worldwatch Institute, Washington, DC. Reprinted by permission.

ecological quality within countries and to protect the global commons, such as the atmosphere and oceans.

As with transboundary and worldwide pollution, national governments acting alone are unable to control the environmental effects of trade, making international cooperation essential. Yet, despite the many interactions between them, trade and environment traditionally have been seen as separate domains in the international arena. When the General Agreement on Tariffs and Trade (GATT) [now called the World Trade Organization] was created in 1948, its main task was lowering the tariff barriers erected in the 1930s that were widely blamed for the global depression. The environment was scarcely a national concern then, let alone an international one.

Now, though, as ecological issues achieve a new prominence on the international agenda and increasingly bump up against trade agreements, the world is beginning to take note of the connections. Such matters have become a major feature of several ongoing negotiations—the talks on expanding GATT, debate over Europe's single market, and discussions about the North American Free Trade Agreement (NAFTA) among Canada, Mexico, and the U.S. In these and other forums, governments are struggling to reconcile antiquated trade rules with present-day environmental realities.

In the postwar era, free trade sometimes has been pursued as an end in itself, rather than a means to an end. This approach is beginning to give way to the view that trade is a tool for shaping a world that is ecologically sustainable and socially just. Governments are recognizing sustainable development as an overriding goal of the world community. Now, policymakers must get on with the task of determining how the rules of trade can be revised to help achieve it.

TRADE AND THE GLOBAL RESOURCE BASE

Much of the commerce in primary products takes place between industrial countries, while developing nations are net exporters of food, raw materials, minerals, and fuels to the industrial world. In the Third World, primary products tend to dominate exports. More than 98% of the exports of Bolivia, Ethiopia, Ghana, and Nigeria fall into this category, compared with 24% of U.S. exports and two percent of Japan's. Many developing countries thus are particularly vulnerable to trade-inflicted damage to their natural resource bases, yet depend heavily on the foreign exchange exports can generate, making policies that promote sustainable production over the long run especially important.

The tropical timber trade demonstrates many of the pitfalls of natural resource-based exports, beginning to fall as commercially valuable forests are decimated to please consumers in Europe, Japan, and North America. In Nigeria, exports have dropped precipitously over the past decade in response to overlogging, and Thailand and the Philippines—once wood exporters—have become net importers due to the ravaging of their forests. Several other countries, including Côte d'Ivoire and Ghana, soon will make the same transition.

In Malaysia, at least half the trees felled for timber are exported, bringing in $1,500,000,000 in foreign exchange. The East Malaysian states of Sarawak and Sabah, which supply Japan with more than 90% of its tropical imports, have been particularly hard hit. In Sarawak, environmentalists predict there will be no trees left to cut in as little as five years, bringing about the destruction of the homeland of the local Penan people, who aggressively are fighting to save it.

One of the victims of deforestation induced by the tropical timber trade and other forces is the Earth's biological wealth, as plants and animals in the forest are driven to extinction. Biodiversity suffers from another type of trade as well—commerce in wildlife and wildlife parts. For some species that particularly are prized on the international market, such as the Orinco crocodile and Sumatran rhinoceros, trade is a leading threat. For others, it is an added pressure that can push to extinction a species already threatened by habitat loss and other forces.

Global wildlife trade is valued at $5–8,000,000,000 annually, about 70% of which is legal. Each year, 30,000 monkeys and other primates are shipped across international borders, along with 20–30,000,000 pelts, 500,000 parrots, 400–500,000,000 ornamental fish, 1–2,000 tons of raw coral, 7–10,000,000 cacti, and 1–2,000,000 orchids. Nations have had some success, through the Convention on International Trade in Endangered Species of Wild Flora and Fauna, in controlling commerce in products from certain particularly well-known species, such as the African elephant and the snow lion. However, trade in many other threatened species continues apace.

Regional trade pacts may exacerbate the difficulties in controlling the trade in wildlife. For instance, the elimination of all border controls between European Community (EC) [now the European Union] countries may impede efforts at monitoring wildlife trade. In North America, a World Wildlife Fund study

projects that the increased tourism and transport likely to result from NAFTA—as well as tariff reductions it mandates—will lead to more trade, both legal and illicit, in furs, exotic leather goods, parrots, stuffed birds of prey, sea turtle products, and other valuable and endangered species.

Many agricultural exports have important environmental implications. In Costa Rica, the lure of the export market encouraged people to clear the rain forest for cattle ranching. During the 1960s and 1970s, the nation's rain forest was reduced to 17% of its original size through agriculture and grazing. The country exported between one- and two-thirds of its beef, in part to whet the almost insatiable demand for hamburgers in the U.S. In Botswana, land degradation from overgrazing partially is attributed to trading arrangements with the EC, as nearly half its beef production is exported for the European market.

Overfishing of certain species such as cod and haddock also is being spurred by trade. In Iceland, which relies on fish exports for more than half its foreign exchange, a 40% quota cut thought necessary to restore the health of the local cod fishery would have caused the gross national product to decline by four–five percent. Faced with this, the government restricted the cut to 27% for 1993. As stocks are depleted in industrial nations' waters and world fish prices rise as a consequence, northern consumers increasingly are turning to developing countries to help meet the rapidly growing demand for fish. Prawn farming in Asia and Latin America for the export market has led to the clearing of large areas of coastal mangrove swamps that help protect biologically diverse coral reefs and other coastal habitats from storm damage and marine pollution.

The production of ores, minerals, and metals for export is responsible for large amounts of environmental degradation. Mining and mineral processing have a variety of ecological impacts, ranging from the destruction of huge tracts of land to the generation of prodigious quantities of waste and the creation of large amounts of air and water pollution. A single copper mine in Papua New Guinea, for instance, yielded 40% of the nation's export earnings, but dumped 130,000 tons of metal-contaminated tailings into the Kawerong River per day. The mine finally was closed in 1989, but only after a civil war ignited at least in part by local people's anger over the environmental damage it caused forced the government from power.

Most unexploited mineral reserves are in developing countries, meaning these nations will account for a growing share of the total damage from mineral extraction in the years ahead. A World Wide Fund for Nature study found that refined copper production grew by 33% during the 1980s in developing countries, compared to 13% in the industrial nations. The share of aluminum production centered in developing countries increased from 14% in 1980 to 35% in 1990 and is projected to climb to 44% by 1995.

Like most commerce, trade in energy has a considerable impact on environmental quality. Some energy trade can have beneficial ecological effects. For example, natural gas use produces fewer air pollutants than coal or oil do. Transporting it internationally by pipeline could allow gas to be substituted for these more polluting alternatives. The Organisation for Economic Co-operation and Develop-

ment (OECD) estimates that burning gas from the Commonwealth of Independent States instead of coal in 20% of Western Europe's power plants would cut carbon emissions from the utility sector by eight percent, sulfur dioxide emissions by 20%, and nitrogen oxides by eight percent.

On the negative side, though, the damage wreaked by oil and gas exploration and coal mining is experienced in the exporting country, while the importer gains the economic benefit of using the fuel without suffering many of the ecological consequences. For example, the U.S.S.R. long supplied large quantities of oil to Eastern and Western Europe. This provided a key source of foreign exchange, but also left a ruinous environmental legacy. Only recently has the extent of the destruction from this industry in the former Soviet Union begun to come to light.

Trade and investment in manufactured goods play an integral role. The ecological issues associated with industrialization include energy use, air and water pollution, toxic chemical production, and waste disposal. The global marketplace means that environmentally harmful goods and processes can follow the path of least resistance to countries most willing to accept such hazards in order to reap an economic reward.

The export of waste is perhaps the most celebrated example. According to Greenpeace, at least 10,000,0000 tons have been exported over the last several years, more than half of which have gone to Eastern Europe or developing countries, where regulation tends to be lax. There is reason for concern that trade agreements will make it tougher to control dumping. The removal of border controls in Europe and the greater traffic across borders in North America and elsewhere could create difficulty in controlling illicit traffic. Moreover, these agreements could dictate that waste is a "good" not dissimilar to others in international commerce, making it hard for nations unilaterally to ban exports or imports.

Many other hazardous goods are sold on the world market. Faced with declining sales at home in response to health concerns, the Canadian asbestos industry has joined forces with the government to promote sales abroad. Ninety-five percent of the asbestos Canada produces is exported, more than half of it to the Third World. The government has been known to offer free samples to targeted countries, such as Thailand and India, to entice them to buy Canadian-produced asbestos. Export of pesticides banned or restricted for domestic use is big business in many nations. The banned pesticides sometimes return on imported food, a phenomenon known as the "circle of poison."

Freer trade and investment can influence where goods are manufactured, and thus where the pollution burden associated with production is located. Some forms of manufacturing increasingly are concentrating in developing countries, including textiles, leather, iron and steel, and chemicals. The growth has a number of explanations. Development planners have touted manufacturing as the route to prosperity in these nations. Other factors include cheaper labor or energy, accessibility of raw materials, and the shift toward services and high-tech industries in the industrial world.

The extent to which regulations in developed countries might be affecting these trends has been the subject of considerable debate over the years. In the 1970s, when the U.S. was beginning to pass stricter environmental legislation, businesses claimed that these laws would disadvantage domestic companies in foreign competition and cause the loss of many jobs as polluting industries moved elsewhere to escape regulation. Some feared that poorer countries deliberately would keep environmental standards lax in order to attract investment by becoming pollution havens.

Whatever the reason, manufacturing, some of it hazardous, is on the rise in much of the Third World. The debate over the North American Free Trade Agreement focused attention on one area where these forces are readily apparent. The border region between the U.S. and Mexico is home to nearly 2,000 manufacturing plants known as *maquiladoras*—branches of companies that are allowed to import duty-free components for processing in Mexico on the condition that the final product be exported back. Almost all the plants are foreign-owned, drawn there by wages as low as seven percent of what is paid for comparable work in the U.S., as well as by the preferential tariff treatment and proximity to markets. More than half of the 100 largest U.S. companies operate assembly plants in Mexico.

On the books, Mexico's environmental laws are roughly comparable and in some cases stricter than U.S. ones, but enforcement has been lax. Though *maquiladoras* are required to return to the U.S. any waste they generate, compliance with this mandate is believed to be the exception rather than the rule.

Investigations by a number of groups have revealed alarming conditions in the area. At three-quarters of the *maquiladoras* sampled in 1991, the U.S. National Toxics Campaign discovered toxic discharges—including chemicals that cause cancer, birth defects, and brain damage—being emptied into open ditches running through settlements near the factories. The American Medical Association describes the border area as "a virtual cesspool and breeding ground for infectious diseases," in no small measure due to the fact that the population there has swelled to twice its former size over the last two decades, while sewage treatment remains practically nonexistent. Investigations by medical teams on both sides of the border have revealed alarming public health conditions, including elevated rates of hepatitis A and tuberculosis, in part because some of the pollution drifts or flows back and forth across the national boundary.

Mexico has announced its intention to tighten enforcement and explicitly ruled out becoming a "pollution haven" under NAFTA—a promise environmentalists will try to hold the government to. Under the pact, it will be considered a violation to relax such standards or enforcement in order to encourage investment.

In countless other places, companies locating overseas are causing environmental harm. Japan has come in for heavy criticism from environmentalists in Southeast Asia for allegedly locating extremely harmful processes abroad because they no longer can pass environmental muster at home. A Malaysian subsidiary of the Mitsubishi Kasei Corp. was forced by court order to close after years of protests by local residents that the plant's dumping of radioactive thorium was to blame for unusually high leukemia rates in the region. Several multinational corporations operating in South Africa, including local subsidiaries of the Bayer pharmaceuticals concern and a Duracell battery plant, have been implicated by local environmentalists in toxic catastrophes that they believe have caused cancer and other severe health problems among workers.

Despite the threats, international markets also help diffuse many environmentally helpful products around the world. Trade in pollution control technologies is on the rise, particularly as environmental laws are strengthened in developing countries. International trade also can put pressure on companies to match the environmental innovations of their international competitors, as in the U.S. car industry's response to Japan's advances in fuel efficiency.

Meanwhile, there are indications that, contrary to some people's expectations, being open to foreign investment can help prevent the creation of pollution havens, rather than cause them. Research by Nancy Birdsall and David Wheeler of the World Bank found that dirty industries developed faster in Latin American economies relatively inhospitable to foreign investment than in open ones. Another World Bank study looked at the rates at which 60 different countries adopted a cleaner pulping technology and concluded that the new technology made its way to nations open to foreign investment far more rapidly than to those closed to it.

The authors of these studies suggest several possible explanations for such trends. For one, closed economies might protect capital-intensive, pollution-intensive industries in situations where low-cost labor otherwise would have been a draw to less polluting industries. Second, companies trying to sell their goods in industrial-country markets need to please the growing number of "green consumers" there. Finally, the equipment used by multinationals tends on balance to be newer and cleaner than that employed by national industries....

Because the failure to consider the ecological impacts of trade agreements could have dire consequences, integrating environmental considerations into their fabric would yield sizable environmental returns. Trade must become a vehicle for promoting products and technologies that will help ensure ecological health, not those that undermine the prospects for an environmentally sustainable future.

NO

Julian L. Simon

MORE PEOPLE, GREATER WEALTH, MORE RESOURCES, HEALTHIER ENVIRONMENT

INTRODUCTION

This is the economic history of humanity in a nutshell: From 2 million or 200,000 or 20,000 or 2,000 years ago until the 18th Century there was slow growth in population, almost no increase in health or decrease in mortality, slow growth in the availability of natural resources (but not increased scarcity), increase in wealth for a few, and mixed effects on the environment. Since then, there has been rapid growth in population due to spectacular decreases in the death rate, rapid growth in resources, widespread increases in wealth, and an unprecedentedly clean and beautiful living environment in many parts of the world, along with a degraded environment in the poor and socialist parts of the world.

That is, more people and more wealth has correlated with more (rather than less) resources and a cleaner environment—just the opposite of what Malthusian theory leads one to believe. The task before us is to make sense of these mind-boggling happy trends.

The current gloom-and-doom about a "crisis" of our environment is all wrong on the scientific facts. Even the U. S. Environmental Protection Agency acknowledges that U.S. air and our water have been getting cleaner rather than dirtier in the past few decades. Every agricultural economist knows that the world's population has been eating ever-better since World War II. Every resource economist knows that all natural resources have been getting more available rather than more scarce, as shown by their falling prices over the decades and centuries. And every demographer knows that the death rate has been falling all over the world—life expectancy almost tripling in the rich countries in the past two centuries, and almost doubling in the poor countries in just the past four decades.

The picture also is now clear that population growth does not hinder economic development. In the 1980s there was a complete reversal in the consensus of thinking of population economists about the effects of more people. In 1986, the National Research Council and the National Academy of Sciences completely overturned its "official" view away from the earlier worried view expressed in 1971. It noted the absence of any statistical evidence of a negative connection between population increase and economic growth. And it said that "The scarcity of exhaustible resources is at most a minor restraint on economic growth."

This U-turn by the scientific consensus of experts on the subject has gone unacknowledged by the press, the antinatalist [anti-birth] environmental organizations, and the agencies that foster population control abroad.

Here is my central assertion: Almost every economic and social change or trend points in a positive direction, as long as we view the matter over a reasonably long period of time.

For proper understanding of the important aspects of an economy we should look at the long-run trends. But the short-run comparisons—between the sexes, age groups, races, political groups, which are usually purely relative—make more news. To repeat, just about every important long-run measure of human welfare shows improvement over the decades and centuries, in the United States as well as in the rest of the world. And there is no persuasive reason to believe that these trends will not continue indefinitely.

Would I bet on it? For sure. I'll bet a week's or month's pay—anything I win goes to pay for more research—that just about any trend pertaining to material human welfare will improve rather than get worse. You pick the comparison and the year.

THE FACTS

Let's quickly review a few data on how human life has been doing, beginning with the all-important issue, life itself.

The Conquest of Too-Early Death

The most important and amazing demographic fact—the greatest human achievement in history, in my view—is the decrease in the world's death rate.... It took thousands of years to increase life expectancy at birth from just over 20 years to the high 20's about 1750. Then, about 1750, life expectancy in the richest countries suddenly took off and tripled in about two centuries. In just the past two centuries the length of life you could expect for your baby or yourself in the advanced countries jumped from less than 30 years to perhaps 75 years. What greater event has humanity witnessed than this conquest of premature death in the rich countries? It is this decrease in the death rate that is the cause of there being a larger world population nowadays than in former times.

Then starting well after World War II, since the 1950s, the length of life you could expect in the poor countries has leaped upwards by perhaps fifteen or even twenty years, caused by advances in agriculture, sanitation, and medicine.

Let's put it differently. In the 19th century the planet Earth could sustain only one billion people. Ten thousand years ago, only 4 million could keep themselves alive. Now, 5 billion people are living longer and more healthily than ever before, on average. The increase in the world's population represents our victory over death.

Here arises a crucial issue of interpretation: One would expect lovers of humanity to jump with joy at this triumph

Figure 1
Copper Prices Indexed by Wages

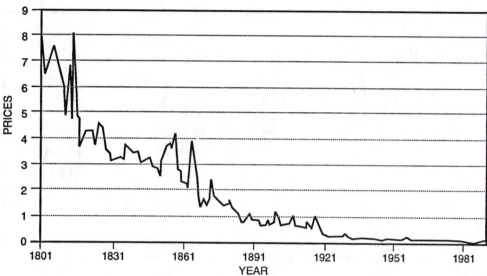

of human mind and organization over the raw killing forces of nature. Instead, many lament that there are so many people alive to enjoy the gift of life.... And it is this worry that leads them to approve the Indonesian, Chinese and other inhumane programs of coercion and denial of personal liberty in one of the most precious choices a family can make—the number of children that it wishes to bear and raise.

The Decreasing Scarcity of Natural Resources
Throughout history, the supply of natural resources always has worried people. Yet the data clearly show that natural resource scarcity—as measured by the economically-meaningful indicator of cost or price—has been decreasing rather than increasing in the long run for all raw materials, with only temporary exceptions from time to time. That is, availability has been increasing. Consider copper,

which is representative of all the metals. In Figure 1 we see the price relative to wages since 1801. The cost of a ton is only about a tenth now of what it was two hundred years ago.

This trend of falling prices of copper has been going on for a very long time. In the 18th century B.C.E. [before the Common Era] in Babylonia under Hammurabi—almost 4000 years ago—the price of copper was about a thousand times its price in the United States now relative to wages. At the time of the Roman Empire the price was about a hundred times the present price.

In Figure 2 we see the price of copper relative to the consumer price index. Everything that we buy—pens, shirts, tires —has been getting cheaper over the years because we know how to make them cheaper, especially during the past 200 years. Even so, the extraordinary fact is that natural resources have been get-

Figure 2
Copper Prices Divided by CPI

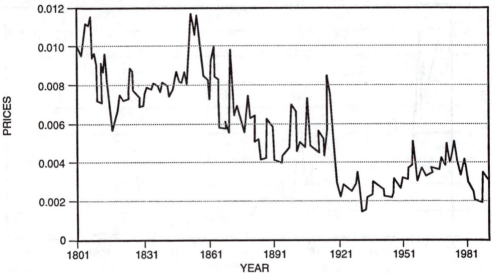

ting cheaper even faster than consumer goods.

So by any measure, natural resources have been getting more available rather than more scarce. . . .

Regarding oil, the shocking price rises during the 1970s and 1980s were not caused by growing scarcity in the world supply. And indeed, the price of petroleum in inflation-adjusted dollars has returned to levels about where they were before the politically-induced increases, and the price of gasoline is about at the historic low and still falling. Concerning energy in general, there is no reason to believe that the supply of energy is finite, or that the price of energy will not continue its long-run decrease forever. . . .

Food is an especially important resource. The evidence is particularly strong for food that we are on a benign trend despite rising population. The long-run price of food relative to wages is now

only perhaps a tenth as much as it was in 1800 in the United States. Even relative to consumer products the price of grain is down, due to increased productivity, just as with all other primary products.

Famine deaths due to insufficient food supply have decreased even in absolute terms, let alone relative to population, in the past century, a matter which pertains particularly to the poor countries. Per-person food consumption is up over the last 30 years. And there are no data showing that the bottom of the income scale is faring worse, or even has failed to share in the general improvement, as the average has improved.

Africa's food production per person is down, but by 1994 almost no one any longer claims that Africa's suffering results from a shortage of land or water or sun. The cause of hunger in Africa is a combination of civil wars and collectivization of agriculture, which periodic droughts have made more murderous.

Here let us digress from the general discussion to a resource which has been of special historical interest... in the Netherlands—agricultural land. Let's consider it as an example of all natural resources. Though many people consider land to be a special kind of resource, it is subject to the same processes of human creation as other natural resources. The most important fact about agricultural land is that less and less of it is needed as the decades pass. This idea is utterly counter-intuitive. It seems entirely obvious that a growing world population would need larger amounts of farmland. But the title of a remarkable prescient article in 1951 by Theodore Schultz tells the story: "The Declining Economic Importance of Land."

The increase in actual and potential productivity per unit of land have grown much faster than population, and there is sound reason to expect this trend to continue. Therefore, there is less and less reason to worry about the supply of land. Though the stock of usable land seems fixed at any moment, it is constantly being increased—at a rapid rate in many cases—by the clearing of new land or reclamation of wasteland. Land also is constantly being enhanced by increasing the number of crops grown per year on each unit of land and by increasing the yield per crop with better farming methods and with chemical fertilizer. Last but not least, land is created anew where there was no land.

There is only one important resource which has shown a trend of increasing scarcity rather than increasing abundance. That resource is the most important of all—human beings. Yes, there are more people on earth now than ever be-

fore. But if we measure the scarcity of people the same way that we measure the scarcity of other economic goods—by how much we must pay to obtain their services—we see that wages and salaries have been going up all over the world, in poor countries as well as in rich countries. The amount that you must pay to obtain the services of a barber or a cook has risen in India, just as the price of a barber or cook—or economist—has risen in the United States over the decades. This increase in the price of peoples' services is a clear indication that people are becoming more scarce even though there are more of us.

About pollution now: Surveys show that the public believes that our air and water have been getting more polluted in recent years. The evidence with respect to air indicates that pollutants have been declining, especially the main pollutant, particulates. (See Figure 3.) With respect to water, the proportion of monitoring sites in the United States with water of good drinkability has increased since the data began in 1961. (See Figure 4.)

Every forecast of the doomsayers has turned out flat wrong. Metals, foods, and other natural resources have become more available rather than more scarce throughout the centuries. The famous Famine 1975 forecast by the Paddock brothers—that we would see millions of famine deaths in the United States on television in the 1970s—was followed instead by gluts in agricultural markets. Paul Ehrlich's primal scream about "What will we do when the [gasoline] pumps run dry?" was followed by gasoline cheaper than since the 1930s. The Great Lakes are not dead; instead they offer better sport fishing than ever. The main pollutants, especially the particulates which have killed people

Figure 3

National Ambient Concentrations of Pollutants

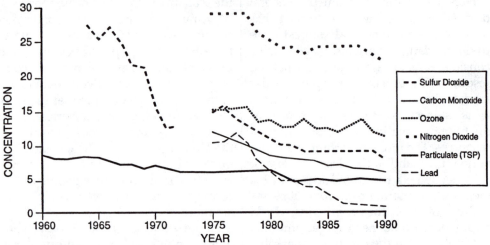

Source: Council on Environmental Quality, Environmental Quality, 22nd Annual Report, 1992, p. 276
Council on Environmental Quality, Environmental Quality 1981, 12th Annual Report, 1981, p. 243
Sulfur 1964 through 1972: EPA (1973): 32 stations

for years, have lessened in our cities. (Socialist countries are a different and tragic environmental story, however!)

... But nothing has reduced the doom-sayers' credibility with the press or their command over the funding resources of the federal government....

With respect to population growth: A dozen competent statistical studies, starting in 1967 with an analysis by Nobel prizewinner Simon Kuznets, agree that there is no negative statistical relationship between economic growth and population growth. There is strong reason to believe that more people have a positive effect in the long run.

Population growth does not lower the standard of living—all the evidence agrees. And the evidence supports the view that population growth raises it in the long run.

Incidentally, it was those statistical studies that converted me in about 1968 from working in favor of population control to the point of view that I hold today. I certainly did not come to my current view for any political or religious or ideological reason.

The basic method is to gather data on each country's rate of population growth and its rate of economic growth, and then to examine whether—looking at all the data in the sample together—the countries with high population growth rates have economic growth rates lower than average, and countries with low population growth rates have economic growth rates higher than average. All the studies agree in concluding that this is not so; there is no correlation between economic growth and population growth in the intermediate run.

Of course one can adduce cases of countries that seemingly are exceptions to the pattern. It is the genius of statistical inference, however, to enable us to

Figure 4

National Ambient Water Quality in Rivers and Streams, 1973–1990

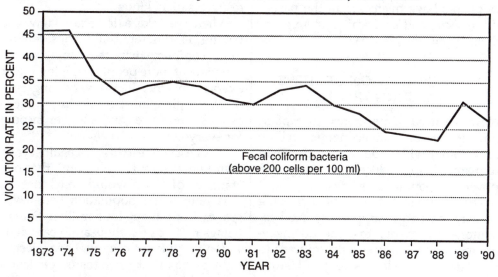

Source: Statistical Abstract of the United States, various issues

draw valid generalizations from samples that contain such wide variations in behavior. The exceptions can be useful in alerting us to possible avenues for further analysis, but as long as they are only exceptions, they do not prove that the generalization is not meaningful or useful.

The research-wise person may wonder whether population density is a more meaningful variable than population growth. And indeed, such studies have been done. And again, the statistical evidence directly contradicts the common-sense conventional wisdom. If you make a chart with population density on the horizontal axis and either the income level or the rate of change of income on the vertical axis, you will see that higher density is associated with better rather than poorer economic results....

The most important benefit of population size and growth is the increase it brings to the stock of useful knowledge. Minds matter economically as much as, or more than, hands or mouths. Progress is limited largely by the availability of trained workers. The more people who enter our population by birth or immigration, the faster will be the rate of progress of our material and cultural civilization.

Here we need a qualification that tends to get overlooked: I do not say that all is well everywhere, and I do not predict that all will be rosy in the future. Children are hungry and sick; people live out lives of physical or intellectual poverty, and lack of opportunity; war or some new pollution may finish us off. What I am saying is that for most relevant economic matters I have checked, the aggregate trends are improving rather than deteriorating.

Also, I don't say that a better future happens automatically or without effort. It will happen because women and men will struggle with problems with muscle and mind, and will probably overcome, as people have overcome in the past—if the social and economic system gives them opportunity to do so.

THE EXPLANATION OF THESE AMAZING TRENDS

Now we need some theory to explain how it can be that economic welfare grows along with population, rather than humanity being reduced to misery and poverty as population grows.

The Malthusian theory of increasing scarcity, based on supposedly-fixed resources—the theory that the doomsayers rely upon—runs exactly contrary to the data over the long sweep of history. Therefore it makes sense to prefer another theory.

The theory that fits the facts very well is this: More people, and increased income, cause problems in the short run. Short-run scarcity raises prices. This presents opportunity, and prompts the search for solutions. In a free society, solutions are eventually found. And in the long run the new developments leave us better off than if the problems had not arisen.

To put it differently, in the short-run, more consumers mean less of the fixed available stock of goods to be divided among more people. And more workers laboring with the same fixed current stock of capital mean that there will be less output per worker. The latter effect, known as "the law of diminishing returns," is the essence of Malthus's theory as he first set it out.

But if the resources with which people work are not fixed over the period being analyzed, then the Malthusian logic of diminishing returns does not apply. And the plain fact is that, given some time

to adjust to shortages, the resource base does not remain fixed. People create more resources of all kinds.

When we take a long-run view, the picture is different, and considerably more complex, than the simple short-run view of more people implying lower average income. In the very long run, more people almost surely imply more available resources and a higher income for everyone.

I suggest you test this idea against your own knowledge: Do you think that our standard of living would be as high as it is now if the population had never grown from about four million human beings perhaps ten thousand years ago? I don't think we'd now have electric light or gas heat or autos or penicillin or travel to the moon or our present life expectancy of over seventy years at birth in rich countries, in comparison to the life expectancy of 20 to 25 years at birth in earlier eras, if population had not grown to its present numbers....

THE ROLE OF ECONOMIC FREEDOM

Here we must address another crucial element in the economics of resources and population—the extent to which the political-social-economic system provides personal freedom from government coercion. Skilled persons require an appropriate social and economic framework that provides incentives for working hard and taking risks, enabling their talents to flower and come to fruition. The key elements of such a framework are economic liberty, respect for property, and fair and sensible rules of the market that are enforced equally for all.

The world's problem is not too many people, but lack of political and economic freedom. Powerful evidence comes from an extraordinary natural experiment that occurred starting in the 1940s with three pairs of countries that have the same culture and history, and had much the same standard of living when they split apart after World War II—East and West Germany, North and South Korea, Taiwan and China. In each case the centrally planned communist country began with less population "pressure," as measured by density per square kilometer, than did the market-directed economy. And the communist and non-communist countries also started with much the same birth rates.

The market-directed economies have performed much better economically than the centrally-planned economies. The economic-political system clearly was the dominant force in the results of the three comparisons. This powerful explanation of economic development cuts the ground from under population growth as a likely explanation of the speed of nations' economic development.

THE ASTOUNDING SHIFT IN SCHOLARLY CONSENSUS

So far we've been discussing the factual evidence. But in 1994 there is an important new element not present twenty years ago. The scientific community of scholars who study population economics now agrees with almost all of what is written above. The statements made above do not represent a single lone voice, but rather the current scientific consensus.

The conclusions offered earlier about agriculture and resources and demographic trends have always represented the consensus of economists in those fields. And ... the consensus of popula-tion economists also is now not far from what is written here.

In 1986, the U.S. National Research Council and the U.S. National Academy of Sciences published a book on population growth and economic development prepared by a prestigious scholarly group. This "official" report reversed almost completely the frightening conclusions of the previous 1971 NAS report. "Population growth [is] at most a minor factor.... The scarcity of exhaustible resources is at most a minor constraint on economic growth," it now says. It found benefits of additional people as well as costs.

A host of review articles by distinguished economic demographers in the past decade have confirmed that this "revisionist" view is indeed consistent with the scientific evidence, though not all the writers would go as far as I do in pointing out the positive long-run effects of population growth. The consensus is more toward a "neutral" judgment. But this is a huge change from the earlier judgment that population growth is economically detrimental.

By 1994, anyone who asserts that population growth damages the economy must either turn a blind eye to the scientific evidence, or be blatantly dishonest intellectually.

SUMMARY AND CONCLUSION

In the short run, all resources are limited. An example of such a finite resource is the amount of time allotted to me to speak. The longer run, however, is a different story. The standard of living has risen along with the size of the world's population since the beginning of recorded time. There is no convincing economic reason why these trends toward a better life should not continue indefinitely.

The key theoretical idea is this: The growth of population and of income create actual and expected shortages, and hence lead to price run-ups. A price increase represents an opportunity that attracts profit-minded entrepreneurs to seek new ways to satisfy the shortages. Some fail, at cost to themselves. A few succeed, and the final result is that we end up better off than if the original shortage problems had never arisen. That is, we need our problems though this does not imply that we should purposely create additional problems for ourselves.

I hope that you will now agree that the long-run outlook is for a more abundant material life rather than for increased scarcity, in the United States and in the world as a whole. Of course such progress does not come about automatically. And my message certainly is not one of complacency. In this I agree with the doomsayers—that our world needs the best efforts of all humanity to improve our lot. I part company with them in that they expect us to come to a bad end despite the efforts we make, whereas I expect a continuation of humanity's history of successful efforts. And I believe that their message is self-fulfilling, because if you expect your efforts to fail because of inexorable natural limits, then you are likely to feel resigned; and therefore to literally resign. But if you recognize the possibility— in fact the probability—of success, you can tap large reservoirs of energy and enthusiasm.

Adding more people causes problems, but people are also the means to solve these problems. The main fuel to speed the world's progress is our stock of knowledge, and the brakes are (a) our lack of imagination and (b) unsound social regulations of these activities. The ultimate resource is people—especially skilled, spirited, and hopeful young people endowed with liberty—who will exert their wills and imaginations for their own benefit, and so inevitably they will benefit not only themselves but the rest of us as well.

REFERENCES

Schultz, Theodore W., "The Declining Economic Importance of Land," *Economic Journal*, LXI, December, 1951, pp. 725–740.

National Research Council, Committee on Population, and Working Group on Population Growth and Economic Development, *Population Growth and Economic Development: Policy Questions* (Washington, D.C.: National Academy Press, 1986).

POSTSCRIPT

Is There a Global Environmental Crisis?

"You can't have your cake and eat it too" is a trite phrase. Such bits of folk wisdom, though, often get to be trite because there is a kernel of truth to them that is worth repeating. The environment is akin to our common cake. People have been consuming it gluttonously during the past century, and that certainly cannot go on any longer. The question is whether or not we have to go on a bread-and-water diet. Also, can we ask the world's less developed countries to forgo cake when the economically developed countries have already consumed so much?

Some, such as French, say we have exceeded the boundaries of responsibility. Simon and other technological optimists contend that we have or can develop the technology to continue our development and enhance the existence of less developed countries while protecting—even improving—the environment.

Even if Simon is correct, it is important not to ignore the costs of sustainable development. Simon does not deny that these exist. Because of population and economic development patterns, the less developed countries require particular care and assistance. It is easy to preach about not cutting down Brazilian rain forests, but what do you say to the poor Brazilian who is trying to scratch out a living by clearing the rain forest for cropland or grazing land? Questions such as this have brought environmental issues much closer to the forefront of world political concerns. See, for example, Stephen Viederman, "Sustainable Development: What It Is and How Do We Get There?" *Current History* (April 1993).

The point is that environmental protection is not cost free. This is because environmentally safe production, consumption, and waste disposal techniques are frequently much more expensive than current processes. The less developed countries have precious few financial resources to devote to developing, constructing, and implementing environmentally safe processes. Therefore, if the changes that need to occur are going to be put in place before further massive environmental degradation occurs, there will have to be a massive flow of expensive technology and financial assistance from the developed to the less developed countries. The EDCs resisted LDC demands for vastly increased aid at the Rio Conference. Based on their perceived economic self-interest, countries watered down the global warming and biodiversity treaties. Some refused to sign one or the other of them. To learn more about UNCED, see James Gustave Speth, "A Post-Rio Compact," *Foreign Policy* (Fall 1992) and the symposium issue "Environment and Development: Rio and After" in the *International Journal* (Autumn 1992).

ISSUE 18

Is the United Nations Advocating Objectionable Policies to Control World Population Growth?

YES: John Paul II, from *International Conference on Population and Development: Letter to President Clinton and Address to Dr. Nafis Sadik* (Vatican City, March 18/19, 1994)

NO: Jessica J. Kulynych, from "Population Control and Women's Rights," An Original Essay Written for This Volume (July 1994)

ISSUE SUMMARY

YES: John Paul II, pontiff of the Roman Catholic Church, charges that the draft document for the United Nations International Conference on Population and Development (ICPD) is disturbing in that it contains concepts and wording that, if pursued and promoted, could cause a moral decline and result in a serious setback for humanity.

NO: Jessica J. Kulynych, a doctoral student in political science at the University of Connecticut and holder of a prestigious American Association of University Women fellowship, replies that the proposals before ICPD empower women and represent an important, necessary, and humane change for population programs.

There is no debate over some of the basic statistics of the world population and its growth. First, on July 11, 1987, the estimated world population hit the 5 billion mark, and by mid-1994 it stood at approximately 5.5 billion. Second, the rate of world population growth has expanded rapidly in this century. It took all of human history, about 14 million years, before the world population reached 1 billion in 1800. Another 130 years passed before the population rose to 2 billion in 1930. Just 30 years then passed before 1960 and 3 billion people. That time span was halved to 15 years when the population reached 4 billion in 1975, and dropped to 12 years for the 5 billion milestone in 1987. If sustained, the annual 1987–1991 increase of 96 million works out to a world population of 6 billion people in October 1997. A 1992 report issued by the UN Population Fund, which Nafis Sadik heads, estimated that in the next 30 years the world population would grow to 8.5 billion. Long-range population projections are difficult, but what the UN describes as a "medium" projection puts the world population at 10 billion in the year 2050.

A third statistical fact is that the population growth is not evenly distributed across the globe. The 1992–2000 projected average annual population increase is 1.5 percent. The regions that mostly include less developed countries (LDCs) are expanding the most rapidly. Sub-Saharan Africa has the highest projected regional annual growth rate at 2.8 percent; and the largely Muslim countries of North Africa and the Middle East have a 2.5 percent rate. China, which contains one-fifth of the world's population is growing at 1 percent annually. By contrast, the annual growth rate of the industrialized, economically developed countries (EDCs) is 0.5 percent, and some of these (such as Germany, Italy, and Spain) are at 0 percent, or what is called replacement rate.

The causes of the still rapidly increasing population are more controversial, but there are hard statistics. The 1992 birthrate (annual live births per 1,000 population) is still high in some parts of the world, with a rate of 44 in sub-Saharan Africa being the highest. This is compared to a rate of 13 in the EDCs. But the rate has declined somewhat, from a world rate of 43 in 1940 to 25 in 1992, and from 47 to 44 for those years in sub-Saharan Africa. Also, ironically, improvements in Third World health standards are exacerbating population growth. The world infant (0–5 years old) mortality rate per 1,000 dropped 38 percent from 97 to 60 between 1970 and 1992. Moreover, those who live through their infancy can expect a longer life. In sub-Saharan Africa, for example, life expectancy at birth improved from 42 to 52 years between 1970 and 1992 as the death rate (per 1,000 population) declined 25 percent from 20 to 15. In sum, the population is growing in significant part because improved health standards mean that fewer people are dying.

Population growth and the causal relationship between poverty and population set the stage for this debate. As of this writing, the ICPD, scheduled to convene in September 1994 in Cairo, Egypt, has not yet been held. The conference will consider the so-called Cairo Document, a draft of which is the document that is the subject of the comments of John Paul II and Jessica Kulynych. According to ICPD secretary-general Sadik, the conference will consider a wide range of matters, including lowering both infant and maternal mortality rates, increasing life expectancy, and increasing educational levels for children. These matters are not controversial, although some will add to population pressures. What is controversial is the Cairo Document's announced goals of enabling contraception to reach a much higher percentage of the world population, of making family planning information services universally accessible, and of eliminating unsafe abortions. John Paul II argues that such measure are objectionable on a number of grounds and that they deny the human right of people to procreate and of unborn infants to live. The pontiff favors development as a better way to foster natural population control. Jessica Kulynych argues that the Cairo Document is moving in the right direction because a truly effective and nondiscriminatory population program must change the focus of population policy by including broad reproductive rights for women as an integral part of the effort.

YES

John Paul II

ADDRESS OF POPE JOHN PAUL II

LETTER TO PRESIDENT CLINTON

The draft document for next September's International Conference on Population and Development in Cairo, Egypt, is "a disturbing surprise," Pope John Paul II said in a March 19 [1994] letter sent to President Clinton. The letter was released April 5 by the U.S. Embassy to the Vatican. In his "urbi et orbi" Easter message May 4, the pope said he was "sending a letter to all the world's heads of state on the occasion of the International Year of the Family" asking "that every effort be made to ensure that the value of the human person is not diminished." Here is the text of the letter Clinton received.

The international community recently began its celebration of the International Year of the Family, a timely initiative promoted by the United Nations.

The International Conference on Population and Development, also organized by the United Nations and to be held in Cairo in September 1994, likewise represents one of the important events of this year. International leaders will thus have an opportunity to reconsider the reflections and commitments of the previous conferences on these themes held in Bucharest (1974) and Mexico City (1984). But public opinion is especially looking to the Cairo meeting for guidelines for the future, conscious as it is of the important matters everyone clearly recognizes to be at stake, including the well-being and development of peoples, the growth of world population, the rise of the median age in some industrialized countries, the fight against disease and the forced displacement of whole peoples.

The Holy See [the see of the Pope; "see" being a seat of a bishops's office, power, or authority], in conformity with its mission and using the means at its disposal, willingly associates itself with all these efforts to serve the human family throughout the world. Last Dec. 26, the Catholic Church also inaugurated a "Year of the Family" for the purpose of encouraging all the faithful to engage in a deeper spiritual and moral reflection on this human reality, fundamental to the lives of both individuals and societies.

From John Paul II, *International Conference on Population and Development: Letter to President Clinton and Address to Dr. Nafis Sadik* (Vatican City, March 18/19, 1994). Copies available from Permanent Observer Mission of the Holy See to the United Nations.

I myself decided to address all families personally by writing them a letter. It restates the fact that every human being is "called to live in truth and in love" (No. 16), and that the family unit continues to be the "school of life" where the tensions between independence and communion, unity and diversity are lived out on a unique and primary level. It is in the family, I believe, that we find a human resource which produces the best creative energies of the social fabric. This is something which every state ought carefully to safeguard. Without infringing on the autonomy of a reality which they can neither produce nor replace, civil authorities have a duty, in effect, to strive to promote the harmonious growth of the family, not only from the point of view of its social vitality but also from that of its moral and spiritual health.

This is why the draft of the final document of the forthcoming Cairo conference was of particular interest to me. I found it a disturbing surprise.

The innovations which it contains, on the level both of concepts and wording, make this text a very different one from the documents of the conferences of Bucharest and Mexico City. There is reason to fear that it could cause a moral decline resulting in a serious setback for humanity, one in which man himself would be the first victim.

One notes, for example, that the theme of development, on the agenda of the Cairo meeting, including the very complex issue of the relationship between population and development, which ought to be at the center of the discussion, is almost completely overlooked, so few are the pages devoted to it. The only response to the population issue and to the urgent need for an integral development of the person and of societies seems to be reduced to the promotion of a lifestyle the consequences of which, were it accepted as a model and plan of action for the future, could prove particularly negative. The leaders of the nations owe it to themselves to reflect deeply and in conscience on this aspect of the matter.

Furthermore, the idea of sexuality underlying this text is totally individualistic, to such an extent that marriage now appears as something outmoded. An institution as natural, fundamental and universal as the family cannot be manipulated by anyone.

Who could give such a mandate to individuals or institutions? The family is part of the heritage of humanity! Moreover, the Universal Declaration of Human Rights clearly states that the family is "the natural and fundamental group unit of society" (Art 16.3). The International Year of the Family should therefore be a special occasion for society and the state to grant the family the protection which the universal declaration recognizes it should have. Anything less would be a betrayal of the noblest ideals of the United Nations. Even more serious are the numerous proposals for a general international recognition of a completely unrestricted right to abortion: This goes well beyond what is already unfortunately permitted by the legislation of certain nations.

Indeed, reading this document—which, granted, is only a draft—leaves the troubling impression of something being imposed: namely a lifestyle typical of certain fringes within developed societies, societies which are materially rich and secularized. Are countries more sensitive to the values of nature, morality and religion going to accept such a vision of man and society without protest?

As we look toward the year 2000, how can we fail to think of the young? What is being held up to them? A society of "things" and not of "persons." The right to do as they will from their earliest years, without any constraint, provided it is "safe." The unreserved gift of self, mastery of one's instincts, the sense of responsibility—these are notions considered as belonging to another age. One would have liked, for example, to find in these pages some attention to the conscience and to respect for cultural and ethical values which inspire other ways of looking at life. We may well fear that tomorrow those same people, once they have reached adulthood, will demand an explanation from today's leaders for having deprived them of reasons for living because they failed to teach them the duties incumbent upon being endowed with intelligence and free will.

In writing to you, I have not only wished to share my deep concern about the draft of a document. Above all I have wished to draw your attention to the serious challenges which need to be faced by those taking part in the Cairo conference. Questions as important as the transmission of life, the family, the material and moral development of societies: All these undoubtedly call for deeper reflection.

That is why I am appealing to you, who are concerned for the good of your own people and of all humanity. It is very important not to weaken man, his sense of the sacredness of life, his capacity for love and self-sacrifice. Here we are speaking of sensitive issues, issues upon which our societies stand or fall....

* * *

[On March 19, 1994, Pope John Paul II sent a letter to President Clinton about the International Conference on Population and Development. The day before, on March 18, John Paul II released an address to Dr. Nafis Sadik, the Secretary General of the Conference and the Executive Director of the United Nations Population Fund. In it, he covers in greater detail arguments against the approach to global population issues planned by the conference. Here is the text of the address to Dr. Sadik.—Ed.]

ADDRESS TO DR. NAFIS SADIK

I greet you, Madam Secretary General, at a time when you are closely involved in preparing the 1994 International Conference on Population and Development, to be held in Cairo in September. Your visit provides an occasion for me to share with you some thoughts on a topic which, we all agree, is of vital importance for the *well-being and progress of the human family.* The theme of the Cairo Conference takes on a heightened significance in the light of the fact that the gap between the rich and the poor of the world continues to widen, a situation which poses an ever increasing threat to the peace for which mankind longs.

The global population situation is very complex: there are variations not simply from continent to continent but even from one region to another. United Nations studies tell us that a rapid decrease in the global rate of population growth is expected to begin during the 1990s and carry on into the new century. At the same time, growth rates remain high in some of the least developed nations of the world, while population growth has declined appreciably in the industrialized developed nations.

Basic Ethical Principles

The Holy See has carefully followed these matters, with a special concern to make accurate and objective assessments of population issues and to urge global solidarity in regard to development strategies, especially as they affect the developing nations of the world. In this we have derived benefit from participation in the meetings of the United Nations Population Commission and from the studies of the United Nations Population Division. The Holy See has also participated in all the regional preparatory meetings of the Cairo Conference, gaining a better understanding of regional differences and contributing to the discussion on each occasion.

In accordance with its specific competence and mission, the Holy See is concerned that proper attention should be given to *the ethical principles* determining actions taken in response to the demographic, sociological and public policy analyses of the data on population trends. Therefore, the Holy See seeks to focus attention on certain *basic truths:* that each and every person—regardless of age, sex, religion or national background—has a dignity and worth that is unconditional and inalienable; that human life itself from conception to natural death is sacred; that human rights are innate and transcend any constitutional order; and that the fundamental unity of the human race demands that everyone be committed to building a community which is free from injustice and which strives to promote and protect the common good. These truths about the human person are the measure of any response to the findings which emerge from the consideration of demographic data. It is in the light of authentic human values —recognized by peoples of diverse cultures, religious and national backgrounds across the globe—that all policy choices must be evaluated. No goal or policy will bring positive results for people if it does not respect the unique dignity and objective needs of those same people.

Human Development and the Family

There is widespread agreement that a population policy is only one part of an overall development strategy. Accordingly, it is important that any discussion of population policies should keep in mind the actual and projected development of nations and regions. At the same time, it is impossible to leave out of account the very nature of what is meant by the term "development." All development worthy of the name must be integral, that is, it must be directed to the true good of every person and of the whole person. True development cannot consist in the simple accumulation of wealth and in the greater availability of goods and services, but must be pursued with due consideration for the social, cultural and spiritual dimensions of the human being. Development programs must be built on justice and equality, enabling people to live in dignity, harmony and peace. They must respect the cultural heritage of peoples and nations, and those social qualities and virtues that reflect the God-given dignity of each and every person and the divine plan which calls all persons to unity. Importantly, men and women must be active agents of their own development, for to treat them as mere objects in some scheme or plan would be to stifle that capacity for freedom and responsibility which is fundamental to the good of the human person.

Development has been and remains the proper contest for the international community's consideration of population issues. Within such discussions there naturally arise questions relating to the transmission and nurturing of human life. But to formulate population issues in terms of individual "sexual and reproductive rights," or even in terms of "women's rights" is to change the focus which should be the proper concern of governments and international agencies. I say this without in any way wishing to reduce the importance of securing justice and equity for women.

Moreover, questions involving the transmission of life and its subsequent nurturing cannot be adequately dealt with except in relation to *the good of the family:* that communion of persons established by the marriage of husband and wife, which is—as the *Universal Declaration of Human Rights* affirms—"the natural and fundamental group unit of society" (Art. 16.3). The family is an institution founded upon the very nature of the human person, and it is the proper setting for the conception, birth and upbringing of children. At this moment in history, when so many powerful forces are arrayed against the family, it is more important than ever that the Conference on Population and Development should respond to the challenge implicit in the United Nations' designation of 1994 as the "International Year of the Family" by doing everything within its power to ensure that the family receives from "society and the State" that protection to which the same *Universal Declaration* says it is "entitled" (*ibid*). Anything less would be a betrayal of the noblest ideals of the United Nations.

Responsible Parenthood

Today, the duty to safeguard the family demands that particular attention be given to securing for husband and wife the liberty to decide responsibly, free from all social or legal coercion, the number of children they will have and the spacing of their births. It should not be the intent of governments or other agencies to decide for couples but, rather, to create the social conditions which will enable them to make appropriate decisions in the light of their responsibilities.... What the Church calls *"responsible parenthood"* is not a question of unlimited procreation or lack of awareness of what is involved in rearing children, but rather the empowerment of couples to use their inviolable liberty wisely and responsibly, taking into account social and demographic realities as well as their own situation and legitimate desires, in the light of objective moral criteria. All propaganda and misinformation directed at persuading couples that they must limit their family to one or two children should be steadfastly avoided, and couples that generously choose to have large families are to be supported.

In defense of the human person, the Church stands opposed to the imposition of limits on family size, and to the promotion of methods of limiting births which separate the unitive and procreative dimensions of marital intercourse, which are contrary to the moral law inscribed in the human heart, or which constitute an assault on the sacredness of life. Thus, sterilization, which is more and more promoted as a method of family planning, because of its finality and its potential for the violation of human rights, especially of women, is clearly unacceptable; it poses a most grave threat to human dignity and liberty when promoted as part of a population policy. Abortion, which destroys existing human life, is a heinous evil, and it is never an acceptable method of family planning, as was recognized by consensus at the Mexico City United Nations International Conference on Population (1984).

To summarize, I wish to emphasize once again what I have written in the Encyclical *Centesimus Annus:* "It is necessary to go back to seeing the family as the sanctuary of life.... In the face of the so-called culture of death, the family is the heart of the culture of life. Human ingenuity seems to be directed more towards limiting, suppressing or destroying the sources of life—including recourse to abortion, which unfortunately is so widespread in the world—than toward defending and opening up the possibility of life" (No. 39).

Status of Women and Children

As well as reaffirming the fundamental role of the family in society, I wish to draw special attention to *the status of children and women,* who all too often find themselves the most vulnerable members of our communities. Children must not be treated as a burden or inconvenience, but should be cherished as bearers of hope and signs of promise for the future. The care which is essential for their growth and nurture comes primarily from their parents, but society must help by sustaining the family in its needs and in its efforts to maintain the caring environment in which children can develop. Society ought to promote "social policies which have the family as their principal object, policies which assist the family by providing adequate resources and efficient means of support, both for bringing up children and for

looking after the elderly, so as to avoid distancing the latter from the family unit and in order to strengthen relations between generations" (*Centesimus Annus,* 49). A society cannot say that it is treating children justly or protecting their interests if its laws do not safeguard their rights and respect the responsibility of parents for their well-being.

It is a sad reflection on the human condition that still today, at the end of the twentieth century, it is necessary to affirm that *every woman* is equal in dignity to man, and a full member of the human family, within which she has a distinctive place and vocation that is complementary to but in no way less valuable than man's. In much of the world, much still has to be done to meet the educational and health needs of girls and young women so that they may achieve their full potential in society.

In the family which a woman establishes with her husband she enjoys the unique role and privilege of motherhood. In a special way it belongs to her to nurture the new life of the child from the moment of conception. The mother in particular enwraps the newborn child in love and security, and creates the environment for its growth and development. Society should not allow woman's maternal role to be demeaned, or count it as of little value in comparison with other possibilities. Greater consideration should be given to *the social role of mothers,* and support should be given to programs which aim at decreasing maternal mortality, providing prenatal and perinatal care, meeting the nutritional needs of pregnant women and nursing mothers, and helping mothers themselves to provide preventive health care of their infants. In this regard attention should be given to the positive benefits of breastfeeding for nourishment and disease prevention in infants, as well as for maternal bonding and birth-spacing.

Valid Implications of Population Growth

The study of population and development inevitably poses the question of *the environmental implications of population growth. The ecological issue too is fundamentally a moral one.* While population growth is often blamed for environmental problems, we know that the matter is more complex. Patterns of consumption and waste, especially in developed nations, depletion of natural resources, the absence of restrictions or safeguards in some industrial or production processes, all endanger the natural environment.

The Cairo Conference will also want to give due attention to morbidity and mortality, and to the need to eliminate life-threatening diseases of every sort. While advances have been made that have resulted in an increased life span, policies must also provide for the elderly and for the contribution that they make to society in their retirement years. Society should develop policies to meet their needs for social security, health care and active participation in the life of their community.

Migration is likewise a major concern in examining demographic data and the international community needs to ensure that the rights of migrants are recognized and protected. In this regard I draw special attention to the situation of migrant families. The State's task is to ensure that immigrant families do not lack what it ordinarily guarantees its own citizens, as well as to protect them from any attempt at marginalization, intolerance or racism, and to promote an attitude of convinced and active solidarity in their regard (cf. *Message for World Migration Day*, 1993–94, No. 1).

Moral Significance of Conference Issues

As the preparations for the *Cairo Conference* proceed, I wish to assure you, Madam Secretary General, that the Holy See is fully aware of the complexity of the issues involved. This very complexity requires that we carefully weigh the consequences for the present and future generations of the strategies and recommendations to be proposed. In this context, the draft final document of the Cairo Conference, which is already being circulated, is a cause of grave concern to me. Many of the principles which I have just mentioned find no place in its pages, or are totally marginalized. Indeed, certain basic ethical principles are contradicted by its proposals. Political or ideological considerations cannot be, by themselves, the basis on which essential decisions for the future of our society are founded. What is at stake here is the very future of humanity. *Fundamental questions* like the transmission of life, the family, and the material and moral development of society, *need very serious consideration.*

For example, the international consensus of the 1984 Mexico City International Conference on Population that "in no case should abortion be promoted as a method of family planning" is completely ignored in the draft document. Indeed, there is a tendency to promote an internationally recognized right to access to abortion on demand, without any restriction, *with no regard to the rights of the unborn,* in a manner which goes beyond what even now is unfortunately accepted by the laws of some nations. The vision of sexuality which inspires the document is individualistic. Marriage is ignored, as if it were something of the past. An institution as natural, universal and fundamental as the family cannot be manipulated without causing serious damage to the fabric and stability of society.

The seriousness of the challenges that governments and, above all, parents must face in the education of the younger generation means that we cannot abdicate our responsibility of leading young people to a deeper understanding of their own dignity and potentiality as persons. What future do we propose to adolescents if we leave them, in their immaturity, to follow their instincts without taking into consideration the interpersonal and moral implications of their sexual behavior? Do we not have an obligation to open their eyes to the damage and suffering to which morally irresponsible sexual behavior can lead them? Is it not our task to challenge them with a demanding ethic which fully respects their dignity and which leads them to that self-control which is needed in order to face the many demands of life?

I am sure, Madam Secretary General, that, in the remaining period of preparation for the Cairo Conference, you and your collaborators, as well as the nations which will take part in the conference itself, will devote adequate attention to these deeper questions.

None of the issues to be discussed is simply an economic or demographic concern, but, at root, each is a matter of profound moral significance, with far-reaching implications. Accordingly, the Holy See's contribution will consist in providing an ethical perspective on the issues to be considered.

NO

Jessica J. Kulynych

POPULATION CONTROL
AND WOMEN'S RIGHTS

For more than a decade international coalitions of women's organizations have been working patiently to redefine the focus of population policy. These efforts have culminated in widespread support among United Nations member states, population experts, and women's organizations for a radically new approach to population control that is premised on empowering women. This approach, which is described in the United Nations proposal for population policy, represents an important, necessary, and humane change of direction for population programs.

TWO TRADITIONAL APPROACHES TO POPULATION CONTROL

Until now, the population debate had crystallized around two positions; the contraception approach and the development approach. The contraception approach to population control assumed that controlling fertility in countries with high birth rates was the key to slowing population growth. These early population programs concentrated primarily on the widespread distribution of female birth control methods, and on the development of predominantly female sterilization programs. On the other hand, advocates of the development approach argued that population growth would stabilize as economic development improved, and those who endorsed this approach suggested that the United Nations should focus its efforts on increasing the economic prosperity of less developed countries. However, as feminist scholars, development workers, and women's organizations worldwide have pointed out, both of these approaches to population control discriminate against women. Approximately half the world's population is female. Yet for too long population control efforts have treated women merely as a means to achieving population goals.

The contraceptive approach, although somewhat successful in slowing population growth, typically employed top-down family planning programs that placed control in the hands of bureaucrats and medical experts, who were inclined to treat women as problems to be solved rather than independent actors. Contraception-centered efforts were targeted predominantly at women in less developed countries, and often resulted in forced or manipulated sterilizations, coerced abortions, and the misuse or disuse of contraceptive devises. Often the women targeted for these contraceptive programs were not provided with accurate or complete information on the side effects of the oral contraceptives or intrauterine devices [IUDS] with which they were provided. Others were encouraged by international organizations, such as the World Health Organization, to receive the injectable hormone contraceptive Depo-Provera, which was considered a health hazard and was not approved as a contraceptive in industrialized countries such as the United States.[1]

The sterilization programs undertaken in Bangladesh in the early 1980s are a frightening example of the dangers of the contraceptive-centered approach. The forms of coercion used on women in Bangladesh ranged from compulsory sterilizations organized by the military to more subtle "incentives" for voluntary sterilization. Such incentives included the withholding of "emergency food aid provided by the U.N. World Food Program" and the provision of "compensation payments" of money and clothing in return for sterilization.[2] Apart from their coercive nature, these contraceptive efforts fell short primarily because they attempted to control women's fertility without "examining the social conditions which structure their [women's] behavior."[3]

Similarly, the development approach also discriminated against women. Economic development programs, unlike contraceptive programs, were targeted primarily at men. Modern tools and farming methods, for example, were provided to men, ignoring the economic activities of millions of the world's women. In many developing countries, women who had previously had significant control over agricultural production were ignored as agents of modernization by world development agencies. The loss of traditional spheres of power and autonomy resulted in a reduction in women's status that ultimately hindered population control efforts. The development approach fatally underestimated the relationship between women's status in society and population growth.

REDEFINING REPRODUCTIVE RIGHTS: THE NEW APPROACH

A truly effective and nondiscriminatory population program must change the focus of population policy by including broad reproductive rights as an integral part of population control. The U.N. "Program of Action" for population policy expands the definition of reproductive rights to include expanded health services for women as well as a substantial investment in furthering women's political and legal rights. Accordingly, population programs, as advocated in the U.N. proposal, should include preventive gynecological care, prenatal care, child immunizations, counseling about sexually transmitted diseases and birth control, and broadly available contraceptives, including safe and legal abortion services.[4] These health services should be accompanied by a commitment to furthering women's educational opportunities, legal rights to property ownership and divorce, and their representation in positions of political power. The 1994 U.N. draft proposal for population policy is a crucial first step toward achieving effective and just population control.

The arguments for changing the focus of population policy fall into two categories: (1) ethical, human rights arguments; and (2) instrumental, pragmatic arguments. On the one hand, furthering the basic human rights of half the world's population is one of the fundamental responsibilities of the United Nations. The new population proposal is a step toward achieving this goal. On the other hand, the pragmatic goal of controlling population cannot be achieved without the proposed change in focus. Development concerns cannot be separated from issues of reproductive freedom. Without improving women's status worldwide, population efforts will fall on deaf ears.

REPRODUCTIVE RIGHTS AS HUMAN RIGHTS: THE ETHICAL ARGUMENTS

Security of Person

In 1948 the United Nations adopted the Universal Declaration of Human Rights. This declaration committed the United Nations to the "promotion of universal respect for and observance of human rights and fundamental freedoms."[5] Included in these rights are the right to "life, liberty, and security of person."[6] In order for women to enjoy "life, liberty, and security of person", they must be able to make autonomous decisions, especially over choices involving the use of their own bodies. The right to security of person guarantees all humans the right not to have their physical bodies violated or used without their consent, as occurs in cases of rape and torture. Yet women's bodies have been routinely violated by coerced sterilizations, misused contraceptives, and unwanted pregnancies. In all of these cases women have

had parts of their bodies destroyed, removed, or utilized in ways they did not desire. Women, as much as anyone else, have a fundamental right to control their own destiny. They cannot do that unless they have the right to control their own bodies.

Women are still the world's childbearers. This simple fact means that "the advantages and disadvantages—as well as the benefits and risks associated with reproduction and its prevention—do not accrue equally to both sexes."[7] The risks and costs of reproduction for women are expansive. The risks differ across the world, but in all cases they constitute a significant burden. In less developed countries, where women are often chronically tired, malnourished, and underweight, pregnancy can easily become a serious health hazard. The "complications of pregnancy account for between 10 and 30 percent of all deaths of women of reproductive age in areas of Asia, Africa, and Latin America."[8] Even in industrialized countries, where the immediate physical risks of pregnancy are diminished, women bear the economic costs of lost work time and reduced earning potential. So-called corporate mommy tracks steer women into career positions with less opportunity for advancement, creating an economic "glass ceiling" for mothers. Additionally, pregnant women and mothers face subtle forms of discrimination when they are harassed for nursing in public or refused service when they order a drink. Women worldwide also bear the social stigma of illegitimacy and child welfare support, and the emotional costs of injury or death to the child. And, in most cases, women retain primary responsibility for childcare even in the face of divorce or abandonment. Given this expan-

sive set of risks that accompany reproduction, it is imperative that women be
granted the fundamental right to decide
for themselves whether or not to take on
these risks. In practice, this right means
that women must not be forced to become pregnant, forced to continue a pregnancy, or forced to end a pregnancy. In no
other situation do we expect a person to
"give or lend his/her body or parts of it
for another's use" without their "uncoerced consent."[9] Unless women are given
the right to make uncoerced decisions regarding reproduction they cannot and do
not enjoy the security of person guaranteed in the U.N. Universal Declaration of
Human Rights.

Equality
Women are also guaranteed a fundamental human right to political equality.[10]
But political equality cannot be separated from economic and marital equality. When women are no longer legally or
economically subject to their husband's
control, they can more freely assert their
political opinions and interests. Reproductive control is an important step toward achieving equality for women for
a number of reasons. First, reproductive
control separates sex from reproduction.
Effective contraception, including safe,
legal, and accessible abortion, enables
women to choose when to have children.
Women who have access to reproductive
control can choose marriage more freely,
without being forced to marry in order to
avoid the economic deprivation or societal consequences of bearing a child out of
wedlock. Indeed, reproductive control is
a necessary condition for free and equal
marriages. Second, reproductive control
can also reduce economic dependence.
In the industrialized world, women who
can plan their pregnancies can more eas-

ily enter the workforce as equals to men,
plan for career advancement, and postpone pregnancy until they are more fi-
nancially secure. Similarly, women in
developing countries, who often begin
reproducing in their teens, can postpone
having a child until they have an education and a means of financial support. Although equal employment opportunities
and equal educational opportunities are
conditions for economic independence,
reproductive control is also a crucial element, and one without which women
can never achieve the economic independence necessary for political equality.

Critics of reproductive freedom argue
that marriage is a private, cultural institution that should be free from the dictates
of the United Nations. This argument is
doubly flawed. On the one hand, preserving the sanctity of marriage does not benefit women and men equally; rather, it often serves merely to preserve male power.
The presumption that families and marriages are private institutions has often
been used as the justification for society to
ignore domestic violence, especially marital rape, spousal abuse, and child abuse.
Law enforcement officers and judges
have used the sanctity of the home as
explanation for their reluctance to intervene in domestic disputes. Similarly,
practices such as bride burning, female
infanticide, and genital mutilation have
been justified because they are part of
various countries' cultural traditions and,
therefore, to object, to urge "western" notions of women on these countries, is a
form of cultural imperialism. But arguments against cultural imperialism and
preserving "family values" crumble in
the face of the significant data that has
been gathered which indicates a desire
for reproductive freedom and contraceptive education on the part of women

worldwide. The World Fertility study indicated that "nearly half the women questioned wanted no more children, and that younger women especially tended to desire a smaller family."[11] Additionally, interviews with women worldwide indicate a widespread desire for information on safe and effective family planning.[12] According to Dr. Nafis Sadik, the secretary general of the U.N. population conference, "we have to realize that in many parts of the world, women want [birth control] methods they can hide from their husbands and families. Many of them are desperate, saying, 'Can't you give me an injection, or a pill, because I don't want to be pregnant again.' "[13] Advocating reproductive freedom looks like cultural imperialism if we listen only to the voices of men.

Democracy

A population policy that emphasizes reproductive freedom is also an important part of furthering women's equality generally. The draft proposal created by the U.N. reflects the principles of democracy. This proposal represents the first time women from all parts of the world have participated significantly in the creation of population policy. Although women still make up only a minority of the delegates responsible for the draft, women's organizations, such as the International Women's Health Coalition, were the force behind the new proposal. The substantial contribution of women worldwide to this population plan reflects a central principle of democracy: representation. As Martin Luther King, Jr., wrote from his Alabama jail cell, any law that is "inflicted" upon a group who "had no part in enacting or creating [it]" is an "unjust" law.[14] Since population policies have been targeted directly at con-

trolling women's fertility, the absence of women from the decision-making process violates the principle of representation. Denying women input into policies directed primarily at them results in unjust and undemocratic population policy. Who is better able to judge what is in the interest of women than women themselves? The resounding voices of women echoing in this proposal are, by themselves, enough to justify its adoption.

EFFECTIVE POPULATION CONTROL: THE PRAGMATIC ARGUMENTS

As political theorists Mary Wollstonecraft and J. S. Mill so clearly recognized, arguments about the moral imperative for women's rights often fall on deaf ears unless those changes can be shown to have practical use as well. Wollstonecraft, an eighteenth-century British theorist and author of *A Vindication of the Rights of Woman,* and Mill, a nineteenth-century British theorist and author of *The Subjection of Woman,* were two early proponents of women's suffrage, and their writings have had a profound effect on how society views women. Both these theorists argued that not only was it a matter of principle and a necessary right to grant women the right to vote, but also that women's participation would be beneficial for all of humankind. The relationship between reproductive freedom, gender equality, and population control is also a positive one. The new approach to population policy is ethically correct, and it is also the best way to achieve population goals. Neither the contraceptive approach nor the development approach can, by themselves, significantly curb world population growth. Improving women's status generally is the only way to effectively achieve population control.

Contraception Is Not Enough

The U.N. proposal is a departure from both the contraception-centered and the development-centered approaches to population policy. Attempts to control women's fertility through contraception, though somewhat effective, cannot really succeed without improving women's status through a broad reproductive health policy that provides expansive reproductive freedom and education. To begin with, women can hardly be expected to make responsible reproductive decisions without adequate information on the benefits and risks of pregnancy and the high costs of soaring birthrates. Educating women on all aspects of reproduction, not just handing them contraceptives or encouraging sterilization procedures that they do not understand, will enable women to make autonomous and responsible decisions.

Second, women, who have significantly less power than men worldwide, often do not have the power to use contraceptives or to refuse sexual relations with their husbands or mates. Critics of female reproductive control, who talk about "marital" decisions regarding procreation, ignore the power inequities within many marriages, and thereby perpetuate women's low status. "Marital" decisions are often male decisions, a fact that is particularly insidious when most of the risks of those decisions are born almost exclusively by women. Women are routinely physically coerced into reproduction. Domestic violence is epidemic in many countries across the globe. Women who fear for their lives are in no position to discuss abstinence or birth control as equal partners with their husbands.

For example, providing women with condoms is of little use when they have no power to make men use them. As long as women remain second-class citizens, efforts to get women to change their reproductive behavior, which will impact global population rates, will remain futile.

Additionally, in many societies, women depend on children, especially male children, for economic survival. As long as economic opportunities are severely limited for women, and the loss of a husband results in severe poverty, women will be forced to ensure their economic survival through producing children who can contribute labor power to the family, and provide care for aging parents. Obviously, broader social changes will be necessary to completely equalize status, but the U.N. focus on reproductive freedom is an important first step. The U.N. proposal addresses the issue of the low status of women by making an international commitment to reproductive freedom and the advancement of political and legal rights for women. The guarantee of a sphere of reproductive control for women sets an important example, and raises the status of women to the level of international concern.

Development Is Not Enough

The U.N. proposal also departs from the pure development approach to population control. According to development theory, since high birthrates are often necessitated by economic considerations, such as the need for labor power, increasing prosperity will reduce the impetus for large families. Critics of the United Nations focus on reproductive freedom argue that issues of development are separate from reproductive rights issues. However, when it comes to controlling population, the two sets of issues cannot be separated. Economic development cannot by itself control population. Some wealthy countries, Arab nations for example, have high birth rates, while other, extremely poor nations, such as Indonesia, parts of India, and Bangladesh, have successfully reduced population growth. In these cases it would appear that other factors, such as contraceptive programs, the status of women and their level of education, have a more determining effect than economic prosperity alone. According to the U.N. population fund, countries with high literacy rates and a large percentage of women with formal schooling tend to have significantly lower infant mortality rates and lower fertility. This theory is born out in the state of Kerala in India, which boasts a female literacy rate much higher than the rest of India, and a much lower fertility rate. As the U.N. proposal states, "economic growth and improvement of quality of life have been fastest in those areas where women have higher status, and slowest where they face the greatest disadvantages." Economic prosperity must be accompanied by a recognition of the value of women in society. Women who are considered assets to society, not only for their wombs but also for their skills and intellects, are the real key to population control.

CONCLUSIONS

The dilemmas of global population control are real and often overwhelming. The United Nations has presented us with a glimpse into the future of population control, and that future does give reason for optimism. A broad-based approach to population control that includes an expansive definition of reproductive freedom and a commitment to improving women's status through education and investment in women's political and legal rights is the best approach to population control, both ethically and practically. The current draft proposal works to fulfill the United Nations's obligation both to protect human rights and to address a very real population dilemma. The U.N. "Program for Action" reflects the goal of women's empowerment. The proposal moves beyond insular development and contraceptive approaches to one that is broad-based to a policy that integrates concerns for reproductive health, economic and political opportunities, and educational improvements. This program, which is a comprehensive population strategy, makes important linkages between development, democratization, and population control. For the first time, women are the subjects and not just the objects of population policy. Women across the world have demanded recognition of their fundamental right to control their own destiny. And they have done so in a way that advances the cause of population control. With so much to gain, a renewed and revitalized U.N. population policy should be a cause for support, not for strife and disunity.

NOTES

1. Betsy Hartmann describes the failings of contraceptive programs in detail in *Reproductive Rights and Wrongs: The Global Politics of Population Control and Contraceptive Choice* (New York: Harper & Row, 1987), pp. 186–196.

2. Ibid., pp. 214, 218.

3. Sandra Schwartz Tangri, "A Feminist Perspective on Some Ethical Issues in Population Programs," *Signs* 1, 4 (Summer 1976): 903.

4. The U.N. draft proposal deals delicately with the issue of abortion, stressing attempts to prevent the need for abortion, but carefully preserving freedom of choice.

5. *Universal Declaration of Human Rights,* preamble.

6. *Universal Declaration of Human Rights,* Article 3, Article 16.

7. For this argument I draw heavily on Sandra Tangri's "A Feminist Perspective on Some Ethical Issues in Population Programs," pp. 896–897.

8. Hartmann, *Reproductive Rights and Wrongs,* p. 46.

9. Ibid.

10. *Universal Declaration of Human Rights.*

11. Hartmann, *Reproductive Rights and Wrongs,* p. 45.

12. Ibid., p. 46.

13. "Still Ticking," *Mother Jones* 18, 4 (Mar/Apr 1993), pp. 70–71.

14. Martin Luther King, Jr. "Letter From a Birmingham City Jail."

POSTSCRIPT

Is the United Nations Advocating Objectionable Policies to Control World Population Growth?

Is the world population growing rapidly? Yes. Is this a problem for less developed countries? Yes. Are population and poverty related? Yes. John Paul II, Jessica Kulynych, Nafis Sadik, and virtually everyone else agree on these points.

Beyond these points of consensus, the population issues become much more controversial. In the debate on the environment, Julian Simon argues that population growth provides expanding human resources and that fears of a population-glutted world are unfounded. Population optimists like Simon can cite the high standards of living in densely populated countries such as Japan and the Netherlands as proof of this point. And they are correct that if Chad achieved an economic vitality equal to that of Japan, many of its population problems would be lessened. The living conditions of Chad's people would certainly be better and various socioeconomic factors would almost certainly cause a decline in the fertility rate.

There are some problems with this line of thought, however. One has to do with the prospects for development. At best, it will take a very long time, even under optimal conditions, for many LDCs to approach the development levels of Japan or the Netherlands, and in the meantime, LDC population continues to rocket upwards. It may even be that, given resource availability and other factors, some LDCs will never become fully developed.

Even if we could agree that there needs to be a sharp decline in population growth, methods for bringing about a decline are controversial. Economic development, contraceptive education, and such methods are worthwhile, but they take time. Then there is the issue of abortion, and many who object to abortion, including the pope, believe that the United Nations should not promote programs that are either immoral or that violate the religious or ethical standards of many people. If women have a reproductive right to an abortion, for example, then are countries that ban such procedures, such as some Muslim countries, in violation of women's rights? If so, should the world impose sanctions on them until they change their policies? Which rights are inviolate and should be enforced by international action? Which are discretionary? Should the UN be making these choices?

Those who worry about an emphasis on contraception, abortion, and other medical/technical methods of population control are also concerned that there will be increasing pressure on couples not to have children. These pressures might even include sanctions, such as tax disincentives or fines, as have been utilized in China. Another concern is this: Where does society draw the line between encouraging having fewer children and using social or legal coercion to achieve that goal through enforced sterilization, mandatory abortions, and other procedures? There have been charges (and denials) that such practices have occurred in China.

There are several sources to consult for recent information and views on the population issue. The most current source of statistics is the most current edition of *The State of World Population* (United Nations Population Fund, published annually). Also see such monthly journals as *Population Today*. For a view that the world is at a crucial juncture in its population and efforts to control it, read Sharon L. Camp, "Population: The Critical Decade," *Foreign Policy* (Spring 1993).

ISSUE 19

Is Self-Determination a Right of All Nationalities?

YES: Michael Lind, from "In Defense of Liberal Nationalism," *Foreign Affairs* (May/June 1994)

NO: Amitai Etzioni, from "The Evils of Self-Determination," *Foreign Policy* (Winter 1992/1993)

ISSUE SUMMARY

YES: Michael Lind, executive editor of *The National Interest*, writes that nationalism, "the idea that every nation should have its own state," is the most powerful idea in the contemporary world. Prejudice against nationalism is a mistake, he argues; for practical, strategic reasons, and for reasons of principle, the United States should support legitimate efforts at self-determination.

NO: Amitai Etzioni, a professor of sociology at George Washington University and the editor of the journal *Responsive Community*, contends that self-determination movements have exhausted their legitimacy. It is time to see them for what they are—destructive.

President Woodrow Wilson stood before a joint session of Congress on January 8, 1918, to outline the goals of the United States in World War I. Trying to set America's war aims apart from what he saw, and rejected, as the power plays and land grabs that had long sullied and bloodied Europe, Wilson outlined a program that became known as the Fourteen Points. Wilson called for the self-determination of nationalities within the Austro-Hungarian, German, and Ottoman empires with which the United States was at war.

Not long before, Nikolai Lenin had similarly called for self-determination. Writing in his epic work *Imperialism*, the Bolshevik leader condemned colonialism as the domination of proletariat people by bourgeois, imperialist countries, and he advocated revolution and freedom for oppressed nations.

The idea of self-determination it dates back to the mid-1700s and the idea of popular sovereignty. This concept rejected the theory of the divine right of kings to hold power, to control and even to own people within their realms. The theory of popular sovereignty holds that a people should be free from outside control and should control their own governments. The theory of self-determination was one of the ideological underpinnings of the late eighteenth-century democratic revolutions in the United States and France.

Western-based ideas about independence spread around the world and gave intellectual justification to the ancient, some would argue instinctive, urge by groups of people not to be dominated by others. In the time of Wilson and Lenin there were about 40 independent countries; now there are nearly 200. The Spanish and Portuguese empires in the Americas collapsed in the early 1800s; the German, Austro-Hungarian, and Ottoman empires collapsed during World War I; the African and Asian colonial empires of the British, French and other European imperialists collapsed in the 30 years following the end of World War II. Finally, in 1991, the Soviet Union collapsed. Some countries formed with a mix of various religious and ethnic groups have recently fallen apart or descended into internal warfare. The Czechs and Slovaks managed a national divorce peacefully, to their credit. The Bosnians, Croats, and Serbs were neither that lucky nor that civilized in Yugoslavia.

The debate at issue here is whether or not the idea of self-determination is a standard which we should support. It is important to clear up a few terms before proceeding. The word *state,* as used by political scientists, means country. A state is a physical and political entity that possesses, most importantly, sovereignty. *Sovereignty* means autonomy, freedom from outside control. *Nations* and *ethnic groups* (tribes) are groups of people who share a mutual identity based on some combination of history, culture, language, religion, and other characteristics. What differentiates nations and ethnic groups is that a nation can be said to have some sense of wanting independence or at least political autonomy, which is not necessarily the case for ethnic groups.

To return to the idea of national self-determination, it has evolved in this century mostly as an affirmation that nations have the right to break free from empires. That is what Wilson and Lenin were advocating; that is what has been affirmed by the United Nations in its 1960 declaration on the independence of colonial peoples and in various UN-sponsored human rights conventions. While old-style empires have disappeared, multiethnic and/or multinational states are still commonplace. Africa, for example, is a maze of cross-cutting ethnic and political boundaries created by the Europeans who carved the continent up with little or no regard to its population distribution. The periodic fighting since the late 1950s between the Hutus and Tutsis in what are now Burundi and Rwanda is part of that legacy. India, which has 24 different languages spoken by a million or more people, is considered an ethnic powder keg by many. The point is that the drive for self-determination did not end with the demise of traditional empires.

Michael Lind and Amitai Etzioni take up the debate about what our attitude should be as we approach the twenty-first century. Lind does not favor indiscriminate support for separatism. But he argues that U.S. interests may be better served by those who seek to break up multinational states than by those who seek to preserve them. Etzioni disagrees strongly, contending that we should oppose those forces that seek fragmentation and tribalism and support those that promote multicultural tolerance.

YES

Michael Lind

IN DEFENSE OF LIBERAL NATIONALISM

THE WORLD'S MOST POWERFUL FORCE

The simple idea that every nation should have its own state—accompanied by the corollary that one ethnic or cultural groups should not collectively rule over another—has been the most powerful political force of the past two hundred years. While particular nationalisms vary, this basic nationalist conception of an ideal world order has been remarkably unchanged for well over a century. "The world should be split into as many states as humanity is divided into nations," the Swiss international lawyer Johann Caspar Bluntschli wrote in 1870. "Each nation a state, each state a national being." When he wrote, nationalism as a considered doctrine, with its roots in the thought of Rousseau, Herder, Fichte and Mazzini, was already generations old. National sentiments, of course, long predated the doctrine, despite recent attempts to claim that national feelings are purely modern fabrications.

The nationalist ideal has survived one universalist assault after another: the Concert of Europe, which Metternich saw as a way of repressing anti-dynastic nationalism and republicanism; Hitler's supranational racist imperialism; the doomed Soviet effort to replace national loyalties with commitment to socialist universalism. Even the failure of the European Community to become a genuine federal state was foreseeable long before the troubles afflicting the Maastricht treaty and the crisis of the European Monetary System. It seems unlikely that liberal universalism will succeed where illiberal universalisms failed, in attempting to transfer loyalties from nations to supranational entities.

Despite all the evidence of the enduring power of nationalist sentiment, many statesmen, scholars and opinion leaders continue to treat nationalism as an anachronistic or dangerous relic of a previous age. Translated into policy, this prejudice against national self-determination usually means supporting the efforts of regimes to suppress secessionist movements by national minorities. The widespread conviction that nationalist secession is in itself dangerous and regressive helps explain the vehemence with which many observers blamed Germany for its allegedly premature recognition of

Slovenia, Croatia and Bosnia, and the criticism directed at the United States for allegedly engineering the independence of Eritrea.

This prejudice against nationalism—even liberal, democratic, constitutional nationalism—is a mistake. Reflexive support for multinational political entities, especially despotic ones, is as misguided as the automatic rejection of movements that seek the sovereignty of national homelands. For practical strategic reasons, as well as reasons of principle, the United States should identify itself with the most powerful idea in the contemporary world.

THE GREAT ILLUSION

Having survived so many setbacks since the wars of the French Revolution, will nationalism now end up in the dustbin of history along with its defeated universalist rivals? Scholars and writers... have been predicting the imminent obsolescence of the nation state for most of the twentieth century. In most cases, they have rested their argument on the economies of scale made possible by advances in technology—the transoceanic cable of yesterday, the computerized stock exchange and satellite television of today.

But this "interdependence" school, like Marxism, is based on a contradiction. It is simultaneously deterministic and prescriptive. If the world is inevitably growing more interdependent, then there is no reason to oppose particular nationalisms that are doomed in the long run anyway. Why oppose what is bound to wither away? On the other hand, if effort is needed to promote transnational integration, then clearly such integration is not preordained.

The mistake of prophets of a postnationalism world has been to leave out moral and political economies of scale. As a purely technical matter, it has probably been possible since Genghis Khan—certainly since Napoleon—for the earth to be governed from a single capital. That all attempts at world conquest have failed has nothing to do with technology and everything to do with the determination of diverse peoples not to be ruled by the conquering nation of the day. This is true of the latest attempt at world hegemony as well. Superior technology made it possible for the Western alliance to outinnovate and outproduce the Soviet bloc, but it was American, German and Japanese desires to protect national autonomy that kept those countries in a four-decade alliance. Why nations that will fight to the death to prevent surrendering their sovereignty to a conqueror would voluntarily surrender it to a supranational bureaucracy or a global elite of financiers and industrialists is a mystery that interdependence theorists have yet to explain.

THE 'STABILITARIANS'

A somewhat more plausible case against nationalism is made by "stabilitarians," or defenders of the present-day territorial status quo. The harmful effects of alteration of existing borders—even peaceful alteration—would, it is thought, outweigh the benefits. Every viewpoint has an address, of course. A national leader will view stability differently, depending on whether he thinks of his state as a status quo or a revisionist power. The belief of the Bush administration that the United States was a status quo power explains its efforts to keep both the Soviet empire and the Yugoslav federation intact.

While the breakup of a multinational state may create a regional power vacuum or a new balance-of-power pattern among its successor states, these results may be strategically desirable for some countries. Britain, for example, sought the independence of the Low Countries, the Hapsburgs the fragmentation of Italy, and successive Chinese empires the disunity of the nomads [to the northwest] in the Tarim Basin. A state may easily conclude that a power vacuum in a particular region is preferable to a rival power center. Given the threat the Soviet Union posed to the United States (and the threat its predecessor, the Romanov empire, posed to Great Britain) it is by no means clear that a consolidated entity on the territory of the Soviet Union is preferable to a balance-of-power system of rival successor states.

Assertions that successful secession by one or a few nations will produce runaway disintegration, thanks to the demonstration effect, deserve to be greeted with the same skepticism that should be directed at other straight-line extrapolations. The domino theory of nationalist disintegration is no more persuasive than similar domino theories. Secessionist activity tends to come in limited bursts: decolonization, the disintegration of the Soviet bloc and empire.

The potential for global disorder inherent in a world community with more states than exist at present is easy to exaggerate. To begin with, the number of possible new nation states is in the dozens, not the hundreds or thousands. While there are thousands of ethnic nations in the world, there are at most only dozens of national groups numerous, unified and compact enough conceivably to serve as the nuclei of sovereign nation states. The impossibility of basing nation states on tiny minorities like Sorbs or Wends in Germany or the Amish in the United States in no way discredits the potential for statehood of the Kurds [mostly in Turkey, Iraq, and Iran] or the Ibo [in Nigeria] or the Tibetans.

Even if the number of nation states were to increase by a dozen or two in the next few decades, through the peaceful or violent partition of several multinational countries, the very inequality of power among states would prevent too great a degree of disorder. A world of 200 or 250 effectively equal states would indeed be unmanageable, but not a world of the same number of nominally independent states, in which real power inheres in a handful of great powers, blocs and alliances. The breakup of nineteenth- and twentieth-century empires has produced, to date, almost two hundred states —well short of the 300 independent political units that existed in early-modern Germany, or the 500 that Charles Tilly has identified in the Europe of 1500. If the world survived the rapid expansion of the number of U.N. member states from 52 in 1946 to 183 today, surely it can survive a more incremental expansion by a dozen or two more.

Would the replacement of some of today's multinational states by new nation states lead to an increase in interstate war? History since the great wave of postwar decolonization in Africa and Asia gives some cause for reassurance in this regard. While many postcolonial states have been riven by ethnic conflict (reflecting the fact that they themselves are often ethnically heterogeneous), major interstate wars have been relatively infrequent.

Although prophets must be careful, it is possible that there would be less interstate conflict in a world of relatively homogeneous nation states than there is intrastate conflict between ethnic groups in multinational states. There are powerful incentives against engaging in cross-border war, whereas the penalties against a dominant ethnic group crushing others in the state it controls are very weak indeed.

Opponents of secessionist nationalism frequently argue that larger minorities, once they gain independence, may in turn oppress smaller minorities in the new national territory. The Quebecers, if independent, might be more inclined to oppress American Indians in Quebec. (The Balkan war is not terribly relevant, inasmuch as Slovenes, Croats and Yugoslav Muslims seceded in the first place to escape oppression in a multinational federation dominated by Serbs.)

Without condoning any injustice, the fact that a secessionist nation engages in oppressive behavior does not mean its complaints about its own oppression at the hands of a central government or dominant imperial ethnic group are not legitimate. Even criminals may be victims of crime. Inevitably, the replacement of a multinational empire or federation by a group of nation states will leave minorities that are too small or too dispersed without states of their own. This, in itself, is no argument for holding the multinational structure together, unless the multinational elite is significantly more virtuous than the successor national elites, which is rarely the case.

The relatively bloodless dissolution of the Soviet Union into its constituent republics, the separation of the Czech and Slovak republics, the accession of East Germany and, earlier, the Saarland to the German Federal Republic, as well as a number of cases of postcolonial independence, prove that national self-determination need not be accompanied by violence. Those concerned that national self-determination will lead to violence should support the strengthening of peaceful constitutional and diplomatic procedures for increasing the congruence of borders and nations, rather than support the status quo at all costs.

SMALL IS VIABLE

Is there a lower limit to the size of a viable nation state, imposed by the needs of defense or economics or minimum international order? If the viability of a state is defined as its military invulnerability in the absence of allies and economic autarky, then the only viable states would be isolationist, continental superpowers (rather like the Eastasia, Eurasia and Oceania of Orwell's *1984*).

As long as states are willing to cooperate in security alliances and engage in mutually beneficial trade, there is no reason why a small state like Portugal or Croatia should not be as viable as a great power like the United States. In an integrated North American market, an independent Quebec might prosper, even while preserving its distinctive French-American identity (though the transition might be painful). Indeed, smaller states may have advantages over the populous when it comes to economic progress (contrast Singapore and Hong Kong with China). Instead of specializing in one or a few crops, like states in a federation or provinces in an empire, an independent nation can take steps to diversify its economy as a buffer against market shocks. A sovereign state can also have a certain amount of leverage in both economic and military diplomacy—an advantage denied to a region subordinated to a single capital.

It might be thought that the costs of defense for a small nation state would be prohibitive. In fact, experience shows that small nation states do not spend more on defense as a share of GDP [gross domestic product] than do large countries. Indeed, during the Cold War the United States spent proportionately more on defense than its medium-sized allies like Germany and Japan, or small allies like Denmark and Portugal. A small state can act as a free rider, taking advantage of a powerful neighbor's interest in defending not only itself but its region. Of course such a neighbor may be a threat as well as an ally—but this is a risk that might be worth taking. After all, Kurds would be safer from Baghdad even in a weak Kurdish nation state than they can ever be as part of Iraq.

At any rate, an argument for the benefits of scale is an argument against small states of any kind—against small multinational states, like Switzerland, as much as small nation states like Slovenia. It is not in itself an argument against making nationality the basis of statehood wherever substantial geographical concentrations of linguistically and culturally similar people exist.

LIBERAL VS. ILLIBERAL NATIONALISM

Support in some circumstances for national self-determination need not mean support for nationalism in its tyrannical or imperial manifestations. It is important to draw a distinction between liberal and illiberal nationalism. Liberal nationalists tend to favor a linguistic-cultural definition of nationality and a liberal-constitutional (though not necessarily democratic) organization of the state. Illiberal nationalists (who might more accurately be described as nativists, to employ a term that originated in American politics) favor a religious or genetic definition of nationality, as in Iran or Serbia, and usually (though not always) an authoritarian-populist constitution. It is as great a mistake to confuse liberal nationalism with illiberal nativism as it is to identify social democracy with Leninist communism. Illiberal nationalism is often responsible for terrible atrocities, as the carnage in Bosnia has shown. The problem, however, is with illiberalism and militarism, not with nationalism as such.

Liberal nationalism holds that, far from being a threat to democracy, nationalism —the correspondence of cultural nation and state—is a necessary, though not sufficient, condition for democracy in most places today. Modern democracy presupposes a degree of extrapolitical community. The linguistic-cultural nation is today generally accepted as the basis for the political community because it is the largest particular community that can still command sentimental loyalty and the smallest comprehensive community that still has features of universality, combining all ages and classes. The nation is a small humanity and a large association. "Few will burn with ardent love for the entire human species," Tocqueville observed. "The interests of the human race are better served by giving every man a particular fatherland than by trying to inflame his passions for the whole of humanity."

Some claim that national loyalty is irrational and atavistic, compared to "rational" patriotism or allegiance to a state that is not identified with any predominant linguistic or cultural group. There is nothing at all "irrational," however, about making the suprafamilial community with which one identifies the cultural nation, rather than the territorial state in the abstract. Quite apart from the psychological reasons, there are practical reasons. One is usually born into a cultural nation for life, but the state to which one owes allegiance may alter its borders, change its constitution, change its name, even cease to exist through conquest or merger. National communities, while by no means immortal themselves, tend to be more stable and long-lived. This being the case, to identify primarily, not with a historic linguistic-cultural nation, but with a possibly transient government or a paper constitution, would be the height of irrationality.

MULTINATIONAL DEMOCRACY IS NEITHER

The evidence that democracy almost never works in societies that are highly divided along linguistic and cultural lines is overwhelming. Examples of multinational countries that have failed are numerous: Cyprus, Lebanon, Sri Lanka, Sudan, the Soviet Union, Yugoslavia, Czechoslovakia (India increasingly looks like another failure). Nevertheless, many persist in arguing that multinational democracy not only is possible but represents the wave of the future. Multinational despotisms, they argue, should not be partitioned into nation states that (in some cases) may become democracies. Rather, they should be transformed from multinational despotisms into multinational democracies.

As examples of successful multinational federations, proponents of multinational democracy usually point to three countries with elaborate ethnic power-sharing arrangements: Switzerland, Belgium and Canada. The very fact that only three successes can be found, out of dozens of multinational states, in itself suggests the difficulty of getting linguistically and culturally distinct nations to cohabit peacefully under a common democratic constitution. In reality, these three examples hurt the multinationalist case more than they help it. Switzerland, for example, is better described as a confederation of relatively homogeneous territorial nation states (the cantons) than as a truly multiethnic society. Belgium is a society deeply troubled by its linguistic and political divisions, and Canada recently almost came apart over the Quebec question. The two "founding nations" of Canada may yet go their separate ways, like the Czechs and Slovaks did.

The fact that Switzerland and Belgium are small countries (and Canada a huge country with a small population) tends to contradict another argument made in favor of holding multinational entities together: the argument that more populous states benefit from economies of scale. While there are economic and military returns to scale, these may be neutralized if they are accompanied by the costs of increased ethnic diversity accompanied by ethnic conflict. All other things being equal, a large homogeneous nation state may well be preferable to a small homogeneous nation state. But a small nation state may be better off, in terms of prosperity and governability if not necessarily defense, than a gigantic state riven by ethnic and linguistic conflicts.

Those who call on nondemocratic multinational states to adopt Swiss- or Canadian-type power-sharing arrangements as an alternative to partition seldom describe the policy to be pursued if their constitutional panaceas fail (as they have in most cases). If elaborate power-sharing schemes are rejected, or tried and found not to work, is partition or secession then in order, as a second-best option? Or should multinational states like Iraq that cannot be held together by democratic and federal means be held together by force and terror?

Those who seek to promote democracy and at the same time to preserve multinational entities intact will discover that in many cases these goals cannot be reconciled. A world of liberal nationalist states, including many that are nondemocratic, is much more likely to develop into a world of democracies, as Franco's Spain would attest. For this reason, proponents of democratization are justified in encouraging liberal nationalism even where democracy is not yet possible. This might be the case, for instance, in Algeria or Egypt. Conversely, it may be a waste of time to try to hold together and democratize a multinational state, even a relatively liberal one, where a common national identity is lacking. This might be the case in the future in South Africa. Instead, it often makes more sense to promote liberal and constitutional nationalism, with or without electoral democracy. First comes the nation state, then a liberal constitution reinforced by a liberal political culture, and only then, if at all, democracy. For many, living as the citizen of a liberal but nondemocratic nation state is preferable to being the subject of an illiberal multinational despotism that can only be held together by force.

NO LONGER A LAST RESORT

To substitute indiscriminate support for national self-determination for reflexive defense of the territorial status quo around the world would be a mistake. Rather than strict principles, a few rules of thumb are in order. To begin with, the United States should refrain from making gratuitous statements in favor of state unity.... Even if American policy is to favor state unity in a particular case, the United States might lose some of its leverage if this preference is too obvious. Even worse, the United States may appear to license vicious repression, as the Bush administration's statements in favor of Yugoslav unity may have convinced Serb nationalists that they would not be penalized seriously for attacking Slovenia and Croatia.

In the civil wars where ethnic or cultural differences are at issue, partition should no longer be considered the last resort. It might sometimes be wise to stress national self-determination above free elections, during the terminal crisis of a state that is both multinational and undemocratic. Oppressed nations seeking to escape from a multinational empire should not be told that they will be free to vote on everything except their independence. Since democracy and liberal constitutionalism work best in relatively homogeneous nation states, in most of the world democratic constitution-writing should follow national independence, not be promoted as an alternative to it. Indeed, it is not only futile but insulting for policymakers and academics in Western capitals and campuses to design democratic federal constitutions like the Vance-Owen plan for Bosnia and try to impose them on Kurds, Kosovars or Kashmiris as alternatives to national independence. Where a multiethnic federation has utterly collapsed, it may be better to create two or more new, relatively homogeneous nation states than to try to piece the wreckage together with ingenious but unworkable power-sharing schemes.

The corollary of support for national self-determination in the form of secession is support for the enlargement of nation states through peaceful and democratic accession or annexation, like the unification of Germany. The United States enlarged itself in this manner as recently as 1958 (with the statehood of Alaska and Hawaii); President Bush called for statehood for Puerto Rico. If east Germany can join west Germany, by what reasoning can the 90 percent majority of ethnic Albanians in Kosovo [a province of Yugoslavia] be denied accession to Albania, if they choose and can make their choice effective? How can compact populations of Bosnian Croats be forbidden by the international community from voluntarily merging with Croatia (the very international borders of which are recent and fluid)? States should be allowed not only to shrink but to expand, so long as the expansion is undertaken peacefully and with the consent of majorities (or perhaps supermajorities) of those affected. The difficulties attending European unification suggest that we need not fear the creation of possibly overpowerful bureaucratic superstates like the Third Reich and the Soviet Union through purely voluntary mergers.

The United States may legitimately refuse to support nationalist movements that define the nation in narrow racial or religious terms, rather than in inclusive linguistic and cultural terms, as well as movements that threaten minorities with persecution or genocide. Also, as a condition of admitting new nation states to the international community, outsiders may legitimately insist that states protect the rights of association of individual members of cultural minorities, such as private religious or language instruction. It would be a mistake, however, for the international community to attempt to promulgate a general duty of states not only to tolerate but to subsidize and promote minority cultures. Such policies, whether undertaken as a result of international or purely domestic pressure, tend only to inflame majority resentment without accomplishing any important goals that cannot be achieved by less intrusive, more voluntary means.

The wave of disintegrative nationalism that ripped apart the former Soviet Union and the Yugoslav federation will not be the last. In all likelihood, the next few decades will see increasingly determined secessionist movements in the multiethnic successor states of the European empires: India, Pakistan, South Africa, Iraq, perhaps even the Russian federation. In such countries, as dominant elites, seeking new formulas for legitimacy to replace fading secular and socialist philosophies, make more concessions to the national and religious sentiments of ethnic majorities, minority nationalisms may grow more bitter and intense in response. The fact that in many, perhaps most, cases central authorities will prevail will not prevent secessionist nationalism from being a major source of terrorism and civil war in the 21st century. The United States does not need to become an exporter of secession. Washington should recognize, however, that in particular cases American values, as well as American interests, may be served by those who seek to break up multinational states rather than by those who seek to preserve them.

NO

Amitai Etzioni

THE EVILS OF SELF-DETERMINATION

Self-determination movements, a major historical force for more than 200 years, have largely exhausted their legitimacy as a means to create more strongly democratic states. While they long served to destroy empires and force governments to be more responsive to the governed, with rare exceptions self-determination movements now undermine the potential for democratic development in nondemocratic countries and threaten the foundations of democracy in the democratic ones. It is time to withdraw moral approval from most of the movements and see them for what they mainly are—destructive.

All people must develop more tolerance for those with different backgrounds and cultures; with compromise, ethnic identities can be expressed within existing national entities without threatening national unity. If tolerance between groups is not fostered, the resulting breakups will not lead to the formation of new stable democracies, but rather to further schisms and more ethnic strife, with few gains and many losses for proponents of self-government. The United States, then, should use moral approbation and diplomatic effort to support forces that enhance democratic determination and oppose those that seek fragmentation and tribalism.

Historically, the principle of self-determination served well those who sought to dissolve empires—governments of one people imposed on another that lacked economic reciprocity between the metropolitan center and the outlying colonies. While historians tend to treat as distinct the emergence of nation-states from the Ottoman and Hapsburg empires and the liberation of former colonies in Asia and Africa following World War II, there are actually great sociological similarities between the two movements. In the Balkan peninsula, foreign empires imposed themselves on the indigenous people, roughly in the area of the modern-day countries of Albania, Bulgaria, Greece, Romania, and what used to be Yugoslavia. The foreign imperialists gained dominance by conquest, and the metropolitan core drew significant economic benefit from the "colonies," although that term is not usually used. When nationalism strengthened the self-awareness of the Balkan people in the late nineteenth century, they rebelled against colonial rule. By 1914, Albanians,

Bulgarians, Greeks, Montenegrins, Romanians, and Serbians had established their independence. Similarly, undemocratic, imperially imposed governments in Africa and Asia led to demands for, and eventually the establishment of, more fully representative governments. In discussing Africa and Asia in the post–World War II era, historians argued that the quest for a new self-expression and self-awareness was at the heart of those self-determination movements. In retrospect, it seems that the metropolitan government's failure to represent and respond to the needs and demands of the various subgroups constituting the empire's population was at least as important.

Nationalism, then, functioned not only as a way to gain one's own flag, national hymn, and other symbols of selfhood, but, perhaps even more important, as a way to lay the foundations for a responsive government. It is true that not all emergent nation-states fashioned democratic governments, but where democracy was absent, the struggle for democratic self-determination continued. The wars of national liberation after World War II that yielded new countries from the former colonies of the British, Dutch, French, Germans, Italians, and Portuguese parallel the historical development of the Balkans in important ways. In both cases, the metropolitan countries were remote and at least in some ways exploitative. While some of the metropolitan governments, especially Britain's, were democratic, their democracy did not embrace the people of their colonies. Moreover, in Africa in particular, the demands for national self-expression were weak because the colonial borders drawn by the empires paid little attention to tribal, cultural, and linguistic lines. Most

of today's African nationalism was generated after independence. In short, the driving force behind the wars of liberation was the desire for democratization and a responsive government, not for ethnic self-determination.

That pursuit parallels the American quest for independence from Great Britain in the late eighteenth century. The American colonial rebellion was most openly and directly a call for representation, not for national expression. Many pre-independence "Americans" saw themselves as British. The American sense of nationhood remained rather tentative, even during the Revolutionary War period, and grew largely after independence. The remoteness and unresponsiveness of the British government, not strong American nationalism, motivated the colonists' revolt.

The world witnessed the final round of the thrust against imperial governments in a most dramatic fashion from 1989 to 1991, as the Soviet empire crumbled with a speed only possible because the imposed government lacked legitimacy. The breakaway of Bulgaria, Czechoslovakia, East Germany, Hungary, Poland, and Romania can easily, though mistakenly, be understood simply as a result of repressed nationalism. Closer examination, however, reveals that another factor was the unresponsiveness of remote and exploitative Muscovite rule. The unresponsiveness of the "local" East European governments explains the collapse of Communist regimes in each of those countries; however, the breakdown of the Soviet-led system was rooted in the member countries' overwhelming sense that the system was dominated by an exploitative USSR that ignored their needs. The same must be said about the breakaway of Estonia, Latvia, and Lithuania.

With the latest attempts at independence, though, there are signs of a new and unproductive strain of self-determination. Far from enhancing democratic government, the drive to dismember the USSR has so far resulted in a shift of power away from the reforming parliament, the most freely elected to date, and toward a small group of republic heads, many of whom were not democratically elected.

There are so far precious few indications that the governments of the 12 non-Baltic republics will be more democratic than the Soviet government they replace. Uzbekistan, for example, remains firmly under control of the former Communist leadership, and even by late 1992 it showed very few signs that it would soon institute the kinds of democratic reforms evident at the federal level. Georgia also remains under one-party rule, and rebels ousted a president who was elected with 87 per cent of the popular vote. Several of the new republics outlawed the main opposition party (the Communist party), and in some the press is often muzzled. President Boris Yeltsin has reminded the Russian parliament that it contains many Communists, and he demands that his powers be increased whenever the parliament does not favor his policies. In short, self-determination in the former USSR often weakens democracy.

INDEPENDENCE WITHOUT DEMOCRACY

Those concerned with promoting responsive governments, by and for the people, can no longer assume that breaking up larger entities provides movement in the desired direction. One may favor or oppose replacement of an empire with a group of local tyrannies; some-times, it is said, at least they are "ours." But replacing a metropolitan democratic government, into which, for instance, the USSR was beginning to evolve, with a bunch of local autocrats hardly constitutes progress toward genuine self-determination.

True, some pockets of empire remain. The people of Tibet and Inner Mongolia may well need to break away from the remote, imposed, exploitative, and undemocratic Chinese empire. And the Kurds may never find a responsive government in tyrannical Iraq or authoritarian Iran. Turkey, however, given its close relationship to the United States and its interest in democracy, may be persuaded to be more tolerant of and responsive to the Kurds, and to grant them more local autonomy. If it becomes clear that the international community would discourage a Kurdish drive for independence from Turkey, reconciliation and compromise between the Turks and the Kurds would be more likely....

The need to tilt in favor of fuller representation, responsiveness, and democratization—and against self-determination by fragmentation—is most evident in those countries that are already basically democratic but within which one subgroup is, or feels that it is, underrepresented or isolated. African Americans were among the first to understand that point. While some flirted with the notion of a separate black state within the United States during the 1960s, and while others had previously promoted a separate state in Liberia, most African Americans quickly realized that their needs would be better served by a racially mixed state—as long as discrimination could be brought to an end. In India, with many ethnic groups competing for resources and recognition, democracy continues to be far from perfect; however, few can expect it to benefit if more territories, such as Kashmir, were to break away and form their own states. The peoples of India desire and deserve a government that is responsive to them, but not necessarily a separatist one. Areas such as Kashmir should be allowed more autonomy and proper participation in national politics, but they should not be encouraged to break up the country into a jigsaw puzzle of hostile, undemocratic, and potentially warring territories.

Yugoslavia was at best a partial democracy; it required much restructuring to make its government responsive to the groups that made up the country—to allow a truly free press, free elections, and the other elements of democracy. However, one thing stands out so far: The governments of the new, fragmented countries that dismembered the Yugoslav federation are even less democratic, and more murderous. . . .

The Parti Québécois self-determination movement in Canada, though not now violent, poses similar dangers to the Canadian federation and Canadian citizens. However legitimate one judges the complaints of French-speaking Canadians to be, it is hard to compare their lot to that of Czechs or Hungarians under Soviet occupation, or even to that of Indians under British colonial rule. One must consider the danger of less democracy in a separatist Quebec, if not for the French-speaking Québécois, then for the English speakers. The merits of enhancing Ottawa's responsiveness and allowing for some redefinition of the central government's role far outweigh the benefits of dismembering the union.

The success of the Flemings and the Walloons in Belgium provides a paradigm for other countries. While the Flemings and the Walloons do not live together in what might be characterized as one big happy community, a democratic government, responsive to both major ethnic groups, has enabled them to avoid the terrible fate of the people of Lebanon, who were relieved from years of horrendous interethnic civil war only by Syrian occupation. Indeed, changes in the structure of the Belgian government in recent years led its two groups toward more satisfactory self-expression—without separation and within the framework of a shared, democratic government. Switzerland, now held up as a model of a country containing people of different origins, ethnicities, languages and cultures, was possible only after the ethnic groups that fought each other for nearly 1,000 years were able to agree on a common democratic government.

Self-determinists often say that they seek to preserve a separate ethnic culture, tradition, religion, or language. They argue, for instance, that Macedonian distinctiveness is threatened within a Greek state. However, as the preceding examples suggest, within a truly democratic state patterns of integration can be created that preserve distinct identities without breaking up the encompassing societies. In a truly democratic state, there is no reason for one culture to try to suppress others, as long as the others seek self-expression rather than cultural dominance or territorial separatism.

It is impossible to sustain the notion that every ethnic group can find its expression in a full-blown nation-state, fly its flag at the United Nations, and have its ambassadors accredited by other nation-states; the process of ethnic separation and the breakdown of existing states will then never be exhausted. Many countries in the world continue to contain numerous ethnic enclaves. Even within those enclaves, further ethnic splinters exist. Moreover, new ethnic "selves" can be generated quite readily, drawing on fracture lines now barely noticeable. Subtle differences in geography, religion, culture, and loyalty can be fanned into new separatist movements, each seeking their own symbols and powers of statehood. Few saw the potential for three countries in Iraq until it nearly broke into a Shiite southern state, a northern Kurdish state, and a central Iraqi Sunni state after the 1991 Persian Gulf war. In the United Kingdom, Scots and Welsh are again asserting themselves. The former Yugoslavia, already riddled by division, may fragment further still; for instance, Albanians, Yugoslavia's third largest and Serbia's second largest ethnic minority, have elected a shadow government in Kosovo and are agitating for independence but have so far stopped short of armed rebellion. And so it goes throughout the world. In most places centrifugal forces, forever present, are accelerating.

Indeed, as most drives to break away from existing states or coalesce in new ones advance, groups line up to tear the emergent state into segments. New divisions often take place long before ethnic groups accord the new entity even a limited opportunity to develop a responsive, democratic government.

A good example would be the Sorbians in eastern Germany who want to establish the state of Lusatia. Though one may not take their claims seriously, Alfred Symank, a Sorbian and the chief lobbyist for a group known as Sorbian Nationality for Autonomous Lusatia, argues that Sorbians "are a legitimate nation" and "want the world to recognize that Germany isn't just made up of Germans.

The Sorbs are here too!" Symank speaks of the oppression of the Sorbs at the hands of the Prussians, Saxons, Nazis, communists, and now unified Germany. He wonders, "If Lithuania succeeds, if Slovenia succeeds, why can't we?" All that before the ink had even dried on German unification.

Much more serious are the demands of various groups within the former Soviet Union's republics. For example, the southern Ossetians in Georgia are in violent battle with the majority Georgians, and the ethnically Turkish Gagauz have already proclaimed independence from the Moldovan majority in Moldova. Continued ethnic strife destablizes a region and makes it unlikely that the new states will survive as more ethnic groups emerge and demand further fragmentation.

Even the romantics of self-determination may pause before the prospect of a United Nations with thousands of members. The world may well survive the creation of ever more toy states, smaller than Liechtenstein and less populated than the South Pacific island-country of Nauru (population 9,300), but what meaning does self-determination have when minuscule countries are at the economic and military mercy, even whim, of larger states—states in whose government they have no representation at all?

If the world is to avoid such chaos, the call for self-determination should no longer elicit almost reflexive moral support. We should withhold political and moral support unless the movement faces one of the truly exceptional situations in which self-determination will enhance democracy rather than retard it. Generally, people who see themselves as oppressed put great value in gaining the moral support of others. As a rule, though, we should encourage groups to work out their differences within existing national communities. Also, to further discourage fragmentation, the economic disadvantages of separatism should be made evident. Finally, governments that face ethnic challenges, like Canada, should be urged to provide more local autonomy and more democratic federalism in order to prevent dissolution.

THE ECONOMICS OF SECESSION

Objectively assessed, the economic disadvantages of fragmentation stand out. Countries that fragment into smaller economies pay heavy economic penalties. For instance, Slovakia, a source of many raw materials,... split from the Czech republic, a place where raw materials have been turned into finished products. Also, the pipelines that carry oil from the former USSR to the Czech republic run through Slovakia, and Slovakian independence [could] pose a potential security threat to the Czechs' oil supply.... [Conversely,] the Czechs supply much of the Slovaks' electricity....

In another case, Quebec's ardor for separation seems to have cooled recently as its business leaders have recognized the great economic losses independence could entail. Even the mere possibility that Quebec could secede has pushed up the cost of its credit. When it issued bonds in 1990, it had to offer higher interest rates than the other Canadian provinces.

Theoretically, in a world of truly free trade, it does not matter where national borders are drawn. However, under existing conditions, national borders retain considerable economic significance, ranging from the subtle—such as the tendency of citizens to buy domestically pro- duced products, even when there are no legal restrictions on imports—to overt industrial policies aimed at giving domestic producers a competitive advantage. National borders continue to affect not only the economy, but also the environment. Many environmental issues cannot be dealt with by fragments of countries: The acid rain produced in one rains on the other; the pollution dumped into a river by one country can appear in the drinking water of another downstream. Of course environmental issues also pose a problem for long-established countries, but their new prominence demonstrates the need for more cross-national community building and the difficulties posed by additional fragmentation.

Some argue that groups like the Croatians and Slovenians will first find their nationalist self-expression and later form common markets. However, the argument is akin to suggesting that a married couple running a mom-and-pop store will, after divorce, be more able to work together on behalf of their joint business than during marriage. It rarely happens that way. Indeed, the African experience makes evident the great difficulty, indeed near impossibility, of forming new unions once various territories have become independent states. Some experts once considered independent states a transitional stage between Western colonialism and African unity. Instead, the African states have been independent for decades now and show very few signs of moving toward a new political African union.

Providing yet another argument for the large, multiethnic state and the development of international communities, economies of scale are becoming increasingly important. Economists long stressed the efficiency of large-scale divisions of labor and exchange. However, it is only in the last decades that we have developed the technologies of communication and management that allow us to run enterprises on a truly continental, even inter-continental, scale. In recent years, even many of the world's strongest economies, like those of Western Europe, have found it advantageous to join together and have cooperated on high-tech and industrial ventures. For its part, the United States has responded to economic competition by forming a free-trade area with Canada and... Mexico.

It must be acknowledged that economies of scale are not the only factor in determining economic success. Some small countries, like Singapore, are doing relatively well, while much larger ones, like Brazil, are doing poorly. Holding all other factors constant, though, few would contend that countries like Brazil would benefit from being broken into parts—or that smaller countries would not benefit from economic mergers. Economics has motivated many countries to form, or at least to try to form, economic unions. (Brazil is hoping to join with Argentina, Paraguay, and Uruguay by 1995.) From a sheer economic viewpoint, the way to well-being is not fragmentation but its opposite: community.

Moreover, it is highly questionable whether groups of autonomous countries successfully develop common economies, a process that entails far more than shared markets and trade zones. The European Community is now considering, albeit with difficulty, varying degrees of political union because of the difficulty of maintaining an economic union without broader integration. Because governments routinely seek to affect the rate of inflation, interest rates, unemployment, economic growth, and other economic fundamentals, a successful economic policy requires a political consensus and a specification of shared goals. It would be the ultimate irony of history for countries to dismember existing states, such as India, only to discover that the resulting entities must reunite politically to provide their citizens with the blessings of a modern economy. Though such irony may satisfy the observer and provide social scientists with a fascinating experiment, it would impose pervasive suffering on the people involved.

Although the economic penalties paid by splinter states may be painful, they are not the primary cost of disunion. Excessive self-determination works against democratization and threatens democracy in countries that have already attained it. Self-determination movements challenge democracy by chipping away at its structural and socio-psychological foundations.

Structurally, democracy depends on more than regular elections. Elections were conducted frequently by... the communist USSR. A true democratic structure requires that nonviolent change of those in power can be made in response to the people's changing preferences. Such changes ensure that the government can continue to respond to the needs and desires of the people, and that if the government becomes unresponsive it will be replaced without undue difficulties.

To ensure that the variety of needs within a population find effective political expression, democracies require that the sitting government not "homogenize" the population in some artificial manner, like imposing one state-approved religion. Only a plurality of social, cultural, and economic loyalties and power centers within society make it possible for new groups to break upon the political scene, find allies, build coalitions, and effect change. The Great Society reforms of the mid-1960s in the United States demonstrate the importance of a plural, fluid system. Rising African American groups formed a coalition with white liberals and labor unions to advance a common agenda, increasing political participation and preventing a political explosion.

Aside from keeping the government and its closest allies in the population in check, the pluralistic array of groups that thrive in a truly democratic society also keep one another in check. When historical processes or deliberate government policies leave only one group of supporters organized and weaken all other groups, as the Nazis did in post–World War I Germany, they undermine the foundations of democracy. In short, social pluralism supports democratic government.

While there are many ways the coalitions needed for social pluralism can be built, the best are those that cut across existing lines of division, dampening the power of each and allowing for a large number of possible combinations of social bases to build political power. Thus, a society rigidly divided into two or three economic classes may have a structure that is somewhat more conducive to democratic government than a society with only one class. However, the potential for democracy in such a society increases when there are other groups that draw on members from various classes, so that loyalty to them cuts across class lines.

In the United States, ethnic loyalties have historically cut across socioeconomic strata, dampening both class and ethnic divisions. Thus, American Jews may be largely middle and upper-middle class, but most people in those classes are not Jewish, and there are Jews in the other classes. White Anglo-Saxon Protestants may be over-represented in the upper classes, but they are also found in large numbers in all other classes, and so on. The fact that both economic and ethnic loyalties cut across regional boundaries further cements the foundations of pluralism and, hence, of democracy.

In contrast, breakaway states based on ethnicity tend to fashion communities that are more sociologically monolithic than their parent states. Quebec, obviously, would be more "French"— and the remaining Canada more "English"—than the current composite. The great intolerance breakaway states tend to display toward minority ethnic groups heightens the polarization. Ethnically based breakaway states generally result in more ethnic homogeneity and less pluralism, meaning that they often lack the deeper sociological foundations of democracy.

Democracy requires tolerance to function because tolerance provides the socio-psychological bases for compromise, such as the willingness to accept the outcome of an election even if it favors a party one opposes. Community requires the same basic psychological mindset because tolerance is inherent in the ability to work out differences with people whose religions, histories, and habits one does not share and is vital to the process of uniting people of different backgrounds and traditions. When tolerance is absent, as it often is in breakaway states, the predisposition toward further fragmentation is strong. Since the ultimate purpose of self-determination is not self-determination per se but a responsive government, mutual tolerance might be what many countries and ethnic groups need most and first.

At least before self-determination groups take a wrecking ball to their countries, it seems reasonable to expect them to try to work out their differences by reforming the existing government to render it more responsive, for example changing its structures to make it less unitary and more federal. If that truly doesn't work, we must insist that the newly formed communities take special pains to nurture the tolerance they will need to stay together.

In earlier historical periods the people favoring self-determination tended to be internationalist. As long as the leaders of various national movements were largely poets, philosophers, and intellectuals rallying against dominant empires, their causes seemed appealing and just. However, as nationalism—and especially micronationalism—has spread increasing hostility, ethnic fragmentation has opened the door to great new violence. In Moldova, the Russian minority and the Gagauz people face discrimination and outright violence. The same holds for the ethnic Turkish minority in Bulgaria, Romanians in Hungary, and Hungarians in Romania. Civil wars among ethnic entities within the newly independent African states are commonplace. And in India, though the Sikhs have not yet obtained independence for Punjab, subgroups are already at each other's throats.

A DEMOCRATIC MOSAIC

Self-determination should not be treated as an absolute value, trumping all others. Self-determination is meant to enhance justice in the world through self-government. However, in spite of its positive role in previous periods, the violence and destruction—even war—it now incites greatly undercut its legitimacy.

Pluralism can exist, even flourish, within a unified state; ethnic groups and other subgroups need not be suppressed or dissolved to maintain community. The best solution to the worldwide ethnic crumble is not total assimilation. In fact, ethnic groups should continue not only to exist, but to thrive and enrich the cultural mosaic. They form the foundation of democratic pluralism, as long as their sociological scope does not expand to the point where it cuts into the community's sustaining bonds.

Ethnic expressions can include many things: the maintenance of traditional cuisine, music, dance, religious rituals, and mutual aid associations. Ethnic groups should accept those values embedded in the shared national constitution (like respect for individual and minority rights), a limited set of ultimate values (like the defense of one's country), and, in most countries, a shared language. However, those minimum requirements still leave room for free cultural expression, assuming ethnic groups coexist in an environment of mutual tolerance. The preservation of a national community or democracy does not demand the assimilation or the elimination of ethnic groups, though it does require that some basic limits be placed upon them.

Those who seek to bolster national unity often argue for the imposition of one language while those seeking to maintain their own ethnic cultures strongly oppose the introduction of a language other than their own, and they see efforts to do so as a major attack on their unique cultural identity.

They may point to the experiences of Belgium and Switzerland, which show that a country can sustain government responsiveness and unity even in face of separate languages.

The principle of pluralism within unity provides a guideline for consideration. Countries that encourage their citizens to acquire one common language facilitate communication and community building. But they should not discourage subgroups from maintaining their own languages. Quebec can encourage its citizens to learn and speak French but should not make taboo the use of English as a second language on its shop and restaurant signs. The Soviet government, after all, oppressed Jews not by expecting them to learn Russian but by prohibiting the teaching of Yiddish and Hebrew.

Clearly, the moral support historically granted to self-determination movements was based on the often-correct belief that empires deny minorities their right to a responsive, democratic government forcing them to break away. Self-determination movements gained support because they fought against oppression, not because they fought for separatism.

Now, in most states of the world, further fragmentation is likely to imperil democratic forces and endanger economic development. Only when secessionist movements seek to break out of empires—and only when those empires refuse to democratize—does self-determination deserve our support. Otherwise, democratic government and community building, not fragmentation, should be accorded the highest standing.

POSTSCRIPT

Is Self-Determination a Right of All Nationalities?

The issue of self-determination presents a particularly emotional conundrum. One the one hand, the idea that people should be free to govern themselves is very appealing. Also, for Americans and others, opposing self-determination puts them in a position of arguing against the very principle that once led them to independence.

On the other hand, self-determination has its drawbacks. First, countries are becoming integrated economic units, and rendering them asunder often creates great hardship for all. Second, the various claims of nations/ethnic groups/tribes are hard to unravel in an even-handed and just manner. In central Africa, the Tutsis have recently suffered amazing cruelty at the hands of the Hutus. But the Hutus, a majority, were long dominated by the Tutsis, who invaded the region, probably from Ethiopia, in the sixteenth century. The Tutsis were also used by European colonial powers as the local enforcers of their oppressive rule. Then again, the Hutus also are invaders who long ago conquered the area and its indigenous people the Twa. Would it be reasonable to return control of Rwanda and Burundi to the Twa? A third drawback of self-determination is that it leads to so-called microstates. There are some 38 countries with populations of less than 1 million. Many of these microstates have marginal economies that are too small to sustain the diverse base necessary to build a modern economy and compete in world commerce. Also, the ability of these microstates to defend themselves against outside domination is negligible. In an ideal world, size would not be an issue. In the real world, microstates tempt the powerful, and an ensuing struggle could set off a wave of conflict among the major powers. As one scholar has put it, "microstates can cause macropolitical havoc."

Few people advocate unrestrained self-determination or absolutely oppose it. Lind and Etzioni both avoid those extremes. Yet, once one begins to make choices between the two, other issues arise. Most of us might readily agree, for example, that the white minority in South Africa should not be able to break away and establish a white state, as some there want to do. How about the Zulus, though? Should that black nation be supported in a claim for independence? Should English-heritage Canadians be willing to let the largely French-heritage province of Quebec declare independence?

Further complicating the debate is whether or not the tolerance that Etzioni laudably advocates is even possible. For more on the origins and nature of ethnicity and nationalism, you may wish to read George M. Scholl, Jr., "A Resynthesis of the Primordial and Circumstantial Approaches to Ethnic

Group Solidarity," *Ethnic and Racial Studies* (April 1990); Paul Brass, *Ethnicity and Nationalism* (Sage Publications, 1991); Liah Greenfeld, *Nationalism* (Harvard University Press, 1992); and Walker Connor, "Beyond Reason: The Nature of the Ethnonational Bond," *Ethnic and Racial Studies* (July 1993).

ISSUE 20

Are U.S. Efforts to Promote Human Rights Culturally Biased and Self-Serving?

YES: Bilahari Kausikan, from "Asia's Different Standard," *Foreign Policy* (Fall 1993)

NO: Aryeh Neier, from "Asia's Unacceptable Standard," *Foreign Policy* (Fall 1993)

ISSUE SUMMARY

YES: Bilahari Kausikan, director of the East Asian and Pacific bureau of the Ministry of Foreign Affairs of Singapore, contends that international human rights advocates ignore cultural differences and seek to impose rules that reflect the "individualistic ethos of the West" on the more "consensus-seeking" societies of East and Southeast Asia.

NO: Aryeh Neier, president of the Open Society Fund, an organization that promotes the development of civil society in formerly repressive countries, argues that there are fundamental human rights, such as the right of all persons to be free from cruel and arbitrary punishment, that define us as human beings and transcend the cultural values of any one society.

Take a survey of your friends. Ask them if they are in favor of justice, in favor of morality, in favor of human rights. It would be surprising if any of the people you asked came out solidly against human rights. Nevertheless, although most people say they are in favor of justice, morality, and human rights, these standards are not universally followed.

Why is there a gap between what people say regarding support for justice, morality, and human rights and what happens in practice? There are two reasons. One, of course, is that some organizations or individuals really do not mean what they say. The second reason is a lot more complex and is the focus of this issue. It may be that "violations" of human rights are, to a degree, a matter of perception and culture. It may be that practices that we in the West sometimes condemn are not universally seen as abuses. Rather, they may be things we disapprove of because of our cultural biases.

Where do rights, concepts of morality, and standards of justice come from in the first place? Some people would argue there is such a thing as "natural rights." The *naturalist school* of human rights contends that rights are based on the essence of being human and are theoretically possessed by people when they live in a true "state of nature," that is, before they join into governments. The "right to life" is one possible inherent right. Philosophers such as Jean-Jacques Rousseau (1712–1778) and John Locke (1632–1704) believed that people joined in societies and created governments to improve themselves. It was, therefore, illogical to argue that people would surrender any of their rights. This contention is central to the argument that there are intrinsic human rights that cannot be violated regardless of any cultural context. Many of those who take this view maintain that democracy and justice based on human rights are necessary to societies if they are to progress socially, economically, and politically.

Needless to say, this view of human rights based on natural rights is not accepted by everyone. Other philosophers, such as Thomas Hobbes (1588–1679), have argued that people submitted to government for protection from a state of nature that was brutal, not idyllic. As such, individuals traded away some of their rights in order to gain protection from the state.

Yet other people contend that rights are not inherent, at least for the most part. Instead, those who hold this view argue that rights, or at least many of them, are culturally based. This is called the *positivist school* of human rights. Positivists point out that differing standards prove the cultural origins of rights. Western, especially American, culture, for example, places a high value on individual rights. The right of the individual comes before the good of the society or any class of citizens. Many other cultures place a much higher value on communitarian values. This means that when the rights of the individual and the good of the society clash, the presumption is that societal good is the more important standard. When students protesting for democracy in Tiananmen Square and elsewhere in China were attacked and killed by government troops in 1989, the West condemned China for violating the right to democracy, the right to free speech, and other human rights. From the point of view of the Chinese government, however, the students' rights did not extend to trying to undermine the socialist movement, which had done much to benefit Chinese society.

The contention by the positivist school that rights are culture-based, and therefore not universal, means that anyone who insists that others abide by his or her standards of justice, morality, and human rights is guilty of cultural imperialism.

The issues are thus complex. Bilahari Kausikan contends that Asia's communitarian standards are very different from the West's emphasis on individualism. The West will have to accept that no universal consensus may be possible and that states can legitimately disagree without being guilty of sinister designs or bad faith, he argues. Aryeh Neier accuses Kausikan of being guilty of just such bad faith by using cultural relativism to rationalize the abuses of his country (Singapore), and he argues that the welfare and dignity of the people of Asia should be the true standard of justice.

YES
Bilahari Kausikan

ASIA'S DIFFERENT STANDARD

East and Southeast Asia must respond to a new phenomenon: Human rights have become a legitimate issue in interstate relations. How a country treats its citizens is no longer a matter for its own exclusive determination. Others can and do legitimately claim a concern. There is an emerging global culture of human rights, and a body of international law on human rights has gradually developed, codified in the United Nations Charter, the Universal Declaration of Human Rights, and other international instruments. The United States and many European countries increasingly emphasize human rights in their foreign polices. Of course, human rights are not, and are not likely to become, a primary issue in international relations. Their promotion by all countries will always be selective, even cynical, and concern for human rights will always be balanced against other national interests. Nevertheless, the Western emphasis on human rights will affect the tone and texture of post–Cold War international relations.

In response, East and Southeast Asia are reexamining their own human rights standards. Of the noncommunist states in the region, only Japan, South Korea, and the Philippines are parties to both the International Covenant on Civil and Political Rights and the International Covenant on Economic, Social and Cultural Rights. Seoul and Manila have also accepted the Optional Protocol to the International Covenant on Civil and Political Rights. Tokyo has partially adopted the Western approach to human rights. But there is a more general acceptance of many international human rights norms, even among states that have not acceded to the two covenants or are accused by the West of human rights abuses.

The human rights situation in the region, whether measured by the standard of civil and political rights or by social, cultural, and economic rights, has improved greatly over the last 20 years. As countries in the region become more prosperous, secure, and self-confident, they are moving beyond a purely defensive attitude to a more active approach to human rights. All the countries of the region are party to the U.N. Charter. None has rejected the Universal Declaration. There are references to human rights in the constitutions of many of the countries in the region. Countries like China, Indonesia,

From Bilahari Kausikan, "Asia's Different Standard," *Foreign Policy*, no. 92 (Fall 1993). Copyright © 1993 by The Carnegie Endowment for International Peace. Reprinted by permission of *Foreign Policy*.

and even Burma have not just brushed aside Western criticism of their human rights records but have tried to respond seriously, asserting or trying to demonstrate that they too adhere to international human rights norms. They tend to interpret rather than reject such norms when there are disagreements. They discuss human rights with Western delegations. They have released political prisoners; and Indonesia, for instance, has even held commissions of inquiry on alleged abuses and punished some officials found guilty.

Abuses and inconsistencies continue. But it is too simplistic to dismiss what has been achieved as mere gestures intended to appease Western critics. Such inclinations may well be an element in the overall calculation of interests. And Western pressure undeniably plays a role. But in themselves, self-interest and pressure are insufficient and condescendingly ethnocentric Western explanations. They do less than justice to the states concerned, most of which have their own traditions in which the rulers have a duty to govern in a way consonant with the human dignity of their subjects, even if there is no clear concept of "rights" as has evolved in the West. China today, for all its imperfections, is a vast improvement over the China of the Cultural Revolution. So too has the situation in Taiwan, South Korea, and the Association of Southeast Asian Nations (ASEAN) improved. Western critics who deny the improvements lose credibility.

As countries in East and Southeast Asia position themselves more in the international human rights mainstream, they are trying to stake out distinctive positions in line with their own cultures, histories, and special circumstances. Like all states, East and Southeast Asian countries still subordinate human rights to other vital national interests, such as the territorial integrity of the state or the fundamental nature of their political systems. Moreover, the movement toward greater emphasis on human rights is not even. But in that respect the region is no different from the West. Such imperfections are inescapable political realities; it does not advance human rights to ignore the real progress that has occurred in the name of a pristine, but unattainable, ideal.

The diversity of cultural traditions, political structures, and levels of development will make it difficult, if not impossible, to define a single distinctive and coherent human rights regime that can encompass the vast region from Japan to Burma, with its Confucianist, Buddhist, Islamic, and Hindu traditions. Nonetheless, the movement toward such a goal is likely to continue. What is clear is that there is a general discontent throughout the region with a purely Western interpretation of human rights. The further development of human rights there will be shaped primarily by internal developments, but pressure will continue to come from the United States and Europe.

HUMAN RIGHTS AS A TOOL

Human rights did not evolve in a vacuum. During the Cold War, the Western promotion of human rights was shaped by and deployed as an ideological instrument of the East-West struggle. The post–Cold War human rights dialogue between the West and Asia will be influenced by the power structure and dynamics of a more regionalized world, built around the United States, Europe, and Asia, which is replacing Cold War alliances and superpower competition. Trade and security will, as always, be foremost on the international agenda, and human rights will not be an issue of the first order. But human rights touch upon extraordinarily delicate matters of culture and values. And human rights issues are likely to become more prominent.

An additional factor affecting the prominence of human rights is that Western governments need no longer be constrained in their efforts to advance their fundamental values for fear of driving countries into Moscow's arms. Even if Western foreign ministries find it imprudent or difficult to shake off ingrained habits of caution, there will be pressure from Western publics, human rights nongovernmental organizations (NGOs) and other interest groups, and the news media to take an active approach. It will be more difficult for Western governments to find politically compelling arguments to ignore human rights violations, particularly in an age when modern communication technologies allow images and information to travel almost instantaneously around the world. Even without popular pressure, some Western governments may find it useful for other reasons to selectively inject a greater human rights component in their relations with East and Southeast Asia. New governments may, for example, trumpet human rights in order to distinguish themselves from their predecessors—early Clinton administration rhetoric being a case in point....

Meanwhile, relations among the United States, Europe, and Asia may lead the West to use human rights as an instrument of economic competition. As American and European apprehensions about their competitiveness rise, the West is emphasizing values like openness and equal opportunity and relating them to broader issues of freedom and democracy. Japan's commitment to such values is already being questioned and its cultural traits criticized as deviations from allegedly "universal" norms. The French prime minister has accused foreigners in Asia with "different values" of undermining France's prosperity.

The lengthening catalogue of rights and freedoms in international human rights law now encompasses such matters as pay, work conditions, trade unions, standard of living, rest and leisure, welfare and social security, women's and children's rights, and the environment. The pressures and temptation to link economic concerns with human rights will certainly rise if economic strains increase. That is not to say that the West is insincere in its commitment to human rights. But policy motivations are rarely simple; and it is difficult to believe that economic considerations do not to some degree influence Western attitudes toward such issues as, say, the prison labor component of Chinese exports, child labor in Thailand, or some of the AFL-CIO [American Federation of Labor and Congress of Industrial Organizations] complaints against Malaysian labor practices....

But efforts to promote human rights in Asia must also reckon with the altered distribution of power in the post–Cold War world. Power, especially economic power, has been diffused. For the last two decades, most of East and Southeast Asia has experienced strong economic growth and will probably keep growing faster than other regions well into the next century....

East and Southeast Asia are now significant actors in the world economy. There is far less scope for conditionality and sanctions to force compliance with human rights. The region is an expanding market for the West. Global production networking makes the region an important source of intermediate goods for Western industry. It is also becoming a source of capital. What hurts East and Southeast Asia will also pain the West....

The United States is the only remaining superpower capable of exercising global leadership. Many European countries may well take their cues from how the Clinton administration implements its human rights polices. The United States will be a major influence on human rights debates in the U.N., International Monetary Fund, World Bank, and other international forums. Since most East and Southeast Asian countries regard a continued U.S. presence in Asia as desirable, it is not entirely unreasonable for the Clinton administration to ask that its own interest in promoting human rights and democracy be taken into account in some way. But how it does so is critical.

... The proclivity of American politicians to narrow political debate to the dimensions of sound-bites and the propensity for human rights rhetoric to be presented in legalistic and absolutist terms do not make for a nuanced public understanding of complex issues and diminish the room for compromise—the more so since U.S. leverage is limited.

Most of the outside leverage that now exists clearly belongs to Japan, the world's largest aid donor. Although Tokyo has made human rights one of the yardsticks for its official development assistance, it will certainly implement its human rights policies according to its own assessments. Unlike the West, Japan cannot escape the consequences if pressing human rights or forcing the pace of political change in its Asian

neighbors leads to instability. Distance makes it easier to be virtuous; proximity makes for prudence. If, for instance, tough sanctions break the grip of the State Law and Order Restoration Council in Burma or the Communist party in China, the results could be violent. If disorder breaks out in Burma or China, it is not the United States or Europe that will pay the immediate price. Is the West prepared to intervene and remain engaged, perhaps for decades, to restore order? China will be a formidable political and economic force by the turn of the century. That does not mean human rights abuses in China must be overlooked. But if the promotion of human rights ignores Chinese realities and interests, expect China to find ways to exert countervailing pressures. And it will have the wherewithal to try to reshape any international order it sees as threatening.

East and Southeast Asia are now capable of exerting considerable influence on the international politics of human rights, and their interests, values, and cultures cannot be disregarded. Most of the region's countries can no longer be pushed or coerced. Unlike Eastern Europe, Russia, or many states of the former Soviet Union, Asians do not wish to be considered good Westerners, even if they are friendly to the West. At least two countries, Japan and China, have the power to make a major impact on the international system.

For the first time since the Universal Declaration was adopted in 1948, countries not thoroughly steeped in the Judeo-Christian and natural law traditions are in the first rank: That unprecedented situation will define the new international politics of human rights. It will also multiply the occasions for conflict. In the process, will the human rights dialogue between the West and East and Southeast Asia become a dialogue of the deaf, with each side proclaiming its superior virtue without advancing the common interests of humanity? Or can it be a genuine and fruitful dialogue, expanding and deepening consensus? The latter outcome will require finding a balance between a pretentious and unrealistic universalism and a paralyzing cultural relativism. The myth of the universality of all human rights is harmful if it masks the real gap that exists between Asian and Western perceptions of human rights. The gap will not be bridged if it is denied. . . .

CULTURE AND HUMAN RIGHTS

Most Western governments are well informed about political and economic conditions in East and Southeast Asia. Most therefore try to pursue nuanced policies on human rights. But what Western governments would consider a sophisticated appreciation of the complexities and realistic policies, their publics, media, and human rights NGOs often dismiss as timidity. The Western media, NGOs, and human rights activists, especially in the United States, tend to press the human rights dialogue beyond the legitimate insistence on humane standards of behavior by calling for the summary implementation of abstract concepts without regard for a country's unique cultural, social, economic, and political circumstances. And it is precisely those NGOs and media that are most influential in shaping the public attitudes to which Western governments must respond. In the post–Cold War world, advocacy organizations can be expected to seize the opportunity to push harder.

For many in the West, the end of the Cold War was not just the defeat or collapse of communist regimes, but the supreme triumph and vindication of Western systems and values. It has become the lens through which they view developments in other regions. There has been a tendency since 1989 to draw parallels between developments in the Third World and those in Eastern Europe and the former USSR, measuring all states by the advance of what the West regards as "democracy." That is a value-laden term, itself susceptible to multiple interpretations, but usually understood by Western human rights activists and the media as the establishment of political institutions and practices akin to those existing in the United States and Europe.

There is good reason to doubt whether the countries of the former USSR and Eastern Europe will really evolve into "democracies" anytime soon, however this term is defined, or even whether such a transformation would necessarily always be for the better, given the ethnic hatreds in the region. But the Western approach is ideological, not empirical. The West needs its myths; missionary zeal to whip the heathen along the path of righteousness and remake the world in its own image is deeply ingrained in Western (especially American) political culture. It is entirely understandable that Western human rights advocates choose to interpret reality in the way they believe helps their cause most.

But that is not how most East and Southeast Asian governments view the world. Economic success has engendered a greater cultural self-confidence. Whatever their differences, East and Southeast Asian countries are increasingly conscious of their own civilizations and tend to locate the sources of their economic success in their own distinctive traditions and institutions. The self-congratulatory, simplistic, and sanctimonious tone of much Western commentary at the end of the Cold War and the current triumphalism of Western values grate on East and Southeast Asians. It is, after all, a West that launched two world wars, supported racism and colonialism, perpetrated the Holocaust and the Great Purge, and now suffers from serious social and economic deficiencies. It has difficulty competing economically and is unwilling to come to grips with many of its own domestic problems, all too prone to blame others for its own failings, and apparently exhausted of everything except pretensions of special virtue.

The hard core of rights that are truly universal is smaller than many in the West are wont to pretend. Forty-five years after the Universal Declaration was adopted, many of its 30 articles are still subject to debate over interpretation and application—not just between Asia and the West, but within the West itself. Not every one of the 50 states of the United States would apply the provisions of the Universal Declaration in the same way. It is not only pretentious but wrong to insist that everything has been settled once and forever. The Universal Declaration is not a tablet Moses brought down from the mountain. It was drafted by mortals. All international norms must evolve through continuing debate among different points of view if consensus is to be maintained.

Most East and Southeast Asian governments are uneasy with the propensity of many American and some European human rights activists to place more emphasis on civil and political rights than on economic, social, and cultural rights. They would probably not be convinced, for instance, by a September 1992 report issued by Human Rights Watch entitled *Indivisible Human Rights: The Rela-*

tionship of Political and Civil Rights to Survival, Subsistence and Poverty. They would find the report's argument that "political and civil rights, especially those related to democratic accountability," are basic to survival and "not luxuries to be enjoyed only after a certain level of economic development has been reached" to be grossly overstated. Such an argument does not accord with their own historical experience. That experience sees order and stability as preconditions for economic growth, and growth as the necessary foundation of any political order that claims to advance human dignity.

The Asian record of economic success is a powerful claim that cannot be easily dismissed. Both the West and Asia can agree that values and institutions are important determinants of development. But what institutions and which values? The individualistic ethos of the West or the communitarian traditions of Asia? The consensus-seeking approach of East and Southeast Asia or the adversarial institutions of the West? ...

Poverty, insecurity, and instability breed human rights abuses, while wealth creates the stability of Western societies and allows the operation of political institutions that in less-favorable circumstances could lead to disaster. Only America's wealth, for example, allows it to operate a political system that elevates conflict to the status of principle and makes a virtue of a tendency toward paralysis in all but exceptional circumstances. Wealth makes political institutions almost irrelevant to the well-being and happiness of the majority in many Western societies. Many Americans do not even bother to vote and the popular estimation of American politicians is low. Those are among the luxuries that wealth buys. But the costs are already becoming evident.

As the international distribution of power and wealth changes, the West ought to subject itself to a probing and unsentimental analysis. It should ask itself whether many of its persistent problems and its lack of economic competitiveness compared to several East and Southeast Asian countries are not in part due to its tendency to transform every social issue into an uncompromising question of "rights" and place the claims of the individual and special interests over those of society. There are grounds to question whether, viewed against the continuing march of history, the Western type of "democracy" provides optimal societal arrangements or even whether it can endure in its present form.

At any rate, many East and Southeast Asians tend to look askance at the starkly individualistic ethos of the West in which authority tends to be seen as oppressive and rights are an individual's "trump" over the state. Most people of the region prefer a situation in which distinctions between the individual, society, and state are less clear-cut, or at least less adversarial. It will be far more difficult to deepen and expand the international consensus on human rights if East and Southeast Asian countries believe that the Western promotion of human rights is aimed at what they regard as the foundation of their economic success. In fact, many Asians perceive the values and practices insisted upon by Western human rights purists as exacerbating the thorny problems faced by the West.

There is, however, a natural tactical convergence of interests between the Western media and human rights activists and those aspiring Asian elites who are challenging established governments. Such elites seek sympathy and legitimacy abroad by espousing human rights, just as the rhetoric of anticommunism served to gain support in the West during the Cold War and nationalist leaders of an earlier generation employed the ideology of liberalism to undermine the legitimacy of illiberal colonial regimes. Thus the popular image is created of repressive Asian governments holding down the masses yearning to be free, occasioning cheers when they fail and condemnation when they succeed. Such are, for example, some common popular Western interpretations of events in China in June 1989.... Such images are not always entirely wrong, ... but they often have a political significance that bears little relationship to their accuracy.

If dramatic scenes of the "Goddess of Democracy"—cleverly modeled after the Statue of Liberty—and students shouting defiance in Tiananmen Square in Beijing stirred Western hearts, the emotion obscured the fact that the vast peasantry of China—among the first beneficiaries of Deng Xiaoping's reforms —were largely unmoved. Sympathy for the students came, if at all, after the massacre and probably had more to do with the disproportionate use of force against them than with their ideas. What may have struck a chord with the peasants was not "democracy," but complaints against inflation, corruption, and nepotism....

One explanation of the contradictions in Asian attitudes is that popular pressures against East and Southeast Asian governments may not be so much for "human rights" or "democracy" but for good government: effective, efficient, and honest administrations able to provide security and basic needs with good opportunities for an improved standard of living. To be sure, good government, human rights, and democracy are overlapping concepts. Good government requires the protection of human dignity and accountability through periodic fair and free elections. But they are not always the same thing; it cannot be blithely assumed, as many in the West have, that more democracy and human rights will inevitably lead to good government, as the many lost opportunities of the Aquino government demonstrated. The apparent contradictions mirror a complex reality: Good government may well require, among other things, detention without trial to deal with military rebels or religious and other extremists; curbs on press freedoms to avoid fanning racial tensions or exacerbating social divisions; and draconian laws to break the power of entrenched interests in order to, for instance, establish land reforms.

Those are the realities of exercising authority in heterogeneous, unevenly modernized, and imperfectly integrated societies with large rural populations and shallow Western-style civic traditions. The competing Asian elites who today use human rights rhetoric to advance their causes may find good reason to retain and use such measures if ever they come to power and encounter the realities of governance. Espousing or claiming rights in the midst of political struggle does not mean they will or can be granted once the struggle is won. After all, their predecessors found it prudent to retain colonial laws that had been used against them and that they too denounced as contrary to human rights. Disagreements over human rights may therefore not be resolved even if the current generation of East and Southeast Asian leaders is replaced. The conviction that these countries are inevitably evolving toward Western-style democracy is unwarranted. Greater convergence with the West is possible, but a perfect fit is unlikely.

ROOM FOR DEBATE

For East and Southeast Asia, the challenge will be to devise credible, distinctive, and coherent positions within the parameters of international law on human rights. Most East and Southeast Asian governments sincerely want to protect and advance the human dignity of their citizens, even if they must do so within the constraints of their circumstances. Their good faith is less likely to be questioned if they accept the framework of the two U.N. human rights covenants. Those documents are flexible enough to accommodate a diversity of political institutions, cultures, and traditions. There is sufficient provision for reservation and derogation and room for further interpretation to ensure that special conditions are acknowledged and vital interests need not be compromised. Working within existing international law on human rights will also ameliorate what could otherwise be the overwhelming influence of the area's most powerful states, Japan and China, on the evolution of a regional position.

The challenge for the West is far more difficult because it requires wrenching psychological adjustments. The West must internalize the reality of diversity in all its dimensions and acknowledge that, notwithstanding the existence of a body of international law on human rights, many rights are still contested concepts where a consensus of meaning is coupled with equally important, and perhaps unresolvable, conflicts of interpretation. The West is no more or less special than any other region. It must recognize that the main influence on the development of human rights in East and Southeast Asia will be internal and difficult for the West to reach. Abrasive or ill-considered attempts to influence that dynamic are not only unlikely to succeed but could set back acceptance of human rights by arousing nationalistic responses. Progress will entail eschewing transcendent crusades or dramatic confrontations for patiently and quietly building consensus on modest, specific objectives through a still-evolving process of international lawmaking. The result will not always reflect Western preferences.

Future Western approaches on human rights will have to be formulated with greater nuance and precision. It makes a great deal of difference if the West insists on humane standards of behavior by vigorously protesting genocide, murder, torture, or slavery. Here there is a clear consensus on a core of international law that does not admit of derogation on any grounds. The West has a legitimate right and moral duty to promote those core human rights, even if it is tempered by limited influence. But if the West objects to, say, capital punishment, detention without trial, or curbs on press freedoms, it should recognize that it does so in a context where the international law is less definitive and more open to interpretation and where there is room for further elaboration through debate. The West will have to accept that no universal consensus may be possible and that states can legitimately agree to disagree without being guilty of sinister designs or bad faith. Trying to impose pet Western definitions of "freedom" and "democracy" is an incitement to destructive conflict, best foregone in the interest of promoting real human rights.

The international law on human rights provides a useful, relatively precise, and common framework for the human rights dialogue between West and East. It helps prevent "human rights" from becoming a mere catchphrase for whatever actions the West finds contrary to its preferences or too alien to comprehend. But the implementation, interpretation, and elaboration of the international law on human rights is unavoidably political. It must reflect changing global power structures and political circumstances. It will require the West to make complex political distinctions, perhaps refraining from taking a position on some human rights issues, irrespective of their merits, in order to press others where the prospects for consensus are better.

... [T]he West can legitimately object to the torture or murder of Tibetans or point out defects in the administration of justice in China. If done with patience and finesse, there is some chance of improving conditions as China develops. But to demand independence for... Tibet is an entirely different matter. It is a fantasy to believe that any... Chinese government would do anything but reject that outright, no matter what the West does. And it is not self-evident that the cause of human rights will really be advanced if China... which contain[s] a diversity of ethnic groups, disintegrates under such centrifugal pressures, generating instabilities across the region. It is immoral for the West to give... Tibetans false hope by encouraging wild dreams of self-determination. Better to help the... Tibetans improve their lot within the existing system.

Unfortunately, it is not obvious that Western governments are free to adopt such hard-headed policies of political triage. It goes against the most deeply held Western notions of human rights: individualism, the idea that rights are held against the state, the primacy of civil and political rights, and universalism. It will be complicated by the temptation to use human rights to pursue other interests. And it raises difficult questions about the role of human rights NGOs in mobilizing public and media pressures on Western governments to take action. Precisely because they are advocacy organizations, NGOs must adopt a strident, adversarial stance; they are impatient of nuance; they must define issues in stark moral outline; and they are usually quick to dismiss interpretation and exception as self-serving. For them, to do otherwise is to risk diminishing their influence and lose public support in a maze of moral ambiguities and contradictions.

Yet it is only through such thickets of compromise, contradiction, and ambiguity that further progress on human rights can be made. Those in the West concerned about human rights in East and Southeast Asia, therefore, must be asked a simple question: Do you ultimately want to do good, or merely posture to make yourselves feel good?

NO

Aryeh Neier

ASIA'S UNACCEPTABLE STANDARD

Bilahari Kausikan contends that international human rights advocates ignore cultural differences and seek to impose rules that reflect the "individualistic ethos of the West" in East and Southeast Asia, where the tradition is that of "consensus seeking." He argues that the authoritarian systems of Asia have produced stability and prosperity for their people and that Asia will resist Western efforts to promote human rights, particularly if they are seen to threaten the foundations of Asian economic success.

But Kausikan paints with too broad a brush. He characterizes the West as "individualistic" or "adversarial" and the East as "communitarian" or "consensus seeking." In fact, each region has its individualistic and communitarian traditions. Hong Kong's entrepreneurs, who have made that colony an outstanding economic success, are as individualistic as their Western counterparts. And seminal figures in the development of the West's rights-based traditions, such as John Locke and Thomas Jefferson, also had their communitarian sides. Each believed that a functioning civil society was essential to the exercise of individual rights and that a central purpose of those rights was the establishment of good government. The views they espoused, which helped shape the international agreements on rights in our time, are characterized as individualistic principally because of their belief that a ruler's authority was conditional, not absolute, and that the individual did not give up all rights in entering civil society.

Kausikan uses the term "consensus seeking," but "consensus imposing" is a more fitting description of some governments in East and Southeast Asia. "Consensus seeking" implies that all citizens may express their views and that, having heard one another, as in a Quaker meeting, they attempt to arrive at a consensus. The press freedoms that seem anathema to Kausikan are essential to such a process. If one fears that an article in the press critical of government policy will prevent a consensus from forming, that concern may mean that a society does not seek consensus.

An example of the way governments in East and Southeast Asia impose consensus is Malaysia's suppression of public discussion of logging in the Borneo state of Sarawak. Indigenous residents of the rainforests that are being destroyed have been detained without charges or trial in order to prevent them from speaking out. Local publications, as well as such foreign magazines as the *Economist* and the *Far Eastern Economic Review*, have been banned in order to suppress information about the despoliation of the environment and the enrichment of government officials who own vast timber concessions in Sarawak. Such are the measures that Kausikan seeks to mask with claims that the governments of the region are upholding communitarian and consensus-seeking values.

Are authoritarian systems required to maintain the economic success of East Asia and Southeast Asia? And does the promotion of human rights undermine that success? Such claims seem questionable at best.

The main reason to promote human rights worldwide is that intrinsic values are at stake—namely the right of all persons to be free from cruel and arbitrary punishment; to be able to express themselves freely; and to matter equally regardless of race, ethnicity, religion, or gender. Those rights are fundamental because they define us as human beings. By and large, people will not consent to a denial of such rights except in the face of superior force.

That said, the case that human rights are also instrumental in such achievements as economic success seems far stronger than the case Kausikan makes to delay human rights pending prosperity. Open societies around the world are flourishing economically to a far greater extent than closed societies or societies that were closed until recently. There are, of course, exceptions. They demonstrate that political freedom, by itself, is no guarantee of prosperity and that the denial of political freedom does not ensure

economic failure. Some of the exceptions are states in East and Southeast Asia. Yet even within that region, the mightiest economic power is Japan, a society that is not welcoming to outsiders but that generally respects the rights of its own citizens. In Japan, press criticism of governmental corruption that would not be tolerated in China, Indonesia, Malaysia, or Singapore is published freely. The Japanese government's peaceful critics are not jailed arbitrarily. In another example, Hong Kong, though not a democracy, has a far freer press than Singapore, and the colony is thriving. South Korea and Taiwan have not suffered economically as they have started to make the transition from authoritarianism to relative openness. In contrast, countries with repressive governments, such as Burma, Cambodia, Laos, and Vietnam, are among the world's poorest. Even in China, most people remain impoverished despite the recent economic boom.

Kausikan tells us that it is Western wealth that "allows the operation of political institutions that in less-favorable circumstances could lead to disaster." There is an element of truth here, but his argument carries the ahistorical implication that the West's wealth came before its embrace of human rights. Actually, the two proceeded in tandem and it is virtually impossible to separate cause from effect. Great Britain acquired great wealth during the seventeenth and eighteenth centuries, the period when its dissenters and philosophers were laying the foundation for the legal recognition of human rights. Similarly, in the United States, rights were codified at about the time the country began to achieve great prosperity.

Kausikan [argues] that the pursuit of civil and political rights may be incompatible with stability and economic success in East Asia. The [argument] could be turned around. Under Ferdinand Marcos [for example] the Philippines suffered from despotic and spectacularly corrupt rule for two decades before his ouster in 1986. No proponent of human rights would argue that the mere removal of Marcos could have produced an instant transformation, with respect to either human rights or national prosperity. Such a legacy will be felt for some time, and placing the blame for the difficulties of the Philippines on civil and political rights, which are by no means regularly respected in that country, is unfair to say the least.

Finally, it is worth noting that some inhabitants of East and Southeast Asia have endured great costs for present-day economic advances. As discussed in the Human Rights Watch report that Kausikan singles out for criticism, *Indivisible Human Rights*, between 15 and 30 million Chinese lost their lives in the famine of 1958–61 created by Mao Tsetung's "Great Leap Forward." During that disastrous period of ill-conceived industrialization and agricultural collectivization schemes, few in China spoke out in protest. The reason is not hard to find. In the late 1950s, thousands who had been encouraged to speak out during the short-lived period of "Let a hundred flowers bloom and a hundred schools of thought contend" found themselves denounced, imprisoned, or even executed. So, by the time the policies that caused the famine were instituted, few were willing to criticize them openly. Even when the famine was underway, Beijing got false information from rural cadres who felt obliged to report that Mao's programs were a great success. When it became aware of the famine, Beijing shrouded the information in secrecy to avoid discrediting Mao, thereby making it impossible to launch relief efforts. It was such disasters that made Human Rights Watch conclude that "rights are not luxuries to be enjoyed only after a certain level of economic development has been reached."

Kausikan writes that the Western media, non-governmental organizations (NGOs), and human rights activists "press the human rights dialogue beyond the legitimate insistence on humane standards of behavior by calling for the summary implementation of abstract concepts without regard for a country's unique cultural, social, economic, and political circumstances." Those groups, he writes, exercise undue influence, creating a climate of public opinion that shapes the way Western governments use human rights issues internationally.

Kausikan accepts that every government should be held to certain standards. Indeed, he asserts that it is not only legitimate that genocide, murder, torture, and slavery should be prohibited, but also that the West has a "moral duty" to insist on the elimination of such practices. One wonders why it is not also a moral duty of the East. What legitimates campaigns to end such abuses, he writes, is that "there is a clear consensus on a core of international law that does not admit of derogation on any grounds."

I cannot speak for such broad categories as Western media, NGOs, and human rights activists generally; nor would I wish to do so. It seems sufficiently presumptuous to try to represent the views of the relatively small number of NGOs based in the United States or Western Europe that systematically attempt to promote human rights worldwide in accordance with recognized international standards. Even within that group of organizations there are significant differences of opinion. Nevertheless, on the questions Kausikan addresses, there is a broad consensus within the mainstream of the international human rights movement, which, for purposes of brevity, I will call "the movement."

Kausikan exaggerates his own quarrel with the movement, which accepts that its core concerns worldwide are torture, murder, and disappearances. (Slavery would be in the same category if its practice were comparably widespread.) Documenting and campaigning against those practices constitute much of the day-to-day work of the movement.

Kausikan points out that the Reagan and Bush administrations focused much of their own effort in the human rights field on the anticommunist struggle and that the post–Cold War trend is now away from rights that are "relatively precisely defined in international law toward the promotion of hazier notions of 'freedom' and 'democracy.'" Many in the movement might have the same criticism. Whether the Clinton administration will follow the Reagan-Bush path is not yet clear. But by and large the human rights movement would prefer not to be associated with a global crusade to promote democracy up to and including self-determination; in discussions with the Clinton administration, its members have urged that U.S. human rights efforts be focused on the kinds of abuses that Kausikan accepts as legitimate foreign policy concerns. The movement's agenda is broader than what he favors, but not as broad as he suggests.

The Reagan and Bush administrations argued that promoting electoral democracy worldwide would empower critics of such practices as torture to mobilize opposition in their own countries. The right to take part in free and fair elections then became the ultimate human right from which all other rights would flow. In consequence, so the argument went, it was not necessary for the United States to publicly criticize violations of human rights in countries with democratically elected governments: The self-correcting mechanisms of the democratic system itself would deal with such abuses.

The movement objected that this approach politicized human rights: The same abuse was denounced publicly in an autocratic country and passed over in silence when it took place in a democratic country. That problem was further exacerbated by the tendency of the Reagan and Bush administrations to affix the democratic label on a wide range of governments that hardly deserved the honor yet were geopolitically aligned with the United States. Unfortunately, the human rights progress the Reagan and Bush administrations said democratic government would bring did not always accord with the movement's observations. During the Reagan years, much debate focused on Central America, where the advent of elected governments did not radically reduce torture, murder, and disappearances. The movement also called attention to the high level of violent abuses in other countries where democratic governments had recently come to power, as in Turkey and Brazil, and in such longer-established democracies as India. To the movement, the Reagan-Bush emphasis on democracy often seemed not only a means of manipulating human rights for political purposes, as Kausikan suggests, but also a pretext for not taking a strong stand on systematic violations of core human rights in countries identified as democratic.

The Universal Declaration of Human Rights does commit the countries of the world to representative government, and the International Covenant on Civil and Political Rights commits the 120 countries that are party to it to periodic free and fair elections. Nevertheless, there is division within the movement about whether human rights organizations should promote democracy. Some fear that associating themselves with the espousal of democracy would align them with the political opponents of nondemocratic governments and, thereby, diminish their credibility in criticizing violations of core human rights. Others consider that support for the right of citizens to take part in self-government is legitimate in that it is analogous to, and an extension of, their efforts on behalf of the freedom of expression recognized in international law. Even those within the movement who fall into the latter camp readily agree, however, that promoting democracy is far less central than stopping torture, murder, and disappearances.

Kausikan writes that the countries of East Asia and Southeast Asia would "reject outright" efforts by the West to promote independence for territories such as ... Tibet in the name of human rights. What is misleading in his essay is the implication that the movement takes a different position. When the Asia Watch division of Human Rights Watch issues reports on ... Tibet, it not only refrains from supporting independence but is explicit in disclaiming any stand on such issues....

The [human rights] movement's refusal to take stands on self-determination reflects a recognition that the history, geography, demography, culture, economy, and politics of particular territories determine such questions, not simply the terms of international covenants. Some outside the mainstream of the international human rights movement invoke human rights to promote independence. They find support for their use of the term human rights in that regard in the International Covenant on Civil and Political Rights and in the International Covenant on Economic, Social and Cultural Rights. In each document, Article I provides that "all peoples have the right of self-determination." But the incorporation of that provision in the covenants, which were adopted by the United Nations General Assembly in 1966, is not a consequence of a Western conspiracy. It reflects the insistence by the former colonial states of Africa and Asia that self-determination is an intrinsic component of human rights. Probably few among the countries that then advocated such a status for self-determination envisaged a day when some of their number would be challenged as colonial oppressors by groups marching under human rights banners.

The most important differences between Kausikan and the movement concern such matters as detention without trial and press freedoms. Should those be on the international human rights agenda? Kausikan says no; the movement says yes.

Kausikan makes two arguments in that regard. He contends such matters are not part of the "hard core of rights that are truly universal." Unlike the prohibitions of torture and murder, the international agreements on human rights allow derogation—that is, suspension in certain circumstances—of rights in those areas. And he argues that "good government may well require, among other things, detention without trial to deal with military rebels or religious and other extremists; curbs on press freedoms to avoid fanning racial tensions or exacerbating social divisions; and draconian laws to break the power of entrenched interests." In other words, the ends for which those means are used may be worthy.

Now, international agreements on human rights do permit derogation of those rights. Yet derogation is hardly to be casual; the circumstances in which it is permissible are extreme. The International Covenant on Civil and Political Rights permits derogation only "in time of public emergency which threatens the life of the nation" and, even then, only "to the extent strictly required by the exigencies of the situation." Does a right lack universality because it may be suspended at such a dire moment? That seems a peculiar position. A better test might be whether U.N. members have generally proclaimed their acceptance of certain rights. Not only have a majority ratified the International Covenant on Civil and Political Rights, but, in addition, the Universal Declaration of Human Rights was adopted by the U.N. General Assembly in 1948 with no dissents and with abstentions from only the Soviet bloc, South Africa, and Saudi Arabia. Also, press freedoms and protections against detention without trial have been incorporated in such regional human rights agreements as the European Convention on Human Rights, the American Convention on Human Rights, the African Charter of Human and Peoples' Rights, the Conference on Security and Cooperation in Europe (the Helsinki Accord), and the Cairo Declaration on Human Rights in Islam. The great majority of the countries of the world are party to one or more agreements protecting those rights. There is no Asian declaration of rights, but it is partly because Asia has not clearly identified itself as a region as have other parts of the world. The provisions of the international agreements may be widely disregarded in practice, but the same is true of the prohibitions on torture and murder. The test of whether a right is universal is whether states universally assert an obligation to respect it. Thus, press freedom and the prohibition on detention without trial, except in the most exigent circumstances, are universal rights.

Kausikan's other argument asks us to presume that governments are wise and benign in denying those rights. Regrettably, that is often not the case. His own government in Singapore imprisoned a peaceful political dissenter, Chia Thye Poh, a former opposition member of parliament, for 22 years without charge or trial. The Singapore government only released him when it seemed that the impending release of Nelson Mandela in South Africa might focus international attention on other governments holding political prisoners for an extremely long time. In Malaysia, as noted, detention without trial and the denial of press freedoms have been used to silence critics of the despoliation of the rain forests of Sarawak. In Indonesia, the targets have often been critics of the corruption of Suharto's family and cronies. In China, criticism of the Three Gorges dam project, which would displace 1.2 million people, may not be published. And so on.

Kausikan's main concern, in sum, is to delegitimate international efforts to address the abuses that particularly characterize his own government and its regional allies: detention without trial and denial of press freedoms. Although the issues he raises are worthy of serious consideration, it is not out of order for the international human rights movement to call attention to such matters—not if the welfare and dignity of the people of Asia are our foremost concerns.

POSTSCRIPT

Are U.S. Efforts to Promote Human Rights Culturally Biased and Self-Serving?

The points discussed in the selections by Bilahari Kausikan and Aryeh Neier are not just matters of abstract concern. Instead, they are significantly related to the conduct of international relations. Many have argued that countries should make foreign policy decisions based at least partly on considerations of morality. What is more, that view has gained strength in the last few years in the aftermath of the end of the cold war. During the cold war, the United States and other Western countries were frequently willing to overlook the abuses of allies because they were seen as lesser evils in the fight against the greatest evil, the Soviet communist menace. That is changing. In 1993, for example, Haiti's military government was being forced to yield to pressure from the United States and other countries who insisted on the restoration of Haiti's last elected president. In 1994, when a Singapore court sentenced a resident American youth, Michael Fay, to six lashes on the buttocks by a cane for vandalism, President Bill Clinton protested to the government of Singapore: "This punishment is extreme, and we hope very much that somehow it will be reconsidered." Singapore rejected what one editorial called U.S. "interference," said Clinton was making a grandiose gesture to deflect American attention from the "deepening personal crisis" that scandals had brought to his administration, and pointed out that, unlike American cities, Singapore was "orderly and relatively crime free."

The point is that standards of justice sometimes govern foreign policy. More insight on this is available in Terry Nardin and David R. Mapel, eds., *Traditions of International Ethics* (Cambridge University Press, 1992) and Felix Oppenheim, *The Place of Morality in Foreign Policy* (Lexington Books, 1991).

Among other reasons that human rights standards are important is that there are those within most domestic political systems who argue that their government should make policy based on moral evaluations, and sometimes countries do act on human rights. Thus, human rights is not merely an abstract question of justice; it is a matter of foreign policy choice. More insight on this is available in Thomas M. Franck, *Political Questions/Judicial Answers: Does the Rule of Law Apply to Foreign Affairs?* (Princeton University Press, 1992).

The view of what constitutes abuses of human rights continues to be controversial. According to the 1993 annual report of the international monitoring group Amnesty International, at least 110 governments still engage in chronic human rights abuses. The countries labeled as human rights abusers included the United States, characterized as having had a year (1992) of "appalling human rights catastrophes." Among the actions characterized as abuses were the forced repatriation of Haitian refugees and the U.S. Supreme Court decision allowing the execution of convicted juveniles and mentally retarded persons.

More evidence of the controversy about human rights arose when the UN World Conference on Human Rights convened in Vienna, Austria, in June 1993. It was attended by more than 5,000 delegates representing more than 170 countries and nearly 1,000 nongovernment organizations, such as Amnesty International and the International Red Cross. The conference drafted for UN consideration language that supported greater protection for women and children. See Rebecca J. Cook, "Women's International Rights Law: The Way Forward," *Human Rights Quarterly* (Spring 1993). The conference made less progress on the idea of appointing a UN commissioner to oversee human rights and on proposals to increase UN enforcement of human rights by imposing economic and diplomatic sanctions, and taking other actions against abusive countries. Part of the resistance came from some Third World representatives who worried that the creation of universal human rights standards would mean that the dominant Western powers of Europe and North America would force their values on other cultures.

For discussions of universal law and suggestions for global standards, see Jonathan I. Charney, "Universal International Law," *American Journal of International Law* (October 1993) and Dipak K. Gupta, Albert J. Jongman, and Alex P. Schmid, "Creating a Composite Index for Assessing Country Performance in the Field of Human Rights," *Human Rights Quarterly* (April 1993).

CONTRIBUTORS
TO THIS VOLUME

EDITOR

JOHN T. ROURKE, Ph.D., is a professor of political science at the University of Connecticut for campuses in Storrs and Hartford, Connecticut. He has written numerous articles and papers, and he is the author of *Congress and the Presidency in U.S. Foreign Policymaking* (Westview, 1985); *The United States, the Soviet Union, and China: Comparative Foreign Policymaking and Implementation* (Brooks/Cole, 1989); and *International Politics on the World Stage*, 5th ed. (The Dushkin Publishing Group, 1995). He is also the coauthor, with Ralph G. Carter and Mark A. Boyer, of *Making American Foreign Policy* (The Dushkin Publishing Group, 1994). Professor Rourke enjoys teaching introductory political science classes—which he does each semester—and he plays an active role in the university's internship program as well as advises one of its political clubs. In addition, he has served as a staff member of Connecticut's legislature and has been involved in political campaigns on the local, state, and national levels.

STAFF

Mimi Egan   Publisher

Brenda S. Filley   Production Manager

Libra Ann Cusack   Typesetting Supervisor

Juliana Arbo   Typesetter

Lara Johnson   Graphics

Diane Barker   Proofreader

David Brackley   Copy Editor

David Dean   Administrative Editor

Richard Tietjen   Systems Manager

AUTHORS

ROGER C. ALTMAN is the deputy secretary of the treasury for the Clinton administration.

DOUG BANDOW is a senior fellow of the Cato Institute in Washington, D.C., a public policy research foundation, and a member of the State of California Bar Association and the U.S. Court of Appeals for the District of Columbia. He is the author of *Beyond Good Intentions* (Crossway Books, 1988) and *The Politics of Plunder: Misgovernment in Washington* (Transaction Publishers, 1990).

JAGDISH BHAGWATI is the Arthur Lehman Professor of Economics at Columbia University in New York City and a former economic policy advisor to the director-general of the General Agreement on Tariffs and Trade.

BOUTROS BOUTROS-GHALI, a former foreign minister of Egypt, is the secretary-general of the United Nations. He holds the distinction of being the first Arab, the first African, and the sixth secretary-general of the United Nations. He received a law degree from Cairo University in 1946 and a doctorate in international law from the University of Paris in 1949. He has also been a professor at Cairo University and a president of the Center of Political and Strategic Studies.

JEREMY BRECHER is a historian and the coeditor, with Tim Costello, of *Building Bridges: The Emerging Grassroots Coalition of Labor and Community* (Monthly Review, 1990).

MICHAEL CHEGE is a visiting scholar in the Center for International Affairs at Harvard University in Cambridge, Massachusetts. He is a former, director of the Institute of International Studies at the University of Nairobi, and from 1988 to early 1994, he served as a Ford Foundation program officer in charge of governance and international affairs in eastern and southern Africa.

PETER F. DRUCKER is the Clarke Professor of Social Science and Management at the Claremont Graduate School in Claremont, California.

JOHN L. ESPOSITO is a professor of religion and international affairs at Georgetown University in Washington, D.C., and the director of the Center for Muslim-Christian Understanding: History and International Affairs at Georgetown University's Edmund A. Walsh School of Foreign Service. He is a former president of the Middle East Studies Association of North America and of the American Council for the Study of Islamic Societies. His publications include *Islam and Politics* (Syracuse University Press, 1991) and *The Islamic Threat: Myth or Reality?* (Oxford University Press, 1992).

AMITAI ETZIONI, a senior advisor to the White House from 1979 to 1980, is a professor in the Department of Sociology at George Washington University in Washington, D.C., where he has been teaching since 1968. He is also the founder of the Society for the Advancement of Socio-Economics and the founder and director of the Center for Policy Research, a nonprofit organization dedicated to public policy. His publications include *A Responsive Society: Collected Essays on Guiding Deliberate Social Change* (Jossey-Bass, 1991).

HILARY F. FRENCH is a senior researcher at the Worldwatch Institute in Washington, D.C. She is the author of *Clearing the Air: Worldwatch Paper 94.*

FRANCIS FUKUYAMA, a former deputy director of the U.S. State Department's policy planning staff, is a consultant for the RAND Corporation in Washington, D.C. He is the author of *The End of History and the Last Man* (Free Press, 1992).

EJUP GANIC is the vice president of the republic of Bosnia and Herzegovina.

PATRICK GLYNN is a resident scholar at the American Enterprise Institute in Washington, D.C., a privately funded public policy research organization. His publications include *Closing Pandora's Box: Arms Races, Arms Control, and the History of the Cold War* (Basic Books, 1992).

JAMES P. GRANT is the executive director of the United Nations Children's Fund.

JOHN F. HILLEN III is a lieutenant in the U.S. Army and a Ph.D. candidate in St. Anthony's College at Oxford University in Oxford, England.

DANIEL JAMES is an advisor to Carrying Capacity Network in Washington, D.C., an organization that focuses on issues pertaining to the carrying capacity of the Earth, including immigration, population, and the environment. He is the author of *Illegal Immigration—An Unfolding Crisis* (University Press of America, 1991).

JOHN PAUL II, a former archbishop of Kraków, Poland, is the pope of the Roman Catholic Church and an outspoken commentator on world events.

ROBERT D. KAPLAN is a contributing editor of *The Atlantic Monthly.*

BILAHARI KAUSIKAN is the director of the East Asian and Pacific bureau for Singapore's Ministry of Foreign Affairs.

SAMUEL S. KIM is a senior research scholar at Columbia University's East Asian Institute in New York City. He received a Ph.D. from Columbia University in 1966, and he has also taught in the Woodrow Wilson School of Public and International Affairs at Princeton University. He is the author or editor of over a dozen books on Chinese foreign policy and world order studies, including *China's Quest for National Identity* (Cornell University Press, 1993), coauthored with Lowell Dittmer.

JESSICA J. KULYNYCH is a doctoral candidate in political science at the University of Connecticut where she teaches politics and political theory and women.

KAREN LaFOLLETTE is a research associate for the Institute for Political Economy in Washington, D.C.

ANTHONY LAKE is the assistant to the president for National Security Affairs for the Clinton administration.

MICHAEL LIND is the executive editor of *The National Interest.*

JEAN CLAUDE MALLET is the director of strategic policy for France's Ministry of Defense.

JOHN McCAIN is a senator (R) from Arizona (1987–present; term ends 1999).

JUDITH MILLER is a fellow of the Twentieth Century Fund in New York City and a writer for the *New York Times.*

STEPHEN MOORE is an economist with the Cato Institute in Washington, D.C., a public policy research foundation.

ARYEH NEIER is the president of the Open Society Fund, an organization that promotes the development of civil society in formerly repressive countries. He is also a former executive director of Human Rights Watch.

MICHAEL QUINLAN is the director of the Ditchley Foundation in England. A noted thinker on the philosophy of deterrence, he worked on defense-related issues for over 40 years, including serving as permanent undersecretary of state in Great Britain's Ministry of Defense.

MARCUS RASKIN is the cofounder of the Institute for Policy Studies and a member of the editorial board of *The Nation*. His publications include *Essays of a Citizen: From National Security State to Democracy* (M. E. Sharpe, 1991).

GEORGE SHULTZ is a professor of economics at Stanford University. He has held various positions in the U.S. government for a number of years, including secretary of labor (1969–1970) and secretary of state (1982–1988)

JULIAN L. SIMON is a professor of economics and business administration in the College of Business and Management at the University of Maryland at Col-

lege Park. His research interests focus on population economics, and his publications include *The Economic Consequences of Immigration* (Basil Blackwell, 1989), *Population Matters: People, Resources, Environment, and Immigration* (Transaction Publishers, 1990), and *The Ultimate Resource*, 2d ed. (Princeton University Press, 1994).

CYRUS R. VANCE is a lawyer and a partner in the law firm of Thacher and Bartlett in New York City. He was the secretary of state under President Jimmy Carter from 1977 to 1980.

REX A. WADE is a professor in the Department of History at George Mason University in Washington, D.C.

LINCOLN WOLFENSTEIN is a professor of physics at Carnegie Mellon University in Pittsburgh, Pennsylvania, and a member of the National Academy of Sciences. He received a Ph.D. in physics from the University of Chicago in 1949.

R. JAMES WOOLSEY is the director of the Central Intelligence Agency for the United States.

ZHAO XIAOWEI is a prominent member of the Chinese Democratic Liberal Party, and he has written widely for Chinese publications.

INDEX